# DYNAMICS OF INTERNATIONAL TRADE AND ECONOMY: AN INQUIRY INTO EMERGING MARKETS

# DYNAMICS OF INTERNATIONAL TRADE AND ECONOMY: AN INQUIRY INTO EMERGING MARKETS

RAJAGOPAL

Nova Science Publishers, Inc.
*New York*

**LIBRARY OF CONGRESS CATALOGING-IN-PUBLICATION DATA**
*Available upon request*

ISBN 13: 978-1-60021-707-4
ISBN 10: 1-60021-707-9

*Published by Nova Science Publishers, Inc. ✢ New York*

# CONTENTS

# BIOGRAPHIC SKETCH OF THE AUTHOR

Dr. Rajagopal is Professor of Marketing at Monterrey Institute of Technology and Higher Education (Instituto Tecnologico y de Estudios Superiores de Monterrey - ITESM) in Mexico City and Fellow of the Royal Society for Encouragement of Arts, Manufacture and Commerce, London. He is also associated with many national and international organizations of repute in various capacities. He teaches Competitor Analysis, Marketing Strategy, Advance Selling Systems, International Marketing, Services Marketing, New Product Development and other subjects of contemporary interest to the students of undergraduate, graduate and doctoral programs. Dr. Rajagopal holds masters and doctoral degrees in Economics and Marketing respectively from Ravishankar University in India. His specialization is in the fields of Marketing Management, Rural Economic Linkages and Development Economics. He has to his credit 27 books on marketing and rural development themes and over 300 research contributions that include published research papers in national and international refereed journals. He has imparted training to senior executives and has conducted over 55 management development programs. His research contributions have been recognized by the Government of Mexico and he has been awarded the status of National Researcher (SNI-level II) since 2004.

# PREFACE

Countries of transitional economies and emerging markets have broadly focused structural reforms in five major areas comprising international trade, financial markets, labor markets, and the generation and use of public resources. Consequently, the financial development in these countries has improved the intensity of financial intermediation, private sector participation in banking, and the size and activity of stock markets. The economic integration and structural reforms in Eastern European countries and Latin America have considered that import substitution in manufacturing sector would be synonymous with industrialization, which in turn was seen as the key to development. As far as efficient generation and use of public resources are concerned, much has been done to make the value-added tax system efficient and to privatize public enterprises during the process of economic reforms.

Liberalization process has also triggered off opportunities of international trade in the countries of Central and Eastern Europe, Asia and Latin America to look for new business partnering countries and expand their international trade relations. Many countries in Latin American region began to open their international business opportunities to the rest of the world in 80's. This process has made significant improvement in the structural adjustments program along with the debt management strategies. In these countries, structural reforms have been set off as growth drivers towards macroeconomic activities, international trade, financial markets, generation and use of public resources, governance, and labor markets. The macroeconomic policies adopted during the reforms process in these countries intend to maximize growth curbing rise in inflation and unemployment. Most common form of economic reforms include process of trade liberalization and reducing financial barriers required for investment and production operations to support the international trade movements.

During early stage of economic transition, it was presumed that the newly liberalized economies in Central and Eastern Europe would experience high rates of sustained economic growth, with rapid convergence towards trade and economy of the major industrialized economies in the West. A key factor of the transition process is the structural change consisting in the reallocation of resources on the basis of market incentives. Variability in the production and consumption behavior is therefore a potentially useful concept in analyzing the structural changes that have actually occurred in Eastern European transition economies. Among the Central and Eastern European countries, the Polish transition can be viewed as the most successful one in terms of growth levels. Overall impact of political and economic disintegration on trade among the former constituent republics of three demised federations in central and Eastern Europe, the Soviet Union, Yugoslavia, and Czechoslovakia has been followed by a sharp fall in trade intensity, although the legacy of a common past remains strong. However, the process of integration into the world economy has not been uniform across transition countries. After long inward-looking trade policies and import-substituting industrialization, several Latin American countries undertook comprehensive trade liberalization and macroeconomic adjustment in the 1980s and the experience of these countries has been relevant for the economies in Eastern Europe and the former Soviet Union in transition from socialism to market economies.

Regional trade has emerged as an important move of globalization which has been induced collectively with shared norms and political leadership in respective regions. Informality has appeared to be a representative common norm which played a catalytic role in first nurturing communication for regional cooperation framework to enhance the international trade opportunities with emerging countries as business partners. The political leadership shown by China and Japan has played a vital role in promoting the regional integration initiatives. It has also helped the Latin American countries to overcome the industrial and trade policy of import substitution of over four decades. During the late 80's and early 90's a large number of countries began to lower their levels of protection and bent their energies towards international trade reforms with the increasing assistance of the multilateral institutions. Trade reforms process proceeded at a faster pace and tariff barriers were reduced significantly. There has been a significant transition in the international relations and business partnering of Latin American countries with the rest of the world in the post 80's period that has reflected in the economic and technological growth of some countries like Mexico, Brazil, Chile and Peru. There has been a rapid proliferation of bilateral free trade agreement (FTA) in East Asia and the Asia-Pacific regions since 1990s and the this trend has further intensified enhancing the scope of advance regional co-operation and integration.

The most common pattern of economic reforms in Latin America has been, first, radical liberalization, and second, implementation of prudential norms that moderated the initial liberalization. The policy changes related to the financial system include removal of interest-rate controls, elimination of mandated credit to "priority" sectors, privatization of state banks, liberalization of the foreign investment regime, and more recently, improvements in the regulatory framework, which have improved both the banking system and the stock market. It has been observed that Latin American countries are moving in sensible directions by emphasizing well-publicized actions against price fixers, by undertaking competition advocacy programs, and by targeting public sector restraints on competition. A positive trend in the behavior of trade flows has been observed during the reforms period, resulting from the increased openness of these economies to international markets. There is a striking difference between the behavior of export and import volumes around the devaluation episodes. Exports tend, on average, to increase in the year of the devaluation and the following two years. Only in Argentina, Peru and Venezuela negative export growth has been observed in the second year after the devaluation, and this probably has more to do with the circumstances in world markets at that time. However, entire economic progress may not be interpreted as an outcome of the reforms. The growth and development may result to be slower in a country or region in a normal process than stirred process of reforms.

The Asia-Pacific countries have shown extraordinary success in diversifying their exports and in raising their stakes in the world economy, while at the same time their domestic market is largely protected against import competition. Such trade policies of this region have also alarmed the concerns for global partnering and business expansions. Instruments such as tariff, non-tariff barriers, Trade Related Investment Measures (TRIMS) and barriers to domestic distribution still play an import role in these countries, although there are important cross-country differences in their timing, scope and magnitude. China has emerged as a major player in the global economy with a key position in global production, trade and, increasingly, finance. In the context of large imbalances in world growth rates China has helped in sustaining world economic expansion, especially in the Asia Pacific region and has emerged as an important global financial force by pulling enormous amount of inflows of foreign direct investment.

In Asia, the most significant arrangement is among the countries of South-East Asia. Association of South-east Asian Nations (ASEAN) was formed in 1967 to promote economic, social and cultural cooperation among Indonesia, Malaysia, Philippines, Singapore and Thailand. In 1978, ASEAN put into force a preferential trading arrangement granting a margin of preference of 10 to 15 per cent on selected products to members. In the early 1990s, the arrangement was upgraded into the ASEAN. Membership of ASEAN has also expanded to include Brunei Darussalam, Viet Nam, Lao People's Democratic Republic, Myanmar and Cambodia. Another integration arrangement among the developing countries of the region that is potentially significant is the South Asian Association for Regional Cooperation (SAARC), whose membership includes Bangladesh, Bhutan, India, Maldives, Nepal, Pakistan and Sri Lanka. A decision was taken in 1992 to form the SAARC Preferential Trading Arrangement (SAPTA) and in 1995, the group agreed to move towards a free trade area. However, political differences between India and Pakistan have impeded the effectiveness of the arrangement. In the meantime, India and Sri Lanka have moved separately to form a free trade area. The importance of the Asia-Pacific is most marked for Chile, which exported 29 percent of its exports to Asia-Pacific, as well as for the Mercosur countries, which sent 15 percent of their exports to the Asia-Pacific basin in 2003. The economic integration arrangements in the Latin American and Asian regions have been established mainly at the sub-regional level. Over years, inter-regional cooperation has intensified on the trans-Pacific agenda in recent years. Latin America and Asia-Pacific have created various platforms to deal with bilateral economic and political issues.

There is a fast change observed in the world markets resulting into the new emerging markets across the countries. In this century China, India and Latin America and the emerging market based economies in Eastern Europe promise new opportunities for global trade. The European Union provided an outlet, initially for unskilled-labor intensive products of Central and Eastern European countries and more recently for skilled-labor intensive and technology-based products. Knowledge-intensive imports from the European Union have also contributed to industrial realignment in the Central European countries. The growing trade agreements in the countries indicate some likelihood of success because when the level of tariff and non-tariff barriers is already low, a preferential agreement is more likely to have an adverse impact than a beneficial one. However, the reduction in the tariff barriers, duties and liberalization process worldwide has further given a stimulus to the international marketing across regional boundaries.

This book discusses a research analysis based on extensive survey of literature and statistical analysis of the data available from secondary sources and argues the strategic partnership model developed by analyzing the functional gap-map in reference to the political, economic, legal and trade related factors. The analysis emphasizes the evolution of productivity and exports, and discusses factors variability in the transitional economies and emerging markets on the basis of spatial and temporal data. The principal data sets have been used from the published resources of Economic Commission on Latin America and Caribbean (ECLAC), World Development Reports, World Trade Reports and World Economic Outlook for the reference period 1950-2003. The role of strategic alliances in the trade liberalization and international partnering variables has been analyzed in the study in reference to non-parametric measures and the recent trends towards economic appreciation observed in these countries have been put through the process of appropriate qualitative and quantitative test to support the development of the model. The research study analyzed in the book discusses economic integration between two economies, distinctively one central, with a large local market, and the other peripheral, with a small local market. Each economy has an imperfectly competitive manufacturing sector. It has been observed that trade liberalization creates a strong incentive for the imperfectly competitive industry to concentrate in the central region, near the large market.

Literature on the trade and economic growth of transitional economies and emerging markets need more emphasis and analytical insights over the days to come to support the needs of students of international relations, research and policy makers. This book offers contemporary reading on the transitional economies and emerging markets for undergraduate and graduate students of international economy, international business and international trade. In addition, this book would serve as a reference book for doctoral and post-doctoral research scholar. Major discussions in the book is woven around like trade openness, foreign direct investment, production portfolios, debt, terms of trade, GNP, foreign reserves, savings, exports share, imports and foreign exchange rates. Analysis of critical issues in the book have been carried over in reference to the total factor productivity, trade competitiveness, revealed comparative advantage, trade performance index and measurement of welfare benefits (as Nash equilibrium). The discussions in this book have been organized in a systematic way in three parts-global environment and transition, analysis of research study and synthesis presenting future perspectives of trade and economy in the countries of transitional economies and emerging markets. Organization of chapters in the book in the above patterns allows readers to move from macro to micro learning environment within the subject.

In pursuing this research project, I was benefited from the discussions with Dr. Rodolfo Loyola, Dr. Teresa Liedo, Dr. Macario Schatino, Dr. Pedro Marqez and other faculty members of ITESM, Mexico City Campus. I extend my sincere thanks to the Research Committee of the ITESM for sponsoring this research project. I have also learnt from the external referees' comments at various stages of project during data analysis and interpretations. I acknowledge the academic support provided by Dr. Maria Guisen Carmen, Faculty of Economics and Business, Universidade de Santiago de Compostela, Spain and Dr. Erdener Kaynak, Professor, School of Business Administration, Pennsylvania State University at Harrisburg as a principal referee for extending their suggestions to improve the analytical contents of the study. I acknowledge the efforts and time invested by Engineer Ananya Rajagopal in developing theoretical contruct of the study and performing the commendable job of computation of data using SPSS and ARC software, testing the mathematical models and drafting the tables which have been incorporated in the report. Finally, I express my gratitude to Nova Science Publishers, New York for agreeing to publish this academic work.

Rajagopal
February 06, 2007

# PART I
# GLOBAL ENVIRONMENT AND TRANSITION

*Chapter 1*

# THE DEBATE: FOR AND AGAINST GLOBALIZATION

Globalization in economic reference may be explained as a historical process which has emerged, as the result of continuous development of civilization, human needs, innovation and technological progress. It endorses integration of various types of economies around the world- developed, developing and transitional, particularly through the flow of trade and financial operations. The term *globalization* often draws out the expression towards immigration of people and spread of technology as core knowledge of the society, across international borders. However, there are also broader cultural, political and environmental dimensions associated with the process of globalization. Among many, the most striking aspect of this has been the integration of financial markets made possible by modern electronic communication that took off the globalization concept in the middle of $20^{th}$ century. Globalization aimed at offering extensive opportunities with outward-oriented policies which were designed to bring dynamism and greater prosperity to reach developing countries. Its effects became visual as the time advanced which, has been evidenced by East Asia, transforming it from one of the poorest areas of the world. Living standards in the east-Asian region rose and it became possible to make progress on democracy and economic issues such as the environment and work standards.

Early twentieth century had the central challenge facing the postwar trading system to prevent a return to protectionism - a path which had led directly to the Great Depression of the 1930 and ultimately to the descent into world war. In the inter-war era, the global concern was back on internationalism or globalization as we find now and countries which were observing closed economies, protectionism and pervasive capital controls were interlocked in their own state of economy. This was a major factor in the devastation of this period, when per capita income growth fell to less than 1 percent during 1913-1950. For the rest of the century, even though population grew at an unprecedented pace, per capita income growth was over 2 percent, the fastest pace of all coming during the post-World War boom in the industrial countries[1]. Gaps between rich and poor countries, and rich and poor people within countries, have grown. Over a long period by the 60's of $20^{th}$ century, the deep levels of economic integration have been pumped in many ways to overcome the post-war political and economic crisis. Large number of developing countries has made slow progress or has lost ground in the race of global competition. In particular, per capita incomes in Africa have

[1] International Monetary Fund (2002): Globalization-Threat or Opportunity, Staff Working Paper, IMF.

declined relative to the industrial countries and in some countries have declined in absolute terms. Untill 1980s, many emerging markets were characterized by heavy state-ownership and intervention; in a number of respects the transition economies were only the extreme case, although the absence of entrepreneurial skills, the reach of state planning and the degree of autarchy represent particular weaknesses. In many developing economies, populism led to over-expansive macro-economic policies, relying on deficit financing and generalized controls, which took little account of basic economic equilibria[2].

People around the globe are now more connected to each other than ever before. Information and money flow more quickly than ever. Goods and services produced in one part of the world are increasingly available in all parts of the world. International travel is more frequent. International communication is commonplace. This phenomenon has been titled "globalization." While sometimes globalization is endorsed as primarily a synonym for global business, it is much more than that. The same forces that allow businesses to operate as if national borders do not exist also allow social activists, labor organizers, journalists, academics, and many others to work on a global stage. We live in a world which is very different today from the one that existed half a century before - a multi-polar world of multiple interests bound together by trade, investment and technology as never before. Nevertheless, it is also a world whose security and equilibrium is no less dependent on a strong transatlantic partnership where not only interests but also values and visions are shared[3]. Contemporary economies of many countries are operating at the leading edge of economic integration, and the accelerating pace of globalization gives work an importance which reaches well beyond the regional dynamics.

## Concerns for Globalization

Globalization can be described as combined influences of trade liberalization, market integration, international finance and investment, technological change, increasing distribution of production across national boundaries and emergence of new structures of global governance. Global market place equipped with the application of global communications has become the focus of the global business arena that makes the world markets remain open and involve in the fair competitive practices. At the same time the anti-globalization moves also exist in the process of development that protest against the hazards of suppressive strategies of the global companies affecting the regional trade entities. Efficient multinational companies from the leading countries enter the secured country markets and drain out the regional players from the benefit market segments. However, many Japanese companies have not lived to the anticipated success against the international competition. Consequently, Japanese markets that were long protected under various tariff and non-tariff barriers were removed by the government nodding to the global business trends of liberalizations. Globalization concept has strong arguments in favor of developing the trade and economy of developing countries by way of flexible trade and capital movements,

---

[2] Zdenek Drabek and Sam Laird (1997), *The Neo Liberalism: Trade Policy Developments in Emerging Markets*, Staff Working Paper ERAD 9707, World Trade Organization, 1-30.

[3] Renato Ruggiero(1997): Regional initiatives, global impact: cooperation and the multilateral system, Speech of former Director General, World Trade Organization, , WTO News, 07 November.

migration of human and technology resources and sharing of knowledge. The composition of export of developing countries largely consists of primary commodities including agricultural produce and raw material. It has been observed that there has been steep decline of export of these products from developing countries in the world exports. Globalization may liberalize the trade movement for the basic export products of developing countries. However, after introducing economic reforms by many developing countries, prominent rise in the export of manufactured goods has been observed. Foreign direct investment has become the most important contribution enhanced in the globalization process which would help developing countries to increase their foreign reserves, strengthen their economy and maintain sustainable growth. Both portfolio investment and bank credit rose but they have been more volatile, falling sharply in the wake of the financial crises of the late 1990s.

Supporters of globalization concept also argue that allowing free trade and capital movement would also favor workers to move from one country to another, partly to find better employment opportunities. The numbers involved are still quite small, but in the period 1965-90, the proportion of labor forces round the world that was foreign born increased by about one-half. Most migration occurs between developing countries. However, the flow of migrants to advanced economies is likely to provide a means through which global wages converge. There is also the potential for skills to be transferred back to the developing countries and for wages in those countries to rise. Transfer of knowledge on managerial skills, technology and production process is a necessity for development which is made easy through globalization process. Knowledge about production methods, management techniques, export markets and economic policies is available with the developed country relatively at a low cost, and it may be regarded as a valuable resource for the developing countries. Typical arguments that have been put forth by leading movement leaders in various countries towards far and against globalization are illustrated in Exhibit 1.1.

Prominent business moves of the multi-national companies include Japanese electronics and automobile companies, Germany's BMW, Ciba –Geigy, Nestlé, Proctor and Gamble etc. Operating in the global environment requires mastered skills to penetrate in the host countries particularly during the conditions when the trade barriers and government protections have been removed and business policies have been restructured. The phenomenon of the global customer is growing in importance every day and so too is the global-customer-centric organization. Yet, many companies especially those designed according to function, country and business unit, are having difficulty re-designing and aligning their structure with the needs of the global customer. The reasons of the globalization of business have been revealed in many ways, of these the significant variables include:

- market saturation in home country
- trade deficit and long disequilibrium in the balance of trade
- increasing foreign competition
- emergence of new markets
- globalization and free trade zones
- opportunities via foreign aid programs

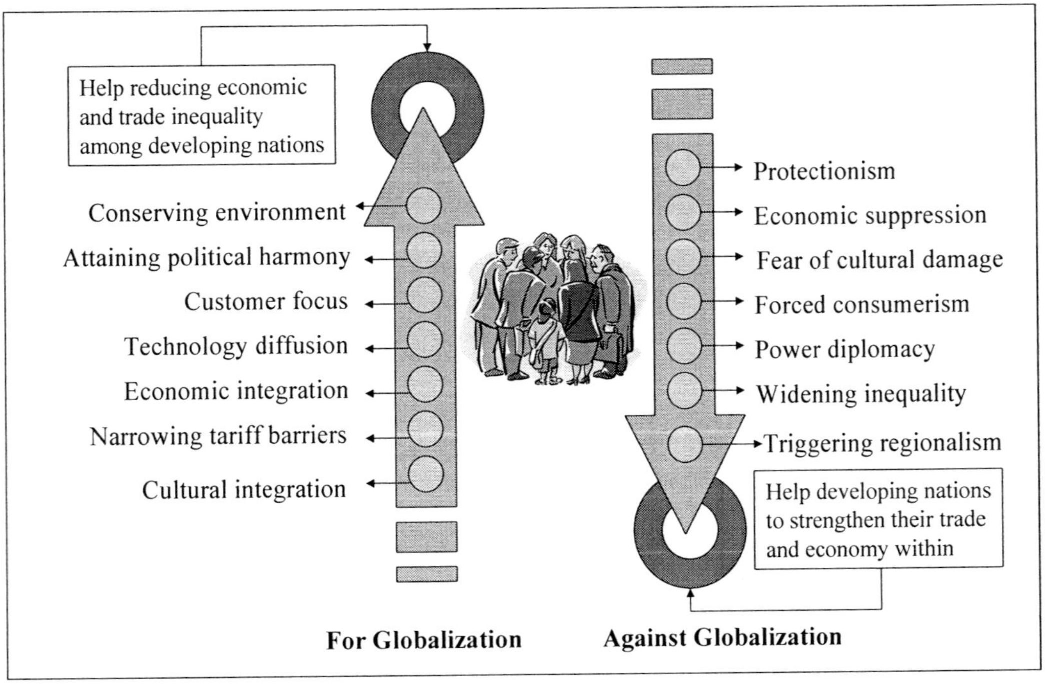


Exhibit 1.1. Debate on Globalization: Emerging issues on for and against.

Problems in the developing world manifest themselves in different ways, apart from falling incomes and the absence of growth. In a number of cases there were serious balance of payments crises (Indonesia, Mexico, and Nigeria); in Latin America there was acute hyper-inflation (Argentina, Bolivia, and Peru). Macro-economic instability usually has serious consequences for a country's balance of payments and trade. Domestic imbalances translate into current account imbalances, and then foreigners are often blamed for unfair trade practices and the like. The greatest risk of slippage in trade policy occurs where there is a lack of fiscal and monetary discipline, and the real exchange rate is allowed to appreciate sharply, i.e., nominal exchange rates are not allowed to compensate fully for the differentials in inflation between the home and foreign markets[4]. However, in emerging markets need to analyze achievements of the fast growing economies in East Asia, which were either open as Singapore, Hong Kong or introduced economic reforms much earlier like Korea, Chinese Taipei), albeit with different emphases in key elements.

Globalization and its impacts have profound implications for a broad range of issues important to the funding community. These issues range from the sustainable use of the worlds' resources and the protection and preservation of the environment, to the need to improve living standards, safeguard human rights, promote and protect cultures, and ensure democratic and responsive global governance. While the idea of globalization has only recently captured public attention, "globalization" has been occurring for centuries.Globalization of market opportunities were observed as the outgrowth of the above factors and the scope of such marketing opportunities has increased with the continued

[4] Zdenek Drabek and Sam Laird (1997), *The Neo Liberalism: Trade Policy Developments in Emerging Markets*, Staff Working Paper ERAD 9707, World Trade Organization, p. 2-4.

deregulation of the significant functional sectors like financial services, leisure industry, information technology etc.

Largest and powerful multinational business houses prefer to be aggressive to dominate over the most demanding and emerging sectors. General Motors for example is offering credit cards and supermarket groups routinely now offer gasoline, banking, pensions and saving plans apart from the manufacturing and marketing of automobiles. Privatization of the state and public sector ventures like energy, transport and communication led to industry restructuring and further allowed the multinational companies to compete in these countries. Entry to the liberalized state and public sector industries brought more professional rules and guidelines for implementing the quality standards like ISO. Nevertheless, there has been a backlash against liberalism. The traditional calls for intervention to "save" jobs or redistribute wealth still strike a chord. Moreover, many people dislike the fact that seemingly impersonal market forces hold sway over their lives, even though markets in fact reflect the combined preferences of millions of ordinary people.

Globalization is not new, but it is more pervasive than before. A century ago, for instance, there was more cross-border migration than there is now. Throughout the past century, new technologies have continuously caused upheaval. Now in the media age, people are constantly confronted with change that they would otherwise not be aware of. There has been a strong social and political reaction in the initial phase of building the concept of globalization across the countries. The anti-globalization arguments were cropped up in reference to economic integration, social integration, and political integration. A study using panel data for 123 countries in 1970-2000 analyses empirically the effects of the overall index of globalization as well as sub-indexes constructed by measuring the single dimensions on economic growth. The results show that globalization promotes growth - but not to an extent necessary to reduce poverty on a large scale. The dimensions most robustly related with growth refer to actual economic flows and restrictions in developed countries. Although less robustly, information flows also promote growth whereas political integration has no effect[5]. The globalization of capital and product markets has many implications for economic welfare. Countries can specialize in the production of goods for which they have comparative advantages, and capital is allocated more efficiently. However, one potentially adverse effect of globalization is the possibility that business cycle volatility might increase. Rapid and badly coordinated capital account liberalization has been blamed for enhancing the vulnerability of emerging markets to unstable international capital flows. At the same time, business cycle volatility in OECD countries seems to have been on a decline in the past decades.

There has been substantial thinking blown in favor of the globalization. Economists, management experts and statisticians were of the strong notion that big demographic and social lifestyle shifts will impact business in this new decade, century, and millennium: fickle fashions, ageing but wealthy populations, retired people inheriting trillions of dollars, an aggressive war for top talent, female consumer influence, human cloning, medical breakthroughs, and a host of other factors, including the huge untapped challenge of mega-city markets in emerging economies. These changes are fundamental to the shape of business because they will alter the way people think and feel. Soft factors may create greatest new

---

[5] Axel Dreher (2003): Does Globalization Affect Growth?, Working Paper, University of Mannheim, Germany, 1-33.

business opportunities. Nevertheless, are teams gearing up to exploit them? Fears that globalization is imposing a deadening cultural uniformity are as ubiquitous as Coca-Cola, McDonald's, and Mickey Mouse. Many people dread that local cultures and national identifies are dissolving into a cross-regional consumerism. That cultural imperialism is said to impose American values as well as products, promote the commercial at the expense of the authentic, and substitute shallow gratification for deeper satisfaction. The core issues woven around globalization are that it can free people from the tyranny of geography. Just because someone was born in France, does not mean they can only aspire to speak French, eat French food, read French books, and so on. That we are increasingly free to choose our cultural experiences enriches our lives immeasurably. We could not always enjoy the best the world has to offer. Technology is reshaping culture: Just think of the Internet. Individual choice is fragmenting the imposed uniformity of national cultures. New hybrid cultures are emerging, and regional ones re-emerging. National identity is not disappearing, but the bonds of nationality are loosening. Some of the questions that have strong hold in the debate of globalization seem to be more lashing against the western influence on pushing global trade. Questions that have emerged during the thought process of globalization may be stated as whether globalization and international trade is destroying local cultures and diversity. Does the market expand our positive liberties and increase the menu of choice? Does trade in cultural products support the artistic diversity of the world or destroy it? More generally, are market exchange and aesthetic quality allies or enemies.

Cultural diversity has multiple meanings and diversity within a society refers to the richness of choice within that society. Globalization focuses on diversity across societies, that is, whether societies are becoming more similar. Cross-cultural exchange tends to favor diversity within a society but not across societies. Trade tends to increase diversity over time by accelerating the pace of change and bringing new cultural goods with each era or generation. Cultural similarities tend to come together over time across the regions. That is, although chain restaurants take an increasing percentage of restaurant sales, growth in dining out has led to an expansion of specialty food opportunities. While cross-cultural exchange alters and disrupts each society it touches, it also supports innovation and creative human energies. The author's views are definitely positive on the benefits of cross-cultural exchange. *Creative destruction* of the market creates a plethora of innovative and high-quality creations in many different genres, styles, and media cross-cultural exchange expands the menu of choice, at least provided that trade and markets are allowed to flourish[6]. Since globalization gathered pace in the 1980s, world inequality has also increased. Strong arguments against the globalization move, argue that while some developing countries were able to take advantage of trade to improve their standard of living, many fell further behind as they depended on a single commodity. Rich countries invested erratically and selectively in developing countries and continued to protect their own markets. However, anti-globalization movement argues that the world trading system is unfair, undemocratic and unsustainable.

Few subjects polarize public opinion as much as the role of globalization in developing countries. Foreign direct investment boosts their economic performance by endowing them with new skills, new technologies, and new jobs—all of which increase their standard of living. In reality, global corporations and the developing countries where they invest have

---

[6] Tyler Cowen (2002): Creative Destruction: How Globalization Is Changing the World's Cultures. Princeton, NJ: Princeton University Press. P 65.

symbiotic objectives. Globalization brings broadly positive economic benefits to developing economies, which in turn represent the best hope for the future of global companies. Both sides should recalibrate their approach. Advantages of the globalization may be viewed as it gives ambitious companies access to the best capital, talent, markets, and resources that the world has to offer. On the contrary, it generate neck-to-neck competition for survival as for some companies, at least—is that every organization is essentially competing against the best in the world. In this adaptation process from *Race for the World*, globalization explores the economic benefits of free trade and look at how the changing landscape will force many companies to reevaluate their strengths and weaknesses. Globalization is both irreversible and unsustainable in its present form.. What will come after it is far from determined. It could be a war of all against all, world domination by a single superpower, a tyrannical alliance of global elites, global ecological catastrophe, or some combination thereof[7]. Hence, at the positive end globalization gets mixed reviews. However, increasing interconnectivity among the world's people seems to promise a *global village* in which the destructive antagonisms of the past can be left behind, replaced by global cooperation and enriching diversity.

## DETERMINANTS OF GLOBAL TRADE

The concept of globalization is characterized with variety of contradictions prominently pertaining to standardization and simultaneously catering to the local needs. Over the period of global thinking, it has been encapsulated that the true nature of globalization should reflect in the attributes "think global, act local". The major determinants of the globalization are as below:

- Market access
- Market opportunities
- Industry standards
- Technology, research and development
- Resource management – internal and external
- Products and services
- Customer prerequisites and needs
- Competition
- Business alliances and cooperation
- Distribution and logistics
- Communication
- Strategy implementation and control process

Globalization has increased the access to the markets as the remote markets have been reduced following the political and economic changes world-wide. The market access has also been improved by growing trade blocks at the regional level. Such accessibility to the markets is further reinforced by reducing the trade barriers through far-reaching business

[7] Jeremy Brecher, Tim Costello and Brendan Smith (2001): Globalization from Below – The Power of Solidarity, South End Press , Cambridge, MA

communication strategies, product and market development programs and customer relations. This situation has given a boost in determining the market opportunities as narrowing the trade barriers helped in deregulating certain sectors of trade such as financial services. The technical operating standards and protocols are being widely adapted to synchronize with the global industry standardsand resources are managed externally to a large extent as the best and low cost materials are procured locally by the multinational companies. Benefits of global sourcing for such companies include low cost labor, uniform quality, innovative ideas, access to local markets, economies to scale, lower taxes and duties, lower logistics costs and more consistent supply. However, there are also some risks in global sourcing that might be political, economic, exchange or supplier risks. In globalization, the product life cycles are getting shorter as the new products are penetrating with higher speed in the markets due to technological development and scale of operations. In this process, many products are dropped off the product life cycle either at the stage of introduction or growth. There are few products that sustain till the mature stage is passed. Growth of technology and its dynamic synchronization with the industry is converging fast leading towards quick adaptations of global products. Globalization of customer requirements is resulting from the identification of worldwide customer segments of homogeneous preferences across the territorial boundaries. Business-to-consumers and Business-to-business markets are powered by the consumer demands from the global companies, as they are perceived more value oriented and of added benefits.

The global competition is observed on both aggressive and defensive dimensions in the market. Companies that are capable of managing appropriate diffusion of technology and adaptation process among the customer segments are found to be highly successful. Competition among multinationals these days is likely to be a three-dimensional strategic game wherein the moves of an organization in one market are designed to achieve goals in another market in ways that aren't immediately apparent to rivals[8]. There is growing consensus among international trade negotiators and policymakers that a prime area for future multilateral discussion is competition policy. Competition policy includes antitrust policy (including merger regulation and control), but is often extended to include international trade measures and other policies that affect the structure, conduct, and performance of individual industries. The leading alliances between the major multinational enterprises may be seen in reference to production, finance, and technology and supply chain along with other complementary activities. To compete in the major global markets the multinational companies manage with substantial financial resources. Logistics and the supply chain management is an art of management of flow of materials and products from the source of production to the end user. This system with the multinational companies includes the total flow of material right from the stage of acquisition of raw materials to the delivery of finished products to the customers. The function of distribution is a combination of activities associated with advertising, sales and physical transfer of the goods and services to the retail and wholesale delivery points as is being observed by the global companies in order to establish their competitive strength in the market. Logistics management is an important function handled by such business companies in the marketing process and effective logistics management improve both cost and customer service performance of the company.

[8] Ian C. MacMillan, Alexander B. van Putten and Rita Gunther McGrath (2003): Global Competition- What is the First Move, HBS Working Knowledge, Harvard Business School, June 23

Globalization of distribution is particularly important for companies using internet for e-commerce as they can operate on economies of scale with wider reach of customers.

The rationale of international marketing is governed by factors of comparative advantages, sustained product life cycle, production sharing and extent of internalization. The concept of comparative advantages states that even if a country is able to produce all its goods at lower costs than that of another country, the trade still benefits mutually based on the comparative costs. It may be stated that the comparative costs help in determining the companies to produce goods in the foreign countries that have comparative advantages over the others and decide either to export goods and services or produce therein. The major variables to measure the comparative advantages are land, labor, capital resource, cost of infrastructure, energy and tax structure. The internalization factor is a prerequisite for a prospecting company to go global. A multinational firm can serve a market across national boundaries either by exporting from a production facility located in the country of the parent company, or from a third country subsidiary or it can set up production facilities in the market itself. The sourcing policy of the firm is the result of the firm's decisions as to which of its production facilities will service its various final markets. Thus, the firm establishes an international network linking production to markets. Major issues associated with the concepts of internalization of the firms may be observed towards:

- Extension of direct operation of the firm
- Common ownership
- Control the activities of the market
- The companies have the global horizon
- Firms choose the least-cost location for each functional activity
- Benefit-cost equilibrium
- Focuses on motives and decision process

Such a network enables the firm to grow by eliminating external markets in intermediate goods and subsequently by *internalizing* those markets within the firm. When international markets are internalized the transfer of goods and services may take place. Internalization of markets is more significant wherever the research inputs and proprietary technology are an important part of the manufacturing process. The theoretical dimensions of internalization provides an economic rationale for the survival of the multinational companies considering the industry-specific factors ( nature and type of product), region-specific product (territorial advantage), country specific factors (SLEPT[9] factors) and company specific factor reflecting on its managerial know-how.

> Maquiladora comes from the Spanish word *maquilar* meaning to perform a task for another. In Mexico, the word referred to the portion of grain collected by millers from grinding other farmers' grains. Today, *maquiladora* refers to a Mexican corporation, wholly or predominantly owned by foreigners, which assemble products for export to the U.S. or other foreign country. The *maquila* industry has transformed the border area of Baja California, which includes the cities of Tijuana, Ciudad Juarez and Mexicali from tourist and agricultural areas into thriving industrial centers. As of February 2001, there are nearly 4000 *maquiladora*

[9] SLEPTsignifies Social, legal, economic, political and technological factors.

plants employing over 1.6 million people in Mexico. The shelter concept divides the operations in the Mexican facility between production functions and administrative functions. The shelter company typically supplies the plant, handles human resources and administrative tasks such as accounting, legal issues, permits, tariffs, transportation and customs issues. Under the North American Free Trade Agreement (NAFTA), U.S. businesses are generally encouraged to source more of their raw materials products within North America, and in most cases, only pay customs duties on any non-U.S. portion of their products. For manufacturers, it is a way to remain competitive without moving operations to Asia and face complicated, time consuming, expensive transportation and customs. The close proximity of Mexico allows easy, inexpensive transportation back into the U.S. Plus, the labor force is adult and plentiful. That's why in the more than 30 years since *maquiladoras* were introduced, there are more than 3,500 companies, including Sony, Ford, General Electric, General Motors and Zenith, that have set up *maquila* operations in Mexico[10].

Production sharing is the contemporary global economic trend that is based on the concepts of comparative advantages that offers economic advantages by stages of the production process. The strategy of production sharing has emerged as a solution to an economic problem in developing countries where the absorption of the surplus manpower in industry is a national economic issue. Consequently, the developing countries turn to the developed countries as major cost effective labor market in order to share production of labor orient products. Investment in production sharing operations has become an integral part of global efforts to reduce manufacturing costs and has contributed to the accelerated pace of cross-border integration of manufacturing in North America and the Caribbean Basin. Currently, production sharing seems to be a growing practice. This practice offers both the developed and developing countries a scope to share their resources and strengths for the mutual benefits.

## Global Trade Dynamics

Since World War II, international marketing has received increased attention from the governments of developing countries who wish to revamp their economy. Many geo-political changes have taken place in the global marketing scenario because of the external affairs policies of developed nations. Exports have been one of the major determinants to measure the economic growth of a country. Hence international marketing rose into prominence in the global economic order and emerged as a discipline in itself for studying the technical, managerial, socio-cultural and economic processes of a country. Observing the dynamism of the international market was viewed as a major strategy to control a substantial share of the trade of a country in the world market. Such attempts were made by the developing nations in the eighties. Later, in the early nineties, the new GATT proposal and evolution of the WTO opened new horizons in the field of international marketing by pushing the export oriented economy worldwide. Today, the scope of international marketing has grown and includes the manufacturing sector and its services. International marketing broadly includes export and import activities that govern the marketing environment.

[10] North American Production Sharing Inc. www.napsmexico.com

Outreach of the global market place has increased manifolds with the emergence of a more open world economy, relaxed trade and tariff barriers, growing customer needs, inter-dependency and inter-communication factors among the countries. The global marketplace consists of population over 6 billion people which is projected to touch the mark of 10 billion people by 2050 according to the estimation of the United Nations. Such a large global market place is becoming economically, culturally and technologically inter-dependent as the convergence of marketing activities have become more effective due to telecommunication and popularity of the electronic commerce. Leading corporations around the world have turned their attention towards expansion of their business activities in order to maintain their competitive edge and retain the customer loyalty. The global business activities in the current period have been described as the second industrial revolution.

Markets today not only provide the multiple goods and services to the customers but also expose their behavior to the cross-cultural differences and innovations. Specialization of the production process has also brought such cultural changes by business penetrations in the low production skills regions across the countries. Apparel from Asian countries like Indonesia, Korea and all type of consumer goods from China, electronics from Japan, perfumery from France may be the good examples to explain the specialization and cross-culture sharing of consumer behavior. Conducting business is a creative enterprise and doing it out of one's own country is more demanding. The industry structure varies dramatically across the countries in the world and a global enterprise to strive against odds requires strong adaptation behavior. In the international business, a company needs to best prepare itself to achieve competitive advantage in the marketplace. The global business has controllable factors that a company needs to adjust within and build its organization within largely uncontrollable marketing environment comprising of SLEPT factors. International marketing involves the companies in making one or more marketing –mix decisions across national boundaries in view of the controllable and non-controllable factors of the market environment. The term international business refers to a wide range of activities involved in organizing business transactions across the boundaries. In international marketing non-controllable factors differ significantly among the markets however, the controllable factors in terms of cost and price structures, opportunities for advertising and distributive infrastructure need marginal adjustments. Global marketing is still larger focus and more complex wherein the companies coordinate, integrate and control a series of marketing programs for sustaining competition and augmenting growth. Hence, international marketing refers to exchanges across national boundaries for the satisfaction of human needs and wants.

## Global Trade and Economy

International trade rebounded in 2002 from its contraction in the preceding year, growing at about 2.5 per cent in volume terms, which was faster than the growth of global output. This rebound occurred despite the weakness of the global economic recovery, greatly reduced capital flows, major changes in exchange rates, increased restrictions on international trade transactions to mitigate risks from terrorism, and rising geopolitical tensions.

## Trade

Trade growth was strong in Asia and the transition economies, largely reflecting better economic performance in those regions. However, trade was stagnant in Western Europe, and contracted in Latin America as a result of economic turmoil in a number of countries in the region. North America's imports recovered in line with stronger domestic demand, while exports continued to decrease in 2002. Many countries seem to be taking the multilateral trading system for granted, while pursuing their commercial interests on a preferential basis in the belief that this will not jeopardize multilateral, non-discriminatory trade relations[11]. Countries of South-East Asia are home to some 500 million people and have a combined GDP of more than $700 billion. Their largely young populations, with large numbers of well-educated and hard-working people, helped to make the region one of the fastest-growing in the world. Until 1997 there was a feeling that the economic order was changing; that the West seemed to be in decline, and that the Asian century was about to dawn. All the lines on the flip-charts about business prospects in South-East Asia pointed one way: upwards. No one believed that the boom could stop. Australia stood out with strong GDP growth in 2002 (both in excess of 3 per cent). In marked contrast to the industrial economies, the recovery in the advanced developing economies in Asia was strong. With the two most populous countries in the world – China and India , growing very rapidly, the gains in output experienced by developing Asia exceeded that of all other regions.

Severity of the downturn in world trade values was even more pronounced than in volume terms, as dollar prices of internationally traded goods decreased in 2001. Merchandise exports recorded a decrease of 4.5 percent, the steepest decline in more than a decade, contrasting sharply with the 6.5 percent average expansion recorded in the 1990s. Commercial services exports, which expanded at the same rate as merchandise trade between 1990 and 2000, declined marginally in 2001. This was the first decrease in world exports of commercial services since 1983 as exhibited in Table 1. The pattern of world merchandise exports by product category in 2001 reflects the main features of the slowdown in the global economic activities in 2001. Firstly, the burst of the IT bubble and the decline in IT expenditure caused an unprecedented shrinkage of international trade in office and telecom equipment of nearly 14%[12]. The decline in crude oil prices by 9% has been the major factor in the 8% decrease of world fuels exports, as the volume of fuels traded remained roughly unchanged during 2002. Among other products, textiles recorded an above average export decrease in 2001, confirming a long-term trade pattern where trade growth consistently lags behind global trade expansion. Since 1990, the share of textiles in world merchandise trade fell from 3.1% to 2.5% in 2002. A noteworthy performance was recorded in respect of agricultural products, for which the export decrease in 2001 was small enough to increase its share in world exports for the first time since 1994. The major economic drivers in the global trade are observed as:

- Reduction in trade and investment barriers

[11] World Trade Organization (2004): World Trade Report-2003, WTO, Geneva p 22.

[12] World exports of all three major IT product groups, i.e. computers (SITC 75), telecom equipment (SITC 76) and semiconductors, and transistors (SITC 776) fell at double digit rates. Exports of semiconductors and other electronic components shrank by more than one fifth.

- Rapid growth and increase in size of the economies of developing countries and their impact on global production capacity
- Innovations in technologies involving transport and communications

The most prominent explanations, often interrelated, for the retardation in the global economic recovery included erosion of trust in institutional pillars such as public and corporate governance, weakening consumer and investor confidence and rising geopolitical risks. The weakness of fixed investment expenditure – particularly pronounced for non-residential investment – contributed significantly to sluggish overall growth in the industrial countries. Investment expenditures play a critical role in the business cycle. There have been problems in sustaining the recovery once inventory levels had been re- established during the recent past. Investment activity generally picks up when prospects for profitable investment opportunities increase and the utilization of existing production capacities reaches a level that calls for a further increase of these capacities. Global output and trade grew more strongly in 2004 than in the previous three years. Global GDP growth amounted to 4 per cent in 2004, providing a solid basis for strong trade growth. For some regions, notably Central and South America and the Commonwealth Independent States (CIS), this represented the best growth for more than a decade. Real merchandise trade grew by 9 per cent, the best performance since 2000 and the third highest rate over 1990's. In line with the prevailing post-war pattern, trade growth outstripped GDP growth by a significant margin by 5 percentage points. The most dynamic traders in 2004 were in Asia, South and Central America, and the CIS. Average trade growth in all of these regions was in double digits. Africa's trade grew strongly on average in 2004, buoyed in part by firmer commodity prices, particularly for oil and metals. North America's exports gained further momentum in 2004 compared to previous years, but growth was below the global average.

Consumer confidence in the major industrial economies improved only temporarily in the first quarter of 2002 and declined or stagnated thereafter. Marginal employment gains in some countries and rising unemployment rates in others led to only moderate increases in wage incomes and depressed private consumption expenditure. In some countries, this led to an increase in precautionary savings. The deterioration in the labor markets of industrial economies with rapidly aging populations rendered their already fragile social security systems even more precarious. General public is increasingly aware that profound adjustments are needed to restore financial sustainability to social security systems and that these adjustments can have a significant impact on future contributions and benefits. The clouded prospects of social security, and in particular pensions systems, contributed to the erosion of consumer confidence and exerted a negative impact on private consumption expenditure. Price movements and exchange rates exerted a significant influence on trade flows measured in current dollar terms[13]. Prices of primary commodities increased faster than prices for manufactured goods. The most notable exchange rate development in 2004 was the weakening of the dollar, resulting in a marked appreciation of European currencies against the dollar. World merchandise exports increased by 21 per cent in 2004, amounting to $8.88 trillion as compared to the growth in commercial services trade of 16 per cent in 2004, reaching $2.1 trillion. However, North America and Europe observed below average nominal export and import growth in 2004. Consumer confidence was also negatively affected by the

[13] World Trade Organization (2006): World Trade Report-2005, WTO, Geneva, xxiii-v.

wealth effect of continuing falls in stock prices, although in some countries (e.g. the United States and the United Kingdom) this was compensated for by rising house prices.

## Direct Investment

Economic growth in the transition economies in 2002 was second only to developing Asia and continued to exceed the global average. Nevertheless, there was a deceleration in the region's economic growth, which can be largely attributed to developments in the Russian economy. Economic growth in Africa and the Middle East remained roughly unchanged in 2002, at about 3 per cent. The moderate gains in regional per capita incomes are unlikely to have a significant impact on poverty levels in the region and one should not lose sight of the large variations in the economic performance of individual African countries. Latin America was the weakest part of the global economy in 2002, recording a decline in output and a steep contraction in imports. Unsustainable, large public sector debt, political instability, sizeable external account imbalances and a reduction in private sector net-capital inflows have contributed to severe slumps in output in a number of South American countries. During the course of 2002, the US dollar depreciated against major currencies like the euro and the yen. Total foreign direct investment (FDI) flows fell by about one quarter in 2002, to roughly $500 billion, with both developed and developing regions suffering sharp reductions. Only China and Central /Eastern Europe attracted larger FDI inflows than in the preceding year. Given the strong correlation between FDI flows and current and future trade flows, this development contributed to the weakness in trade growth in regions other than China and Central /Eastern Europe. One factor contributing to this outstanding performance was the high level of FDI inflows driven by the relocation of labor-intensive manufacturing sectors from Japan and other advanced economies in Asia into China's coastal areas.

Total FDI flows surged from about $200 billion in the early 1990s to almost $1.2 trillion in 2000. In 2001, the value of these flows collapsed by about 50 per cent, and in 2002, by another 25 per cent, falling back to about $500 billion, a level first reached five years ago. Both developed and developing regions have been affected by the reduction in FDI flows. Only FDI inflows to China and to Central /Eastern Europe continued to increase. China's FDI inflows rose by 19 per cent, to $ 52.7 billion, and those to Central /Eastern Europe increased by 9 per cent, to $30 billion[14]. The sharp decline in nominal terms of global FDI flows can be attributed to the end of the frenzied boom of mergers and acquisitions and the lower market values of corporations listed on global stock markets. Between the end of 2000 and the end of 2002, the valuation of global stock markets decreased by about 40 per cent, which automatically lowered the transaction value of FDI flows for buying corporations listed on equity markets[15]. It was observed that there has been a moderate increase in global FDI inflows in 2004, after a steep fall over three years, also suggests improved business confidence in the state of the world economy[16]. The United States, a number of Asian

[14] The Vienna Institute for International Economic Studies, press release, February 2003: FDI in Central and Eastern European Countries in 2002: Record Inflow Concentrated in a Handful of Countries. http://wiiw.ac.at.

[15] Estimates based on the average decrease of four major stock market indices: NYSE-Composite, FTSE 100, Frankfurt DAX and Tokyo Topix. Source: World Federation of Exchanges at http://www.world-exchanges.org.

[16] UNCTAD, Press Release 11/01/05.

developing countries, and also some Latin American countries were the principal beneficiary of the increase in global FDI flows. One of the new developments in global FDI flows was the emergence of China as an investor in natural resources in a number of developing countries[17]. Domestic inflation picked up moderately in the course of 2004, under the impact of strengthened economic activity and the increase in world fuel prices.

Marked differences in domestic demand growth between the United States, developing Asia and the transition economies on the one hand, and Japan, Western Europe and Latin America on the other, contributed to major shifts in trade and current account balances. Japan and Western Europe recorded an expansion in net exports. Consequently, the trade and current account surpluses of Japan and the EU widened with increases equivalent to 1 per cent and 0.7 per cent of GDP respectively. Under the impact of sharply lower capital inflows, Latin America had to cut its imports, which led to a trade surplus and reduced the region's current account deficit. The US current account deficit widened to more than $500 billion or 5 per cent of GDP, which was a historic peak in absolute and relative terms. Given that the aggregate deficit for the OECD area remained almost unchanged in relative terms in 2002, this implied that the level of net imports from developing areas also stayed unchanged. Developing Asia again recorded a substantial current account surplus. Japan, the four advanced developing Asian economies (Hong Kong, China; Korea, Rep. of; Singapore; Chinese Taipei) and China reported large current account surpluses, indicating that these economies had become the principal suppliers of capital to the rest of the world[18].

## INTERNATIONAL COMPETITION

Emergence of virtual shopping, liberalization of economic policies in the developing countries all over the world competition has become like a traditional derby in which many companies participate for neck to neck race. In this business game the rules are subject to change without notice, the prize money may change in short notice, the route and finish line is also likely to change after the race begins, new entrants may join at any time during the race, the racers may form strong alliances, all creative strategies are allowed in the game and the governmental laws may change without notice and sometimes with retrospective effect. Hence, to win the race any company should acquire the strategies of outwitting, outmaneuvering and outperforming the competitors. In this process, a company must understand thoroughly all the moves of the rival firms from various sources. The locales of the business rivalry have to be spotted to assess their strengths.

Competing firms pay more attention to the sources of factors, quality thereof, cost and management of the factors in order to prove better over each other. Customer, the end user is the ultimate target of competitor for building aggressive and defensive strategies in business. Such competing firms try to attract the customers by various means to polarize business and earn confidence in the market place. It is necessary for the successful business companies to look for such a place of business which provides them more location advantage and holds the

[17] The agreement reached between IBM and the Chinese firm Lenovo on the sale of the IBM's PC business in December 2004 indicates that China's foreign direct investment is not limited to primary commodities.

[18] The foreign exchange reserves of the five Asian developing economies increased by about $50, while Japan's international reserves increased by $30 billion in 2002.

customers for their goods and services. Business cordoning or securing the trade boundaries is an essential decision to be taken for building competitive strategies to attack rivals across regions. Even the small business company can compete globally with the firms of all sizes through the internet. The distribution channels, franchisees, carrying and forwarding agents, retailers and mailers with value added services represent an increasingly intense business rivalry or competition in all markets or competitive domains. Many firms like Godrej (Diversified Products), Proctor and Gamble (Consumer Goods), Compaq (Computers) reward their managers handsomely for winning the business battles in their channel wars. In succeeding to the market competition, the institutional and political patronage provides long run support to the companies[19].

Many organizations feel that in growing competition establishing strategic alliances would better check the competitor's penetration than the own brand or technology driven company. They recognize that alliances and relationships with other companies of repute are fundamental to outwit, outmaneuver and outperform the competitors by ways of better branding, better service and tagging global brands for assuring the quality of goods and services. Alliances and relationships thus transform the concept of competitor. In international marketing many industries, face fierce competition leading to price wars. The foreign manufacturers penetrate in the international markets by offering low priced, high – quality products. The Xerox Corporation despite this philosophy can not guarantee the market leadership. In a crowded field with some 14 competitors from Japan alone, it faces the toughest market in the USA in the copier machines markets. Retail sales of food and drink in Europe's largest markets are at a standstill, leaving European grocery retailers hungry for opportunities to grow. Most leading retailers have already tried e-commerce, with limited success, and expansion abroad, often with more. However, almost all have ignored the big, profitable opportunity in their own backyard: the wholesale food and drink trade, which appears to be just the kind of market retailers need. Recently even some of the hi-tech industries have become susceptible to the competition, as the competitive situation has forced some of them to shift their consumer electronics manufacturing to the Far-East as it is at the losing edge in USA. As the retail community shrinks, they put greater emphasis on their suppliers for quality products at a competitive price that enables them to make healthy margins to attract consumers. If one manufacturer cannot supply the necessary ingredients, retailers will look for other alternatives. This environment has provided an opportunity to shake up an otherwise mature and stable industry such as the photographic industry and has paved the way for a viable competitor to Kodak such as Fuji Photo Film U.S.A. The phenomenon has contributed to Fuji making significant inroads into Kodak's once commanding U.S. market share in particular and to its global share in general.

The relationship between Kodak and Fuji had always been adversarial, as competitors naturally are; however, it took a very serious turn in May 1995 when Kodak filed a Section301 petition under U.S. trade law. The petition claimed that Kodak's 7-10 percent market share in Japan was not a result of consumer choice and marketing efforts but rather a result of four principle Japanese wholesalers, backed by the Japanese government, that are exclusive Fuji film supporters. The success of Wal-Mart has taught retailers that diversification, scrambled marketing and "one-stop" shopping are important to consumers. As consolidation sweeps the nation in mass merchants, food and drug accounts, retailers realize

[19] Rajagopal (2000): Marketing Management-Text and Cases, Vikas Publishing House, New Delhi, , , pp 91-113.

they must maintain their competitive advantage or close shop. To survive, they are squeezing manufacturers for quality products at competitive prices to capture profit margins for expansion within the industry. This environment has provided an opportunity for Fuji film to prosper in an otherwise stable and mature photographic industry.

Globalization has shown many advantages of economic growth for the developing countries but also posed threats to the regional business environment. The competition among firms is increasingly shifting from company *vs.* company to supply chain *vs.* supply chain. Benefits can be grouped as customer-oriented benefits, productivity benefits, and innovation related benefits. Factors supporting collaboration are observed as trust, common goals for cooperation, and existence of cooperation mechanisms, while barriers are related to three factors such as lack of trust, risk-benefit evaluation, and lack of common goals for cooperation[20]. The collaboration in the business strategy may be considered analogous with the cooperation in the reference to prevailing concerns of the globalization. On the contrary, heavy competition in India in almost all product categories has been experienced due to diversification by large and medium companies and increased entry of multinationals which has restricted the growth of domestic companies. Previously, large companies enjoyed high profit margins by targeting premium priced products in the upper strata of Indian society. High levels of competition from equally reputed brands have not only decreased the companies' market share but also created price wars, reducing profit margins and limiting market growth. This has motivated companies to consider the lower classes and the rural segments, which they had previously ignored[21]. In the growing competitive markets the large and reputed firms are developing strategies to move into the provision of innovative combinations of products and services as 'high-value integrated solutions' tailored to each customer's needs than simply 'moving downstream' into services. Such firms are developing innovative combinations of service capabilities such as operations, business consultancy and finance required to provide complete solutions to each customer's needs in order to augment the customer value towards the innovative or new products[22]. Competition may be characterized as striving together to win the race not to destroy the other competitors from the point of view of the supporters of globalization. The local market competition is targeted towards the customers and the competitors strive to win the customer, temporarily or permanently. However, in business - to - business process, the competition may turn more tactical and strategic in order to outperform the rivals firms. In this way, competition can be seen as regulated struggle. Competitive roles can be radically altered with technological advances or with the right marketing decisions[23].

An all-out war has emerged today,while Kodak and Fuji fight for market share, the real winner and benefactor is the consumer. "Retailers and consumers will be the big winners in this struggle for market share among the big players," says one retailer. "We are going to get

---

[20] Cetindamar Dilek, Catay Bülent and Basmaci O Serdar (2005), Competition through Collaboration-Insights from an Initiative in the Turkish Textile Supply Chain, Supply *Chain Management -An International Journal*, 10 (4), April, 238-240.

[21] Dubey Jayshree and Patel Rajani P (2004), Small Wonders of the Indian Market, *Journal of Consumer Behaviour*, 4 (2), December, 145-151.

[22] Rajagopal and Rajagopal Ananya (2006), Competition vs. Cooperation: Analyzing Strategy Dilemma in Business Growth under Changing Social Paradigms, *International Journal of Business Environment*, 1 (4), Forthcoming.

[23] Rajagopal (2006), Measuring Customer Value Gaps: An Empirical Study in Mexican Retail Markets, *Economic Issues*, 11(1), March, 19-40.

more incentives to sell merchandise and the consumer is going to see a lot more new products at lower prices[24]." Kodak and Fuji deny that they are engaging in a price war, but for each move Fuji makes, Kodak counters with a counter strategy. "Smack them until they figure it out," is how Fuji describes its strategy[25].

## OUTGROWTH OF NEW MARKETS

The World Development Report for 2003 states that "Considerable uncertainty clouds trade growth prospects for 2003. The expectations of a war in Iraq caused a sharp increase of oil prices in the first quarter of 2003 and had a detrimental effect on business confidence and global stock markets. Oil prices started to weaken in the second half of April but remained above the preceding year's level. Information on economic activity in the industrial countries in the first months of 2003 has led to a marked downward revision of output growth in 2003, in particular for Western Europe. As Western Europe accounts for more than 40 per cent of world merchandise and commercial services trade, global trade will suffer accordingly[26]." The global scenario is changing very fast in the emergence of the new markets. The new business opportunities developed from European Community enhanced by the reunification of Germany and the thriving economies of the Pacific Rim countries during 90's. Countries which have prospects in international business are China, Latin America and the emerging market-based economies in the Eastern Europe. However, the growing momentum towards the privatization and liberal policies show further promising markets in the developing countries.

The story of how Schultz & Co. transformed a pedestrian commodity into an upscale consumer accessory has a fairy-tale quality. Starbucks has grown from 17 coffee shops in Seattle 15 years ago to 5,689 outlets in 28 countries. Sales have climbed an average of 20% annually since the company went public 10 years ago, to $2.6 billion in 2001, while profits bounded ahead an average of 30% per year, hitting $181.2 million last year. To duplicate the staggering returns of its first decade, Starbucks has no choice but to export its concept aggressively. Indeed, some analysts give Starbucks only two years at most before it saturates the U.S. market. The chain now operates 1,200 international outlets, from Beijing to Bristol. That leaves plenty of room to grow. Indeed, about 400 of its planned 1,200 new stores this year will be built overseas, representing a 35% increase in its foreign base. Starbucks expects to double the number of its stores worldwide, to 10,000 in three years. During the past 12 months, the chain has opened stores in Vienna, Zurich, Madrid, Berlin, and even in far-off Jakarta. Athens comes next. And within the next year, Starbucks plans to move into Mexico and Puerto Rico. But global expansion poses huge risks for Starbucks. For one thing, it makes less money on each overseas store because most of them are operated with local partners. While that makes it easier to start up on foreign turf, it reduces the company's share of the profits to only 20% to 50%.

---

[24] *Supermarket Business*, February 1999, p47.
[25] *The Wall Street Journal*, 18 November 1998.
[26] World Trade Organization (2004): World Development Report-2003, WTO, Geneva, p 5.

Emerging Markets, in partnership with business leaders, had pursued a variety of initiatives that had cut costs and provided new customer focused products and services. It was not yet clear, however, what new business model would emerge:

> Today's marketplace isn't where clients are at all ready to pay explicitly for anything. But, in time, it is possible our clients will pick and choose. They might get their sales advice from one place and their research from another and they might trade in a third place and clear through a fourth entity— really unbundling the value proposition. So the challenge for us is to try to re-bundle things back together in intelligent ways that continue to add value to clients[27]. (*Simon Lack, Managing Director, Chase Manhattan Bank)*

Companies having an objective of territorial expansion used a three-pronged attack in its strategy to penetrate into the emerging markets: offensive, defensive, and efficiency initiatives. Offensive initiatives were intended to gain market share where the company had not traditionally been a leader, and thus bring new revenues into the bank. Defensive initiatives attempted to preempt competitors' moves into markets where the company had traditionally dominated. Efficiency initiatives delivered cost savings to the bank from customer self-service or from straight-through processing that squeezed costs out of back office processes. Asian markets for US companies are growing faster than other countries as the European market is declining for US products. It has been found that the European market has declined from 31 to 20 percent for the US products while the share going to Asia has increased from 20 to 30 percent in the same period. Asian markets are very sensitive to most of the top brands of the western companies. The markets in Asian countries including Japan shoulder one third of the luxury goods and fashion business and by 2005, this region will make up to the half of the global business of the luxury goods[28]. However, there remains absence of well-functioning product markets in transition economies as a sufficient condition under which big bang reduces output initially, while a Chinese-style reform increases output. Big bang dismantles central planning or centralized organization of production, permitting monopolistic and vertically interdependent enterprises to pursue their own monopoly profits by restricting output and inter-firm trade to the detriment of the economy as a whole. The Chinese reform, by maintaining central planning but allowing enterprises to produce for the emerging product markets after they have fulfilled their output quotas under planning, gives enterprises incentives to expand output beyond planned targets[29].

## DEFINING CONCEPTS OF GLOBAL TRADE

Contemporary global business models explain that the firms tend to structure themselves as one of four organizational types: international, multidomestic, global and transnational. Depending on the type, a company's assets and capabilities are either centralized or decentralized, knowledge is developed and diffused in either one direction or in many, and the importance of the overseas office to the home office varies. International marketing refers

[27] Jeanne Ross and Richard Woodham (2001): Chase Global Markets: Defining New Business Models in the Investment Bank Industry, MIT Sloan School of Management, Working Paper 454-01, August, 1-11.

[28] Asia's Brand Barons Go Shopping, *The Economist*, March 28, 1998, p 60.

[29] Wei Li: A Tale of Two Reforms, Rand Journal of Economics, 30 (1), 1999, 120-136.

to exchanges across national boundaries for the satisfaction of human needs and wants. Various marketing functions coordinated and integrated across the multiple country markets may be referred as *global marketing*. The process of such integration may involve product standardization, uniform packaging, homogeneity in brand architecture, identical brand names, synchronized product positioning, commonality in communication strategies or well coordinated sales campaigns across the markets of different countries. The term 'global' does not convey the literal meaning of penetration into all countries of the world. However, it need to be understood in relative sense and even a regionalization or operating in a cluster of countries may also be taken as a global operation in an applied perspective. The regional marketing efforts like trans-Asian or Pan-European marketing operations may also be viewed as examples of global marketing. Suppliers of products ranging from Budweiser beer to BMW cars have been able to keep growing without succumbing to the pricing pressures of an intensely promotional environment. A strong brand also can open the door when growth depends on breaking into new markets. Starbucks Corporation[30], among the fastest-growing brands, recently set up shop in Vienna, one of Europe's cafe capitals, among 400 new store planed for opening at overseas locations during 2002. The companies succeed in the regional integration across multiple countries markets as they follow the similar strategies and management principals for a cluster of markets. The fourth annual A.T. Kearney/Foreign Policy Magazine Globalization Index[31] in its report on 2004 global trade states "...measures economic, person-to-person, political, and technological integration in 62 countries, accounting for 96 percent of the world's gross domestic product (GDP) and 84 percent of the world's population". Using this system, these countries rank as the most global:

- Ireland
- Singapore
- Switzerland
- Netherlands
- Finland

United States of America has been slowly climbing in this index. Last year it ranked 11th and was 12th the year before. Foreign direct investment (FDI) flows, already down about 40 percent in 2001, slid another 20 percent to $651 billion—the lowest level in five years. The United States and United Kingdom accounted for nearly half the drop, but the trend was felt worldwide, with FDI inflows dropping in two thirds of the countries covered. Global portfolio capital flows also contracted; stock market losses in the United States, Germany, and Brazil erased wealth and risk aversion that grew in the wake of Argentina's economic meltdown. In the developing world, Southeast Asia again ranked as the most globally integrated region, with Singapore and Malaysia placing among the world's 20 most global countries (and the first and second place countries in trade). Central and Eastern Europe registered strong gains and was among the few world regions to see levels of economic integration deepened during the year 2003.

Historically *multinational marketing* is referred to the common strategies in the 'multi-domestic' business environment with strong long preferences. In an applied perspective these

[30] Gerry Khermouch (2002) : The best global brands, Business Week Online, August 05.
[31] Kearney AT *et.al.*(2004): Ireland clings to the top Global, Foreign Policy, February 24. www.foreignpolicy.com

differences are very narrow and they show the natural progress from one function to another. In order to perform the global management tasks successfully, it is necessary to develop adequate acquaintance with the issues of trade barriers, market environments and SLEPT factors including their possibilities of effective coordination with the corporate as well as the home country policies. The salient product beliefs, attitudes and social norms vary largely among the markets. Customers' decision making across the countries depends to a large extent on the quality attributes associated with the product and attitude of the customers towards foreign brands. There are also variations in the sensitivity preferences like taste, touch, appearance, odor etc. If the European consumers prefer a car with a stick shift and tight cornering, the Japanese consumers like to have a soft touch and easy control of the machine. These preference are considerably governed by the traditional, cultural, social and transitional factors thereof like fashion. Such differences drive the marketers to wait for product adaptation in the target segments before setting the volume sales operations.

The *multi-domestic markets* may be defined as the product markets that serve the preferences of the local customers and the functional requirements therein may widely differ from other markets. The products and services such as food and beverages, clothing, entertainment, life-style products may be an appropriate example of the multi-domestic markets which tend to vary considerably across the countries wherein consumers prefer to have the local variants. Philips may be cited as a good example of the company that has followed the multi-domestic strategy. This strategy of the company resulted in promoting innovation from the local research and development process, build entrepreneurial spirit, tailor the products to the individual countries and maintain high quality through backward integration. However, the company had to move on to the challenges that emerged due to the implementation of multi-domestic strategy. The challenging issues before the company include high cost of tailored products and growing fear of duplication across the countries, product innovations were more research based than market driven and the time to market was running slow. The multi-domestic company allows its subsidiaries to develop and exploit local opportunities, expects them to create a local knowledge and competency base, and decentralizes significant decision-making to the subsidiaries. An example of a multi-domestic firm is General Motors, whose extensive European units tend to operate as self-contained entities. Multi-domestic markets reflect various preferential attributes of the consumer decisions. The companies selling into multidomestic markets require localizing and adapting their products and services across the markets in reference to varied customer needs and buying preferences. Multidomestic companies intending for geographic expansion of the business across the countries, largely associate with:

- establishing complete set of value-creation activities—including production, marketing, and R&D—in each major national market
- transferring skills and products developed at home to foreign markets
- Extensively customizing both product offering & marketing strategy

However, the multidomestic strategy of the companies develop into the decentralized federation, suffer lack of control and national subsidiaries of the companies tend to function in an autonomous manner over the period. Often it has been observed that the companies fail to transfer the knowledge to their subsidiaries uniformly to attain the perfect blend of skills and technology to match the local needs. The key differences in the global and multidomestic markets are exhibited in Table 1.1.

**Table 1.1. Key Differences in the Multidomestic and Global Markets**

| Attributes | Market Category | |
|---|---|---|
| | Multidomestic | Global |
| Territorial | Markets are defined within the country borders wherein the customer and competitors are of local origin. | Markets are identified across the country borders. Transactions are held across the borders with the customers and competitors. |
| Target buyers | Heterogeneous customer targets across the countries that are defined locally. | The segments are territorially cut across the countries with similar customer characteristics from different countries. |
| Competition | Cost competition in multidomestic companies creates greater stress. Local firms pose higher threats and strategies need to be planned on country basis. | Competitors are less in number and exist in major markets. Competition is observed on regional or global platforms. |
| Operations | Operating in multidomestic markets will have greater difficulty in achieving parent/subsidiary consistency. Strategies are local and coordinating activities among the markets do not benefit significantly. | Higher advantages in coordinating activities within the region or across the countries in the world. Strategies by the global marketing firms can be built on regional or standardized business goals. |
| Interdependence | Independent operations in local markets. Isolated impact of competition in the market. | Interdependent operations in each country and possess mutual interactions among the markets. |

Global products that are standardized in terms of quality, features and packaging do not succeed in the market as they are of low price or consumer psychodynamics but are often preferred by the buyers as such products are value based and offer competitive advantage on the price and non-price factors thereof. In global product markets the company is required to develop technological capabilities to be able to compete by launching new products. An excellent example of an organization which can be precisely characterized as having multidomestic growth strategy may be Unilever which has specialized in the food and cosmetics products catering to the consumer preferences of each country under its business. The company used the multidomestic strategy to gain competitive advantages in its target country markets.

Similarly, another example may be cited of Asea Brown Boveri (ABB), the engineering and technology company wherein the key factor of the corporate strategy is encouraging the senior managers to be entrepreneurial in responding to the local needs of the customers, comply with industry standards and coordinate at the different stages of economic development. ABB uses a matrix to organize its activities that allows global optimization of the business and maximize performance in each country. However some companies like ABB get into the internal dilemma while streamlining the growth path as they want to be global as well as local, manage large markets as well as prove their brand value in niches and radically decentralize the activities or subsidiaries while also look for centralizing the reporting system to demonstrate effective monitoring and control.

*Transnational companies* have flexible management processes and networks that integrate diverse assets, resources and people into operating units globally. The transnational companies aim at developing the strategic capabilities towards global scaling and competitiveness, national level responsibilities and operational flexibility and cross market capacity to leverage learning on global basis. In the transnational organizations, the ownership of the operations is less clear in terms of manufacturing locations, status of service provider or the manufacturer and marketer of products and services. There is emerging evidence that globalization is beginning to provide new opportunities for global coalitions of advocacy groups to bring market-based pressures to bear upon major transnational firms in a way that promotes higher standards of social and environmental responsibility in production processes and trade relations[32]. The United Nations Conference on Trade and Development in its annual survey of foreign direct investment had constructed an "index of trans-nationality". It works out the ratios of companies' foreign assets to total assets, foreign sales to total sales and foreign employment to total employment; the index is the average of these three numbers[33]. Transnational organizations require highly flexible coordination process to manage the short term assignments and long run realignments of basic responsibilities and interactive relationship. Such companies should have the capability of modifying roles and relationships on the basis of each decision on the market situation.

International Business Machines Corporation (IBM) is a good example of transnational business organization as its functional pattern is strategically divided into the principal and subsidiary organizations. The company strives to lead in the creation, development and manufacture of the industry's most advanced information technologies, including computer systems, software, networking systems, storage devices and microelectronics. We translate these advanced technologies into value for our customers through our professional solutions and services businesses worldwide. Currently the company operates in 160 countries. Some of its marketing, operations and research and development activities are centralized and standardized whereas other units operate with substantial degree of independence. The company has a strong corporate identity and some of its promotional themes are uniform across its subsidiaries. It has also formed strategic alliance with international business partners in the information technology area. The company has 24 manufacturing plants world over that include North America (10), Europe (6) and Asia-Pacific (8). The research and development of IBM is carried out in 8 countries world over. The company had 351,889 employees across the countries.

The imperial Chemical Industries (ICI) a multi-product transnational company would be a good reference to be cited as a network corporation. ICI creates, develops and markets products that make the world look brighter, taste fresher, smell sweeter and feel smoother such as paints, foods, fragrances, personal care and the like. Of course, the ICI Group is a huge international business. ICI was formed in 1926 by the merger of four of the largest

---

[32] Michael E Conroy (2001): Can Advocacy-Led Certification Systems Transform Global Corporate Practices? Evidence, and Some Theory, Political Economy Research Institute, University of Massachusetts at Amherst, Working Paper # 21, , 1-28.

[33] The Economist, 25 September 1997.

chemical companies in the UK. In 70's the inorganic fiber 'Saffil' was launched by the company and is still used in, among other applications, catalytic converters for cars. In 1983, ICI began to abandon its conventional country-by-country organization and established worldwide business units[34].The laboratories of the company across the countries were given independent roles for developing market driven R&D close to the competitors. The company began its transformation from bulk chemical producer to global specialty products and paints leader with its biggest ever acquisition in 1997. It purchased four businesses from Unilever - National Starch and Chemical, Quest International, Unichem and Crosfield - for $8 billion and added them to its own specialty products and paints businesses. Such strategic shifts created drastic changes in the corporate policies that primarily resulted in narrowing down the human resources and increasing per capita productivity. ICI accelerated its exit from the bulk commodity chemicals market by selling its cyclical bulk chemical businesses for value to new owners who were keen to grow and invest in those sectors. ICI accelerated its exit from the bulk commodity chemicals market by selling its cyclical bulk chemical businesses for value to new owners who were keen to grow and invest in those sectors. Divestment proceeds, and a rights issue has been used to repay debt and restore the strength of the balance sheet. ICI today is a collection of world class businesses, many of them leaders in their sectors. The company employs more than 35,000 people worldwide. Their product range is 50,000 strong that took the sales in 2003 to £5.8 billion[35].

## DRIVERS OF GLOBALIZATION

There are over 200 countries in the world and it is difficult for the marketer to determine a critical path of success across the countries or regions. Exceptionally, couple of companies like Fuji, Kodak and Coca-cola that have spread their business in over 100 countries developed gradually. The characteristics of the global market place are diverse and international marketing approaches are differentand companies need to adapt a strong rationale for grouping the countries into segments. The multinational and the global corporation are different as the former operates in a number of countries and carries adjustment in the production and marketing practices in each country at a highly relative costs.[36] Global corporations operate with the stanch loyalty at relatively low costs with standardization. Coca-cola and Pepsi-Cola companies have standardized their products globally according to the regional and ethnic preferences of consumers. Most effective world competitors integrate quality and trust attributes into their cost structure. Such companies compete on the basis of appropriate value of price, quality, trust and delivery systems. These values are considered by the companies in reference to the product design, function and changing consumer preferences like fashion. The multi-national corporations know a lot about the business environment in a country, put their efforts on adapting to the given environment and sets gradual penetration process in the country. On the contrary, the global corporations recognize the absolute need to be competitive and drive through the lower prices

[34] Jeremy Main (1989): How to go global-And why, Fortune, August 28, p.70.
[35] Corporate home page- Group Overview, www.ici.com, 21 May 2004.
[36] Theodore Levitt (1998): *The globalization of markets* in Meloan W Taylor and Graham L John (Eds), International and Global Marketing-Concept and Cases, , Irwin McGraw Hill, Boston, 13-23,

by standardizing its marketing operations. The global corporations treat the world as composed of a few networked and standardized markets than many independent and customized markets.

There are five major categories of drivers that propel companies towards globalization. These drivers include market, competition, cost, technology and government. Of these, the market driver has been considered as one of the strongest forces that push the process of global marketing.

> "The major driver of change for General Motors today is the same as for most companies; it's globalization. Advances in technology and communication are making the 'small world' a reality, and the world will only get smaller and smaller in coming years...This trend towards global integration should be- viewed as an opportunity—not a problem." (*John F. Smith, Jr., CEO of General Motors*)

The *market drives* comprise the needs of common customers, global customers, global channels and transferable marketing. The common customers needs become a compelling factor for the multinational companies when customers of the different countries have the same needs in a product category. The free trade and unrestricted travel has created homogenous groups of customers across the countries in reference to specific industries. However, some markets that typically deal with the culture bound products like food and beverages, apparel and entertainment strongly resist the shift towards globalization and remain multidomestic serving to the different customer preferences and differentiated products across the countries. On the contrary, the global customers need the same products or services in many countries like the case of Kodak films or Hilton Hotels. The global channels, distribution and logistics companies offer seamless transport, storage and delivery services. The companies can expand internationally provided the channel infrastructure is met with the distribution needs of the company. Hence, their integrated networks thrive to bring the multinational companies close to the global distributors, retail stores like super markets and departmental stores in order to generate systems effect. Transferable marketing is applied to the same marketing ideas on brand names, packaging, advertising and other components of marketing-mix in the different countries. Nike's campaign anchoring the basketball champion Michael Jordan pulled-up the brand in many countries. This is how the good ideas of multinationals get leveraged world over.

The *competitive drivers* support companies for matching their strategies appropriately with their moves in the market. The existence of many global competitors indicates that an industry is mature for international business operations. The global competitors operate on cost advantages over the local competitors. The emergence of strong global competitors has served to develop the market infrastructure for the local companies and also help in transfer of technological skills enabling the domestic company to explore the scope of expansion. The competitive efforts put pressure on companies to globalize their marketing activities to derive optimum performance by interpreting appropriately the competitor signals. When Kodak backed out from sponsoring the 1984 Los Angeles Olympics, the Fuji Film entered into the sponsorship issue immediately at the prescribed price and was one of the official sponsors of the Olympics. By the time Kodak reconsidered to participate in this international event, the time overran. However, for the Olympics of 1988 and ABC-TV Kodak become sport program sponsor[37].

The *cost drivers* are largely based on scale of economies that involve the cost of production functions in large and complex industries, cost of outsourcing, diffusion and adaptation of technology, tariffs and taxes and costs associated with the basic and advanced marketing functions. The macro economic factors of the neighboring countries also govern the cost drivers. When a new automobile plant is set-up, it aims at designing, manufacturing or assembling and delivering a particular model by penetrating into the neighboring markets to gain the advantages of economies of scale. The high market share multidomestic companies derive gains from spreading their production activities across multiple product lines or diversified business lines to achieve advantage through the scope of economies. The manufacturing and marketing activities of Proctor and Gamble, Unilever, Colgate-Palmolive may illustrate this global attribute that is explained by the cost drivers. Other cost drivers include global sourcing advantages, low global communications and automation processes. The location of strategic resources to the production plants, cost differences across the countries and transport costs are also some important considerations of the cost drivers.

Lowering of trade barriers made globalization of markets and production a theoretical possibility, and technological change has made it a tangible reality. Since the end of World War II, the world has seen major advances in communications, information processing, and transportation technology including, most recently, the explosive emergence of the Internet and World Wide Web. The *technology drivers* play a significant role in global business. Global expansion of the multinational companies has been highly stimulated by the technological advancements in the designing, manufacturing and marketing of consumer and industrial products. The services were also improved by many technological breakthroughs. The internet revolution has triggered the e-commerce as open access channel as a strong driving forces for the global business in the consumer and industry segments. Improved transport and communication now makes it possible to be in continuous contact with producers anywhere in the world. This makes it easier for companies to split production of a single good over any distance. Storage and preservation techniques have revolutionized the food industry for example, so that the idea of seasonal vegetables is no longer relevant today as anything can be exported all year round from anywhere.

In addition, the IT revolution has made the movement of investment capital around the globe an almost immediate process ensuring that financing opportunities across the developed and developing world have both expanded and become more flexible. However, non-economic drivers of global integration, from travel to telephone traffic maintained their forward momentum, making the world more integrated at the end of 2002 than ever before. Technological upgrading, in the form of introduction of new machinery and improvement of technological capabilities, provides a firm with the means to be successful in competition. In the process of introducing better technologies, new lower-cost methods become available, which allow the firm to increase labor productivity, i.e., the efficiency with which it converts resources into value. Firms will adopt these newer methods of production if they are more profitable than the older ones. The ability of a firm to take advantage of technical progress is also enhanced if the firm improves its entrepreneurial and technological capabilities through

[37] Thomas C Finnerty (2000): Kodak Vs. Fuji – The Battle for Global Market Share, Institute of Global Business Strategy, Lubin School of Business, Pace University, New York, 1-23.

two competitiveness strategies, namely (i) learning and adaptation, and (ii) innovation wherein latter is a process of searching for, finding, developing, imitating, adapting, and adopting new products, new processes, and new organizational arrangements. Because rivals do not stand still, the firm's capacity to develop these capabilities, as well as its ability to compete, depends on the firm's maintaining a steady pace of innovation[38]. Containerization has revolutionized the transportation business, significantly lowering the costs of shipping goods over long distances. Before the advent of containerization, moving goods from one mode of transport to another was very labor intensive, lengthy, and costly. It could take days to unload a ship and reload goods onto trucks and trains. As containerization process has gained efficiency and transportation costs have plummeted, shipping goods around the world has become economical , thereby helping to drive the globalization of markets and production.

The *government drivers* for the globalization include diplomatic trade relations, customs unions or common markets. The government drivers add favorable trade policies, foreign investment regulations, bilateral or regional trade treaties and common market regulations. The introduction of global standard norms like ISO certifications by the respective countries may be one of the effective measures to promote the globalization through uniform quality perspectives. In the past the government barriers to foreign market entry protected the domestic markets and made the global marketing an uphill task. WTO has been instrumental in promoting government drivers for improving trade in the developing countries.

> At the Fourth World Trade Organization Ministerial Meeting held in Doha in November 2001, Ministers launched a comprehensive set of multilateral trade negotiations and a work program. This mandate is sometimes referred to as the Doha Development Agenda, reflecting a shared desire to ensure that the trading system is relevant and responsive to the needs of developing countries. Among the areas covered by the negotiations or the work program are market access in manufactures, agriculture and services, certain rules (including anti-dumping, subsidies and countervailing measures, and regional arrangements), trade and environment, trade-related intellectual property rights, the relationship between trade and investment, the interaction between trade and competition policy, transparency in government procurement, trade facilitation, and dispute settlement. Developing countries were particularly instrumental in putting certain issues on the agenda, including trade and technology transfer, trade, debt and finance, small economies, implementation issues (mostly pending from the Uruguay Round) and special and differential treatment. Between 1990 and 2001, South-South trade grew faster than world trade with the share of intra-developing country trade in world merchandise exports rising from 6.5 per cent to 10.6 per cent. Over this period, developing country economies grew much faster than those of the developed and transition countries. The liberalization of the trade and investment regimes of a large number of these countries has played a significant role in this expansion. Much of this expansion in South-South trade took place in developing Asia (which accounts for more than two-thirds of intra-developing country trade). Manufactures, in particular office and telecom equipment, played a leading role in the growth of intra-developing country trade. This strong performance can be attributed in part to open trade and investment policies in the major developing economies of Asia. Trade liberalization in Asia took various forms in the 1990s: some of it was undertaken on a unilateral basis, some arose from multilateral efforts[39].

---

[38] Asian Development Bank (2003): Drivers of Change. Globalization, Technology and Competition, Section III, Competitiveness in Developing Asia, Asian Development Outlook.

[39] World Trade Organization (2004): World Trade Report-2003, Executive Summary, 14-15.

Integrating a worldwide strategy involves five key dimensions which include selecting markets for their global strategic importance, standardizing products, locating value-adding activities in a global network, using uniform marketing techniques, and integrating competitive moves across countries. Industry globalization drivers that are defined as the industry conditions that determine industry globalization potential and organization and management factors largely determine the use of global strategy. Such drivers have the strongest influence in global trade. Global companies constantly search for opportunities to achieve the benefits of globalization; take a zero-based view of existing activities; flout conventional wisdom and established practices; systematically analyze industry, strategy, and organizational linkages; and make multiple reinforcing changes in strategy and organization[40]. They assume that strategy should be global unless proven otherwise, and they think globally and act locally.

Besides the five drivers discussed above, other there exist reasons to market products and services globally. The major factors that influence the drivers of globalization may be illustrated as under:

- Market Saturation
- Trade Deficit
- Foreign Competition
- Emergence of New Markets
- Globalization of Markets
- Opportunities via Foreign Aid Programs
- Other Reasons

One of the most evident reasons to drive the companies go global is the market potential in the developing countries that constitute as major players in the world market. The companies such as *Nintendo, Disney* and the Japanese Motorcycle industries (Honda, Kawasaki, Suzuki etc.) have been greatly benefited from exploiting the markets of the developing countries and reassuring their growth in the world market to harness the promising market potential. Emerging scope of spatial diversification has also been one of the drivers for enhancing the global business utilizing the additional production capacity at the economies of scale and low-cost outsourcing. The production sharing of *Volvo* industries in India (Bangalore) may be a good example of spatial diversification of multinational companies for aligning developing countries strategically in international business operations. Volvo manufactures engines for its heavy transport vehicles in its factory at Bangalore in India delivering win-win alliance as company enjoys low cost production benefits and offer high-end wage employment to various categories of workforce in India. The company is also engaged in transfer to technology in automobiles manufacturing sector. The thrust of Japanese motorcycle industry in the US markets is aided significantly by its low-cost position. The saturation of the demand for the products and services of a company in domestic market may also be an effective driver to globalization wherein the company looks for building the value for its brand across the boundaries. A product that is near to the end of its life cycle in the domestic market is positioned to operate at growth stage of the product life

[40] George S Yip and Johnny K Johansson (1993): Global marketing strategies of US and Japanese Business, Marketing Science Institute, Cambridge, USA, 93-102

cycle in the overseas market. *Dickson Poon's* export of high brand-value luxury goods from America to the Far-east may be cited as an example of gaining advantage of general rise in the conspicuous consumption that is regarded as a sign of prosperity. Sometimes the cross-culture attributes of overseas markets that become the source of new product ideation, also may be considered as one of the potential drivers for globalization of business and explore the strategic alliances with prominent regional or multinational brands thereof. The tested market entry approaches may be implemented in the emerging markets such as South-east Asia as shown by the Revlon in cosmetics though there exists risk of international currency, legal issues and business protocols. However, the most difficult task for the global companies to develop products with a universal appeal as illustrated by *Gillette* with its fragrances. On the contrary *Lego* is facing hardship in the Far-east markets to popularize its concept of *do it yourself* (DIY) for creative learning against the head-on competition of video games industries attracting the same segment of buyers ( age group 5- 14).

## ORGANIZING GLOBAL MARKETING

Marketing is an integrated effort of various elements linked with the corporate objective of the organization. The marketing environment is volatile and keeps changing according to the business policy of competing firms, fashion, legal interventions and innovations. Thus, in the modern era, most companies put great efforts into organizing their marketing avenues with response to significant changes in the market. In such a process, it is essential to know consumer orientation at the very beginning. The research and development wing of the company needs to concentrate on new ideas and engineer them to manufacture the products desired by the consumers. Some of the essential determinants on the process are as given below:

- Consumer feedback
- Product improvement
- Distribution and purchase
- Marketing set-up
- Zero defects

In a marketing organization, there should be a continuous flow of information from the consumers which will enable the manufacturer to improve the product accordingly. The ideas generated through the feedback of consumers need to be evaluated with the view of accelerating the product improvement process. However, the company should develop a proper match with the supply and distribution system to ensure the availability of the products to the consumers. The marketing department in an organization should consist of a chain of functionaries for managing various marketing operations such as consumer survey, production, research and development.Various business functionaries should have a horizontal and a vertical network in order to perform their tasks efficiently and to provide feedback to the decision managers. Horizontal networking needs to promote product distribution, sales and promotion at a grass-root level. It is better to spread geographically covering all the sensitive marketing points in the hinterland of the operation of the company.

Networking of a marketing organization can also be built in a pyramidal structure wherein the administration, monitoring and evaluation is done in a synchronized manner. The top management exercises the highest powers while the middle and the lower management are answerable to the personnel of the top management. This is a centralized marketing system where the middle and lower levels of management executives are not given functional autonomy. The service functions have to be coordinated, monitored and evaluated at the middle management level while the planning functions need to be taken care of by the top management of the organization. Service functions include—administration of sales personnel, promotion, marketing research and market surveys. Functions pertaining to strategic planning, product planning, marketing research and decisions about the new projects comprising the planning and program functions rest with the top management. The area functionary in a marketing organization should provide regular feedback to the middle management to enable them to evaluate product performance and modify the marketing strategies as and when required. The product manager's role is to develop product plans and to administer them in the selected market segments. Other important functions such as the job chart of the product manager are stated below:

- Formulation of sustainable and competitive product plans
- Formulating annual operational marketing plans
- Forecasting sales
- Planning sales force
- Developing sales promotion strategies
- Managing the market information system
- Analyzing marketing problems, consumer grievances and working out suitable solutions for them
- Suggesting product improvement

The product manager has to interact with different types of interest groups in order to ensure the smooth functioning of a marketing organization. On the product front, the interactions of the product managers are marked with the personnel of research and development, production, distribution, promotion, media, consumer services, packaging, purchase, sales, fiscal and legal department (to ensure that the product on sale is not violating any regulations stipulated by the government).

Often, in a vertical organizational network the problem of striking a balance of operational decisions between the apex and the lower level functionaries occurs. The operational decisions consist of marketing and non-marketing functions. The marketing functions comprise planning, program, implementation, monitoring and evaluation while the non-marketing functions comprise research, development, and public relations. Balance needs to be struck as what mix of these activities will be attended by apex and grassroots level functionaries. An important point to remember is that along with functional decentralization there remain chances of duplication of efforts. In such circumstances, networking decisions have to be taken on the basis of the extent of the expenditure incurred while performing the tasks. However, there exist advantages and disadvantages of functional centralization and otherwise. Some of the main considerations for organizing marketing are as follows:

Lines of authority and tasks need to be unambiguous and clearly stated to the functionaries at various levels.

- The structure of the global marketing organization must be acceptable, conducive and dynamic to perform the functions on time.
- All the sub-activities should be properly coordinated.
- Information on marketing activities needs to be collected by an efficient department of the organization and the relevant facts must be made available to all the functional units to set their strategies.
- It is essential to maintain integrity among the marketing personnel in an organization.

Environmental control in marketing with reference to new entrants, buyers and distributors' lobby and the substitutes of products and technology must be considered while exercising market control approaches. All these areas need to be monitored simultaneously and continuously. It has been observed that new entrants and new technologies work hand in hand and generate latent threats to the existing products. These control operations are termed as strategic control. To achieve such critical control operations successfully, the managers belonging to the strategic level need to look into the following factors:

- Effectively assessing consumerism
- Analyzing the first sight of threats in the market
- Protecting the company's interest on maintaining markets
- Attainment of marketing objectives
- Maintaining the quality of market intelligence
- Keeping the sales level intact.

Operational control in a marketing organization comprises—streamlining of sales, distribution, promotion and product innovation activities. Sales control may be administered by scrutinizing new contracts, competitive sales approaches and new proposals of expanding sales avenues. It is essential to identify brand loyalty among the distributors and encourage exclusive distribution of the product effective monitoring of sales. Promotional control consists of administering effective communication strategies to the distributors and the consumers by way of advertisement, consumer surveys and sales campaigns. Periodical reviews need to be done by the operational control personnel of a company in order to build-up the image of the company and its product thereof in the market. One of the important tasks of operational control is the streamlining of consumer services. This activity can be performed after knowing fully the views of the consumers regarding the services offered by the company through benchmarking. This technique enables one to see at a glance the investment in consumer services providing the value in their perceptions. The marketing manager of a company may prepare a consumer service matrix denoting high, medium and low perceptions of different segments of consumers and thus identify the target area. It is expected of the marketing manager to take clear action if the elements of consumer service fall into certain specific parts of the matrix. The target area emphasizes the importance that needs to be given to the consumers of the "target" segment.

# GLOBAL LOCAL MARKETING

The global growth products of multinational companies are mostly centralized in the country of origin and the products that emerge tend to have FABs (features, advantages, benefits) specified by central marketing system of the company. Hence, key technologies and major product introductions cater primarily to customers in that geographical region. Marketing and customers in other regions are relegated to acceptance of custom modifications; or they have the choice to buy from other local suppliers. The product targeting goes beyond the perceived use values of the customers, local preferences and local language. Expectations regarding size, shape, customized items, price and availability vary widely. Hence, regional markets tend to be dominated by local companies. Often the companies offer locally engineered or customized products at a differential price to win market share. For growth and success in the new global economy, the guiding principle must be *Go Global – think Local!* Automation suppliers must become truly global by allowing local development of products for local markets. The best approach is to develop technology (hardware & software) through global alliances – preferably with relatively small, fast-moving local companies. In a global market, there are 3 keys that constitute the winning difference:

- Marketing abilities that assess correctly the local needs in a global arena.
- Proprietary technology and products targeted specifically for local markets.
- High-value-added services offered through effective local service providers.

In the global village of the new economy, automation companies have little choice – they must find more ways and means to expand globally. To do this they need to minimize domination of the central corporate culture, and maximize responsiveness to local customer needs.

> Ever since Fujifilm began actively exporting its products throughout the world in the early 1960s, it has been one of Japan's leading companies regarding overseas operations. Besides establishing a world-spanning network of local marketing bases, we were among the first Japanese companies to initiate overseas manufacturing, starting with the 1974 construction of a color photographic paper processing plant in Brazil. Since the 1980s, Fujifilm has arranged for Japanese and local technical staff to cooperatively design and construct overseas manufacturing facilities that make appropriate use of the Company's unique technologies in harmony with local conditions. These efforts have enabled the steady expansion and strengthening of Fujifilm's global production, marketing, and service networks. Having consistently placed strong emphasis on understanding regional characteristics and on respecting and adapting to local cultures, Fujifilm has been highly praised for its localization efforts and contributions to the communities in which it operates. The Company views globalization and localization as two equally crucial elements of its overall business strategy. The localization has been done by the companies to serve the markets in Americas, Europe and Asia-Pacific.
>
> As continued growth in the digitization of diagnostic imaging has also supported rising demand for dry medical imaging film in North America, Fuji Photo Film, Inc., based in Greenwood, South Carolina, in the United States, has been proceeding with the expansion of its medical-use film factory. In March 2003, the company completed that facility and began

> operating an integrated manufacturing system that performs a full range of manufacturing processes, from coating to processing. Because the range of products manufactured at the facility has been expanded to include dry medical imaging film, Fujifilm has significantly upgraded its systems for efficiently supplying customers throughout North America with our high-quality medical imaging products and related services. Fujifilm's headquarters in Europe, Fuji Photo Film (Europe) GmbH, recently established marketing companies in Poland, the Czech Republic, Slovakia, and Italy. In view of the huge changes under way in Europe - such as the monetary integration in 2002 and the forthcoming enlargement of the European Union in 2004 - Fuji Photo Film (Europe) has been seeking to expand and strengthen its marketing systems so that it can accurately respond to local needs and expeditiously supply products and services. Fujifilm began marketing the DocuCentre Color series of digital color multifunction machines in the Asia-Oceania region during the current fiscal year 2004. The Company also proactively proceeded with measures to expand its manufacturing and marketing systems in the region, particularly in China, which has markets that are expected to grow greatly. Consolidated revenue in this region rose 13.4%, to ¥279.1 billion[41].

One of the world's most recognized companies and brands, Coca-Cola continues to prosper by innovating and adapting to the local needs of its customers and consumers throughout the world. Despite ferocious competition, significant currency devaluations in key markets, and major acquisition-related write-downs, the company reported first quarter 2002 sales of US$4.08 billion and has predicted long term growth approaching six percent. Global Marketing helps set global marketing strategies and product positioning, which is then implemented locally and adapted to local marketing needs.

## Objectives of Global Marketing

The continuing debate on the global organizations and executives over time there is no definitive answer that may be slated to the question of what is really meant by "global." The dilemma of setting clear objectives of global marketing, some of the corporate leaders feel that they are losing sight of the reality of globalization. However, the companies should pay attention towards globalization as the national barriers are quickly coming down. Global companies integrate assets, resources, and diverse people in operating units around the world. The multinational, multi-domestic and transnational companies can build three strategic capabilities: global-scale efficiency and competitiveness; national-level responsiveness and flexibility; and cross-market capacity to leverage learning on a worldwide basis through a flexible management process, in which business, country, and functional managers form a triad of different perspectives that balance one another. In reference to the benefits of the global marketing, it may be firmly stated that the market overseas goes beyond simple and pure marketing considerations as it stands on the trade-off within the array of gains and risks. The global marketing under such fix may determine the following objectives to sail through the distant and somewhat troubled markets across the countries:

- To exploit market potential and growth to the optimum extent
- To set its marketing operations to gain the advantages of economies of scale

---

[41] Fujifilm Corporte Home page: http://home.fujifilm.com/info/profile/operation.html 27 May 2004.

- To learn from the leading markets through technology, innovation and competition
- To increase competitive pressure in stronghold markets to make space for survival and sustenance
- To explore the score of diversification of products, services and markets, and
- To gain comprehensive knowledge on doing overseas business successfully.

Multinational companies see globalization in general as a matter of replication, spreading a single business model as widely as possible to maximize economies of scale. From this perspective, the key strategic challenge is choosing how much of the model to keep standard and how much to grudgingly adapt to local tastes. Indeed, the scope of generalization or peripheral understanding is as wide as the differences that remain among countries, and those differences continue to be broad and deep with changing customer preferences and competitive moves across the regions. In order to reap the benefits of diplomatic privileges, growing economies and market size a multinational company must properly construct its efforts into its overall organization and perform at the national level but also tailor local strategies, by way of joint ventures, franchising and mitigate risk, in particular the theft of intellectual property.

## REFERENCES

Branch, Shelly. "ACNielsen Gives 43 Brands Global Status". *The Wall Street Journal,* October 31, 2001, p.38.

Czinkota, M.R., and I. Ronkainen. *International Marketing.* 5thed. Fort Worth: Dryden, 1998

Dreher Axel; Does Globalization affect Growth, University at Mannheim, Germany *Working Paper*, 2003, pp 1-33.

Elie Ofek: Customer Profitability and life time Value, *Harvard Business School, Press*, Aug. 2002, 1-13.

Frankel Jaffery A: Globalization of the Economy, working paper 7858, *NBER Working Paper Series*, Cambridge, USA, 2000, pp 1-42.

Giddens, Anthony. *Runaway World.* New York:Routledge, 2000.

Graham, Edward M. *Fighting the Wrong Enemy: Antiglobal Activists and Multinational Enterprises.* Washington DC. Institute for International Economics, 2000.

Micklethwait, John and Adrian Woolridge. *A FuturePerfect: The Challenge and Hidden Promise of Globalization.* New York: Crown, 2000.

Rugman, Alan. *The End of Globalization.* New York: Amacom, 2001.

Rust R Zeithaml V and Lemonk: *Driving Customer Equity: How Customer lifetime value is reshaping corporate strategy*, New York, Free Press, 2000.

Shanklin, William L., and David A Griffith, "Crafting Strategies for Global Marketing in the New Millenium," *Business Horizons,* September-October 1996, p.11-16.

Wind, Jerry, and Vijay Mahajan. *Digital Marketing: Global Strategies from the World's Leading Experts.* New York:Wiley, 2001.

*Chapter 2*

# GLOBAL MARKETPLACE

There is a fast change observed in the world markets resulting into the new emerging markets across the countries. In this century China, India and Latin America and the emerging market based economies in Eastern Europe promise new opportunities for global trade. The Pacific region had shown time-bending leap in the past four decade as significant Asian population participated in the rapid transition in response to the global movement of trade and services. Asia may be portrayed as the fastest growing market for the top brands of western companies and at the same time the Asian companies began penetrating in the western markets at low price-high quality strategy. While the luxury and fashion goods are dominating the Asian and Far-east markets, the specialized product like electronics and automobiles from Asian Markets are trying to capture considerable market share in Europe and North American countries. Emerging markets in the developing countries have shown a strong potential for change in preferences during the late 20$^{th}$ century. In most of the advanced countries the birth rate is declining while it is increasing in the developing countries. It has been observed that the technology has homogenized the world markets for variety of customer and industrial needs. The reduction in the tariff barriers, duties and liberalization process worldwide has further given a stimulus to the international marketing across the regional boundaries.

> Until recently, Honda Motor Co. seemed fast growing. With its sporty Civic compact, stalwart Accord sedan, and a fleet of snazzy sport-utility vehicles and minivans, sales seemed to go nowhere but up. Profits soared, and Honda's U.S. market share rose to 9% in 2003 from 6.7% in 2000. The U.S. problem is twofold: sales of key models are slipping, and the rising yen lowers the value of U.S.-derived profits when they're translated back into the Japanese currency. The company predicts that the strong yen will reduce income by $1.22 billion in the current fiscal year, even worse than the $889 million currency hit in the fiscal year ended Mar. 31, 2005. Today, 80% of the 1.53 million cars Honda sells in North America are made at North American factories, and the parts in Honda's American cars increasingly come from local suppliers[42]. Honda has long been successful because it entered mainstream market segments with offbeat cars. Its high-tech engines offer the better of two worlds: They're zippy and fuel-efficient. The cars handle well, offering a little fun to go with their high quality and utilitarian design. Honda is struggling in newer segments, too. Honda says it would cost too

> much to revamp its factories to produce all-new platforms and big engines for trucks and luxury cars, so a big shift isn't in the cards soon. Company executives, meanwhile, have high hopes for the new Acura RL sedan. The car will feature all-wheel drive, a first for an Acura sedan and its V-6 engine will crank out 300 hp. Dick Colliver, executive vice-president for sales and marketing at American Honda Motor Co observes that this is one of the most powerful engines Honda has ever built and that is the kind of excellence rests with the company. However, the problem is that there are a lot of excellent cars on the road these days[43].

The growing internationalization of business induces changes in the positioning of competitors and appropriate competitive strategies. As the companies attain gradual success in geographically expanding their business and effectively performing international operations, they reach at critical point and would be able to synchronize the proximity to the overseas markets and customer needs. The global companies at this point blue print their successful business systems in the emerging markets by creating relatively decentralized operations in production, marketing and sales.

## KEY ASPECTS OF INTERNATIONAL MARKETING

The term international marketing may be defined as the process of trade exchanges across the national boundaries for the satisfaction of human needs and wants. The pursuit of foreign markets is a function of commitment and the extent of involvement of the company overseas. The foreign involvement of a company may be described in one of the possible categories:

- *Domestic marketing,* wherein the enterprises operate exclusively within a single country may be termed as native country.
- The agencies or individuals operating within the predefined region may be described as *regional exporters*. In this kind of operations, the markets served are economical and culturally homogeneous and turn opportunistic if the activities fall outside the home region.
- *Exporters* deal with the finished goods and operate from their home country office to various destination markets across the countries.
- A firm's *international* involvement reflects in its regional operations in a partially autonomous fashion. However, the key decisions are made in the corporate office with a top-down control strategy. In the process, both the manufactured and intermediate or semi-processed products are exported outside the home region.
- On the other hand, the *global* companies operate with total autonomy through their independent subsidiaries in a cluster of countries. Some key functions such as research and development, outsourcing, promotions and finance functions are managed locally in view of the customer preferences and market driven needs.

[42] David Welch, Ian Rowley and Michael Eidam (2004): How Honda is Stalling in US, Business Week Online, May 24.

[43] Annual report of American Honda Motor Company 2003.

The international marketing activities begin from the home market. Upon saturation, the companies plan to explore the markets across the boundaries in order to search for further growth opportunities. Once the domestic check points are reached, the companies involve in an export activity where the markets are economically and culturally homogeneous. Regional exporters and export companies function from their corporate office locations in the home markets, though some marketing, sales and distribution activities are initiated across the boundaries. The companies gradually succeed in their business operations and at such critical point; they span their wings to achieve grater proximity to the overseas markets. The functions of research and development, manufacturing, marketing, sales and finance are decentralized except the key decisions that are coordinated from the corporate headquarters. Companies that have reached that stage of market progression may be delineated as *international* companies. Later the international companies may follow total standardization in the functional and strategic business disciplines to become *global*. The internal factors primarily refer to the corporate objectives, organizational behavior and resource availability. The nature of decision making in international marketing is like domestic operations barring some considerations on the factors of marketing ambience that call for a philosophical diagnosis. The SLEPT factors should be understood by the international marketing company along with the effect of the international institutions like International Monetary Fund (IMF), World Trade Organization (WTO) and Regional Trade Agreements (RTA).

The Gillette Company[44] today is the global market leader in nearly a dozen major consumer products categories, principally in the grooming, alkaline battery and oral care businesses. Since the company was founded, Gillette has gained, held and strengthened leadership positions through the Company's strategy of managing its business with a long-term, global perspective. This demonstrated ability to generate long-term, profitable growth in a changing global marketplace rests on several fundamental strengths. These include a constantly increasing accumulation of scientific knowledge in core businesses, innovative products that embody meaningful technological advances and an immense manufacturing capability in terms of reliability, cost effectiveness and quality. Skillful marketing of superior technology to achieve worldwide leadership is the goal of The Gillette Company. An array of premium quality of shaving preparations and after-shaves complements the shaving process and rounds out the Gillette grooming franchise. Additional market presence and support is provided by the Company's well-established deodorant/antiperspirant brands. Batteries are another thriving worldwide business in which the Company competes successfully. Duracell, the most popular brand of alkaline batteries in the world, is the clear global leader in the growing alkaline battery market. Oral care offers a comparable opportunity as consumers' trade up from regular Oral-B manual toothbrushes to the premium-priced Cross Action manual toothbrush, and then move on to power-assisted Oral-B toothbrushes—which generate a highly profitable refill brush-head business. The Gillette Company announced in May 2004 an exclusive three-year marketing agreement with football star David Beckham, who will be featured in the Company's worldwide consumer advertising and promotional campaigns for its premium grooming products. Net sales of the company for the first quarter of 2004 was increased by 13 percent amounting to $2.24 billion from $1.97 billion as compared to the above reference period in 2003, with notable strength in Latin America, Russia, Turkey and Eastern Europe. Favorable foreign exchange, in Europe and to a lesser extent in Asia, contributed 7 percentage points to the net sales gain.

[44] www.gillette.com Home page of the company.

International marketing may be best explained with an initial review of the marketing aspects in a domestic context. It may consist of finding and satisfying global customer needs over and above the competition and coordination of marketing activities in the given global environment. Customer needs can be explored through marketing research that helps in mapping the consumer needs, competitive preferences and value perceptions. The customer needs may be understood by the international business organizations by analyzing he market segments seeking to identify the similarities and differences thereof across the countries.

Companies may need to develop the global customer database to build their strategies responding to the customer needs and their purchase behavior. The companies in the international marketing arena may attempt to satisfy the customer needs adapting products and services with appropriate marketing in reference to the spatial and temporal customer preferences in the identified global segments. Strategies towards satisfying the needs of the global customers also include manufacturing and technology decisions in reference to the competitive gains to the customers in price and non-price factors such as quality, uniqueness, availability, convenience, services and warranty. International marketing generates complex environment in view of balancing their business activities across the countries. Such complexities may be reflected in the resources management structure including physical, human and capital resources. Multinational companies build their strategies to resolve the regional disparities in their strategies by coordinating and integrating the strategy implementation activities that involve centralization, standardization, delegation of authority and local responsiveness. The levels of foreign involvement of a company may broadly comprise the following strategic attributes:

- Operate in a Single Country
- Export Regionally
- Export Globally
- International Operations
- International to Global
- Global

International companies, in order to be better among the competition involve significantly in assessing, monitoring and responding to the global competition by offering competitive values, developing superior brand image and positioning the product appropriately, keeping broader product line, adjustable price and keeping the quality of the products relatively high. Thus, it may be stated in brief that for competing globally the international companies should configure their marketing operation as discussed above, coordinate effectively with the domestic, markets across the boundaries, and establish linkage of various marketing activities in different regions in order to sustain the global competition. Networks have made integration systems an essential aspect of doing business. Businesses rely on significant integration of servers to address the business needs of division, partners, distributors, and other affiliated groups to achieve efficient information access, enterprise-wide communication, and business process systems automation. Changing composition of world trade has been accompanied by a shift in production structures and the composition of domestic output. In industrial countries, growth in the information technology sector is rapidly changing with technology and services while developing countries are specializing in areas like apparel, metal products and electronics.

## Global Marketplace

In the highly competitive and *global marketplace* of today, the pressure on organizations to find new ways to create and deliver value to customers grows ever stronger. Global marketplace has been segmented geographically comprising triad market, pacific- rim, post/communist countries, Latin America, China and India. In the last two decades, technological innovation, logistics and supply chain has moved to the center stage. There has been a growing recognition that it is through an effective management of the logistics function and the supply chain that the goal of cost reduction and service enhancement can be achieved. The global market place may be described as spatial network of markets across the countries comprising homogenous and customized segments. Multidomestic and global markets with preferential and standardized products for the marketplace are offered by the multinational companies. A multidomestic market is one that is present in many countries but in which the competition occurs on the basis of country by country. In multidomestic market, the companies may experience the competitive advantage from one time transfer of skills and technology from the home markets of various countries. In the global marketplace, a company's competitive position is significantly influenced by the companies of other countries. In the view to ease the complexities of the global market place in terms of competition and socio-economic conflicts, the international business houses generally cluster the countries by common attributes such as political systems, social structures, economic development and accessibility. Cultural and economic geography that affect the international trade and investment include proximity to the marketplace, common heritage, income levels and ownership of natural resources.

*Shared boarders* of the countries determine the scope of international marketing as proximity to the marketplace influences the functional advantages in performing marketing activities thereof. The proximity lowers the cost of logistics and distribution of goods and services and manages investments in the international markets. Canada and United States are the principal trade and investment partners in North America as are France and Germany. Countries that have common heritage established through homogenous political and ethnic bounds offer strong international business ties. Trade and investment ties in the Commonwealth countries may be an appropriate example to describe the role of common heritage factor in international marketing within the common clusters. Cultural differences between the countries pull down significantly the scope of international marketing. Social and cultural factors of a country include lifestyles, language, and attitude towards foreigners, gender sensitivity, human rights and income equality.

The country posting the highest gross-domestic-product growth since 1966 is Botswana, a landlocked nation in southern Africa that's two-thirds desert. Its economy has expanded an average of 7% a year since it won independence from Britain that year, according to the World Bank. The overall economic growth of the country was projected at 5% during 2002 despite a rampant AIDS epidemic that is now the country's biggest challenge. Botswana keeps taxes low. It respects property rights and hasn't nationalized any businesses. It avoids the

> corruption that easy money encourages, and doesn't waste much money on grandiose air forces or white-elephant industrial projects. Indeed, Botswana is rated Africa's freest economy by the Washington-based Cato Institute in its annual report, Economic Freedom of the World. It boasted just three-and-a-half miles of paved roads and only three high schools in a country of 550,000 people. The per-capita income was $80 a year. Water was so scarce, and valuable, that the currency would later be named the *Pula*, meaning rain. Today Botswana is one of Africa's few enclaves of prosperity. Per-capita income has jumped to $6,600. In a continent of weak currencies, the pula is strong, backed by one of the world's highest per-capita reserves ($6.2 billion). Budget surpluses are the norm, and Moody's Investors Service rates Botswana's government bonds higher than Japan's. Botswana's world-class game parks are so free of poachers that they must cull their elephant herds. As a result, the government is a leader in the fight to expand legal ivory trading[45]. The multinational companies in Botswana largely operate through their franchises and are hesitant of setting-up their own subsidiaries due to the AIDS threat. The Botswana subsidiaries and Botswana companies were concerned about how the pandemic would affect their survival their future financial sustainability and market position and generally reported greater skills shortages than the South African companies surveyed. The South African multinationals are more concerned about the direct costs of HIV/Aids and its effect on productivity[46].

The per capita income determines the purchasing power of the buyers in the international marketplace and similarities thereof demonstrates the commonality in the customer needs and preferences. This phenomenon may be observed with the industrialized and developed countries. Countries which are rich in natural resources attract the international manufacturing and marketing companies as they play key role in the supply of natural resources like crude oil, timber etc. to the rest of the world. Canada is the largest exporter of forest products to the other countries. Governments of respective countries play an important role in protecting natural resources, setting boundaries for business operation such that the necessary resources are available to present and future generations and create an environment conducive to sustainable business practices by harnessing the profit incentive. Global marketplace is also determined by the *demographic* variable along with the other environmental factors that govern the characteristics of the marketplace. Urban population is showing a declining growth trend in European countries as assuming current demographic and economic trends continue. European Union's share of total global output will shrink from 18% today to 10% in 2050. Japan's share would decline from 8% to 4%[47]. On the contrary, population in the less developed countries is becoming an increasingly large proportion of world population, growing from 70% in 1960 to 81% in 2001. The developed global demographic regions include Australia, New Zealand, Japan, Europe and North America, which are collectively home to 1.19 billion people. On average, population growth in these regions is almost 0.3 per cent per year, a rate that is projected to dip below zero before 2025, under all but the highest population projections, as fertility and the proportion of people in their childbearing years continue to decline. Population of less developed regions is estimated to be 4.6 billion and is growing at a rate of 1.6 per cent annually. Africa's high rate of population growth also fluctuates from 2.0 and 1.6 per cent in Northern and Southern Africa to 2.5 and 2.7 per cent in Western and Middle Africa, while the average for the continent is about 2.4 per cent.

---

[45] John Koppisch (2002): Lessons from the fastest growing nations – Botswana, Business Week, August, 26.
[46] Sunday Times (2003): Botswana feel burnt of HIV/AIDS Apathy, December 29.
[47] David Fairlamb (2004): A Global Demographic Time Bomb, Business Week Online, January 23.

Moreover, while higher rates of population growth are to be found in the Comoros, Gambia, Guinea, Libyan Arab Jamahiriya, Mozambique and Western Sahara, fertility is highest in Niger, Malawi, Uganda and Angola, where women have, on an average, about 7 children each. Africa's 1999 population of 767 million people is projected to nearly double by 2035.

After sub-Saharan Africa, the regions with the highest rates of population growth are Western Asia (2.2 per cent), Northern Africa (2.0 per cent), Central America (1.9 per cent) and South-Central Asia (1.8 per cent). Again, there are noteworthy variations among countries. The population of Central Asia region, which includes Indian sub-continent, Iran and five former Soviet republics, is projected to increase by about 50 per cent over the next 30 years, from less than 1.5 billion to 2.0 billion under the United Nations' medium variant. While Pakistan's fertility rates remain obstinately high, family size in Bangladesh is now steadily declining. India presents a mixed picture, with high rates in the north of the country and low ones in the south. Rates of population growth in the rest of Asia range from around 1 per cent in China, South Korea and Thailand to more than 2 per cent in Cambodia, Malaysia and the Philippines. Asia as a whole is home to 60 per cent of the world's people, and while that proportion will not change significantly over the next 30 years, the medium variant projection shows Asia's population increasing by more than 37 per cent, reaching over 4.7 billion people in 2025. In contrast to Asia's demographic size, Latin American and the Caribbean constitute about 8 per cent of the world's population[48]. Overall population of the world is expected to rise by a little more than one third from 2000 to 2030, the urbanization process will continue, albeit at a slower pace than in the recent past. The average rate of increase in the urban population is projected to decline from 2.7 percent per year in 1950-2000 to 1.8 percent in 2000-2030. Urban life offers opportunities for economies of scale, international trade, employment and improvement in living standards. Whether this promise can be realized in developing countries to the extent that it has in the now developed world is a crucial question for coming decades[49]. Considering the factors that are critical of urbanization, consumption patterns, infrastructure development and overall growth in the industrialization, the international marketplace opportunities may be explored by regions.

Growing importance of developing countries as markets is an important development in terms of trade policy conditions. Less developed countries have historically been dependent on preferential market access to developed country markets. Some less developed countries, however, obtained reciprocal market access through trade agreements with developing countries. An example of such a scheme is the Association of South East Asian Nations and their preferential trading agreement, which includes Cambodia and Laos. It has been observed that multilateral, regional and bilateral trade agreements are imposing increasing disciplines on traditional trade-policy instruments. Tariffs are progressively being reduced, quotas are largely prohibited and subsidies are disciplined. Governments make an increasing use of new trade policy tools, in particular export promotion and attraction on foreign direct investment[50].

---

48 UNFPA (1999): Demographic Trends by Region, United Nations Population Fund, Population Issues, www.unfpa.org

49 Don Hinrichsen, Ruwaida M. Salem and Richard Blackburn (2002): Meeting the Urban Challenge, *Population Reports*, 30 (4).

50 Melo, A. (2001) 'Industrial policy in Latin America and the Caribbean at the turn of the Century', *IADB, Research Department Working Paper* No 459, Washington, DC: Inter-American Development Bank.

# TRIAD MARKET

New global marketplace accelerates competition, thereby reducing the lead time for companies with new products, services or technologies to reach and service their target market. To survive and grow in this type of economic environment, a business will need strategic markets where it can expand its sales and be competitive. Businesses, both large and small, are turning to niche markets where competition is reduced. Economic globalization is a new worldwide economic order, in which a majority of nations prescribe to the free enterprise system. The *triad market* refers to the United States and Canada, Japan and Western European countries. This group of countries accounts for approximately 14 percent of the global population and represent about 70 percent of world gross product and absorb the major proportion of capital and consumer products. There are about 92 percent of world computers used by the triad countries Since 1980 three major international trading areas emerged in the world economy in the form of triad that aims at developing uniformity in the markets and currency parity differences across the countries. One of the appealing characteristics of the triad market is the globalization of needs. There are similarities in the demand and lifestyle patterns of triad consumers. The purchasing power of triad residents is more than 10 times higher than the buyers of the developing countries. The technology infrastructure of this group of countries is advanced, as over 70 percent of the households possess modern telecommunication tools and services. The level of buyers in the triad countries is higher as compared to other regions in the world and the social infrastructure like roads, electricity and communication, health and sanitation, housing and transport services are highly advanced. All these factors stimulate the triad to be powerful in doing business among its affiliates and global marketplace.

The triad power may be described as the group of countries performing business operations on a predetermined framework. A Japanese triad power is operative in the United States of America, European community and the Southeast Asia with Japan as a foul point of business operations. Likewise, the American triad power consists of the NAFTA countries (United States, Canada and Mexico), European community and Japan. The triad powers essentially function in the countries of their spatial spread and other regions have become less important for survival and considered as marginal or less opportunistic. In the triad market, time and distance play major role in helping the executives to make quick and appropriate strategic decision. This factor of time and distance may be termed as an *anchorage* perspective in international marketing[51]. However, this base pattern may not be uniform for all the companies of the triad region and there may be some exceptions. For many European companies like Volkswagen Latin America may be more attractive market than Africa and for a British Chocolate company like Cadbury's; India, Australia, Africa and part of Canada may be an attractive market than others. Some American companies heavily depend on the Middle-east markets. The relative strengths of Triad partner countries also reflect on their resources allocation and corporate spending on the research and development and strategic alliances in terms of capital tie-ups, joint ventures and technical tie-ups with the multinational companies of the partnering countries.

[51] Ohmae Kenichi (1985): Triad Power-The coming shape of global competition, Free Press, New York, 35-54.

General Motors, Ford, and Daimler Chrysler announce plans to create an Internet supplier exchange, called Covisint, billed as the world's largest virtual marketplace. Required government approvals are obtained in the fall of 2000. GM increases its equity stake in Japanese automaker Suzuki to 20 percent in 2000 but has been sized down in 2003 as GM reduces its total equity in Isuzu to 12 percent but acquires majority ownership of Isuzu's diesel engine businesses and its Duramax, Circle L 1.7-liter and V-6 diesel engine technologies. The Chevrolet Cruze is launched in Japan in 2001 that has been designed and developed by GM and its alliance partner Suzuki. The Cruze is the first GM vehicle to be built in Japan since the 1930s. On the front of international penetration for more than 40 years, Honda has continued to grow and expand in America. Today, with a presence in all US states, investment in sales, manufacturing and research operations in the U.S. exceeds $5.9 billion. Honda's direct employment in the U.S. rose to 24,000 associates with an annual payroll of $1.2 billion[52].

Additionally, GM has other affiliate companies in Europe as well as in Australia, which is branded as GM-Holden. GM is involved with a joint venture in state-of-art robotics with Fujitsu-Fanuc. The Chrysler is associated with the European automotive manufacturers through the Peugeot of Italy. Canada is the largest foreign market for the US brands and business collaborations and the United Kingdom is the distant second. There has been good market for the Canadian products in Mexico being its NAFTA partner. Canada succeeded with the triad partners also because of the geographical proximity.

## ASIA- CARIBBEAN- PACIFIC RIM COUNTRIES

The countries of Pacific Rim are emerging in the 21st century as the new international business power over the developing countries. The Pacific Rim comprising of South Korea, Singapore, Taiwan, Hong Kong, Malaysia, Thailand, Indonesia and Philippines is growing as an economic powerhouse by improving the regional trade treaties and exports to European and North American countries. These countries have created a strong manufacturing potential in electronics and natural resources. The consumption of construction materials like steel is higher in the region than in the United States and also the demand for semiconductors are increasing over the European Union. The Committee on Trade and Investment (CTI) of Asia Pacific Economic Cooperation (APEC) organization works to reduce impediments to business activity in 15 key areas outlined in the Osaka action agenda - tariffs and non-tariff measures, services, standards and conformance, customs procedures, intellectual property rights, competition policy, government procurement, deregulation, rules of origin, dispute mediation, mobility of business people and implementation of World Trade Organization (WTO) obligations. The committee[53] is focusing on the following priority areas during 2004:

- Trade and investment facilitation (including IPR).
- Implementation of the APEC Transparency Standards.
- Implementation of Pathfinder Initiatives
- Contribution to the APEC Structural Reform Action Plan, and
- Support for World Trade Organization

[52] General Motors Ltd., internet official web site http://www.gm.com/
[53] Asia Pacific Economic Cooperation: APEC Secretariat www.apecsec.org.sg

APEC Member Economies are working to eliminate tariff and non-tariff barriers to trade. Elimination of these barriers will help Asia-Pacific countries to achieve the common goals resolved in various ministerial meetings of the APEC member countries, encourage greater and freer trade and investment flows and create new business opportunities and jobs in the Asia-Pacific region. It has been further resolved by the APEC nations that sustainable economic development requires empowering people and strengthening societies for globalization. This process requires more effective, better focusing and strengthening global economic and technical cooperation. In addition, it has been envisaged that increasing the interaction of Asia-Pacific rim countries with international financial institutions, the private sector, and other outside organizations would pay long-run gains of globalization.

> "A World of Differences: Partnership for the Future," and its sub-themes, following our interactive and meaningful exchange of views, APEC agreed that strong partnership is vital in order to achieve the goals we set out in Bogor[54]. To realize our vision amidst the rapidly changing international environment, we agreed to strengthen our partnership not only to liberalize and facilitate regional trade and investment, but also to protect our peoples and societies against threats to their security, while preparing them to benefit fully from free and open trade. By taking these steps, we can realize the APEC vision, established by Leaders in 1993, of "achieving stability, security and prosperity for our peoples." We reaffirmed the primacy of the multilateral trading system, and agreed that the Doha Development Agenda (DDA) offers the potential for real gains for all economies, particularly developing economies, in the areas of agricultural reform, improved market access for goods and services, and clarification and improvement of trade disciplines. We lent our strong support for continuing the valuable work done at the Cancun Ministerial Conference to advance the DDA. We agreed that for global free trade to flourish, regional and bilateral free trade agreements must be consistent with WTO principles, advance WTO objectives and contribute to the Bogor Goals[55].

The United Nations Economic Council for Latin America and Caribbean (ECLAC) observed that Latin America and the Caribbean accumulated a surplus in goods and services of about $25.5 billion, and a current account surplus of about $2.8 billion during 2003 as exports from the countries of this region grew by 8.3 percent in the same reference period due to better prices and higher-volume sales for basic goods such as copper, oil, coffee, cotton, wool and sugar. Chile secured a "major advance" with its recently implemented free-trade agreement with the United States. El Salvador, Honduras, Guatemala and Nicaragua successfully concluded negotiations in 2003 for a free-trade pact with the United States, joined by Costa Rica and the Dominican Republic in 2004[56]. Productive activities in Caribbean community and common market (CARICOM) also reflect the changing mode of doing business in a globalization environment with Trinidad and Tobago, Jamaica, Bahamas and Barbados being ranked at 1, 11, 23 and 24 respectively with regard to the "transnationality index" of developing economy host territories for the year 1996. The

[54] Bogar is a place in Indonesia where APEC members meeting was held in 1994 that lead to slate declarations on regional trade promotion.

[55] Excerpts from the "Bangkok Declaration on Partnership for the Future" of APEC member countries, Bangkok, Thailand, 21st October 2003; adapted from the on-line document of APEC secretariat http://www.apecsec.org.sg/apec/leaders__declarations/2003.html

[56] UN Economic Commission on Latin America and Caribbean (2000): Caribbean Trade and Investment Report, ECLAC, Santiago, Chile.

transnationality index is based on the average of the share of Foreign Direct Investment (FDI)inflows as a percentage of gross fixed capital formation for the last three years; FDI inward stock as a percentage of GDP; value added of foreign affiliates as a percentage of GDP; and employment of foreign affiliates as a percentage of total employment and the rankings of the abovementioned four countries in 1997 were 1, 15, 20 and 24, respectively[57].

In the framework of the external co-operation and development policies of European Union, the European Investment Bank (EIB) operates in 77 African, Caribbean and Pacific (ACP) countries. The ACP countries, with a population of some 600 million, have established a special relationship with the European Union through successive Conventions; the latest is the 2000 Cotonou Agreement signed in June 2000. The EIB has been the developing partner of most of the ACP countries over 25 years and as many as 40 countries of the region. Under parallel provisions EIB also supports investments in 20 overseas countries and territories mainly in the Caribbean and Pacific which have constitutional links with certain European community countries.

> The Lomé Convention signed in 1975 sets out the principles and objectives of the Union (at the time Community) cooperation with ACP countries. It's main characteristics include the partnership principle, the contractual nature of the relationship, and the combination of aid, trade and political aspects, together with its long-term perspective. The Cotonou, Benin convention held in June 2000 gave more support to the Lomé convention and opened better socio-economic and trade relationship between ACP countries and European countries. In the Caribbean region, Europe remains a necessary partner and a useful counterweight to powerful neighbors. Maintaining relations with Europe is equally vital for the small island economies of the Pacific, which lie scattered at such a distance from the rest of the world, the largest with only four million inhabitants, the smallest a mere two thousand. The new ACP-EC partnership[58] seeks to create a more favorable context for sustainable development and poverty reduction, and to reverse the processes of social, economic and technological marginalization. Political dialogue between the Community and each of the partner States (or regions) will play a key role in determining the nature and objectives of the assistance provided. The partnership aims to encourage greater participation by civil society, the private sector and trade unions. The Agreement is valid for a period of 20 years. It will come into force once it has been approved by the European Parliament and ratified by the national parliaments of the states concerned. It will be open to revision once every five years[59].

---

[57] United Nations Conference on Trade and Development (2000): World Investment Report-2000, UNCTAD, Geneva, p 25.

[58] The 76 ACP countries eligible for Economic Partnership Agreements (EPAs) include Angola, Antigua and Barbuda, Bahamas, Barbados, Belize, Benin, Botswana, Burkina Faso, Burundi, Cameroon, Cape Verde, Central African Republic, Chad, Comoros, Congo (Brazzaville), Congo (Kinshasa), Cook Islands, Côte d'Ivoire, Djibouti, Dominica, Dominican Republic, Equatorial Guinea, Eritrea, Ethiopia, Fiji, Gabon, Gambia, Ghana, Grenada, Guinea, Guinea-Bissau, Guyana, Haiti, Jamaica, Kenya, Kiribati, Lesotho, Liberia, Madagascar, Malawi, Mali, Marshall Islands, Mauritania, Mauritius, Federal States of Micronesia, Mozambique, Namibia, Nauru, Niger, Nigeria, Niue, Palau, Papua New Guinea, Rwanda, Saint Kitts and Nevis, Saint Lucia, Saint Vincent and the Grenadines, Samoa, Sao Tome and Principe, Senegal, Seychelles, Sierra Leone, Solomon Islands, Somalia, Sudan, Suriname, Swaziland, Tanzania, Togo, Tonga, Trinidad and Tobago, Tuvalu, Uganda, Vanuatu, Zambia, Zimbabwe. South Africa and Cuba are also ACP members. However, Cuba is not signatory to the Cotonou Agreement and South Africa has already concluded a Trade and Development Co-operation Agreement (TDCA) with the EU.

[59] The European Commission: New ACP-EU Agreement 2004. Also refer Online documents, Europa/ development, http://europa.eu.int/comm/development/body/cotonou

The Pacific Rim offers a variety of opportunities for American and European companies for the products and services that range from telecommunication instruments to the aircraft seats and banking services and a host of other products. Although it is a competitive market, the region is growing economically cohesive that attracts production sharing possibilities with the industrial countries. Asian producers outside Japan have gained more than one fourth of the global market share for personal computers. Japan and the pacific emerging triad comprising Singapore, Taiwan and South Korea provide most of the capital and expertise for the rest of the countries of the region that have enormous labor and natural resources. Hong Kong also contributes significantly for the development of international trade in the pacific region. Japan is Canada's second largest national trading partner (after the United States), taking 2.1% of total exports, and is the fifth largest source of foreign direct investment (FDI) in Canada. Canada is a leading supplier to Japan of a number of products of key export interest, such as lumber, pulp and paper, coal, meat, fish, oilseeds and prefabricated housing. While resource-based exports continue to represent much of our trading relationship, Canada is an increasingly important source of sophisticated, value-added, technology-driven products and services imported by Japan. In 2003, Canada's total merchandise trade with Japan was $22 billion. Canadian exports to Japan have declined steadily since the mid 1990s, Canadian exports to Japan declined again to $8.1 billion in 2003 from $8.4 billion in 2002 while imports from Japan decreased by 10% in 2003 to $14 billion. In 2003, Canada exported $1.4 billion in services and imported $1.9 billion[60]. The long-term trend in Japan is toward a growing demand for cost-competitive and innovative imports, which represents a significant market opportunity for Canadian exporters. The Asia-Pacific region has been the fastest growing trade block over past three decades though it had experience downturn in 1998 and extended after shocks. East Asia is the principal export market for American goods. The transpacific trade has grown over 50 percent of its transatlantic trade by the end of 20th century.

## POST-COMMUNIST COUNTRIES

The dynamics of the political transformations have always swept the Eastern Europe and the former Soviet Union. By the change of government systems in the countries of these regions, the trade patterns are affected and reshaped over the preventive trade protocols. These frayed and ungrouped countries are moving towards the western economic orbits of North American and west European countries to rebuild their trade and economy. The largest economies like Czech Republic, Hungary and Poland are making headway. On the contrary, Yugoslavia is concentrating on controlling the ethnic conflicts as the top priority over the trade matters and the less developed Romania and Bulgaria have been finding a better administration for moving ahead with their economic development agenda. In the wake of the Soviet bloc's collapse, various post-communist countries rushed to gain greater access to foreign markets. Many of them have made substantial progress in liberalizing commerce, but the movement toward free trade has been by no means universal. One prominent view is that the establishment of democratic institutions has stimulated economic reform in the post-

[60] Government of Canada: Report on Canada's International Market Access Priorities- 2004, Department of Foreign Affairs and International Trade, Opening doors to the world, Chapter 6, 2004.

communist countries[61]. The economies of the post-communist countries are in "transition" and are leading to reform and liberalize their trade programs to allow freer trading among countries. After the fall of communism in 1989, foreign investors diverted their investments to eastern European countries which are still continuing. Once the changeover of the market economy is complete the countries that have emerged in the post –communist era may offer attractive trade terms. Import liberalization forms part and parcel of trade reforms in transition economies. There are, however, significant differences among post-communist countries in the degree of import liberalization. In the last decade, free trade affected the post-communist countries and predominantly among them those, which had a maturated level of stability, economical development and their geopolitical situation is favored[62]. Russia is taking strong steps to liberalize its economy as fast as it can in order to achieve quicker stability of its collapsed economy. It has adopted high risk averse and austerity based programs to support its international trade policies western economies have viewed such perspective as a challenge and opportunity both to extend their trade operations.

> Eastern Europe is a perceived grouping of countries on the European continent. Their populations do not see themselves as Eastern Europeans, and many consider it a pejorative term. Most countries prefer to include themselves in other groups, associating themselves with Germany in Central Europe, with Scandinavia in Northern Europe or with Italy and Greece in Southern Europe. For many years, Europe was divided on a North South axis. With the southern Mediterranean states having much in common, and the northern Atlantic Ocean and Baltic Sea bordering states also having much in common. The term *Baltic* first arose 19th century and to describe an area that was falling behind the rest of Europe economically. Much of Eastern Europe has ties with both the east and west. While all of the countries were heavily influenced by Roman Catholic or Protestant Christianity and have very close historical and cultural ties to Germany, Italy, France or Scandinavia (e.g. the Hanseatic League in the Baltics), many countries also had relations with the East. The concept of Eastern Europe was greatly strengthened by the domination of the region by the Soviet Union after the Second World War and the takeover of the nations of the region by communist governments. The idea of an "Iron Curtain" separating Eastern and Western Europe was an extremely common view throughout the Cold War.

Since Estonia, Latvia and Lithuania have been liberated in 1991, these countries struggled to transform into market-oriented economies. During a decade, the Baltic countries have accomplished an impressive reorientation of foreign trade, and today the European Union represents the most important trading partner of the Baltic countries. However, foreign trade is still far from fully developed, which leaves opportunities for new international players to participate in trade activities to augment the volumes of business operations of the Baltic countries[63]. Since 1989 the largest islands in the Baltic Sea have formed a common interest group- "The Islands of the Baltic Sea", also called Baltic Sea Seven Islands, or just B7. The member islands are Bornholm (Denmark), Gotland (Sweden), Hiiumaa (Estonia), Saaremaa (Estonia), Åland (Åland/Finland), Öland (Sweden) and Rügen (Germany). The Baltic

[61] Fray T and Mansfield E D (2004): Timing is everything: Elections and trade liberalization in the Post-communist world, *Comparative Political Studies*, 37 (4), 371-398.

[62] Rédei Mary (2001): Regional specialization in a transition country-Hungary, European Regional Science Association, *ERSA conference paper*, August.

[63] Larson, Karin and Wikström, Jenny(2002): *The Development of Foreign Trade in The Baltic Countries*, Graduate Business School, Göteborg.

countries have enough opportunities to get into the European trade arena and also take advantage of the emerging Russian market. The five of the former Soviet republic countries namely Azerbaijan, Uzbekistan, Turkmenistan, Kyrgyzstan and Tajikistan have joined Iran, Turkey and Pakistan to become a part of an Islamic market[64]. Simultaneously in the most advanced post-Communist countries of Europe, including Poland, the dynamic growth of the small business sector has been the principal factor driving economic growth since 1992, and has been accompanied by a number of public programs supporting Small and Medium-sized Enterprise (SME) development. Most former Soviet republics have fallen into an economic and political under-reform trap. An intrusive state imposes high tax rates and drives entrepreneurs into the unofficial economy, which further aggravates the pressure on official businessmen. Tax revenues and public goods dwindle, further reducing incentives to register business activity[65].

**Table 2.1. Regional Trade Agreements in Global Market Place (as of January 2003)**

| Period | Developed-Developed | Developed-Developing | Developed-Transition | Developing-Developing | Developing-Transition | Transition Transition | Total |
|---|---|---|---|---|---|---|---|
| 1958-1964 | 2 | 0 | 0 | 1 | 0 | 0 | 3 |
| 1965-1969 | 0 | 0 | 0 | 0 | 1 | 0 | 1 |
| 1970-1974 | 5 | 3 | 0 | 2 | 0 | 0 | 10 |
| 1975-1979 | 0 | 5 | 0 | 1 | 0 | 0 | 6 |
| 1980-1984 | 2 | 1 | 0 | 1 | 0 | 0 | 4 |
| 1985-1989 | 1 | 1 | 0 | 2 | 0 | 0 | 4 |
| 1990-1994 | 3 | 3 | 12 | 5 | 0 | 6 | 29 |
| 1995-1999 | 3 | 7 | 10 | 4 | 12 | 28 | 64 |
| 2000-2002 | 0 | 11 | 4 | 5 | 4 | 6 | 30 |
| Total | 16 | 31 | 26 | 21 | 17 | 40 | 151 |

In this table, developed countries like Canada, USA, EU, EFTA, Japan, Australia, and New Zealand; transition countries include the former Soviet Union, Eastern and Central Europe, the Baltic States and the Balkans; the remaining countries are classified as Developing.

Source: World Trade Report-2003, WTO, P 47.

The post-communist countries need to apply quick structural changes in their transitional economies and develop appropriate strategies to catch-up with the countries of globalization

[64] Jain Subhash (2001): *International Marketing*, South Western, Ohio, 55-63.

[65] Andres Aslund, Peter Bonne and Simon Johnson (2001): Escaping the under-reform trap, IMF Staff Papers, Vol.48, Special Issue, 88-108.

stream exploring alliances and strategic partnerships with the developed trading group like Triad. The transitional countries may emerge as a healthy economy in following two decades provided the countries could stand on a sound political platform and establish trade agreements with the developed countries towards technological, manufacturing and financial partnerships. The regional trade agreements in different types of countries during 2003 have been exhibited in Table 2.1.

Expansion in the number of Regional Trade Centers in the 1990s was because of the collapse of COMECON (the preferential agreement involving the old Soviet Union and the Eastern European Countries) and the alignment of the Central and Eastern European Countries with the European Union. Of the 123 regional trade agreements in force since 1990, covering trade in goods, about a third was signed among transition economies. These new agreements were response to the splintering of COMECON and represented efforts to make up for the forgone preferences. Hence, some of these new RTAs do not necessarily represent increased regionalization of the international trade regime. Another third were the agreements concluded as part of the effort of transition economies to integrate with the European Union[66].

## LATIN AMERICA

There are large differences in gross domestic products by sectors among Latin American countries, and the majority of these differences are due to the value of industrial and service sectors. Although the sectoral economic activity has been increased, in per capita terms this value decreased due to the demographic growth that Latin American countries (mainly Mexico and Brazil) had experienced during the last decades. In terms of external trade, it has been found that the outward orientation as the ratio between total exports and GDP increased from 16.1% in 1990 to 32.7% in year 2000. Panama had the highest level in this area (66.5%). Modest growth returned to Latin America and the Caribbean in 2003 and regional GDP advanced by an average 1.3 percent, after a contraction of 0.6 percent in 2002. Argentina continued recovering rapidly after its acute crisis. Brazil, Mexico and Uruguay shared in the broadening of economic recovery during the year. The Andean countries performed well, with Chile, Colombia and Peru recording growth above 3 percent. However, ongoing political uncertainties caused Venezuela's economy to deteriorate further during the first half of the year. Central America grew by an average 3.1 percent and looks set to sustain growth, thanks to the recently signed Central America Free Trade Agreement[67] (CAFTA).

The Central American Free Trade Agreement (CAFTA) negotiated between the U.S. and Central America offers opportunities and challenges for the five countries including El Salvador, Guatemala, Honduras, and Nicaragua that joined in 2003 and Costa Rica that was included in January 2004. Mexico, Nicaragua, Jamaica and Honduras always were over the mean. During the years 1990, 1995 and 2000, Mexico, Cuba, Panama, Argentina, Brazil, Chile and Uruguay reached incomes above 2000 dollars per capita in the service sector[68]. On the other hand, there are some countries like Haiti, Honduras, Nicaragua and Bolivia with

---

[66] World Trade Report-2003, WTO, P.46.

[67] World Bank (2003): Report on Latin America and Caribbean, Regional Overview.

[68] Guisan, M.C. and Aguayo (2002), "Education, Industary, Trade and Development of American Companies in 1980-99". *Applied Econometrics and International Development*. , 2 (1), 83-106.

incomes below 500 dollars per capita. Latin America's merchandise exports increased slightly as the decline in intra-regional trade was balanced by increased shipments to other regions. Recovery of commodity prices in the course of the year and the upturn in the US economy contributed to this rise. While most Latin American countries saw a reduction or stagnation in their imports, those of Costa Rica increased by 9 per cent. Mexico benefited from the recovery of the US market while for Costa Rica, the recovery in semi-conductor shipments boosted both imports and exports. Despite the continuation of low prices for a number of primary commodities, exports of many Central American and Caribbean countries recovered strongly. Economic activity in Western Europe remained subdued as Germany, the largest economy, experienced declining domestic demand. Domestic demand growth remained positive in the rest of the region, but was sluggish in several other countries. In Euro zone, public consumption was the most dynamic expenditure category while private consumption slowed down and fixed investment in the enterprise sector fell nearly 3 per cent. Amidst poor economic situation, further progress was made towards European integration[69].

Starting in mid-sixties of the 20$^{th}$ century, the European example inspired a number of trade-oriented integration arrangements in the Latin American region such as the Latin American Free Trade Association, which later became Latin American Integration Association (ALADI), Central American Common Market (MCCA), Caribbean Community and Common Market (CARICOM), Andean Group- later known as Andean Community; and more recently, Southern Common Market (MERCOSUR), Group of Three (G3) and Association of Caribbean States (ACS). There are many bilateral alliances as well. Latin American countries have been living a renaissance since 80's. Most economies are stabilized, living standards are higher, direct foreign investment has surged, democracy has been institutionalized and most countries have demonstrated a desire to integrate themselves into the new global economy by opening their economies to international trade and investment. In the 90's the Latin American countries have liberalized their economies, which has been followed by a significant increase in their imports. This improvement was due primarily to three factors including lower inflation, less government intervention, and fewer trade barriers. International trade has been the key indicator of the overall economic growth of Latin American countries. Several regional free trade agreements signed over the past decade-such as MERCOSUR, Central American Common Market, Andean Community, and Caribbean Common Market-demonstrate the region's understanding of the benefits of free trade. Countries like Chile have gone even further in their trade liberalization efforts, signing bilateral agreements with Mexico and Canada after being unable to sign an agreement with the entire NAFTA bloc. In terms of scope, sectors of interest and coverage, there are three levels of sub-regional arrangements: (i) customs unions currently being finalized, e.g., Andean Community, MERCOSUR, MCCA and CARICOM, (ii) first-generation free trade accords with a commercial emphasis, and (iii) new-generation free trade pacts encompassing such sectors as services, investment, intellectual ownership, and state acquisitions. Chile and Bolivia are successfully engaged in negotiations for broader scope aimed at furthering their association with MERCOSUR, establishing free trade areas and bringing other sectors and issues into the accords.

With investor confidence returning in Latin America and domestic conditions improving, gross private financial inflows in 2003 increased by 40 percent over 2002. Moreover, interest

---

[69] World Trade Organization (200$): World Trade Report-2003, 30-42.

rate spreads on sovereign bonds over US treasuries reached record lows. Net foreign direct investment (FDI), however, continued its decline from a peak of $88 billion in 1999 to an estimated $36 billion in 2003. This is partly explained by the end of the privatization boom and the profit crisis in Brazil and Argentina. Export growth outpaced import growth for most countries in 2003, leading to surplus positions on trade and a big improvement in the region's current account deficit, down to 0.5 percent of GDP (compared to 4.5 percent in 1998). Tourism revenues and workers' remittances also improved, and commodity prices were generally strong. Consequent upon falling trade and investment barriers and high growth prospects, the countries of Latin America represent attractive alliance prospects for an increasing number of global firms. The typical objective for these strategic alliances is a basic trade-off wherein local firms seek access to technology and capabilities that are critical for their survival in an environment of increased competition and in return, they offer prospective multinational partners access to a large and growing market. There have been some major factors forming the business environment in most Latin American countries such as:

- Trend of high inflation
- Traditionally closed economies
- Extensive government intervention
- A tradition of family-owned businesses

The region is becoming more attractive to multinationals, as product patent protection is implemented and, more importantly, enforced, in Latin American countries. Mexico, in particular, as a member of NAFTA, is attracting substantial inward investment. This is likely to grow even more rapidly in future, given the recent signing of a trade deal with the European Union. Recent recovery of oil prices has shown a positive sign of growth for a number of countries in the region, particularly Venezuela, Mexico and Colombia.

Corporate networks in Latin America still differ significantly from those in mature countries. Bandwidth usage is symptomatic of this difference. The telecommunication companies in the main markets of the region (Argentina, Brazil, and Mexico, loosely labeled Latin America) enjoy speeds similar to those of developed countries today. Although this may come as no surprise for those familiar with the region, a wide variety of telecom players (ranging from global carriers to Application Service Providers [ASPs]) often disregard this fact and its implications. One of the clearest consequences of the bandwidth lag is that it will constrain the future of applications that can be provided over the Internet (connections over 2 Mbps will still be scarce in Latin America in 2003, while most U.S. and European companies expect to be connecting at this speed by then). Therefore, ASPs should either adapt their business model or simply wait for better timing (when enough bandwidth is available). While the overall level of development and globalization of Latin American countries can explain these differences to some extent, it is believed that factors directly related to the telecom market also play a key role. In particular, the low level of competition in most countries has kept prices artificially high, thus preventing a faster uptake for many products and services. The Yankee Group is a global leader in technology research and consulting. The customers of the company categorically include technology vendors and users, benefit from our accurate, reliable, and trusted research, consulting, and personalized one-to-one client interaction covering communications and IT products and services.

In telecommunications, banking or other sectors that are strictly regulated and where politics plays a role, there's more of a need. Right now in Mexico, which has liberalized many of its rules and regulations and is part of NAFTA, the need for having a local partner has been greatly reduced over the years. Chile may also fall in this category. In other countries, such as Peru, Colombia, Venezuela, Argentina, and Brazil, it is probably more useful to have a strategic partner. The Latin America and Caribbean countries are at a critical juncture that carries risks and challenges but also hopes and motivation. Internationally, these countries supported formation ofWorld Trade Organization (WTO) and hope that new multilateral regulations will lay essential ground rules for international trade.

## African Marketplace

Various initiatives have been undertaken to strengthen Africa's production and trade capacity including the mechanisms as debt cancellation, improved regional cooperation, the Cotonou Agreement and various trade preference schemes. A recent example is the African Growth and Opportunity Act (AGOA) of the United States, which improves the access of African products to US markets. Although the largest part of US imports from Africa is accounted for by fuels, there are some indications that a number of non-oil exporting countries have experienced markedly higher shipments to the United States in 2002. While overall imports of the United States from Africa decreased by 20 per cent, imports from non-oil exporting countries which are full beneficiaries of AGOA preferences rose by 6 per cent. Strongest increases in shipments to the United States were reported by Kenya, Swaziland and Lesotho[70]. However, the available studies suggest that they have not yet succeeded in bringing about sustained growth in trade to the beneficiary countries. This reflects in part the reality that various supply-side constraints are also important to economic growth of Africa and trade performance. The US-African trade is being nurtured under AGOA and the primary U.S. cross-border service exports to Africa included tourism, business services, education, and freight transport. U.S. service imports from Africa were mainly travel and tourism, passenger transport, business services, and freight transport. The largest share of U.S. imports under AGOA came from Nigeria (60.2 percent), followed by South Africa (14.9 percent) and Gabon (12.7 percent). Other major suppliers included Lesotho, Kenya, Cameroon, Mauritius, and Democratic Republic of Congo during 2001-03.

Africa's trade growth lagged behind global trade expansionand merchandise and commercial services trade lagged behind the global trade expansion in 2002. Merchandise exports and imports recorded only marginal gains. South African exports and imports recovered by 2 per cent to 3 per cent from the preceding year's decline. Exports of the other non-oil exporting African countries were much stronger and expanded by about 6 per cent. A strong rebound in exports in 2002 from the preceding years' decline in a number of countries (including Morocco, Egypt, Côte d'Ivoire and Ghana) accounted for most of this strength in the export growth of non-oil exporters in Africa. It has been observed that increase in the prices of cocoa and gold helped export recovery in Côte d'Ivoire and Ghana. However, it is estimated that only six out of 53 African countries comprising Equatorial Guinea, Lesotho, Mozambique, Seychelles, Sierra Leone and Tanzania achieved a sustained expansion of their exports over the 1999-2002 period. Europe is South Africa's biggest source of investment, accounting for almost half of South Africa's total foreign trade. Recently concluded trade agreement between the EU and South Africa removes 90% of all trade barriers over the next decade, 95% of SA goods (including agricultural products), and 86% of EU imports. Africa's overall merchandise import growth was held back by import contraction in Nigeria and Egypt, the third and second largest merchandise importers in Africa in 2001.

## China and India

Since trade reform and globalization policies of China have become one of the concerns of the government, China is moving towards an open market economy in all aspects including its foreign trade. In dealing with antidumping cases, European and American countries pay special attention to freedom in trading, deciding export quantum in reference to export market demands, fixing the terms of prices and sales for export goads, etc. Chinese global trade policies are also determined on the line of European and American patterns. China has adjusted the customs tariffs for several times. At the beginning of 1992, duties of 225 items of import commodities were lowered. The average tariffs (arithmetic average, hereinafter inclusive) dropped down to 43.2 percent; the next year, the duties of 3371 items of imports were reduced, leading to the average tariffs down to 36.4 percent; in 1995, 4997 items were adjusted, accounting for 76 percent of all import tariffs, with the overall tariffs down to 23 percent; in 1997, the tariffs were again widely reduced, with the average tariffs declining by 6 percentage points to 17 percent. By 2001, the average tariffs of China had been lowered to 15.3 percent. The decline of the standard deviation of tariffs from 32.1 percent to 8.73 percent during 1992 - 2001 has indicated that the protection on duties was relaxed significantly. As the reforms in foreign trade system intensified, by 1997, the number of items under quota control dropped to 114 and the value of certificates issued fell to US$32.7 billion, taking an 18 percent share. In 1998, commodities under export control of quota and license were again cut down to 91 items with the value of certificates issued dropping to US$27.2 billion, accounting for 15 percent. The commodities under quota and license control dropped to 73 items in 1999 and in 2000, only 68 items of commodities were still under the control of quotas and license[71]. By 2002, the commodities under license control were further reduced to 53 items. China abolished the import quantity restrictions on some commodities, such as crude oil, steal products, pesticides, asbestos, laminated plywood, tobaccos, polyester chip, acrylon, terylen, and some machinery and electrical appliances, and replaced with voluntary import license control since early 2002.

China's bilateral agreement with the United States was initiated after becoming the member of WTO which reflects the Chinese leadership towards a new growth paradigm. The US-China-WTO agreement of 1999 envisages curbing the tariffs on agricultural and industrial products and eliminating the import quotas by 2005. This agreement also delineates the safeguard and protection[72] measures in implementing the agreement as below:

[70] World Trade Organization: World Trade Report 2003, pp 36-42.

[71] Government of China: Report on the Development of China's Market Economy-2003, Department of Commerce, China Internet Information Center, November 07, 2003 www.china.orgn.cn

[72] USTR, Agreement on Market Access between the People's Republic of China and the United States of America.

- Allows the United States to continue to treat China as a non-market economy in anti-dumping cases for 15 years after accession; this methodology generally results in the application of larger anti-dumping margins against Chinese imports
- Permits the United States to implement a product-specific safeguard to prevent large import surges from China; this safeguard, which allows the United States to impose restrictions on imports from China more easily than imports from other WTO members, would remain in effect for 12 years after China's WTO accession
- Allows the continuation of a safeguard mechanism to prevent textile import surges until the end of 2008; China will be the only WTO member subject to this mechanism

China's WTO accession is expected to boost EU-China bilateral trade, as China's tariffs and non-tariff barriers will be significantly reduced. It is also expected to lead to increase in European direct investment, due to the opening of new sectors of the economy for foreign investment and a general improvement in the regulatory framework. Rapid growth in China's trade volume is directly attributable to the improved trade environment following its entry into WTO in 2002. The agreement between China and the United States on China's entry into the WTO allowed for the United States to adopt emergency measures to limit imports from China if those imports are deemed to be increasing too rapidly and may potentially jeopardize local production. China has become the fourth largest trade body in the world following United States, European Union and Japan. Competition among foreign retailers in China has been growing up since China entered the World Trade Organization (WTO). Global economic activity was strengthened by developments in China and the transition economies. Maintenance of stability combined with substantial market reforms culminating in China's accession to the WTO have contributed to the exceptional output and trade growth recorded by China in the 1990s. One factor contributing to this outstanding performance was the high level of FDI inflows driven by the relocation of labor-intensive manufacturing sectors from Japan and other advanced economies in Asia into China's coastal areas. China's role in international trade has been further enhanced, with its trade expansion last year accounting for more than one-fifth of the increase in world merchandise exports (and imports). China has not only become a major supplier but also a prominent market for many countries[73]. Having overtaken the United Kingdom in 2002, China now ranks as the world's fifth largest merchandise trader. Concerns sometimes expressed about the effects on other economies of China's dynamism, as an exporter should be tempered by the realization that Chinese import demand are also growing at a remarkable pace. According to a survey by the State Economic and Trade Commission (SETC), foreign-funded firms now account for 23 percent of the large-sized supermarkets.

China and India, the two most populous nations in the world contribute substantially to the Asian economy. It has been observed during 2000-03 that while Japanese domestic demand stagnated, China and India continued to grow rapidly. ASEAN countries and other East Asian economies also experienced stronger economic growth in 2002 compared to the preceding year, but for most of them, the expansion was less than the rates of growth achieved in the early nineties. Indian trade reforms focused on liberalization, removing

[73] For eight developing countries China was the principal export market in 2001 and for five other economies, the second largest market.

quantitative restrictions, lowering tariffs and improving the competitiveness of Indian industry to meet global market requirements. The export - import policy over the years has aimed to help strengthen the export production base, give incentives to develop Special Economic Zones, provide procedural simplifications, besides focusing on quality and technological up-gradation. Despite the weak external demand conditions, the Balance of Payments registered an overall surplus in 2001-02. The trade deficit on BOP basis reduced from US$14.4 billion during 2000-01 to US$ 12.2 billion during 2001-02. The BOP position was further strengthened due to the invisible account rising to US$ 14.1 billion in 2001-02 from US $ 11.8 billion during 2000-01.A surplus was recorded on the current account after a period of more than two decades in 2001-02. The new export-import policy (EXIM) of India aims at reducing tariff barriers, identifying new export priorities, simplifications of licensing policies, promoting export processing zones, sector specific trade promotion policies with tax reduction measures and simplification of transaction costs.

South Korean economy surged forward in the 1970s by promoting capital intensive industries. The Korean government exhorted all such enterprises to re-orient themselves with international business approaches. Samsung was one among them. By the mid 70's the government had begun deregulating imports. However, under the protection policies of the government, the subsidized financing and monopoly grants continued. In the late 80's the economic conditions of the country suffered a setback due to inflation overrun and poor fiscal control. This resulted in a steep increase in the prices of raw material, wage rates and internal taxes. Consequently, some of the international marketing firms shifted their manufacturing units to lower wage countries like China and Vietnam. However, the political environment and government decision-making were largely favorable for international business houses in Korea. Of late, the Korean government balancing the growing dominance of domestic business with a handful of international business houses likes Daewoo, Hyundai, Lucky Goldstar (LG) and Samsung. The government wants greater domestic competition and foreign investment. Samsung, a Korean rice trading house, set up in 1938 with an investment of $2000 and 40 personnel became a mammoth export company by the 90's earning world-wide brand recognition. In 1953, Samsung entered the sugar export business, followed by wool processing in 1954. The company had set up a fertilizer plant for entry in to the domestic farm inputs market in 1967 and two years later began manufacturing electronic communication gadgets under the new subsidiary Samsung Electronics Company Limited (SEC). Its heavy industry ventures came-up in 1974 with aerospace products. In 1980, Samsung got into semi-conductors, telecom, computers, automation and genetic engineering. The petro-chemical unit was set up by the company in 1991 and in 1994; Samsung entered the Korean market for commercial vehicles. It spread its international marketing activity by establishing a Joint Venture in India in 1995 as Samsung India Electronics Ltd. (SIEL). SIEL is a 51:49 Joint Venture Company between SEC and the Ahemdabad based Reasonable Computer Solution Pvt. Ltd. manufacturing television, audio-system and frost-free refrigerators.

Economic reforms in India began in 1990 toward globalization and since then the Indian government has taken consistent steps towards a more open and transparent trade regime, leading to a significant increase in U.S.-India trade and investment. In the recent past, India has selectively lowered tariffs on some capital goods and semi-manufactured inputs to help Indian manufacturers. Indian government has steadily reduced the import-weighted tariff from 87 percent in 1992 to level of 25.4 percent by 1999-2000. It has been observed by the international business analysts that despite reforms, Indian tariffs are still among the highest in the world, especially for the goods that are produced domestically. For many years, India maintained a virtual embargo on oranges, lemons, and grapefruit, except for the hotel trade. In March 1999, India lifted restrictions for mandarin oranges (tangerines and satsumas), clementines, lemons, and grapefruit, but it continues to deny market access to navel and valencia oranges. India eliminated restrictions from a large number of products in order to recover the balance of payment disequilibrium, yet variety of other products remain on India's negative list for imports. The negative list is currently divided into three categories: (1) banned or prohibited items (e.g., tallow, fat, and oils of animal origin); (2) restricted items which require an import license; and (3) "canalized" items importable only by government trading institutions that exercise monopolies. Some commodity imports must be channeled ("canalized") through public sector companies, although several "canalized" items have been fully or partially decontrolled recently. Currently, the main "canalized" items are petroleum products, bulk agricultural products (such as grains), and certain pharmaceutical products. The government of India has liberalized many restrictions on the importation of capital goods since 1990. United States and India reached agreement in December 1999, on a schedule to lift quantitative restrictions (QRS) on imports of 1,429 agricultural, textile, and consumer products, following a WTO ruling that these restrictions were no longer justified under the balance of payments provisions of GATT (Article XVIII-B). Opening of India's trade regime has reduced tariff levels, but it has yet to simplify some of the most cumbersome aspects of customs procedures.

Foreign investments for multinational companies are becoming easy in the post-liberalization period as automatic approval is now granted by the Reserve Bank of India for equity investments of up to 51 percent in 48 industries covering the bulk of manufacturing activities. Indian government has also authorized existing foreign companies to increase equity holdings to 51 percent. The government now allows automatic approval by the Reserve Bank of India of equity investments of up to 74 percent in eight categories including mining services, drugs/pharmaceuticals, storage/warehousing, and transport. In addition, 100 percent of FDI is automatically approved in a few sectors like electricity generation and transmission, construction/maintenance of roads, venture capital funds, and business electronic commerce. All sectors of the Indian economy are now open to foreign investment, except those with security concerns, such as defense, railways, and atomic energy. The Association of South-east Asian Nations (ASEAN) and India have set a common thinking that freer global trade and globalization itself do not remain tilted towards the developed countries and towards those who start the game of global competition already far ahead in terms of resources, technology and power. Both wanted to see the better management of international short-term capital flows in order to reduce their volatility[74]. The bilateral trade between India and Europe has surged in early 80's. Indian exports to Europe were a paltry 1.8 billion ECUs in 1980, reached 4.8 billion in 1990 and in 1998 grew to 9.8 billion euro. Indian exports to Europe grew more quickly than to the rest of the world: since 1988, Indian exports in general grew at a rate of 11%, but exports to the EU were even more dynamic with 15% per year. The growth concerned not only traditional products such as textiles and agriculture but almost all product categories (including machinery, cars and chemicals). A parallel trend is noticeable for EU

[74] Rodolfo C Severino (2001): Address by the Secretary General, Association of South-east Asian Nations, Partnership Summit, November 11, www.aseansec.org

exports to India that from 2.4 billion ECUs grew to 6.4 billion in 1990 and reached 9.5 billion euro in 1998.

## Grouping of Countries

Countries of the world can be grouped using the similar criteria as of domestic markets. A multinational company may group the countries on the basis of a single variable like per capita GNP or geographic factors. Similarly, the other variables like political system, religion and culture may also be considered as the criterion for grouping the countries. The choice of an appropriate grouping technique will depend on the nature of products and services of the company. Following methods are commonly used by the multinational companies in grouping the countries for developing appropriate business strategies:

- Economic status grouping
- Geographic grouping
- Political grouping
- Grouping by religion
- Cultural classification
- Multiple variable grouping
- Inter-market segmentation
- Portfolio approach

Grouping of the countries by *economic status* is a simple approach based on the GNP per capita ranks. Accordingly, the countries may be grouped into three categories of low income, middle income and high income classifications. The fast-growing countries are defined as those that have an annual average growth rate above the median and the slow-growing countries grow less than the median. The grouping of countries with this criterion assumes that market behavior is directly related to income. In the case of discrepancies of GNP per capita among the countries or a tie between two or more countries, the parameter of purchasing power might be considered by the multinational companies in forming the groups of the countries. In these clusters each activity benefits from access to inputs produced by others located in the same area and to a pool of skills, infrastructure and business services. A sufficiently large market allows for extensive specialization while each company is still able to exploit economies of scale. Furthermore, when manufacturers have access to a broad variety of specialized inputs their productivity improves, their costs are reduced and they can expand sales. As the market expands, room for more specialized producers is created with a further lowering of costs. Countries that form the consortium on the basis of the economic factors may further lead to various business advantages through economic diplomacy. Another common method that is followed by the multinational companies in grouping the countries is on their geographic position and possible networking. Many international companies organize worldwide operations on the basis of *geographically* determined regions like, South-east Asian, Far-east; eastern, central and western European countries, Pacific and Caribbean countries and the like. Proximity of the countries in such regions help in establishing functional trade blocs and the activities can be monitored and controlled by the predetermined locations. All countries in Latin American region may be well managed by having the business headquarters at Brazil as its proximity to other countries allows the company to establish better transport and communication networking. The regional trade agreements are also made largely on the basis of the geographic locations of the countries like APEC, ASEAN, NAFTA, CAFTA, MERCOSUR. These organizations possess regional economic characteristics and lead to the common business arrangements.

Another way of grouping the countries may be in reference to the commonality in the *political systems* and diplomatic relations. Such consortium may refer to the countries of democratic republic, communist and post-communist governing systems and monarchy. The international trading system has been shaped by a blend of SLEPT principles and pragmatic thinking for mutual benefits. Trade relations cannot be determined solely on the basis of simple grouping techniques consisting of economic, geographic proximity, political and technological convergence that defined and agreed upon in general sense. Practical considerations, politics and particular expressions of the national interest inevitably intervene to determine positions taken by governments. Some commentators reflect this reality when they refer to a government measure or policy approach as "bad economics but good politics". Existing literature on international relations and the theory of politics may offer many rich hypotheses and explanations as to why governments might favor international co-operation. Reasons for such engagements include reciprocity in trade liberalization negotiations, co-operation involving participation, expansion of trade and profit and entering into the stronger international relations for protecting the economic interests of the country and the region against all odds. Grouping the countries by *religion* constitutes an important factor of the society in most of the dominating cultures across the countries. Religion influences the lifestyles and also impedes the liberal decision making as it influences and determines the societal values to a large extent. The religious conglomeration of countries thus provides a better scope for international relations.

*Cultural* grouping also makes sense since culture plays significant role in developing lifestyle. Some societies are associated with the power distance attributes that refers to the degree of acceptable inequality. In societies where a few people make decisions that are followed by the large number of people may be termed as high-power distance groups and in the societies where the decisions are made in a decentralized way may be referred as cultures of low power distance. Some countries would like to play safe and avoid any risks. Countries dominating with such cultural behavior may be grouped or otherwise the societies that possess high risk-high benefits culture may be constituted as a group. However, there are also cultures that exhibit the individualism and function in isolation. Alternatively, *multiple variable approach* of grouping the countries attempts to combine countries with similar socio-economic and political perspectives into segments. However, it assumes that countries are indivisible and are heterogeneous.

Recent segmentation approaches followed by the multinational companies, the consumers who are alike in different countries form homogeneous segments. Such segments are called *inter-market* segments. This segmentation approach may be explained in reference to the pharmaceutical industry that caters to the common needs of the consumers of different countries for its innovative drug formula. Similarly, Mercedes-Benz has a worldwide market niche among the customers of same class. Besides, there are some common characteristics of buyers across the countries that include deal makers, price seekers, loyalists, luxury oriented and experimentalists. The deal makers are value oriented, price seekers exist mainly in competitive and developed markets, the brand loyalists are widespread and the consumers with luxurious values and innovators generally refer to the developed countries. The *portfolio approach* in grouping countries may be explained through a three dimensional matrix comprising the factors of country potential, competitive strength and risk. The country potential approach refers to the market potential for the product or services of the company in a given country based on all economic factors where internal and external factors determine the competitive strength of the market. In a given country, the internal factors constitute the market share of company, resources and facilities while the external factors include industry attractiveness and competition. The risk factor has broad range of factors that include principally, financial, political and business risk in a given country.

## BUSINESS OPPORTUNITIES IN DEVELOPING COUNTRIES

In developing countries the business opportunities may be explored for the two prominent reasons. Firstly, a large number of developing countries are pursuing a growth path. South Korea, Taiwan, Singapore, and Hong Kong were first; Brazil and China followed. Most recently, India and Eastern European countries have also opened-up the gates to globalization in consonance with the neo-liberalism concepts. The developing world is beginning to rely on the international market mechanism to attract foreign investment and technology to become industrialized. Such change proneness has given scope to the increasing demand for the technological and environmental products world over. An example of organic products marketing may be appropriately discussed in this context. Most major markets offer good prospects for suppliers of organic products that are not produced domestically, such as coffee, tea, cocoa, spices, tropical fruits and vegetables, and citrus fruits. There are also very good prospects for foods that are produced in the main markets themselves. These opportunities stem from the simple fact that rapidly growing demand in most markets cannot be met by local supply, at least in the short and medium term. Developing countries produce a wide range of organic products and many are exporting them successfully. And secondly, opportunities in developing countries should be even closely examined than those in advanced countries as the government plays a significant role in business decisions in developing countries. This necessitates dealing with the procedural issues therein in foreign investment with considerable sophistication and confidence.

Each year the World Bank Group lends between US$15-20 billion to developing country governments to fund projects for economic development and poverty reduction. This generates around 40,000 contracts ranging in size from a few thousand dollars to multi-million dollar expenditures for the delivery of a vast range of goods and services. Procurement on a World Bank project is the primary way though which companies get involved with the World Bank. The bank lending generates thousands of contracts worth approximately a total of $12 billion annually to firms worldwide. Loans are made to more than eighty governments and government agencies, which are responsible for procurement under World Bank projects. The World Bank develops procurement policy and guidelines (LINK), issues standard bidding documents, supports executing agencies in developing procurement capacity, disseminates information on procurement matters and maintains contacts with industry to ensure that World Bank policies and guidelines reflect current industry standards. The government of the borrowing country is responsible for all procurement steps, including advertising, prequalification evaluation, preparation of bidding documents, evaluation of bids, and contract awards. In its final form, the Country Assistance Strategy (CAS) document outlines the Bank's planned operations in the country lending, analytical work, and technical assistance. Eighty-five countries are covered by the CAS process.

In an effort to create jobs, diversify and grow the economies, many of the countries in the middle-east region have embarked on economic reform and privatization programs to attract foreign direct investment. Algeria, Kuwait and Saudi Arabia are moving toward opening the development of their oil and gas fields to foreign companies and Qatar and the UAE continue to use foreign companies as partners as they expand the development of their oil and gas industries. In the last five years, Egypt, Morocco, Tunisia and the UAE have undertaken one or more new independent power projects. In recent years, most of the countries have implemented new investment laws that allow foreign ownership of domestic enterprises to the full extent. Better laws and stricter enforcement of intellectual property protection in many of the countries have led to increased investment in the pharmaceutical industry in Jordan and in the high tech industries in Israel and the UAE. The Middle East has become an important region for the development of information technology (IT). Several countries, including Egypt, Jordan and Tunisia, are seeking to develop their IT industries. Two countries, Israel and the UAE, have already taken major steps to create vibrant IT sectors. Israel boasts a high-tech sector that is successfully integrated with the global economy. There are more than 200 U.S. high tech companies in Israel today, ranging from the giants, such as Intel and IBM, to "specialty" companies with only a few employees.

An accelerating growth and poverty reduction requires governments to reduce the policy risks, costs, and barriers to competition facing firms of all types, from farmers and micro-entrepreneurs to local manufacturing and multinational companies. A vibrant private sector creates jobs, provides the goods and services needed to improve living standards, and contributes taxes necessary for public investment in health, education, and other services. Too often governments stunt the size of those contributions by creating unjustified risks, costs, and barriers to competition[75]. However, the policy-related risks dominate the concerns of firms in developing countries. Uncertainty about the content and implementation of government policies is the top-rated concern, with other significant risks including macroeconomic instability, arbitrary regulation, and weak protection of property rights. These risks cloud opportunities and chill incentives to invest productively and create jobs. Nearly 90 percent of firms in Guatemala, and more than 70 percent of firms in Belarus and Zambia, find the interpretation of regulation unpredictable. It has been highlighted in the World Development Report -2005 that more than 80 percent of firms in Bangladesh, and over 70 percent of firms in Ecuador and Moldova, lack confidence in the courts to uphold their property rights. Improving policy predictability alone can increase the likelihood of new investment by more than 30 percent Barriers to competition are also pervasive and dull incentives for firms to innovate and increase their productivity - the key to sustainable growth. High risks and costs restrict competition, while governments also limit competition through policy barriers to market entry and exit. Nearly 90 percent of firms in Poland report strong competitive pressure, more than twice the share of firms in Georgia. Stronger competitive pressure can increase the probability of innovation.

[75] World Bank: World Development Report-2005, News Release 2004/89/S, World Bank, Washington DC.

Tenth Five Year Plan (2002-2007) of Government of India estimates that the Indian economy needs to grow at around 8% per annum over the next decade to create the required 100 million new jobs and reduce the poverty rate to 11%. This would require an increase in agricultural growth from the trend rate of about 3% per annum in the last decade to 4.5% per annum over the next 10 years. Industrial growth would need to increase from 6% per annum in the last decade to 8% per annum in the next decade and services from 7.5% annually in the last decade to 9% per year on an average over the next 10 years[76]. International comparisons indicate that India has intrinsic advantages, such as macroeconomic stability, a large and rapidly growing local market, a large and relatively low-cost labor force, a critical mass of well-educated workers, and abundant raw materials that should allow it to attract and sustain higher levels of private investment, both domestic and foreign. A key challenge for India is to streamline business entry and operation procedures, so as to reduce delays and opportunities for rent seeking.

Promotional efforts to attract foreign direct investment (FDI) have become the focal point of competition among developed and developing countries. This competition is maintained even when countries are pursuing economic integration at another level. Moreover, it often extends to the sub-national level, with different regional authorities pursuing their own strategies and assembling their own basket of incentives to attract new investments. While some see countries lowering standards to attract FDI in a "race to the bottom," others praise FDI for raising standards and welfare in recipient countries. Several trends are reinforcing traditional impulses for foreign direct investment, such as access to natural resources, markets, and low-cost labor. Some countries rely on targeted financial incentives, such as tax concessions, cash grants and specific subsidies. Others have chosen a broader approach that focuses on improving their domestic infrastructure and local skills base to meet the demands and expectations of foreign investors. However, many countries have entered into international governing arrangements to increase their attractiveness as investment locations. Although promoting and arranging such investments are complicated, an effective regulatory environment and strong policy framework can make such investments successful.

World Trade Organization (WTO) has come-up with the rules of trade between nations. In the area of work on trade and investment, it specially focuses on conducting analytical work on the relationships between trade and investment. There are three main areas of work in the WTO on trade and investment:

- A Working Group established in 1996 conducts analytical work on the relationship between trade and investment.
- The Agreement on Trade-Related Investment Measures ("TRIMs Agreement"), one of the Multilateral Agreements on Trade in Goods, prohibits trade-related investment measures, such as local content requirements, that are inconsistent with basic provisions of GATT 1994.
- The General Agreement on Trade in Services addresses foreign investment in services as one of four modes of supply of services.

[76] Carter Michael F: Improving the Investment Climate: Challenges for India, Country Director, The World Bank Group, New Delhi, October 19, 2004 (Address delivered in the OECD Investment Conference).

This agreement was negotiated during the Uruguay Round, which applies only to measures that affect trade in goods. Recognizing that certain investment measures can have trade-restrictive and distorting effects, it states that no member country of the WTO shall apply a measure that is prohibited. The list of TRIMs includes measures which require particular levels of local procurement by an enterprise (local content requirements) or which restrict the volume or value of imports that an enterprise can purchase or use to an amount related to the level of products it exports (trade balancing requirements). Such agreement requires mandatory notification of all non-conforming TRIMs and their elimination within two years for developed countries, within five years for developing countries and within seven years for least-developed countries.

Corporate governance is also one of the measures in the microeconomic environment of the country that affect the foreign investor and an overseas firm seeking to enter to a developing country. The OECD Principles have become the most widely accepted corporate governance benchmark and have influenced the drafting of other codes issued by international organizations, countries, companies and stock exchanges. Codes of best practice are important tools in corporate governance reform that raise awareness and help build consensus and ownership of reform processes and outcomes[77]. These codes are non-binding rules that go beyond the law, take specific country conditions into account and often exceed the standards set by international guidelines like the OECD Principles. While adherence to such codes and standards is voluntary, compliance by specific companies sends a signal to investors to help them identify candidates that match their criteria for investment. One of the central Asian republics Uzbekistan is a small country grappling with a legacy of state ownership of enterprises that has contributed to conflicts between government and market-based business objectives, as well as an unclear division of responsibility for corporate governance[78]. The significance of the corporate governance hence may be reviewed as one of the major parameters in evaluating the business opportunities in the developing countries.

## REFERENCES

Derek S Pugh and Allan R Plath: *International Business and Management*, Internationalization and International Strategy (Vol.1), Sage, London, 2003.

Geert Hofstede : *Cultural Consequences-International Differences in Work Related Values*, Sage, London, 1980.

Henbig P and Day K : Outgrowth of ASEAN- A common market for Pacific, *European Business Review*, 93 (2), 1995, pp 12-23.

Jeannet J P and Hennessey H : *International Marketing Management*, Houghton Mifflin, 1992.

Kenichi Ohmae : *Triad Power*, The Free Press, New York, 1985.

Krugman Paul R : *Geography and Trade,* MIT Press, Cambridge, MA, 1988.

Porter Michael E : *The Competitive Advantage of Nations*, Macmillan, 1990.

[77] OECD (1999): Code of Best Practices, Paris

[78] Broadman Harry G (2002): Competition, Corporate Governance and Regulation in Central Asia: Uzbekistan's Structural Reform Challenges, Working Paper 2331. World Bank, Washington, D.C., May.

Lane Kelley and Reginald Worthley : The Role of Culture in Comparative Management : A Cross Culture Perspective, *Academy of Management Journal*, Vol.1, 1981, pp 164-173.

Lawrence John D : *Can we Compete in the Global Marketplace*, Iowa State University, Department of Economics, Staff General Research Papers, June 2003.

Louis Kraar : The Rising Power of the Pacific, *Fortune*, Pacific Rim Issue, 1990, pp 80-84.

McCallum John : National Boarder Matters : Canada-US Regional Trade Patterns, American Economic Review, 85 (3), 1995, pp 615-623.

The Economist : How not to Sell 1.2 Billion Tubes of Toothpaste, *The Economist*, December 3, 1994.

Vandermevwe S : Strategies for a Pan European Market, *European Journal of Management*, 7 (2), 1989.

Yip George : *Total Global Strategy*, Prentice Hall, Englewood Cliffs, New Jersey, 1992.

*Chapter 3*

# TRADE AND ECONOMY IN EMERGING MARKETS

Macroeconomics is the study of the entire economy in terms of the total amount of goods and services produced, total income earned, the level of employment of productive resources, and the general behavior of prices. Macroeconomics can be used to analyze how best to influence policy goals such as economic growth, price stability, full employment and the attainment of a sustainable balance of payments. It considers the performance of the economy of a country as a whole. Principal macroeconomic topics of a country may include economic growth; inflation; changes in employment and unemployment, trade performance with other countries as reflected in the balance of payments and the relative success or failure of fiscal and monetary policies. The economy of a country is based on allocation and management resources of its livelihood system. As all economies operate at different levels, it is necessary to have a clear idea of the economic situation of a particular host country in order to make appropriate decisions in international marketing.

In the 1990s, macroeconomic policies improved in a majority of developing countries, but the growth dividend from such improvement fell short of expectations, and a policy agenda focused on stability turned out to be associated with a multiplicity of financial crises[79]. Economic advancement of a country may be reviewed in reference to its fiscal, monetary, and exchange rate policies over time, and the effectiveness of the changing policy framework in promoting stability and growth. Contemporary concepts of economic advancement for developed countries include entire range of governmental functions, including sectoral policy reform, economic integration, privatization, public sector enhancement, labor market competitiveness, investment climate enhancement, e-government, soft infrastructures for developing a knowledge economy, macroeconomic management and effective long range planning. The weight of the public sector constitutes a serious impediment to more rapid growth for many countries. Importantly the large expenditure burden it requires does not always translate into an efficient and equitable distribution of services. Such performance is reflected by the public sector efficiency and governance in promoting the economic advancement of a country. The challenges of employment generation, economic growth and societal advancement in changing demographic contexts can only be addressed through productive investment and value building. The climate for

---

[79] Luis Servén, and Peter J. Montiel (2004): *Macroeconomic Stability in Developing Countries: How Much Is Enough?*, Working Paper # 3456, World Bank, November.

investment is therefore critical for the countries which need a strategic direction and an economic concentration on value building rather than value trading, which leads towards the higher degree of economic advancement in a country.

> The Russian economy has been observed growing at a slower rate after the collapse of country's economy in 1998. The economy continued with high commodity prices spur this growth, but increased private consumption and investment also contribute. Significant ruble appreciation since mid 2000 has sharply reduced exports and accelerated imports, but import substitution industries. The economy has continued to benefit from increased monetization of the economy, a substantially improved fiscal situation, and a perception of greater political stability. However, economic advancement of the country depends on several factors, some internal (continued structural reform, domestic investment, improved rule of law) and some external (oil and other commodity prices, foreign investment flows). The Russian economy grew 8.3 percent in 2000. In the first six months of 2001, GDP increased 5 percent (year-on-year) and forecasts for calendar year 2001 are for 5.5 percent GDP growth. However, real appreciation of the ruble in the second half of 2000 due to the strong current account surplus and relaxation of fiscal and monetary policies slowed the growth of export and industrial production. Net exports are a declining but still large contributor to GDP (estimated at 16 percent, down from 24 percent in 2000), as oil and other commodity prices remain relatively high. Imports in dollar terms have only recently begun to rise, although the weakness of the euro against both the dollar and the ruble has masked import volume increases. Domestic demand is increasing and becoming a major economic driver. Total investment also increased substantially in 2001, up eight percent during the first eight months of 2001. Both foreign and domestic investment have shown up-ward trend and increasing amounts went into light industry and food processing, indicating deepening economic recovery. The Russian government in 2001 continued to pursue the course of market economic structural reforms outlined in the government's "Strategy of Development of the Russian Federation through 2010. The plan focuses on modernizing the economy through releasing private initiative and ensuring a favorable environment for economic activity, including fair rules for competition, deepening of the rule of law, integration into the world economy, and reform of Russia's natural monopolies[80].

Economic advancement is directly proportional to the educational and training facilities available in the country. Human resources are not only producers of goods and services, which also play a multifold role in economic development. Economic advancement is characterized by the following factors:

- Allocation of labor force to agriculture
- Energy available in large amounts at low cost per unit
- High level of GDP and income
- High levels of per capita consumption
- Relatively low rates of population growth
- Complex modern facilities for transportation, communication, and exchange
- Substantial amount of capital for investment
- Urbanization based on production as well as exchange

[80] Country Reports on Economic Policy and Trade Practices, Released by the Bureau of Economic and Business Affairs, U.S. Department of State, February 2002.

- Diversified manufacturing that accounts for an important share of the labor force; and technology that includes ample media and methods for experiment.

These factors may be utilized to examine economic standing of the host country and analysis of a large variety of information on these variables may help to categorize the countries on an economic development scale. Besides, there are many historical, geographic, political, and cultural factors intimately related to the economic well-being of a nation.

Changes in large nominal exchange rate affect the behavior of trade flows through their impact on the relative prices of tradable goods in the economy. A change in the nominal exchange rate affects the prices of export and import goods relative to domestically produced goods, which implies changes in the real exchange rate. There is a striking difference, as regards the behavior of the real exchange rate, between the two sets of countries indicated above. In Brazil, Peru, and Argentina home currency goods became more expensive during this episode, due to an even higher domestic inflation rate. For the remaining countries large nominal exchange rate devaluations were transmitted into real exchange rate devaluations. With the notable exception of Brazil and Argentina, all countries had experienced a relative convergence to their initial long-term real exchange rates, with rates of real depreciation much lower than those experienced only two years after the devaluation. In Brazil, the five-year period ended just after the large real depreciation resulting from the collapse of the Real Plan in February of 1999 and some of this depreciation was corrected shortly after that. The adjustment of trade flows to their new equilibrium level does not happen immediately. Exporters and importers need to identify new markets for their products, establish relationships, and develop sales and distribution networks that allow them to find substitutes for their current international partners

Macroeconomic policy refers to the top-down strategy developed and implemented in a country by the government and central banks, usually intended to maximize growth while keeping down inflation and unemployment. Growth factors determining the incentives towards investing in human capital for developing new products include government policies. Countries with broadly free-market policies, in particular free trade and the maintenance of secure property rights typically have higher growth rates. By 1990, most developed countries reckoned to have long-term trend growth rates of 2-2.5% a year. However, during the 1990s, growth rates started to rise, especially in the United States of America. Some economists said it was the result of the birth of a new economy based on a revolution in productivity, largely because of rapid technological innovation but also (perhaps directly stemming from the spread of new technology) due to increases in the value of human capital. At the end of the 20th century, it has been argued that developments in information technology and globalization leading towards free trade through the regional trade agreements, has given birth to a new economy initiated in United States. These developments have shown a higher rate of productivity and growth than the previous economy it replaced. Open economies have grown much faster on average than closed economies.

The main instruments of macroeconomic policy are deviations in the interest rates and money supply, taxation and public spending, known as fiscal policy. It has been observed that with the rise of rate of unemployment and inflation, the growth rate of the economy declines and the GDP of the country falls[81]. This may be an evidence of poorly planned macro-

[81] The Economist (2004): Insecurities, November 11.

economic policy and implementation thereof. Higher public spending relative to GDP is generally associated with slower growth. The rise in the rate of inflation is contributed by the high social expenditure and political instability in a country. However, business cycles may simply be an unavoidable fact of economic life that macroeconomic policy, however well conducted, can never be sure of conquering. The pattern of long run growth and recession in the business that may be explained as boom and bust of the economy of a country or a region may be described as business cycle. There are two main versions of the new paradigm that have attracted followers in America lately over the reactions of the previous business cycles[82]. Of these, one version states that the country's long-term growth rate has shifted upwards while the other reveals that the old pattern of boom and bust has disappeared in the light of the free trade and globalization movement by 2000.

Elsewhere, the reforms did bring lasting benefits. In Chile, an early reformer, fast growth saw poverty halved, to 23%, between 1987 and 1996. Overall, macroeconomic management in the region improved dramatically compared with, say, the 1970s. Partly because governments pulled back from running steelworks and factories, they spent more on education and health. In some countries, such as Brazil and Mexico, new, targeted, anti-poverty programs were introduced. Where income inequality worsened, it was mainly because of recession, not reform. Privatization was not the blanket failure painted by the critics. There is little argument over the sale of state industries. Public utilities are more controversial. In some countries, their sale was badly handled: either tainted by corruption, or by private monopolies, or because regulation has been poor. But private provision of telephones, electricity and water has vastly increased their coverage and quality. However, that has generally come at a price: as subsidies were withdrawn, tariffs often rose, before later starting to fall[83].

A positive trend in the behavior of trade flows has been observed during the reforms period, resulting from the increased openness of these economies to international markets. There is a striking difference between the behavior of export and import volumes around the devaluation episodes. Exports tend, on average, to increase in the year of the devaluation and the following two years. Only in Argentina, Peru and Venezuela we observe negative export growth in the second year after the devaluation, and this probably has more to do with the circumstances in world markets at that time, especially in the United States. In all other cases, exports continue to increase. Import volume, in contrast, behaves quite differently. In most of the devaluation episodes import volume contracted; only in the two devaluations by large countries in the mid 1990s (Mexico and Brazil) was there substantial positive import growth. In all other cases, the import contraction was short-lived. Exports increase faster than average to countries in the region, and especially towards countries that are partners in regional trading agreements. Brazil and Argentina increased their trading flows with each other significantly, and also with other countries in the region such as Chile and Paraguay. There was also a significant increase in regional trade among Central American countries: Honduras, El Salvador and Guatemala, despite suffering an exchange rate crisis, increased their bilateral trade with one another at a rate significantly above the average of their overall trade growth.

---

[82] The Economist (1999): Beyond the business Cycles, October 21.

[83] The Economist: Wanted (2003): A new regional agenda for economic growth, April 24.

**Table 3.1 World Population Growth**

| Year | Population | Average annual growth rate (%) |
|---|---|---|
| 1950 | 2,555,360,972 | 1.47 |
| 1960 | 3,039,585,530 | 1.33 |
| 1970 | 3,707,475,887 | 2.07 |
| 1980 | 4,452,584,592 | 1.69 |
| 1990 | 5,281,653,820 | 1.57 |
| 2000 | 6,079,603,571 | 1.21 |
| 2003 | 6,299,763,405 | 1.15 |
| 2010 | 6,815,892,190 | 1.09 |
| 2020 | 7,541,773,753 | 0.90 |
| 2030 | 8,175,075,482 | 0.71 |
| 2040 | 8,722,646,253 | 0.58 |
| 2049 | 9,147,470,346 | 0.47 |

Source: U.S. Bureau of the Census, International Data Base.

## Demography and Income Distribution

World has 6.4 billion inhabitants today. More than 3 billion will potentially be added to our human family over the next 50 years. For decades, environmentalists have warned that ever-rising number of people and their impact on the Earth's finite resources could lead to disaster, not only for wildlife and ecosystems but also for human populations. Growth in the world population since 1950 and its projections till 2049 has been exhibited in Table 3.1. Besides, the demographic explosion in some countries has led to serious concerns on resources management, consumption levels, income distribution, employment and other macroeconomic factors. These factors, in turn affect the market, as people constitute the market. The world today produces and consumes more than ever before. Modern industrial workers now produce in a week what took their 18th century counterparts four years. Private consumption expenditures—the amount spent on goods and services at the household level—topped more than $20 trillion in 2000, a four-fold increase over 1960. One quarter of humanity—1.7 billion people worldwide—now belong to the "global consumer class," having adopting the diets, transportation systems, and lifestyles that were once mostly limited to the rich nations of Europe, North America, and Japan. Today, China, India, and other developing countries are home to growing numbers of these consumers. Yet the world is one of contrasts. While the consumer class thrives, great disparities remain[84].

Rapid population growth continues to undermine efforts to reduce poverty in Africa and Asia. Poor economic performance, limited natural resources and high rates of population increase have led to declines in per capita income in some countries. Because of continued increases in numbers, many countries will find themselves "running faster in order to stand still" in their efforts to improve access and quality in health services and education until well into the next century. The pace of population growth inexorably affects markets, capital

[84] Gary Gardner, Erik Assadourian, and Radhika Sarin (2004): State of the World -2004, Chapter 1, Worldwatch Institute, Washington DC.

accumulation, labor availability, employment generation, immigration, migration, health care, retirement benefits, education, and a host of other national considerations. The population of western Asia is projected to more than double by 2050, going from 204 million to 418 million. Though economic growth and prices are key drivers of food demand, demographic changes such as urbanization, growth in populations, and changes in age structure of populations, will likely have more profound long-term implications for the food system of the country. Urban growth rates are expected to be the most rapid in China and Southeast Asia; more moderate in Latin America, North America, and Oceania; and slowest in East Asia. Most rapid rates of growth will occur in Vietnam, Indonesia, Singapore, and the Philippines. China's urban population is expected to grow by 300 million people (67 percent) in the next 20 years, a staggering number.

> Pacific region is expected to grow by 400 million people, from 2.6 billion in 2000 to 3.0 billion in 2020. However, population growth throughout the Pacific region will not be evenly distributed. By 2020, the largest absolute increase will occur in China (160 million), followed by Indonesia (60 million) and the United States (50 million). In contrast, Japan's population will begin to decline in 2007. Population growth will undoubtedly place demands on the Pacific agri-food system; more people means more food consumption. But the changing rates and distribution of growth will also have significant implications. Japan's declining population implies lower levels of food demand in this affluent nation, a leading importer of food and agricultural products. More rapid population and economic growth in developing and middle-income economies will increase their influence in the Pacific food system, altering production, consumption, and trade patterns. Marketing food products in the Pacific region will increasingly focus on densely populated urban centers, such as the Hong Kong-Shenzen-Pearl River Delta area, Shanghai, Jakarta, Bangkok, Manila, Santiago-Valparaiso, and Lima-Callao. Many of these urban areas are coastal and have modern port facilities, making them easily accessible to foreign suppliers. In some instances, foreign suppliers are more competitive in these coastal urban markets than inland producers who confront inadequate infrastructure and cost-raising policies, like tolls, in getting their products to market. The changing age structure of the region's population affects food demand directly and indirectly. One direct effect is lower food demand. With an aging population, food demand declines, as activity levels and caloric needs decline. A second direct effect is change in dietary composition and the frequency of eating out. According to ERS research[85], older people eat more fresh fruit, fish, and eggs and eat out less frequently than younger people[86].

In 2002, the world economy grew by 1.9 percent, a slight increase from 1.3 percent in 2001, but below the 2.7 percent annual average in the 1990s. The world's recorded outputand incomegrew by more than $1.1 trillion. Lower-middle-income economies saw the fastest growth, followed by low-income economies. Upper-middle-income economies, affected by slowing investment and widespread uncertainty in financial markets, experienced negative growth. High-income economies, accounting for 81 percent of the world's gross domestic product (GDP), almost doubled their growth over 2001, from 0.9 percent to 1.6 percent. Over the past decade economic growth was fastest in East Asia and Pacific (averaging 7.3 percent a year) and South Asia (5.4 percent). Leading this growth were China and India, each

---

[85] Economic Research Services: United States Department of Agriculture, http://www.ers.usda.gov

[86] Pacific Economic Cooperation Council (2003): Where Demographics will take the Food System, Pacific Food System Outlook 2003-04, October.

accounting for more than 70 percent of its region's output. These two regions even did comparatively well in 2002, with East Asia registering 6.7 percent growth, demonstrating its continuing recovery from the financial crisis in 1998, when annual growth fell to 0.7 percent and a slight decline in the growth over 2001 in South Asia to the extent of 4.3 has been observed[87]. Population growth also affects the pattern of income distribution in a country as aggregate consuming capacity depends on the total population as well as per capita income. Thus, advanced countries where growth of population is low, exhibit high propensity to consume the goods and services. It may be observed that the multinational companies from United States of America are actively performing business in the advanced countries of Western Europe, Japan and Canada where per capita income and propensity of consumption are higher. In contrast, Bangladesh and Bhutan as well as other developing countries do not offer a sizeable market potential for the multinational companies.

The growing population has shown various divulging macroeconomic issues in the developing countries towards the incidence of poverty, low rate of employment, inequality in income distribution and the like. However, it must be noted that many developing countries are slowly emerging from poverty in response to the intervention of international community and World Bank. A carefully designed and implemented trade reforms can support growth and can be a "powerful motor" to reduce poverty. However, the mechanisms through which trade reforms affect the population can have varying impacts on the poor versus the rich. The challenge is to identify the appropriate policies that would have a positive impact on growth and a positive impact on the welfare of the poor. Changes in the trade regime affect the population through two main mechanisms. Firstly, the trade regime affects the prices people pay and receive, as well as the demand for and returns to relevant factors of production. And secondly, the trade regime affects government revenues, and therefore the resources available for the supply of government services. The recent development in the global marketing may be discussed in reference to Western Europe, China and Japan that are becoming more competitive with the United States while the developing countries which have successfully implemented the institutional reforms policies are becoming potential markets. This has already reflected in substantial increase in United States exports to the developing countries since 90's.

> India is central to global stability, peace and economic prosperity, since its development is not just an issue for Indians but for the entire planet. The Government of India's Common Minimum Program showed a country with the vision, resources and capacity to address poverty and the inclusion of the hundreds of millions of rural poor. A recurrent theme is the challenge of a "two-speed" model of India where, one in the global fast lane of entrepreneurial talent and technological creativity, a lane where Indian companies were becoming a global presence. In the other lane were the 600,000 villages of rural India where most of India's over 250 million people live at a substantial lower per capita income[88]. Official estimates show a decline in the poverty rate from 36 percent in the early 1990s to 26.1 percent in 1999/2000, but attempts to adjust the household survey underlying the 1999/2000 figures to make it comparable with earlier surveys result in a smaller degree of poverty reduction; how much smaller is a matter of considerable debate, and estimates vary widely. Recent work suggests that poverty has fallen at a somewhat lower rate—from 36 to 29 percent of the population by

[87] World Bank: World Development Indicators-2004.

[88] Jim Wolfenshon (2005): India – Key to Global Stability and Prosperity, Address of the World Bank President, New Delhi, 17 November 2004 (World Bank New Release No. 2005/164/SAR).

> 1999/2000. Either way, over one quarter of India's population is poor[89]. In parallel with this faster growth, India has made impressive progress towards reducing income poverty, an important element of the Millennium Development Goals (MDGs). Continued progress has also been made on many social indicators, particularly literacy, which rose from 52 percent in 1991 to 65 percent in 2001. These improvements are both real achievements for India—and unquestionably of global significance.

On the contrary, in the North America over 70 percent of the population lives in the urban area. In the United States and Canada, people are moving away from urban cores to sub-urban habitats. In Mexico, the trend of population moves has been found reversed as migration to urban areas remain prevalent. The shifts in the demographic patterns affect the economic activities primarily at the micro level in terms of the use of natural resources, manufacturing and marketing activities. However, in an aggregated manner such micro impacts may be observed at macroeconomic level in reference to change in per capita income, consumption level, GDP and related indicators. Amidst such demographic shifts and variations in the constituents thereof over last couple of decades, the world economy has accelerated sharply in 2004, expanding by an estimated 4 percent. United States of America and Japan, whose economies grew by more than 4 percent, continued to lead Europe in the recovery. Even stronger growth was experienced by a number of large developing countries, notably China (8.8 percent), Russia (8.0 percent), and India (6.0 percent). Their performance helped power developing countries as a whole to an anticipated 6.1 percent growth rate in 2004, which may be described as an unprecedented expansion over the past 30 years. Across the developing world, virtually every region enjoyed substantial growth, and increasing trade volumes thereof played an important role in sustaining the growth in the GDP of these countries.

## STRUCTURE OF CONSUMPTION

Demography, society and production resources largely determine the consumption pattern of a region. A system of consumption depends on production and marketing activities in a region. Hence, every country exhibits specific pattern of consumption potential and structure. The consumption level in a country can be measured in terms of volume and compared with other countries in the region. The structure of consumption in a country may be determined by analyzing the behavioral attributes of the consumers thereof. A country may emphasize producer goods over consumer goods in reference to economic factors; what is considered as necessities in one economy may be luxuries in another. In addition, consumption in most advanced countries is characterized by a higher proportion of expenditures committed to capital goods than in developing countries, where substantially more is spent on consumer goods. The structural differences with regard to expenditures among nations can be explained by a theory propounded by the German statistician Ernst Engel in 1857. The Law of Consumption (Engel's law) states that poorer families and societies spend a greater proportion of their incomes on food than 'well-to-do people'. The Engle's law describes that the people generally spend a smaller share of their budget on food

[89] World Bank (2004): India – Country in Brief, September.

as their income rises. The reason is that food is a necessity, which poor people have to buy. As people get richer they can afford better-quality food, so their food spending may increase, but they can also afford luxuries beyond the budgets of poor people. Hence, the share of food in total spending falls as income grows. Developing countries like the Philippines and Sri Lanka spend a larger percentage on food than countries like the United States.

## ECONOMIC INDICATORS

Economic indicators are the variables that are used to measure the soundness of a country's economy such as GDP per head, the rate of unemployment or the rate of inflation. Such statistics are often subject to huge revisions in the months and years after they are first published, thus causing difficulties and embarrassment for the economic policymakers who rely on them. The analysis of factors of production is an important consideration in the international marketing to optimize the comparative advantages over natural resources, labor, capital and entrepreneurship. Entrepreneurs thus play an important role in enabling the economy to adapt to changing conditions and to new possibilities for material improvements by creating new production organizations, and even to whole new industries. Because of its essential role in initiating the process of production, entrepreneurship is identified by some economists as a "fourth factor of production," alongside land, labor and capital. It may thus be explained that higher the productivity of a factor of production, higher may be the income that accrue to its providers. On the other hand, anything that rises above the expected levels of productivity within a society is responsible for increase in the overall prosperity of the society.

Price indicators in the international markets broadly include export and import price indices, consumer prices, wholesale prices and industrial producer prices. The export and import price indices can be used to determine the impact of exchange rate movements on the prices of exports and imports. International price data have been useful for both multilateral and bilateral trade agreements as often the countries utilize these statistics to negotiate trade agreements for some of the important industrial and consumer products such as construction material, plantation crop products like tea and coffee, cotton textiles, oil, airfreight services etc. A primary reason for measuring import prices is to track the impact they have on domestic inflation. Movements in import prices can often be an indicator of future inflation since some inputs to domestic production, as well as consumption, are imported. Export and import price indices are essential for assessing the impact of international trade on the domestic economy. Among their most important uses are analyzing developments in the trade balance, measuring foreign prices' contribution to domestic inflation, and deflating nominal values of exports and imports for estimating the volume of gross domestic product[90]. The Producer Price Index (PPI) is a family of indices that measures the average change over time in selling prices received by domestic producers of goods and services. PPIs measure price change from the perspective of the seller. This contrasts with other measures, such as the Consumer Price Index (CPI), that measure price change from the purchaser's perspective. Sellers' and purchasers' prices may differ due to government subsidies, sales and excise taxes,

[90] Jemma Dridi and Kimberly Zieschang (2004): Export and Import Price Indices, IMF Staff Working Papers, 51 (1), 1-9.

and distribution costs. It is difficult for a marketer to access information about and review all these indicators from each country. However, at any given time, the choice of economic indicators may be identified to determine the entry strategies of a firm. These indicators may reflect on the marketer's domestic operations and the potential business in the host country.

## FINANCIAL INDICATORS

Financial indicators related to the international marketing consist of corporate bond yield, factor income, value of local currency with reference to US dollars and money supply. Besides, the extent of foreign direct investment in a country also reveals its financial strength. A foreign investment is classified as a direct investment if the foreign investor holds at least 10 percent of the ordinary shares or voting rights in an enterprise and exerts some influence over its management. Higher yields of corporate bonds indicate soundness of the financial conditions in a country. Corporate bond interest rates and associated yield spreads are core topics in financial economics. Factors that affect the level of changes in these variables are important to many financial analysts. An examination of these variables and the relationships between them, as well as possible linkages between yield spreads and stock market behavior, is the focus of major financial analysis. In particular, changes in yield spreads between high and medium quality corporate bonds and treasury bonds are examined, as are changes in the spread between the differing quality corporate bonds. Variations in the interest rates are given in financial market history and are taken for the financial analysis as the guide posts. Changes in macroeconomic factors such as inflation and the business cycle cause these fluctuations. Investor perception of risk, of course, affects both interest rates and stock market valuations. Interest rates tend to move together due to common influences, such as inflation. Although this is true, the difference between corporate and government bond interest rates, and between corporate bonds rates on different quality bonds is not constant Other vital financial indicators include exchange rate, stock trends and long term interest rates. The sensitivity of longer-term interest rates to expectations about future short rates is also operative in a short term. This phenomenon is well illustrated by the rise in Japanese long-term rates during the summer of 1996 when financial markets began to anticipate that monetary policy would be tightened in response to recently published information on growth. In addition, the interdependencies among financial markets have certainly increased with globalization; consequently, the foreign exchange markets and bond markets abroad collectively have become much more sensitive to changes in financial conditions in partner countries. However, long-term interest rates are not fully protected from the influence of external factors even in the developing countries.

## ECONOMIC SYSTEM

Economic system of a country is another important factor that a marketer must understand. Traditionally, there are two types of economic systems that exist prominently - state-owned and capitalist. The state-owned, or Marxist, system is pursued in communist countries, where all activities related to production and distribution are controlled by the state.

The roots of capitalism in the economy and society have deep penetration and patterns of economic activity that characterized the period of state capitalism began to change during the great boom of the 1950s and 1960s. The state capitals increasingly traded with each other – and as they did so the basis was laid for a new internationalization of production. World trade grew, on average, at about twice the rate of world output, until 1970s, trade in manufacturing sector was about the same proportion of world output as it had been in 1900 and 1930. Trade did not contract with the recessions of the mid-1970s and early 1980s as it had in the inter-war years. Despite a contraction of world output and world trade in 1982, trade grew faster than output throughout the rest of the 1980s. The concentration of industry through takeovers and mergers, often under the tutelage of the state, had led to the emergence in particular countries of huge firms, able to channel resources into innovation and productive investment on a scale undreamt of before[91]. In refrence to autpmobiles, Japanese car firms established production facilities in USA, turning out more vehicles than the third biggest American firm, Chrysler; the nationalized French firm Renault began a series of acquisitions in the US, beginning with the small fourth US car firm American Motors; Volvo took over General Motors' heavy truck production in the US; Ford and Volkswagen merged their car production in Brazil; Nissan built an assembly plant in north east England to produce hundreds of thousands of cars a year, while Honda bought a 20 percent stake in Rover.

The living standards of rich and poor countries do not converge at welfare economics standards and most of the gains go to multinationals functioning in the developing countries. Such socio-economic conditions lead towards continuously growing polarization between the rich and the poor countries. Multinational companies are moving to the lowest-cost location implementing their production sharing strategies and emphasize the concept of "knowledge economy" that advocates operations with lesser manpower in order to gain the competitive advantage and streamline their operations[92]. Thus, capitalism in the new global economic order has been characterized largely by private ownership of the means of production and the freedom of transactions in international market governed by the regional trade agreements among the countries with less political interventions. Globalization policies with focus on privatization attempt to overrule the political-economic doctrines that advocate governments to impose political barriers to international trade usually in the form of taxes on imports or quantitative restrictions limiting the volume of legally allowable imports of each particular good in order to "protect" domestic firms manufacturing these same goods from foreign competition and thereby make them more profitable than would otherwise be the case under free competition.

## MACROECONOMIC POLICIES

Macroeconomic policy refers to the top-down strategy developed and implemented in a country by the government and central banks, usually intended to maximize growth while keeping down inflation and unemployment. The growth factors determining the incentives

---

[91] Chris Herman (2002): State and Capitalism Today, Die Roten Internet Archives, 2002, Extracted on 24 November 2004 (http://www.marxists.de/admin/2002en.htm ).

[92] Noreena Hertz (2001): The Silent Takeover - Global Capitalism and the Death of Democracy, William Heinemann. London, 22-76.

towards investing in human capital for developing new products include government policies. The main instruments of macroeconomic policy are deviations in the interest rates and money supply, taxation and public spending, known as fiscal policy. It has been observed that with the rise of rate of unemployment and inflation, the growth rate of the economy declines and the GDP of the country falls[93]. There are two main versions of the new paradigm that have attracted followers in America lately over the reactions of the previous business cycles[94]. Of these, one version states that the country's long-term growth rate has shifted upwards while the other reveals that the old pattern of boom and bust has disappeared in the light of the free trade and globalization movement by 2000.

## TRADE DEVELOPMENT PATTERNS

There are large differences in gross domestic products by sectors among Latin American countries, and the majority of these differences are due to the value of industrial and service sectors. Although the sectoral economic activity has been increased, in per capita terms this value decreased due to the demographic growth that Latin American countries (mainly Mexico and Brazil) had experienced during the last decades. In terms of external trade, it has been found that the outward orientation as the ratio between total exports and GDP increased from 16.1% in 1990 to 32.7% in year 2000. Panama had the highest level in this area (66.5%). Modest growth returned to Latin America and the Caribbean in 2003 and regional GDP advanced by an average 1.3 percent, after a contraction of 0.6 percent in 2002. Argentina continued recovering rapidly after its acute crisis. Brazil, Mexico and Uruguay shared in the broadening of economic recovery during the year. Andean countries performed well, with Chile, Colombia and Peru recording growth above 3 percent. However, ongoing political uncertainties caused Venezuela's economy to deteriorate further during the first half of the year. Central America grew by an average 3.1 percent and looks set to sustain growth, thanks to the recently signed Central America Free Trade Agreement[95] (CAFTA). The rate of change in the merchandize export in the Latin American countries during 2002 shows that most of the countries in the region except Costa Rica, Ecuador, Peru and St. Kit Islands other have shown a downward trend. There are many countries apart from Latin America and Caribbean region categorized as emerging markets. The major attributes of the emerging markets may be understood as below:

- Political Stability in the development process
- (Diplomatic relations, domestic policies, growth related development)
- Industrial reforms [ Infrastructure, free trade, licensing and patenting policies, trade related intellectual property (TRIPs) and trade related investment measure (TRIMs)]
- Economic and legal reforms ( FDI, Forex, Tariff and Taxes, Transfers and Repatriation)
- Planning and entrepreneurship
- Factors of production

[93] The Economist (1004): Insecurities, November 11.
[94] The Economist (1999): Beyond the business Cycles, October 21.
[95] World Bank: Report on Latin America and Caribbean, Regional Overview, 2003.

- Outward orientation (Export promotion)
- Economic incentives on investment
- Privatization
- Regional trade agreements (RTAs)
- Technology development – diffusion and adaptation
- Infrastructure

The Central American Free Trade Agreement (CAFTA) negotiated between the U.S. and Central America offers opportunities and challenges for the five countries including El Salvador, Guatemala, Honduras, and Nicaragua that joined in 2003 and Costa Rica that was included in January 2004. Mexico, Nicaragua, Jamaica and Honduras always were over the mean. During the years 1990, 1995 and 2000, Mexico, Cuba, Panama, Argentina, Brazil, Chile and Uruguay reached incomes above 2000 dollars per capita in the service sector[96]. On the other hand, there are some countries like Haiti, Honduras, Nicaragua and Bolivia with incomes below 500 dollars per capita. Latin America's merchandise exports increased slightly as the decline in intra-regional trade was balanced by increased shipments to other regions. The recovery of commodity prices in the course of the year and the upturn in the US economy contributed to this rise. While most Latin American countries saw a reduction or stagnation in their imports, those of Costa Rica increased by 9 per cent. Mexico benefited from the recovery of the US market while for Costa Rica, the recovery in semi-conductor shipments boosted both imports and exports. Despite the continuation of low prices for a number of primary commodities, exports of many Central American and Caribbean countries recovered strongly. Economic activity in Western Europe remained subdued as Germany, the largest economy, experienced declining domestic demand. Domestic demand growth remained positive in the rest of the region, but was sluggish in several other countries. In the euro zone, public consumption was the most dynamic expenditure category while private consumption slowed down and fixed investment in the enterprise sector fell nearly 3 per cent. In the midst of this poor economic situation, further progress was made in the process of European integration[97].

The region is becoming more attractive to multinationals, as product patent protection is implemented and, more importantly, enforced, in Latin American countries. Mexico, in particular, as a member of NAFTA, is attracting substantial inward investment. This is likely to grow even more rapidly in future, given the recent signing of a trade deal with the European Union. The recent recovery of oil prices has shown a positive sign of growth for a number of countries in the region, particularly Venezuela, Mexico and Colombia.

## International Competition

Competition may be analyzed in reference to the characteristics of products as breakthrough, competitive, and improved. A *breakthrough product* is a unique innovation that is mainly technical in nature, such as the digital watch, VCR, and personal computer. A

---

[96] Guisan, M.C. and Aguayo (2000): Education, Industry, Trade and Development of American Companies in 1980-99, *Applied Econometrics and International Development*. Vol. 2-1,. 83-106.

[97] World Trade Organization: World Trade Report 2003, pp 30-42.

*competitive product* is one of many brands currently available in the market and has no special advantage over the competing products. An *improved product* is not unique but is generally superior to many existing brands. For example, let us assume Aubrey Organics is interested in manufacturing shampoo for tender hair in Turkey and seeks entry into the emerging market in the middle-eastern countries. Company finds that in addition to a number of local brands, Johnson & Johnson's baby shampoo and Helene Curtis Industries' Suave Shampoo are the competitive products in the market. Proctor and Gamble has recently entered the market with its Pantene Pro-V brand, which is considered as an improved product. Most of the competition appears to be addressing the existing demand. However, no attempts have been made to satisfy latent demand or incipient demand. After reviewing various considerations, Aubrey Organics may decide to fulfill latent demand with an improved offering through its Camomile Luxurious brand. Based on market information, the company reasons that a hair problem most consumers face in that part of the world is dandruff. No brand has addressed itself to that problem. Even Proctor & Gamble's new entry mainly emphasizes health of hair. Thus, analysis of the competition with reference to product offerings and demand enables Aubrey Organics to determine its entry point into the market of middle-eastern countries. Companies need to analyze some important issues as below while examining the micro-economic environment:

- Who is the competition now, and who will it be in the future?
- What are the key competitors' strategies, objectives and goals?
- How important is a specific market to the competitors, and are they enough to continue to invest?
- What unique strengths do the competitors have?
- Do they have any weaknesses that make them vulnerable?
- What changes are likely in the competitors' future strategies?
- What are the implications of competitors' strategies on the market, the inc. and one's own company?

One of the appropriate ways to examine the competition is to draw up a demographic profile of the industry. Markets dominated by small, single-industry businesses or small regional competitors differ significantly from those dominated by national or multi-industry companies. The strengths of competitors may be measured by analyzing various functional indicators in marketing as described below:

- Market share
- Differential advantages
- Cost advantages
- Reputation
- Distribution capabilities
- Core competencies
- Perceptions of target buyers
- Competitors' financial strength, which determines their ability to spend money on advertising and promotions, among other things
- Competitor's ability and speed of innovation for new products and services

It is necessary to list the strengths and weaknesses of the competitors from the customer's viewpoint and analyze how a company can capitalize on their weaknesses and meet the challenges represented by their strengths. I Information on the competitor information might be easily obtained by getting a copy of their annual report. It might take analysis of many information sources to understand competitors' strategies and objectives. In an international market, the business takes place in a highly competitive, volatile environment, so it is important to understand the competition. Some questions as illustrated below can help the marketer to map the micro-economic variables in reference to a competitor:

- Who are your five nearest direct competitors?
- Who are your indirect competitors?
- Is their business growing, steady, or declining?
- What can you learn from their operations or from their advertising?
- What are their strengths and weaknesses?
- How does their product or service differ from yours?

The competition in the photo film products has been increasing with competitive price and promotion strategies among the major international brands like Kodak and Fuji. The consumers have found a bona fide competitor to Kodak in the name of Fuji film. Clearly, Fuji film has emerged from a minor player in the early 1980's in American market to take a solid number two position within the US market and has caught the attention, as well as the fury, of Kodak. The success of low priced super stores such as Wal-Mart has taught retailers that diversification, scrambled marketing and "one-stop" shopping are important to consumers. As consolidation in retail industry sweeps in mass marketing, food and drug accounts, retailers realize they must maintain their competitive advantage or close shop. To survive, they are squeezing manufacturers for quality products at competitive prices to capture profit margins for expansion within the industry. This environment has provided an opportunity for Fuji film to prosper in an otherwise stable and mature photographic industry. Though Kodak and Fuji fight for market share, the real winner and benefactor is the consumer, both the companies officially deny that they are engaging in a price war, but for each move Fuji makes, Kodak counters with a strategic move. Kodak and Fuji traditionally enjoyed healthy margins and treated the market as a mutually profitable duopoly[98]. Then in the spring of 1996, Fuji cut prices on film by 10 to 15 percent after Costco Wholesalers decided to go exclusively with Kodak. Fuji had excess inventory of 2.5 millions rolls of film. They distributed the heavily discounted film to other retailers to avoid "expiring" film and thus began a correlation between price cutting and market share. Once consumers tried Fuji, they found they liked the product as long as it was priced lower than Kodak. By 1998, the severe pace of competition between Kodak and Fuji seemed to slow down, with the exception of value packs. However, still the companies are on neck-to-neck competition in the market, though other brands like *Agfa, Konica* have made a dent in the global retailing including American markets.

The soundness of the economy of a country largely governs the consumer confidence, which further determines the buying plans of the consumers. A favorable economic environment helps consumers to optimize their buying decisions and augment propensity to

[98] Finnerty C Thomas (2000): Kodak vs. Fuji: *The Battle for Global Market Share, Institute of Global Business Strategy*, Lubin School of Business, Pace University, 4-23.

spend money. The reverse occurs when economic conditions are unfavorable. The economic environment in Brazil was not encouraging for the various segments of consumers during period 1998-1999 though the inflation was under control. The credit restrictions have had a negative impact on consumption during the above referred period. However, after the country exercised appropriate economic measures to stabilize the economy of the country in the recent past, it has been observed that foreign business corporations consider Brazil to be Latin America's most attractive investment target. International marketers should examine the extent to which their business is vulnerable to economic conditions. For example, in a booming economy, consumers tend to buy durable goods, on the contrary in recession they would avoid spending money. There are many areas in emerging markets as listed below which attract business partnering opportunities with developed countries.

- Turnkey projects
- Process consultancy
- Consortium production and marketing
- Cooperative ventures
- Strategic alliances
- Buyback agreements
- Corporate chains-Technology, retail, consultancy
- Custom hiring- production, branding
- Technology diffusion- creating demand
- Green marketing

The prevailing economic environment is just an indicator to review the business fit in the given region or country. Even if the short-run economic environment is not conducive to profits, a company may decide to enter an overseas market in anticipation of favorable long-term economic prospects in country such as growing political stability, declining inflation or the low wage rates. However, the long-run perspective is the most critical decision factor, which provides the firm sufficient resources to endure waiting for the future favorable environment. The market attractiveness of Brazil may be described from the above point of view. The big emerging markets like Brazil, China, Russia and India have enhanced economic and political attributes as discussed below:

- Physically large markets
- Growing population
- Representing wide range of products
- Strong growth rate
- High participation in economic reforms
- Regional/global political importance
- Regional development drivers
- Lead managers in neighborhood and regional trade
- Contemporary infrastructure
- Liberal policies

An accelerating growth and poverty reduction requires governments to reduce the policy risks, costs, and barriers to competition facing firms of all types, from farmers and micro-entrepreneurs to local manufacturing and multinational companies. A vibrant private sector creates jobs, provides the goods and services needed to improve living standards, and contributes taxes necessary for public investment in health, education, and other services. Too often governments stunt the size of those contributions by creating unjustified risks, costs, and barriers to competition[99]. However, the policy-related risks dominate the concerns of firms in developing countries. Uncertainty about the content and implementation of government policies is the top-rated concern, with other significant risks including macroeconomic instability, arbitrary regulation, and weak protection of property rights. These risks cloud opportunities and chill incentives to invest productively and create jobs.

## POLITICAL FACTORS IN INTERNATIONAL TRADE ALLIANCES

High risks and costs restrict competition, while governments also limit competition through policy barriers to market entry and exit. Nearly 90 percent of firms in Poland report strong competitive pressure, more than twice the share of firms in Georgia. Stronger competitive pressure can increase the probability of innovation. Nearly 90 percent of firms in Guatemala, and more than 70 percent of firms in Belarus and Zambia, find the interpretation of regulation unpredictable. It has been highlighted in the World Development Report -2005 that more than 80 percent of firms in Bangladesh, and over 70 percent of firms in Ecuador and Moldova, lack confidence in the courts to uphold their property rights. Improving policy predictability alone can increase the likelihood of new investment by more than 30 percent Barriers to competition are also pervasive and dull incentives for firms to innovate and increase their productivity - the key to sustainable growth. The reforms were implemented in a relatively unfavorable external environment. The effect of implementing the reforms during 1991–95, instead of in the previous five-year period, was to associate them with an international context that by itself reduced the average growth rates of the reforming countries by about 1 percent. Latin America has not yet reached the levels of performance achieved in faster-growing regions. The results of the study highlights that only about half of the annual growth gap of about 7 percent between Latin America and East Asia during the reform period can be closed by doing more of the same that is, intensifying the reform effort along the lines already undertaken. This remaining gap suggests that the scope of reform in Latin America will need to be broadened. Improvements in macroeconomic management are simply not sufficient for Latin America to achieve long-run growth rates comparable to those achieved in East Asia. Such results have also been evidenced by other research studies[100].

[99] World Bank: World Development Report-2005, News Release 2004/89/S, World Bank, Washington DC.

[100] Fernandez-Arias Eduardo and Montiel Peter (2001): Reforms and Growth in Latin America: All Pains, No Gains? *IMF Staff Working Paper*, 48 (4), 1-25.

## TRADE AND TARIFF STRUCTURES

The trade among the Latin American and East Asian countries certainly exhibit enormous potential and apart from the trading of physical goods the services trade in terms of consultancy, transfer of technology and managerial training may also be explored bi-regionally. However, there exist differences among both the regions in factor endowment between the generally natural-resource-abundant Latin America and the natural resource-scarce Asia-Pacific Geography (*i.e.* distance) and differences in the availability of capital, knowledge (*e.g.* Japan, South Korea and Taiwan) and labor (China) also have been major drivers of the bilateral trade. It has been observed by many researchers that Latin America is aggressively opened up to world trade and investment in the late 1980s and its mixed results have emerged over two decades in expansion, diversification and upgrading its exports. The Asia-Pacific countries have shown extraordinary success in diversifying their exports and in raising their stakes in the world economy, while at the same time their domestic market is largely protected against import competition. Such trade policies of this region have also alarmed the concerns for global partnering and business expansions. Instruments such as tariff, non-tariff barriers, trade related investment measures (TRIMS) and barriers to domestic distribution still play an import role in these countries, although there are important cross-country differences in their timing, scope and importance. China has clearly the more protected market, despite the progress made since the WTO accession in 2001, whereas in the other countries protection is particularly high for agriculture. There still exist wide differences in dynamism between these economies. Latin America has yet to resume the high growth rates of the 1950s-60s, whereas most of the Asian Pacific countries, particularly China, have been growing at a breakneck speed, led by exports.

Past several years have witnessed deep changes in trade policy in the Latin American region; this process has generally been accompanied with other far-reaching macroeconomic reforms. Costa Rica stands out as a determined reformer. From an average tariff of 53% in 1985 this country passed to the lowest level in the region: 3.3% in 1999. The overhaul of the tariff structure included the reduction of the average rate as well as the reduction in its dispersion. Though the gains along this dimension are not very notable throughout the nineties, there is a significant reduction relative to the levels observed during the second half of the eighties. Relative to the Chile's structure –which is almost flat- there is still some room to reduce Central America's tariff dispersion. The Table 3.2 exhibits the tariff dispersion structure among the Latin American countries covered under the present study.

**Table 3.2. Tariff Dispersion among Latin American Countries (Standard deviations)**

| Country | 1985 | 1986 | 1987 | 1988 | 1989 | 1990 | 1991 | 1992 | 1993 | 1994 | 1995 | 1996 | 1997 | 1998 | 1999 |
|---|---|---|---|---|---|---|---|---|---|---|---|---|---|---|---|
| Argentina | 14.5 | 20.5 | 20.5 | 21.5 | 21.5 | 8.6 | 8.6 | 7.4 | 5.0 | 6.7 | 7.6 | 7.0 | 6.8 | 6.9 | 8.3 |
| Brazil | 36.7 | 30.0 | 30.0 | 26.2 | 17.2 | 19.8 | 17.3 | 14.2 | 9.5 | 8.2 | 6.9 | 8.5 | 7.7 | 7.3 | 7.8 |
| Chile | 3.2 | 1.7 | 1.7 | 1.0 | 1.0 | 0.9 | 0.9 | 0.7 | 0.7 | 0.7 | 0.7 | 0.7 | 0.7 | 0.7 | 0.7 |
| Colombia | 28.2 | 16.8 | 16.8 | 17.6 | 17.6 | 14.2 | 8.3 | 6.3 | 6.3 | 6.3 | 4.9 | 6.3 | 6.3 | 6.2 | 6.2 |
| Costa Rica | 27.4 | 11.2 | 8.8 | 8.8 | 8.8 | 8.8 | 8.8 | 8.1 | 6.4 | 6.2 | 8.5 | 6.2 | 5.5 | 4.6 | 7.8 |
| Ecuador | - | 39.0 | 39.0 | 38.6 | 38.6 | 20.4 | 20.4 | 6.0 | 6.0 | 6.3 | 5.6 | 6.4 | 6.4 | 6.4 | 6.3 |
| Mexico | 15.4 | 14.3 | 14.3 | 7.0 | 7.0 | 4.5 | 4.5 | 4.5 | 4.4 | 4.4 | 5.4 | 10.6 | 10.6 | 13.5 | 9.4 |
| Paraguay | - | 15.2 | 15.2 | 15.2 | 15.2 | 13.0 | 1.4 | 7.8 | 6.8 | 7.7 | 6.9 | 7.1 | 6.7 | 6.5 | 7.4 |
| Peru | 26.8 | 25.9 | 25.9 | 27.4 | 27.4 | 22.6 | 22.6 | 4.4 | 4.4 | 4.4 | 4.4 | 4.4 | 4.4 | 2.9 | 2.5 |
| Uruguay | 16.2 | 18.8 | 18.8 | 14.4 | 14.4 | 9.7 | 9.7 | 5.9 | 5.9 | 5.9 | 7.1 | 7.3 | 6.9 | 7.9 | 4.3 |
| Venezuela | 28.6 | 30.2 | 30.2 | 31.4 | 31.4 | 17.1 | 17.1 | 11.3 | 11.3 | 11.3 | 4.8 | 4.8 | 6.1 | 6.1 | 5.9 |

Source: Computed on the data available with ECLAC, UNCTAD, WTO and IDB for the referred periods.

The involvement of Central America's major trading partner, the USA in a trade agreement benefiting neighboring Mexico could have been a source of disruption in the direction and pattern of trade flows in the region. Despite the implementation of NAFTA in 1994, a number of Central American countries (Costa Rica, Guatemala, Honduras, Nicaragua and the Dominican Republic) witnessed throughout the decade an unprecedented increase in trade, both in import and export trade, with the USA[101]. This implies that NAFTA preferential treatment, with its potential trade diversion effect, was to some extent effectively counter balanced. It is notable that only Costa Rica experienced a decline in its market share, but this was probably due to export growth in other sectors of the economy of Costa Rica.

**Table 3.3. Exports from Latin American Countries to Asia-Pacific (1990-2003) (US $ millions)**

| Country | Japan | Korea Republic | China | Hong Kong | Taiwan | Singapore | ASEAN[a] | Asia-Pacific (A) | World (B) | Percent Share (A/B) |
|---|---|---|---|---|---|---|---|---|---|---|
| Argentina | 344 (395) | 434 (51) | 2478 (241) | 98 (60) | 126 (48) | 10 (409 | 1098 (329) | 4588 (1164) | 29566 (12352) | 15.5 (9.4) |
| Brazil | 2311 (2349) | 1223 (543) | 4533 (382) | 694 (271) | 689 (432) | 338 (250) | 1113 (790) | 10900 (5016) | 73084 (31412) | 14.9 (16.0) |
| Chile | 2243 (1384) | 1006 (258) | 1817 (34) | 0 (41) | 583 (279) | 39 (33) | 254 (132) | 5922 (2162) | 20077 (8522) | 29.5 (25.4) |
| Colombia | 202 (259) | 76 (13) | 82 (2) | 16 (16) | 52 (1) | 11 (3) | 18 (9) | 456 (303) | 13092 (6765) | 3.5 (4.5) |
| Costa Rica | 58 (15) | 11 (5) | 89 (0) | 132 (2) | 39 (6) | 24 (1) | 244 (5) | 596 (34) | 5800 (1456) | 10.3 (2.4) |
| Ecuador | 86 (51) | 242 (23) | 14 (0) | 3 (0) | 4 (65) | 1 (0) | 3 (2) | 353 (142) | 6038 (2714) | 5.8 (5.2) |
| Mexico | 607 (1442) | 95 (102) | 463 (65) | 258 (42) | 106 (0) | 183 (33) | 91 (26) | 1803 (1711) | 165395 (26345) | 1.1 (6.5) |
| Paraguay | 5 (21) | 0 (6) | 17 (67) | 9 (17) | 12 (3) | 1 (5) | 9 (5) | 53 (123) | 1242 (1708) | 4.3 (7.2) |
| Peru | 390 (420) | 176 (65) | 675 (55) | 30 (19) | 147 (50) | 16 (0) | 76 (18) | 1511 (628) | 8749 (3313) | 17.3 (19.0) |
| Uruguay | 12 (21) | 6 (6) | 95 (67) | 14 (17) | 5 (3) | 2 (5) | 63 (5) | 197 (123) | 2198 (1708) | 9.0 (7.2) |
| Venezuela | 135 (505) | 15 (6) | 165 (6) | 11 (34) | 37 (57) | 201 (125) | 9 (44) | 571 (777) | 24974 (18044) | 2.3 (4.3) |
| LAC | 6473 (6958) | 3367 (1091) | 10470 (866) | 1278 (507) | 1786 (967) | 832 (495) | 3029 (1376) | 27234 (12261) | 363707 (120916) | 7.5 (10.1) |

Figures in parentheses indicate values for 1990.

Source: IDB-INT calculations based on UN/COMTRADE data published in the official document AB-2370, March 21, 2005: "Asia and Latin America and the Caribbean: Economic Links, Cooperation and Development Strategies".

[101] Leaderman Daniel, Perry Guillermo and Suescun Rodrigo (2002): *Trade Structure, Trade Policy and Economic Policy Options in Central America*, The World Bank, Office of the Latin American and Caribbean Region, Working Paper, November.

Latin America's total exports grew by an annual average 8.9 percent between 1990 and 2003 raising its share of world exports from 3 to 5.4 percent as exhibited in Table 3.3 Mexico has been the indisputable driver of Latin America's export growth, with its share of the regional total rising from a fifth in the early 1980s to 45 percent in 2003. It may be observed from the exhibited data that four big countries which include Mexico, Brazil, Argentina, and Venezuela-today generate more than three-fourths of Latin America's exports. Imports mirror the export patterns. Despite Latin America struggling with anemic economic growth, the region's imports rose by more than exports (an annual average of 10.1 percent in 1990-2003), perhaps reflecting the region's rather aggressive opening and episodes of exchange rate appreciation.

The dynamism of trade notwithstanding, the volume of Latin American exports to Asia-Pacific starts from a relatively low base and is well below the region's exports to North America, the European Union, and intra-regional commerce. In fact, while increasing substantially up to 1991, the importance of Asia-Pacific as a market for Latin America has declined over the past decade. Latin American exports to Asia-Pacific stood at $24 billion in 2003, with the Asia-Pacific accounting for 6.6 percent of Latin America's total exports to the world-a marked drop from Asia-Pacific's share of 9 percent in 1990. Central America did, however, experience slight growth in the share of the Asia-Pacific in total exports in 1990-2003. Of the individual countries, Argentina, Chile, Colombia, Costa Rica, EI Salvador, Guatemala, Jamaica, Paraguay, Peru, Uruguay, and Venezuela did experience a rise in the share of Asia-Pacific in their exports between 1990 and 2003.

The importance of the Asia-Pacific is most marked for Chile, which exported 29 percent of its exports to Asia-Pacific, as well as for the Mercosur countries, which sent 15 percent of their exports to the Asia-Pacific basin in 2003. Arguably, the most vulnerable region right now is Latin America, where most countries are trying to cope with an environment of high economic fragility, partly resulting from the current global slowdown but also reflecting internal political trouble and policy mismanagement. The region’s problems are of a more long-term nature than merely cyclical and therefore need to be tackled accordingly, taking into account country-specific circumstances. Latin America’s large distance from world markets, the region’s complicated topography, and the tropical climate pose particularly important challenges. On the macroeconomic front, the fiscal policy stance has deteriorated significantly in several countries, sending them into a dangerous spiral of increasing debts and deficits despite important efforts to generate primary surpluses in the public budget. However, that encouraging reforms have been implemented in some areas, notably regarding foreign trade and financial liberalization. As a result, exports have increased and became more diversified which augur well when the external environment becomes more favorable again.

## China as Emerging Market

China has emerged as a key player in the determination of global macroeconomic balances and as a major point of reference in the production strategies of the world’s major transnational corporations. At present, 400 of the Fortune 500 companies have set up operations in China. This is not only because of China’s attractive market of 1.3 billion consumers. China has ambitious medium- and long-term goals designed to transform it into an industrial power by 2010 and a technological power by 2015. A particularly noteworthy aspect of Chinese trade development is that, between 1990 and 2004, high-technology exports grew faster than those of other sectors in the economy, while commodity exports fell steeply. The principal trading partners of China are its neighbors in Asia and the Pacific, especially Japan and the nations belonging to the Association of Southeast Asian Nations (ASEAN). These countries supply 56% of China's imports and buy 45% of its total exports. Manufactures represent an extremely high percentage (95%) of these trade flows. The composition of China's trade with other developing countries, primarily of Latin America, Africa and the Middle East, complements these flows, as it is concentrated in commodities and natural resource based manufacturers. These developing nations are thus its main suppliers of copper, iron ore, Soya, petroleum, fishmeal, sugar and a range of other products. China's trade deficit with Latin America alone jumped from US$ 6.37 billion to US$ 10.969 billion between 2003 and 2004. China has emerged as largest investors among Asian countries. Chinese firms are investing via mergers and acquisitions in well-positioned technology intensive enterprises that possess the necessary know-how and have good reputations backed up by established brand names. They are also making green field investments in strategically located research and development centers. This strategy has permitted some firms to enhance their credibility and penetrate more deeply into new markets[102].

China has been increasing its share in Latin American trade during the course of this decade, and by 2003, it accounted for almost 3% of the total exports of the region and 5% of its total imports, thus becoming largest Asian trading partner of the Latin American and Caribbean region. After a period of flat growth that lasted until 1999, Chinese imports from Latin America and the Caribbean began to soar, jumping to almost US$ 5.4 billion in 2000 and to US$ 21.668 billion in 2004. This represented an annual growth rate of 42% between 2000 and 2004, which far outstripped the growth rates of China's imports from the world as a whole (26%). China is an extremely important trading partner for many of the countries in the region today. China absorbs just over 10 percent of exports of Chile compared with less than 1 percent of decade ago. Other countries, including Argentina, Brazil and Peru, are also similarly placed. China is now the third-largest trading partner of Brazil, after the United States and Argentina, and competes with Japan for second place. China's trade with Mexico, Venezuela and Costa Ricahas also increased significantly in recent years[103].

## EMERGING MARKET OF INDIA

India has been a strong advocate of multilateral, rather than regional, trade initiatives and is party to few regional trading agreements. Efforts are nevertheless being made to strengthen regional agreements to which it is party, such as the South Asian Association for Regional Cooperation (SAARC) and the Bangkok Agreement. Under the South Asian Preferential Trade Agreement (SAPTA), the members of the SAARC have completed three rounds of

[102] Economic Commission for Latin America and Caribbean (2004): Latin America and Caribbean in the World Economy, ECLAC Publication, 145-180.

[103] Economic Commission for Latin America and Caribbean (2004): Latin America and Caribbean in the World Economy, ECLAC Publication, 145-180..

trade negotiations and expect to complete the SAPTA in 2002.The Indian economy has grown rapidly over the past decade, with real GDP growth to the extent of 6 percent annually, in part due to the continued structural reform, including trade liberalization. Social indicators, such as poverty and infant mortality have also declined significantly during the last ten years. In order to achieve further significant reductions in poverty, India is currently targeting higher real GDP growth of between 7 percent and 9 percent. However, it is necessary to accelerate the process of institutional reforms and increase trade competitiveness in the country. Government of India has simplified the tariff, eliminated quantitative restrictions on imports, and reduced export restrictions and indications showed to further simplify and reduce the tariff. However, the level of protection through the tariff remains relatively high and the anti-export bias inherent in imports and other constraints still remains. To help counteract this anti-export bias, export promotion measures have gained importance. The Government has recently announced a further increase in these measures and plans to continue reforms of the tariff and other taxes[104].

## INDIAN ECONOMY IN POST-LIBERALIZATION PERIOD

As restrictions on trade and competition have been reduced, constraints associated with infrastructure and regulatory bottlenecks have become increasingly evident and need to be addressed urgently both through regulatory reform and through increased investment. Despite further liberalization of the FDI regime, India's record in attracting investment remains disappointing, with FDI accounting for about 1 percent of GDP. The government has also taken various steps to improve enforcement of intellectual property rights which should help to attract FDI. Tariff and tax reform are also crucial to address the problem of high fiscal deficits, which have continued to grow despite efforts to reduce public spending. Moreover, with the customs tariff accounting for some 30 percent of net government tax revenue, further reform of the tariff may depend on major tax reform. It has been observed that the customs tariff has become the main form of border protection. There have been significant recent efforts to rationalize the tariff, but, with numerous exemptions based on end-use, it remains complex and applied tariffs, which averaged some 32 percent in 2001/02, remains relatively high. As a result of additional bindings taken by India in the WTO, the share of tariff has increased since the previous review, from 67 percent to 72 percent. The average bound rate is 50.6 percent which is higher than what is applied to Most Favored Nations (MFN) rate and this gap has provided ample scope for applied rates to be raised recently on a few agricultural products. The major structural adjustments in the trade and economy appeared in the country towards removal of all import restrictions maintained for balance-of-payments reasons. As a result, the customs tariff has become the main form of border protection. There have been significant recent efforts to rationalize the tariff, but with numerous exemptions based on end-use, it remains complex. Tariffs are relatively high, but the average applied MFN rate fell from 35.3 percent to 32.3 percent between 1997-98 and 2001-02 and expected to fall further, to 29 percent in 2002-03, as the "peak" rate of tariff is reduced from 35 percent to 30 percent. The tariff shows substantial escalation in some sectors, especially for paper and printing,

---

[104] World Trade Organization (2002): Trade Policy Review of India- June 2002, WTO Headquarters, Geneva, Press release # Press/TPRB/195.

textiles and clothing, and food, beverages and tobacco. Government announced recently that it intends to simplify and lower the tariff to two tiers by 2004-05; 10 percent for raw materials, intermediates and components, and 20 percent for final products. In addition to the tariff, importers must pay additional and special duties on a number of products[105].

> India plays key role in regional trade and cooperation among the South-east Asian countries. The ASEAN-India Comprehensive Economic Cooperation covers the issues of strengthening and enhancing economic, trade and investment co-operation. The trade agreement also envisages the cooperation towards the progressive liberalization and promotion of trade in goods and services as well as the creation of a transparent, liberal and facilitative investment environment. Under the agreement it has been emphasized to explore new areas and develop appropriate measures for closer economic co-operation in the region. The role may also be viewed towards facilitating the more effective economic integration of the new ASEAN Member States and bridging the development gap among ASEAN member countries and India. Under the Framework Agreement, ASEAN and India committed to progressively reduce and eliminate tariffs on a reciprocal basis. During January 2006 to December 2011 Brunei, Indonesia, Malaysia, Singapore, Thailand and India would honor the agreement of progressive reduction of the tariffs on reciprocal basis while Cambodia, Lao PDR, Myanmar, Vietnam, Philippines and India would engage in the process of tariff elimination during January 2006-December 2016. A total of 177 manufactured goods from Malaysia are eligible for the preferential tariff treatment under the EHP. The main EHP products exported by Malaysia to India include cocoa butter, cocoa powder, cyclic hydrocarbons, chemical products and preparations, tin and fiber board of wood. Such free trade agreement enables ASEAN and India to share the huge resources available through joint collaboration to promote the further growth of both the manufacturing and services industries[106].

There appears to have been an increase in cross border measures such as anti-dumping conflicts ranging to 250 cases initiated since 1995, though import licensing and tariff restrictions are declining. Internal reforms have concentrated on improving efficiency and competition in the economy. Thus, while industrial policy remains important, its scope seems to have been reduced significantly as number of activities inthe small scale industry have deminished. The need for increased competition is being addressed by gradually reducing the degree of direct government involvement in economic activities, including through a program to restructure and privatize state-owned companies. The privatization program has experienced limited success and stepped up to address the fiscal deficit. In addition, price controls, currently maintained on several products including fertilizers, petroleum products and in agriculture, add to the fiscal burden of subsidies (implicit and explicit subsidies were estimated at some 14.5 percent of GDP in the mid-1990s).

---

[105] World Trade Organization: Trade Policy Review of India- June 2002, WTO Headquarters, Geneva, Press release # Press/TPRB/195.

[106] Directorate of ASEAN Economic Cooperation, Malaysia.

## Sectoral Trade and Growth

Agriculture sector policy in the country has largely been guided by domestic supply and self-sufficiency considerations. Thus, this sector is shielded through import and export controls, including tariffs, state trading, and export restrictions and, until recently, imports restrictions. The result of this policy has revealed in substantial increase in stocks to unsustainable levels and the costs associated with maintaining these stocks. While in services sector, significant reforms have been pursued since the previous review, especially in telecommunications, financial services and, to some extent, in infrastructure services, such as power and transport. Liberalization of telecommunication services has resulted in an increase in availability and a reduction in tariffs. The reduction in telecommunication tariffs is also likely to benefit the software sector, one of the major success stories in recent years. Internal reforms have concentrated on improving efficiency and competition in the economy.. Compulsory licensing now appears to be required mainly for environmental, safety, and strategic reasons. In addition, the number of activities reserved for public sector has been reduced from six to three and the number of sectors reserved for the small-scale industry has been reduced from 821 to 799; another 50 items are expected to be removed from the list of items reserved for the small-scale sector. Price controls are maintained on several products, including fertilizers, petroleum products, and some agricultural products; some of these, including on petroleum and fertilizers, are gradually being phased out.

> India has a huge interest in freer trade in the IT sector. India accounts for a third of the world's software engineers and more are access to computer technology at world prices and efficient, low-cost telecoms. It is one powerful reason why India should be fighting for a new round of negotiations at the WTO. It may be noted that a throw in the prospect of freer trade in agriculture and cuts in industrial tariffs, and the case becomes all the more compelling. The Tinbergen Institute estimates that the annual gains to India from a new round could top $11 billion, raising India's national income by 4.4 percent. A strong push for a new round from India could be decisive. We are approaching a critical juncture at the WTO. Over the past year we have successfully rebuilt confidence in the WTO[107].

The experience of the IT industry in India indicates that increase in temporary movement of persons who move to provide a service, is associated both with inward and outward foreign investment. During the 1990s, there was a large flow of Indian professionals to the United States, the bulk of which were IT specialists. Over the same period, multinationals and investments from non-resident Indians in the IT industry has increased, as the share of US-based non-resident Indians' collaborations in India's IT sector has reached a significant 40 per cent. Many Indian IT professionals who have worked in the United States have had a significant influence on the decision of US multinationals to set up activities in India. At the same time, the large flow of knowledge and technology spillovers including associated exports has facilitated the development of the IT industry in India. Subsequently, Indian IT companies, such as Wipro and Infosys, have established subsidiaries abroad or partnerships. Besides IT, the Indian exports have gained the commendable statues in the global trade. In agricultural and plantation sector, Darjeeling tea is a specialty tea grown in the West Bengal

[107] Mike Moore (2001): The Multi-lateral Trading System: Where are we Headed?, Speech in the Partnership Summit, Hyderabad India, 11th January 2001, WTO Secretariat, Geneva.

region of India. Darjeeling tea is grown on about 19,000 hectares of hilly land (from 700 to 2,000 meters), with production estimated at a little over 5,000 metric tons in 2002. About 70 per cent of production is exported, with the major export markets being the UK, Germany, Japan, the United States, the Netherlands and France. In 1983, a Darjeeling logo was created. This logo was registered as a certification mark in India in 1986. Registration of the logo as a certification mark in major export markets occurred later – in 1988 in the United States and 1997 in the United Kingdom. The Indian Tea Board has also separately registered the word "Darjeeling" as a certification mark[108]. The Indian Tea Board conducts weekly auctions of various grades of tea. The data used are the annual average prices and the quantities sold at auction in Calcutta from 1972 to 2002 of various tea leaves: Darjeeling, Assam, Cachar, Doaars and Terai. The nominal price of Darjeeling tea has shown a pronounced rise since about 1984. However, the deflated price of Darjeeling only rose until 1998 and fell afterwards[109].

Indian Textile Industry is one of the largest segments of Indian economy accounting for over 20 percent of the industrial production as well as providing employment to around 65 million persons. This sector enjoys the distinction of being the highest foreign exchange earner for the country, accounting for nearly one third of the country's total exports. Despite strong domestic demand-pull, textile exports have witnessed steady growth over the years. The share of India's textile exports in the world has grown from 1.8 percent in the beginning of 80's to around 3 percent in 2002. The advantages arising from a strong raw material base, a well established yarn and fabric industry and relatively low labor cost has led to quick growth in textile exports, from an insignificant base of less than US $3 million in the beginning of 70's to nearly US $ 12-13 billion. However, with the lowering of tariff barriers, removal of quantitative restrictions and the phase out of MFA regime, the textile industry is poised to enter an era of fierce competition, not only in exports but in the domestic market as well. All these developments are bound to have some effects on Indian textile trade and industry. To meet the emerging competition, the Government is continuously providing an enabling environment for the industry to be globally competitive[110].

The Indian government has identified certain special focus initiatives for the agriculture, handlooms, handicraft, gems & jewellery and leather sectors with a view to double the share of global trade by 2005 and expanding employment opportunities, especially in semi-urban and rural areas. A new scheme envisaging the Special Agricultural Produce Scheme (SAPS) for promoting the export of fruits, vegetables, flowers, minor forest produce, and their value added products has also been introduced. There are many schemes moved by the Government of India for promoting the export of the unorganized sectors like handlooms and handicrafts. The Market Access Initiative (MAI) scheme is intended to provide financial assistance for medium-term export promotion efforts with a sharp focus on a country and product. A whole range of activities can be funded under the MAI scheme which include market studies, setting up of showroom/ warehouse, sales promotion campaigns, international departmental stores, publicity campaigns, participation in international trade fairs, brand promotion, registration

---

[108] Word Trade Organization (2005): World Trade Report-2004, p 85-86.

[109] Rao, N. (2003) 'Geographical Indications in Indian Context: A Case Study of Darjeeling Tea' Indian Council for Research on International Economic Relations Working Paper No. 110. Paper is available online http://www.icrier.res.in/pdf/ wp110.pdf. Accessed 23/06/04.

[110] Governement of India: Ministry of Textile, Speech delivered by the Minister of Textile in TEXPOCIL Award Function, 30th September 2002 (for details see on-line http://texmin.nic.in/msy_20021009b.htm )

charges for pharmaceuticals and testing charges for engineering products etc. Each of these export promotion activities can receive financial assistance from the Government ranging from 25 percent to 100 percent of the total cost depending upon the activity and the implementing agency, as indicated in the detailed guidelines. Another popular scheme of the government intending to promote the exports is Market Development Assistance (MDA). This Scheme is intended to provide financial assistance for a range of export promotion activities implemented by export promotion councils, industry and trade associations on a regular basis every year.

The social acceptance of trade liberalization is an important issue during the period of adjustment to reform and also after the economy has adapted to the new situation. The adjustment burden of trade liberalization is likely to be concentrated in the import-competing sector and lead to resistance against reform, even though reform is beneficial for the economy as a whole, and also in the long-run for many of the workers employed in the import-competing sector. There are two main approaches to increasing the social acceptance of trade reform. In the field of trade liberalization, joint action among governments to reduce trade barriers helps reduce the risk of obtaining terms-of-trade advantages by some countries at the expense of others, thereby creating an incentive for a mutually advantageous market opening that might not otherwise occur. Joint action to liberalize trade also generates greater domestic support for freer trade by engaging the interests of export industries that stand to gain from reduced barriers in other countries.

## TRADE BARRIERS[111] AFFECTING FOREIGN TRADE IN INDIA

Although India is a proactive member of WTO and an advocate of globalization concept, the country still exercises protections in the sensitive sectors. Many sectors of the Indian economy are now at least partially open to foreign investment, with certain exceptions. The Indian government continues to prohibit FDI in certain politically sensitive sectors, such as agriculture, retail trading, railways, and real estate. Foreign investment is still relatively controlled with various government approvals required for many types of investments. In June 2002, the Indian government opened the news print media sector to FDI of up to 26 percent. FDI is limited to 74 percent in the case of the non-news journals and magazines. In 2001, the government opened the defense equipment industry to private investors with an FDI limit of 26 percent. The government also raised permissible foreign equity in banking to 74 percent from 49 percent, in the interne services provider (ISP) sector to 74 percent from 49 percent, and in pharmaceuticals to 100 percent from 74 percent.

In July 2000, the United States initiated a dispute settlement proceeding in the WTO, later joined by the EU, challenging India's compliance with its commitments under the Agreement on Trade-Related Investment Measures (TRIMS). As a result, on March 14, 2002, India announced a new automobile investment policy. The new automobile investment policy eliminated previous local content and minimum investment requirements. This policy has allowed automatic approval for 100 percent foreign equity investment for manufacturing

[111] For details on trade barriers in India-US international trade, refer Foreign Trade Barriers, US Department of Trade, web link: http://www.ustr.gov/assets/Document_Library/Reports_Publications/2004/2004_National_Trade_Estimate/2004_NTE_Report/asset_upload_file973_4773.pdf

automobiles and components. In August 2002, the Indian government removed export performance requirements for foreign automakers. The Indian Parliament has approved competition legislation in 2002 that provided for a new regulatory authority, the Competition Commission of India (CCI) to replace the Monopolies and Restrictive Trade Practices Commission (MRTPC). The new law does not prohibit monopolies but does charge the CCI with regulating unfair practices and promoting policies that favor competition. The government issued the implementing rules for the Competition Act in April 2003.

The national telecommunications policy allows private participation in the provision of basic, including cellular and value-added telecommunications services. Foreign equity in value-added services is limited to 51 percent. For basic services, the limit is 49 percent. In view of the difficulty to raise the required money to finance the new networks, some creative financing arrangements have been allowed in some cases that extend the limit to 74 percent. Indian government retains a significant ownership stake and interest in the financial health of the dominant telecommunications firms, all of which formerly enjoyed monopoly status in their areas of operation. The government holds a 26 percent position in the international carrier, Videsh Sanchar Nigam Limited (VSNL), a 56 percent position in Mahanager Telephone Nigam Limied (MTNL), which primarily serves the Delhi and Bombay metro areas, and a 100 percent position in Bharat Sanchar Nigam Limited (BSNL), which provides domestic services throughout the rest of India. The government has indicated that it will privatize MTNL and BSNL in the future but has not established a timetable.

India continues to maintain a negative import list. The negative list is currently divided into three categories: (1) banned or prohibited items (*e.g.*, fat and oils of animal origin); (2) restricted items which require an import license (e.g., livestock products); and (3) "canalized" items importable only by government trading monopolies subject to cabinet approval regarding timing and quantity. India has liberalized many restrictions on the importof capital goods. The government allows imports of all second-hand capital goods by actual users without license, provided the goods have a residual life of five years. Some commodity imports must be channeled ("canalized") through public sector companies, although many such items have been decontrolled. Remaining canalized items are primarily petroleum products (although canalization of crude oil was eliminated in April 2002), some pharmaceuticals, and bulk grains (wheat, rice, and maize). Indian Customs requires extensive documentation. The Government of India fixes minimum import prices for certain imported steel products, including hot-rolled steel coils, cold rolled steel coils, hot rolled sheets, tin plates, electrical sheets, and alloy steel bars and rods. However, this issue is being debated extensively in the judicial circles as well as trade associations in the country.

## Regional Trade Cooperation

Trade alliances among the countries have been stronger as the globalization received wider acceptance over years. The impact of increased global economic integration on national and regional environmental standards has been studied in general by a large number of researchers. International trade alliances are formed among two or more countries by developing the Preferential Trade Agreements (PTA) among the trade partners to gain the advantages over tariffs, transfer of factors of production and technology. Tariffs play significant role in determining PTA and attracting foreign direct investment in the host country. Under PTAs, as transport costs fall, the incentive to impose tariffs falls and the benefits on cooperation rise. Thus, in a repeated game in which cooperation is limited by a self-enforcement constraint, a reduction in transport costs facilitates free trade.

> The Thai threat to the Indian auto component industry is felt as serious by the auto parts manufactured real as a result of free trade agreement between India and Thailand. That is the conclusion of consulting agency ICRA Advisory Services, which studied the possible impact of the Indo-Thailand free trade agreement (FTA) on the auto component industry. ICRA, in its report presented to the Automotive Component Manufacturers' Association (ACMA) in January 2004, reveals that there is a significant threat of imports from Thailand and cites three reasons to support its conclusion. Firstly, Thailand enjoys a significant manufacturing cost advantage in relation to India. Secondly, there is surplus capacity available in Thailand that can be used to produce for exports. Finally, vehicle manufacturers with a presence in both countries may decide to source specific components from Thailand under the FTA for assembly in India. The study reveals that Indian companies suffer a cost disadvantage of 15-20 per cent of the total cost over their Thai counterparts mainly due to the adverse tax structure and higher infrastructure costs. Indian companies have limited opportunities for exports to Thailand, as the purchase strategies of Thai vehicle manufacturers will be dictated by their strong links to Japanese majors. Japanese companies such as Toyota, Honda, Suzuki and Isuzu dominate the Thai auto market[112].

It is to be expected that trading partners and neighbors will try to advance liberalization through regional and bilateral trade agreements. There is an array of such initiatives in progress or contemplated at the present time. In all, 162 regional trade agreements notified under the GATT and the WTO are in force across the countries and about 200 new regional trade formations are anticipated by the end of 2005. Regional or bilateral agreements may bring faster results than the multilateral process, may enable parties to conclude levels of liberalization beyond the multilateral consensus, and may be able to address specific issues that do not register on the multilateral menu. The achievements in trade liberalization can be substantial complements to the WTO system, and they can be important building blocks for future multilateral liberalization. The most powerful economic arguments against regional and bilateral trade agreements are that they can cause trade diversion and trade distortions and ultimately undermine the multilateral system because of their discriminatory nature. In some cases, preferential rules of origin have proven to stifle technological developments, networks and joint manufacturing, and to unduly restrict third-country sourcing, leading to trade diversion. Moreover, they can create obstacles to trade facilitation by increasing administrative complexity at customs. The proliferation of different preferential agreements lead to differential trade costs and create complexity in the global marketplace Such effects are not cost effective in business and detrimental to the regional trading prospects. Harmonization and simplification of preferential rules of origin and the accumulation of origin could alleviate some of these obstacles to trade facilitation[113].

---

[112] Raghuvir Srinivasan (2004): Indo-Thai free trade pact – Thai imports may hit auto components companies, *Business Line*, February 04.

[113] International Chamber of Commerce (2002): Regional Trade Agreements and the Multilateral Trading System, Document # 103.

India has trade agreements with many countries world over and has been playing the key role in the regional trade and cooperation among the south-east Asian countries. India plays major role in the following international trade activities.

## ASEAN

India participated at the ASEAN-Post Ministerial Conference (PMC) in Jakarta in July 1996 as a Full Dialogue Partner for the first time. The first ASEAN-India joint Cooperation Committee was held in November 1996 in New Delhi, signaling the operationalization of the main mechanism for Dialogue Partnership and economic cooperation in the agreed areas of trade, investment, science and technology, tourism, infrastructure, human resource development and people-to-people interaction. The Prime Minister of Malaysia delivered the first India-ASEAN Lecture in December 1996 marking the beginning of the India-ASEAN Lecture Series.

> The Association of Southeast Asian Nations or ASEAN was established on 8 August 1967 in Bangkok by the five original Member Countries, namely, Indonesia, Malaysia, Philippines, Singapore, and Thailand. Brunei Darussalam joined on 8 January 1984, Vietnam on 28 July 1995, Laos and Myanmar on 23 July 1997, and Cambodia on 30 April 1999. The ASEAN region has a population of about 500 million, a total area of 4.5 million square kilometers, a combined gross domestic product of US$737 billion, and a total trade of US$ 720 billion[114]. India became a Sectoral Dialogue Partner of ASEAN in 1992, focusing cooperation in economic and development cooperation. This was the first defining moment in ASEAN-India dialogue relations. The second defining moment in ASEAN and India relations came about three years later in December 1995 when India became a full Dialogue Partner of ASEAN. This elevated the interactions between ASEAN and India from the senior official to the ministerial level and enabled cooperation in the political and security field, including India's participation in the ASEAN Regional Forum (ARF), the only such security forum in the Asia-Pacific[115].

The ten economies of ASEAN are working together to enhance their collective competitiveness through various major initiatives such as the implementation of the ASEAN Free Trade Area (AFTA), ASEAN Investment Area (AIA) and the fast tracking of 11 priority sectors. Greater economic integration is not only for industries located in the region but for investors and consumers as well. Liberal trade eases the burden of procuring raw materials and intermediate goods elsewhere and this, for one, would drive manufacturing companies in ASEAN to be more cost competitive and likewise enjoy economies of scale. There is no denying that as a competitive manufacturing sector attracts foreign direct investments (FDI), the growth of supporting industries in the region would be stimulated as well. The ultimate beneficiaries would be the consumers in ASEAN with wider choice of quality goods and services and at competitive prices.

---

[114] ASEAN Secretariat: Basic Data about ASEAN, Headquarters, Jakarta, 2005.

[115] Ong Keng Yong: Advancing the ASEAN-Indian Partnership in the New Millennium, India-ASEAN Eminent Persons Lecture Series, 18th October 2004, New Delhi (Text published by the ASEAN Secretariat, Jakarta www.aseansec.org

## G-15

India led the delegation in the Sixth G-15 Summit, which was held in Harare during November 1996. The G-15 Summit affirmed the viability of the Group as a forum for South-South Cooperation and North-South Dialogue. On North-South issues, India played an active role at the Summit by drawing attention to concerns and prospects of developing countries in the evolving international trading system with special reference to WTO issues. The Summit provided a sharper focus to India's political and economic relations with Africa. A special initiative of a revolving fund for Africa of Rs[116] 1 billion was announced by the Indian government. The G15, a group of 17 developing countries from Asia, Africa and Latin America, was set up to foster cooperation and provide input for other international groups, such as the World Trade Organization and the Group of Seven rich industrialized nations. The G15 is comprised of Algeria, Argentina, Brazil, Chile, Egypt, India, Indonesia, Jamaica, Kenya, Nigeria, Malaysia, Mexico, Peru, Senegal, Sri Lanka, Venezuela and Zimbabwe

## IOR-ARC

The Indian Ocean Rim Association for Regional Cooperation (IOR-ARC) was launched formally in Mauritius on 6 March 1997 at a ministerial level meeting, in which Minister of External Affairs participated. The focus of IOR-ARC is on the large canvas of economic cooperation with special emphasis on trade and investment liberalization, promotion and facilitation; collaboration in human resources development; science and technology and tourism. India is coordinating the Indian Ocean Rim Business Center and IOR-NET electronic data network, studies on investment facilitation and promotion and trade-creating joint ventures and the establishment of an IOR Chair in Indian Ocean Studies and Associate Fellowship Program.

## APEC

India continued to reiterate its interest in membership of Asia-Pacific Economic Cooperation (APEC) on the basis of its geographical location, degree of trade and investment interaction and potential, size of the economy, and ability to contribute to larger neighborhood. The subject of India's membership was raised with individual APEC member economies during high level bilateral interactions. This was also taken up at the Foreign Ministers level during the ASEAN-Post Ministerial Conference in Jakarta in July 1996. India participated in the Working Group on Regional Energy Cooperation in October 1996.

[116] For international comparison Indian currency may be converted in to US dollars. As on 01, April, 2005 the exchange rate was 1 USD = 43.7569 INR. In the text hereafter the monetary values are shown in Rupee- the Indian currency.

## ASEM

The first Asia-Europe Meeting (ASEM) was held in Thailand in 1996. India has taken up the issue of its participation with EU and Asian members of ASEM. India feels that being a "dynamic regional economy"; no ASEM would be complete without its participation.

## OECD

India's economic interaction with the developed countries through the 29-member Organization of Economic Cooperation and Development (OECD) made good progress. The OECD's Policy Dialogue relationship with OECD continued through India's participation in policy dialogue workshops on investment, trade, transfer pricing and steel.

## G-77

India continued to play an important role in the Group of 77(G-77). The Minister of External Affairs attended the meeting of G-77 Foreign Ministers in New York in September 1996. The meeting focused both on issues of South-South Cooperation and North-South Dialogue of interest to developing countries.

Trade is not the only explanation for economic growth. Investment, high savings rates, education, aid, military spending and other factors all play a role in various proportions. Nor should it be forgotten that trade can only flourish in an environment with a conducive security and institutional framework. Even if the gains from trade are theoretically admitted the actual geo-political situation may force governments to take a much more self-reliant economic strategy. The working out of de-colonialization and nationalism in Asia in the post world-war II period is a vital part of the story[117]. However, India, which had traditionally been a much more trade-oriented economy, both under the British and with independence, has become less trade oriented than China over the last 20 years.

# TRADE RELATED ECONOMY

In India, growth has accelerated, reflecting both cyclical and structural factors. The structural factors include the lagged impact of economic liberalization during the 1990s on manufacturing production, the recent further opening up of the external sector, the effect of investment in infrastructure (especially in roads and telecommunications), the corporate restructuring undertaken in recent years, and the impact of the global outsourcing of customer support services on exports. Cyclical and temporary factors include the effect of good monsoon rains on agricultural production, the impact of low interest rates on consumer and real estate credit, and the global recovery. Against this background, further progress in addressing India's large fiscal imbalances is urgent, because the recovery will increase the

[117] Beal Tim: Liberalization of Indian Foreign Trade – Following China through an Open Door into Global Markets, Centre for Asia-Pacific Law and Business, Victoria University of Willington, New Zealand, 2004.

private sector's demand for financing, putting upward pressure on interest rates. The way forward is set out in the recent Fiscal Responsibility and Budget Management Act, which aims to balance the current budget by 2008, an adjustment of about 1 percent of GDP a year. In reference to India's low revenue-to-GDP ratio, the bulk of the adjustment will need to come from revenue-enhancing measures, including improving tax administration, broadening the tax base, and simplifying the tax regime. The appreciation of the Indian currency (Rupee) against the U.S. dollar under the managed float is welcome, and even greater flexibility would be desirable. While progress has been made in strengthening the financial system, vigilance over credit quality will continue to be necessary to limit risks from rapid credit growth[118].

> One of the studies on the role of monetary system on the corporate behavior in India examines the association and corporate behavior for a sample of manufacturing firms in India for the post-reform period 1992-2003. The findings of the study suggest that a contractionary monetary policy may lower overall debt including bank debt, although the lagged response is positive, and listed firms increase their short-term bank borrowings, after monetary tightening. The responses of corporates to a monetary contraction in the post-1997 period have been more pronounced as a major impact on trade and foreign investment. A disaggregated analysis of responses of firms according to size and leverage conducted in the study largely validates these findings. Two policy implications emerge from the analysis which may be described as the interest rate transmission channel has strengthened since 1998, and multinational companies in India, especially the listed ones in the stock markets, seem to exhibit effective relationship towards trade and investment[119]. As an emerging economy India is still not open to foreign goods and services, labor, or knowledge as we should be. On the trade restrictiveness index of IMF, India has a score of 8, which places it amongst the most restrictive countries. India's GDP accounted for 1.6 percent of world GDP in 2003 but its trade accounted for only 0.94 percent of world trade, as per the estimates based on 178 countries and World Economic Outlook data for 2003. And it holds the dubious record of instigating the maximum number of anti-dumping cases under the WTO in the period between 1995 and 2003. India has initiated 379 cases (15.69 percent) of a total 2416, well ahead of the U.S, (329 cases -13.6 percent) during the referred period. India's capital account is still closed. It still places restrictions on foreign entry and participation in various areas of the economy, even those that have little implication for national defense. Moreover, it still extremely wary of advice that may be associated with a foreign hand[120].

India, the focal point of the global trend toward strategic off-shoring, has simultaneously become appealing as a market in its own right. With GDP growth more than double that of the United States and the United Kingdom during the past decade, and with forecast continued real annual growth of almost 7 percent, India is one of the world's most promising and fastest-growing economies where multinational companies are eagerly investing in technology, manufacturing, marketing and services areas. In another estimate, *The Economist Intelligence Unit* forecasts 6.9 percent real GDP growth for India from 2003 to 2008. However, India's per capita income is half of China's and one-fourth of Brazil's, and as much as 80 percent of Indian demand for any industry's products will be in the middle or lower

---

[118] World Economic Outlook,2004, Chapter 1, pp 36-38.

[119] Prasad, A. and Ghosh, Saibal: Monetary Policy and Corporate Behavior in India, International Monetary Fund, IMF Staff Working Papers # 05-25, February 2005.

[120] Raghuram Rajam (2005): India-A Hub for Globalization, Lecture delivered at NRI Conference on January 07, 2005, Text published by External Relations Department, International Monetary Fund.

segments. Indian business would look like; the more successful companies have invested time and resources to understand local consumers and business conditions: tailoring product offers to the entire market, from the high-end to the middle and lower-end segments; reengineering supply chains; and even skipping the joint-venture route[121].

**Table 3.4. Sectoral Growth Rates in India (Average Growth in Percent Per Annum)**

| Sector | Period | | |
|---|---|---|---|
| | 1951-1980 | 1981-1990 | 1991-2000 |
| Agriculture | 2.1 | 4.4 | 3.1 |
| Industry | 5.3 | 6.8 | 5.8 |
| Services | 4.5 | 6.6 | 7.5 |
| GDP | 3.5 | 5.8 | 5.8 |

Source: Computed on the data provided by Central Statistical Organization (CSO) Data for respective periods.

India's economic performance in 2003-04 has placed the country amidst the fastest growing countries in the world. Overall growth acceleration has been high and broad-based across all sectors. However, conventional measures of trend growth and estimates of rain-adjusted GDP suggest that the acceleration in growth was mainly cyclical, led by the rebound in agriculture from drought, and good rainfall, and there is little evidence to suggest that India has yet moved into a new phase of higher trend growth. Nevertheless, indicators that are more recent provide ground for optimism, and suggest that more rapid sustainable growth is within reach, especially with progress on advancing structural reforms. The Table 3.4 exhibits the sector-wise growth in India during the post-independence period (1951-2000).

Various business surveys show capacity utilization at record levels, while import and domestic production of capital goods sustaining double digit annual growth rates during 2002-06. FDI flows have also perked up, rising by over 70 percent in the first quarter of 2003 after years of lackluster performance. Growth in Indian merchandise exports has exceeded 20 percent per annum in three of the last four years. Software service exports have expanded by almost 30 percent per annum over the past two years. Comparing India's growing integration with that of China, Japan, the new industrial economies (NIE) and the ASEAN-4, when their output and growth first started exhibiting sustained growth highlights a number of similarities as well as challenges. India's growth rate is just below that experienced by other Asian economies in the initial phases of take-off. However, India's share of world trade, at 0.8 percent, is still well below that of the other Asian economies at corresponding phases of their integration process when their share of world trade ranged from 1 percent (China) to about 2 percent[122] (Japan, NIEs, ASEAN-4).

There are signs of a recovery in domestic and external investment in India, and exports of goods and services are growing rapidly as it becomes more integrated into the global economy. India is also set to benefit from a rapid expansion in its labor force. The challenge ahead will be to capitalize on these promising beginnings by accelerating the structural reform process. The literature shows that as an economy matures, its sectoral growth pattern

[121] Jain Kuldeep P, Nigel A. S. Manson, and Sankhe Shirish (2005): The Right Passage to India, The McKinsey Quarterly, February.

[122] International Monetary Fund: World Economic Outlook, 2004, IMF.

typically evolves in two stages. In the first stage, both industry and services grow faster than agriculture, and consequently the share of industry and services in output increases. In the second stage, services grow faster than the rest of the economy, and its share in GDP continues to increase, accompanied by a stagnant or declining share of the industrial sector. Though the Indian experience fits in this pattern well, the sectoral transformation in the last decade was more rapid, and occurred at a lower level of income, than in other countries. Consequently, India's services share of GDP is now higher than the average for other low-income countries.

## Architecture of Business Partnering among Asian-Latin American Countries

The Latin American and Caribbean countries have a long history of bilateral and sub-regional preferential agreements on trade and economic integration. Dating from the 1960s and early 1970s, the Latin American Free Trade Area (LAFTA), the Andean Community (AC), the Caribbean Common Market (Caricom) and the Central American Common Market (CACM) rarely met their goals, because of the inherent clash between integration and import substitution industrialization. However, a new wave of preferential agreements rocked the region in the 1990s, now linked to a re-hauling of trade and development strategies. Traditional arrangements, such as the Latin American Integration Association (LAIA) - LAFTA's successor - and the AC, gained strength and Mercosur broke off as an important sub-regional initiative in South America. Various bilateral agreements (many of them under the Montevideo Treaty that created LAIA in 1981) were struck, generally with the goal of establishing free trade areas. Moreover, Mexico negotiated NAFTA with the US and Canada during the 1990s.

> India and Chile have signed a Preferential Trade Agreement (PTA) in early 2006 as part of initiatives to increase trade and investment between the two countries. Chile is a major Latin American country with a GDP of 76.3 billion dollars and a trade of 53.2 billion dollar during 2004. India-Chile trade during 2004-05 stood at 447 million dollars. The PTA strategically positions Chile to access and capitalize on the Indian market and its technological assets. This marks a business ties between the two countries, as it will impart a new dimension to trade relations in times to come. The PTA also provides tariff preferences ranging from 10 to 50 per cent on 178 products to Chile and a similar range of preferences on 296 items to India. It would benefit 98 per cent of items being exported by Chile to India and 91 per cent of the goods being exported by India to Chile. The Framework Agreement also provided for a Joint Study Group to identify the potential for cooperation in trade in goods and services, investments and other areas. The Indian products, which would benefit include textiles, chemicals, pharmaceuticals, engineering and agricultural machinery while Chilean products include copper, newsprint, iodine, fish meal and salmons[123].

In the process of bi-regional business negotiations among the Latin American and Asian countries, Free Trade Agreements (FTAs) were up until recently and signed mainly in reference to the geographically proximate countries. However, FTAs are becoming trans-continental today and such trends may be seen in reference to USA-Australia, USA-Singapore, and Mexico-Israel FTAs, as well as the European Unions (EU's) FTAs with Chile, Mexico, and South Africa. In addition, Latin America and Asia have established trans-continental FTAs. Chile and South Korea signed the first comprehensive FTA between an Asian and Latin American country in 2003, which came in to effect in April 2004. Expanding sunc trans-continental negoitiations Japan and Mexico have concluded FTA talks in early 2006. Latin American and East Asian partners have launched negotiations for three further bi-regional FTAs, including Chile-Singapore-New Zealand, Mexico-South Korea, and Mexico-Singapore FTAs. Chile and Japan have formed a joint study group to explore the feasibility of launching formal FTA negotiations. Latin America-Asia trans-continentalismn has spanned the Asia Pacific basin, with Brazil and India negotiating an FTA. Moreover, plans have been expressed for Chile-Japan, Mexico-New Zealand, Mercosur-India, Mercosur-China, and Chile-China FTAs. The Table 3.5 exhibits the successful trade and economic negotiations since 1980 among the Latin American and Asian countries.

**Table 3.5. Concluded Trade and Economic Partnership among the Latin American and Asian Countries (1980-2004)**

| Trade and Economic Agreements | Year of Entry |
|---|---|
| Asia-Pacific Economic Cooperation (APEC) | 1989 |
| South Korea-Chile | 2003 |
| Taiwan-Panama | 2004 |
| Japan –Mexico | 2004 |

These agreements often managed to form sub-regional free trade areas; many even explicitly seek to become common markets. For example, Mercosur was created to form a common market and similarly Andean Community has reaffirmed its goal of forming a common market in 2005. With ambitious integration goals and modest results, taken together the initiatives present similar trends and prospects, most remain in a free trade, a stage incapable of turning into full-fledged customs unions. Divergent foreign policies, domestic political and economic restraints, and border conflicts plague nearly all. Conflicts flare up from disparities in size, economic structure and patterns of trade, in addition to often contradictory cost-benefit evaluations of undertaking a common external tariff. Moreover, regional agreements risk being drowned out by the deepening of unilateral preferential trade schemes in the US and the EU that benefit the small economies of Central America and the Caribbean.

## Prospects

After many years of effort, a global preferential trade agreement was negotiated in the form of the Global System of Trade Preferences (GSTP), which entered into force in 1989. The preamble of the GSTP agreement embodies the belief that the system is a major instrument of south-south cooperation, for the promotion of collective self-reliance as well as

[123] Times of India, Wednesday, March 08, 2006.

for the strengthening of world trade as a whole. Participation in the GSTP is limited to members of the Group of 77 and only those developing countries that have exchanged concessions are eligible for its benefits. Developing countries, as members of the Group of 77, can become parties to the Agreement individually or as a sub-regional, regional or interregional grouping. This agreement envisages arrangements relating to tariffs; para-tariffs, non-tariff measures, direct trade measures, including medium and long-term contracts, and sectoral agreements. The negotiations can be conducted in accordance with one or any combination of the following modalities:

- Product-by-product negotiations;
- Across-the-board tariff reductions;
- Sectoral negotiations; and
- Direct trade measures.

The GSTP agreement also contains special benefits for the least developed countries by granting exclusive preferential concessions and by stipulating that they must not be required to make concessions on a reciprocal basis. Concessions have been exchanged among 45 developing countries in the first round of GSTP negotiations, which concluded on 30 April 1988 and involved important trading nations from all regions. Among the countries were Argentina, Brazil, Chile, Colombia, Mexico and Peru from Latin America, and India, Indonesia, Malaysia, Pakistan, Philippines, Republic of Korea, Singapore and Thailand from the Asian and Pacific region. Some main features of the concessions granted in the first round of GSTP negotiations were:

- Concessions were confined to tariffs;
- Use of product-by-product negotiations as the modality;
- Limited coverage of concessions for most participants. For example, Argentina had five tariff lines at the 10-digit level; Chile had 10 tariff lines at the eight object level; Indonesia had one tariff line at the seven-digit level; Malaysia had one tariff line at the seven digit level; Philippines had three tariff lines at the seven-digit level and Thailand had 11 tariff lines at the six-digit level. Somewhat more extensive but still quite modest concessions were given by Brazil, 93 tariff lines at the eight-digit level; India gave 32 tariff lines at the six-digit level and Mexico gave 26 tariff lines at seven-digit level. Only the concession granted by Yugoslavia was quite extensive; and
- Concessions were generally in terms of a margin of preference over a range of 10 to 50 per cent.

The first and the most significant developments in Latin America is formation of Mercosur associating Argentina, Brazil, Paraguay and Uruguay as members. Mercosur introduced a common external tariff (CET) in 1995, to be phased over a six-year period. The aim is to eventually create a common market with free movement of goods, labor, services and capital. A feature of the Mercosur policy is that it has either formed a free trade area with other countries (such as Chile) or is actively negotiating such an accord (such as with the

EU). Colombia, Mexico and Venezuela formed another free-trade area, known as the Group of Three in 1994, to be phased over a 10-year period.

> Argentina, Brazil and Chile (ABC) have succeeded in the post-reforms period attracting substantial amounts of foreign direct investment, though these countries have mainly targeted the investment in the primary sectors where competitive advantages already exist. The foreign investments are also promoted by the ABC group of countries to specific segments of the non-tradable sector consisting of mainly infrastructure and banking. Agricultural and food products are the largest contributor to exports in the ABC group of countries and continue to have a strong potential for expansion. First of all, in Argentina and Brazil there is still a large amount of permanent pasture that can be converted into arable cropland. ABC also has room to increase labor and land productivity, and exports of processed food products. In this regard, Chile has succeeded somewhat in developing differentiated products out of primary clusters, the wine industry being a notable, but not unique, example. Competition policy in ABC has evolved from the enforcement of competition on the basis of private claims, to competition advocacy and its contribution to the design of regulatory reforms. However, ABC group of countries still need to strengthen their competition policies and regulatory frameworks, particularly in infrastructure[124].

In Asia, the most significant arrangement is among the countries of South-East Asia. ASEAN was formed in 1967 to promote economic, social and cultural cooperation among Indonesia, Malaysia, Philippines, Singapore and Thailand. ASEAN put into force a preferential trading arrangement granting a margin of preference to members of 10 to 15 per cent on selected products in 1978,. In early 1990s, the arrangement was upgraded into the ASEAN and membership has also expanded to include Brunei Darussalam, Viet Nam, Lao People's Democratic Republic, Myanmar and Cambodia. Another integration arrangement among the developing countries of the region that is potentially significant is the South Asian Association for Regional Cooperation (SAARC), whose membership includes Bangladesh, Bhutan, India, Maldives, Nepal, Pakistan and Sri Lanka. A decision was taken in 1992 to form the SAARC Preferential Trading Arrangement (SAPTA) and in 1995, the group agreed to move towards a free trade area. However, political differences between India and Pakistan have impeded the effectiveness of the arrangement. In the meantime, India and Sri Lanka have moved separately to form a free trade area.

## DEVELOPMENT OF TRADE RELATIONSHIP AMONG ASIAN-LAC COUNTRIES

Trade partnering between Latin America and Asia is yet to be explored while trade between the European Union and Latin America is growing in importance, currently amounting to $100 billion a year. However, there are potential problems for European businesses seeking to move into this market. The North American Free Trade Agreement (NAFTA) linking Canada and the USA with Mexico has had a serious impact on European trade with Mexico and the Free Trade Area of the Americas, which aims to further the

[124] OECD (2004): *Trade and Competitiveness in Argentina, Brazil and Chile*, Agriculture and Food, Organization for Economic Co-operation and Development, Vol. 2004, No. 9, 1-233.

economic integration of the western hemisphere, and an increasing tendency towards dollar orientation in Latin America will pose additional challenges to European trade and investment in the region. The historical perspective of the trade agreements in the global market place is exhibited in Table 3.6.

**Table 3. 6. Regional Trade Agreements in Global Market Place (as of January 2003)**

| Period | Developed-Developed | Developed-Developing | Developed-Transition | Developing-Developing | Developing-Transition | Transition Transition | Total |
|---|---|---|---|---|---|---|---|
| 1958-1964 | 2 | 0 | 0 | 1 | 0 | 0 | 3 |
| 1965-1969 | 0 | 0 | 0 | 0 | 1 | 0 | 1 |
| 1970-1974 | 5 | 3 | 0 | 2 | 0 | 0 | 10 |
| 1975-1979 | 0 | 5 | 0 | 1 | 0 | 0 | 6 |
| 1980-1984 | 2 | 1 | 0 | 1 | 0 | 0 | 4 |
| 1985-1989 | 1 | 1 | 0 | 2 | 0 | 0 | 4 |
| 1990-1994 | 3 | 3 | 12 | 5 | 0 | 6 | 29 |
| 1995-1999 | 3 | 7 | 10 | 4 | 12 | 28 | 64 |
| 2000-2002 | 0 | 11 | 4 | 5 | 4 | 6 | 30 |
| Total | 16 | 31 | 26 | 21 | 17 | 40 | 151 |

In this table, developed countries include Canada, USA, EU, EFTA, Japan, Australia, and New Zealand; transition countries include the former Soviet Union, Eastern and Central Europe, the Baltic States and the Balkans; the remaining countries are classified as Developing.

Source: World Trade Report-2003, WTO, P 47.

The countries of Pacific Rim are emerging in the $21^{st}$ century as the new international business power over the developing countries. The Pacific Rim comprising of South Korea, Singapore, Taiwan, Hong Kong, Malaysia, Thailand, Indonesia and Philippines is growing as an economic powerhouse by improving the regional trade treaties and exports to European and North American countries. These countries have created a strong manufacturing potential in electronics and natural resources. The consumption of construction materials like steel is higher in the region than in the United States and also the demand for semiconductors are increasing over the European Union. The Committee on Trade and Investment (CTI) of Asia Pacific Economic Cooperation (APEC) organization works to reduce impediments to business activity in 15 key areas outlined in the Osaka action agenda - tariffs and non-tariff measures, services, standards and conformance, customs procedures, intellectual property rights, competition policy, government procurement, deregulation, rules of origin, dispute mediation, mobility of business people and implementation of World Trade Organization (WTO) obligations. The committee[125] is focusing on the following priority areas during 2004:

- Trade and investment facilitation (including IPR).
- Implementation of the APEC Transparency Standards.
- Implementation of Pathfinder Initiatives
- Contribution to the APEC Structural Reform Action Plan, and
- Support for World Trade Organization

APEC Member Economies are working to eliminate tariff and non-tariff barriers to trade. Elimination of these barriers will help Asia-Pacific countries to achieve the common goals resolved in various ministerial meetings of the APEC member countries, encourage greater and freer trade and investment flows and create new business opportunities and jobs in the Asia-Pacific region. It has been further resolved by the APEC nations that sustainable economic development requires empowering people and strengthening societies for globalization. This process requires more effective, better focusing and strengthening global economic and technical cooperation. Also it has been envisaged that increasing the interaction of Asia-Pacific rim countries with international financial institutions, the private sector, and other outside organizations would pay long-run gains of globalization.

**Table 3. 7. Merchandize Trade in Latin America (1963-2003) (Share in Percentage)**

| Country/Region | 1963 | | 1973 | | 1983 | | 1993 | | 2003 | |
|---|---|---|---|---|---|---|---|---|---|---|
| | E | I | E | I | E | I | E | I | E | I |
| Mexico | 0.6 | 0.8 | 0.4 | 0.6 | 1.4 | 0.7 | 1.4 | 1.8 | 2.3 | 2.4 |
| Brazil | 0.9 | 0.9 | 1.1 | 1.2 | 1.2 | 0.9 | 1.1 | 0.7 | 1.0 | 0.7 |
| Argentina | 0.9 | 0.6 | 0.6 | 0.4 | 0.4 | 0.2 | 0.4 | 0.4 | 0.4 | 0.2 |
| Latin America & Caribbean | 7.0 | 6.8 | 4.7 | 5.1 | 5.8 | 4.5 | 4.4 | 5.1 | 5.2 | 4.8 |
| North America | 19.3 | 15.5 | 16.9 | 16.7 | 15.4 | 17.8 | 16.6 | 19.7 | 13.7 | 20.5 |
| World | 100 | 100 | 100 | 100 | 100 | 100 | 100 | 100 | 100 | 100 |

E =Exports,
I =Imports.
Source: World Trade Statistics 2004, WTO.

The performance of merchandize trade in Latin America during the past five decades has been exhibited in Table 3. 7. The data reveals that Mexico is the largest exporting countries among the other LAC countries. The recovery in the region's merchandise trade was held back by the sluggish growth of shipments to North America, its principal market, and the failure of some countries in the region to grasp the opportunities provided by the rise in global demand for primary commodities, in particular fuels. The recovery in intra-regional trade, by 9 percent in 2003, did not fully offset its contraction in 2002. The share of intra-regional trade in exports stayed at 15.6 percent in 2003 or more than five percentage points below the 1977 peak level of 21 percent. Merchandise shipments to Western Europe and Asia advanced by 17

[125] Asia Pacific Economic Cooperation: APEC Secretariat www.apecsec.org.sg

percent and 20 percent, to new record levels. Exports to China, the region's largest market in Asia, surged to $9.2 billion, only slightly less than the region's shipments to Africa and the Middle East combined. Exports to the transition economies and Africa rose by more than one third, but even combined account for less than 3 per cent of the region's merchandise exports.

> Canadian companies have been able to expand their sales in the US thanks to innovative design and high quality products. Exports of men's and boy's tailored clothing have been particularly successful abroad, accounting for 32.5% of total foreign shipments. Besides these products, Canada is also renowned for its outerwear, furs, leather goods and children's wear. With NAFTA, the apparel industry has become very trade-oriented: exports represented over 41.0% of total shipments in 2000 compared to 17.4% in 1994 and only 5.0% in 1989. Exports of Canadian apparel have risen over 180% since the inception of North American Free Trade Agreement (NAFTA), mostly as a result of increasing shipments to south of the border. In 2000, Canadian shipments made up 1.9% of the US import market (up from 1.2% in 1994). Exports to the European Union, Canada's second market, have increased more moderately (17.1%) in the past five years and have actually declined since 1998, as a combination of trade barriers, strong local industry, and a relative depreciation of the Euro (especially in the past two years) have dampened the competitiveness of Canadian firms. Since NAFTA, American companies have been restructuring their operations by shifting a growing part of their productive capacity to Mexico and the Caribbean (there is a bilateral trade agreement with the region), decreasing their dependence on supplies from Asia. As a result, imports from Mexico to the US have grown strongly since 1994, causing their share of the American import market to rise from 5.7% to 15.8% in 2000. By the same token, US-bound shipments from Asia made up 19.4% of that market in 2003, down from 34.0% in 1994. Unlike their American and European counterparts, Canadian apparel companies have not resorted extensively to offshore production[126].

In the framework of the external co-operation and development policies of European Union, the European Investment Bank (EIB) operates in 77 African, Caribbean and Pacific (ACP) countries. The ACP countries, with a population of some 600 million, have established a special relationship with the European Union through successive conventions and the latest Cotonou Agreement signed in June 2000. The EIB has been the developing partner of most of the ACP countries over 25 years and as many as 40 countries of the region. Under parallel provisions, EIB also supports investments in 20 overseas countries and territories mainly in the Caribbean and Pacific which have constitutional links with certain European community countries. The Pacific Rim offers a variety of opportunities for American and European companies for the products and services that range from telecommunication instruments to the aircraft seats and banking services and a host of other products. Although it is a competitive market, the region is growing economically cohesive that attracts production sharing possibilities with the industrial countries. The Asian producers outside Japan have gained more than one fourth of the global market share for personal computers Japan and the pacific emerging triad comprising Singapore, Taiwan and South Korea provide most of the capital and expertise for the rest of the countries of the region that have enormous labor and natural resources.

Hong Kong also contributes significantly to the development of international trade in the pacific region. Japan is Canada's second largest national trading partner (after the United

---

[126] Export Development Council: The Canadian Apparel Industry, EDC, 2000 (http://www.edc.ca )

States), taking 2.1% of total exports, and is the fifth largest source of foreign direct investment (FDI) in Canada. Canada is a leading supplier to Japan of a number of products of key export interest, such as lumber, pulp and paper, coal, meat, fish, oilseeds and prefabricated housing. While resource-based exports continue to represent much of our trading relationship, Canada is an increasingly important source of sophisticated, value-added, technology-driven products and services imported by Japan. In 2003, Canada's total merchandise trade with Japan was $22 billion. Canadian exports to Japan have declined steadily since the mid 1990s, Canadian exports to Japan declined again to $8.1 billion in 2003 from $8.4 billion in 2002. In 2003, Canada exported $1.4 billion in services and imported $1.9 billion[127]. The long-term trend in Japan is toward a growing demand for cost-competitive and innovative imports, which represents a significant market opportunity for Canadian exporters. The Asia Pacific region has been the fastest growing trade block over past three decades though it had experienced downturn in 1998 and extended after shocks. East Asia is the principal export market for American goods. The transpacific trade has grown over 50 percent of its transatlantic trade by the end of 20th century.

## REFERENCES


Barro Robert J (1991), Economic Growth in a Cross Section of Countries, *Quarterly Journal of Economics*, 106, pp 407-443.

Beaulieu, Eugene, Yatawara, Ravindra and Wang, Wei Guo: Who Supports Free Trade in Latin America?, *The World Economy*, Vol. 28, No. 7, 2005, 941-958.

Bruce Owen M (2003): *Competition Policy in Latin America, Institute of Economic Policy Research*, Stanford University, Working Paper # 268.

Collie David and Hviid Morten(1993), Export Subsidies as Signals of Competitiveness, *Scandinavian Journal of Economics*, Vol.95, No.3, pp 327-339.

Edwards S (1992), Trade orientation, Distortions and Growth in Developing Countries, *Journal of Development Economics*, 39, pp 31-57.

Frankel Jaffery A and Romer David (1999): Does Trade Cause Growth? *American Economic Review*, Vol. 89, No. 3, pp 379-399.

Haar Jerry and Buonafina Moria Ortiz (2002), Entrepreneurial Exporters: The Canadian Experience, *The International Trade Journal*, Vol. 16, No.1. pp 31-71.

Kamin Steven B(1998), *A Multi Country Comparison of the Linkages between Inflation and Exchange Rate Competitiveness*, Federal Reserve bank of US, International Finance Discussion Paper No. 603.

Omen C (1999): *Policy Competition and Foreign Direct Investment*, OECD Development Centre, OECD, Paris.

Perroni Carlo and Whalley John (1996), How Severe is the Global Retaliation Risk under Increasing Regionalism, *American Economic Review*, Vol. 86, No. 2, pp 57-61.

Rajagopal (2005), Institutional Reforms and Trade Competitiveness in Latin America, *Applied Econometrics and International Development*, Vol. 5, No.1 pp 45-64.


---

[127] Government of Canada: Report on Canada's International Market Access Priorities- 2004, Department of Foreign Affairs and International Trade, Opening doors to the world, Chapter 6, 2004.

Sanchez Blanca R and Clavo Marta Bengoa (2003): Foreign Direct Investment, Economic Freedom and Growth, *European Journal of Political Economy*, Vol. 19, No. 3, September, pp. 529-545.

Tussie, Diana (1987): *The Less Developed Countries and the World Trading System: A Challenge to the GATT*. New York: St. Martin's Press.

Vogel David (1997): Trading Up and Governing Across – Transnational Governance and Environment Protection, *Journal of European Public Policy*, Vol.4, No.4, pp 556-571.

Zheng Ping, Siler Pamela and Giorgioni G (2004): FDI and the Export Performance of Chinese Indigenous Firms: A Regonal Approach, *Journal of Chinese Economic and Business Studies*, Vol. 2, No.1, pp 55-71.

*Chapter 4*

# GROWTH IN TRANSITIONAL ECONOMIES

Regional trade has emerged as an important move of globalization which has been induced collectively with shared norms and political leadership in respective regions. Informality has appeared to be a representative common norm which played a catalytic role in first nurturing communication for regional cooperation framework to enhance the international trade opportunities with emerging countries as business partners. The political leadership has been shown by China and Japan has played a vital role in promoting the regional integration initiatives. There has been a rapid proliferation of bilateral free trade agreement (FTA) in East Asia and the Asia-Pacific regions since 1990s and the this trend has further intensified enhancing the scope of advance regional co-operation and integration. However, after experiencing the regional financial crisis of 1997–98 many Asian economies underscored the need of expanding their trade and economy consciously and aggressively moved towards exploring alternative liberalization paths. At this juncture, the new regionalism or new regional trade agreements became relevant[128].

The development of international trade in the eastern and central Europe has been found to be slow due to transition in the regional economy and political situations. Major crises observed in Central and Eastern European countries (Czech Republic, Hungary, Slovak Republic) and two CIS countries (Russia and Ukraine) can be explained by inconsistencies in the domestic policy mix and by the deterioration of macroeconomic fundamentals. The transitional economies in eastern and central Europe are emerging with new agenda for inter-regional trade development promoting a liberal internationalist agenda[129]. There is a fast change observed in the world markets resulting into the new emerging markets across the countries. In this century China, India and Latin America and the emerging market based economies in Eastern Europe promise new opportunities for global trade. The European Union provided an outlet, initially for unskilled-labor intensive products of Central and Eastern European countries and more recently for skilled-labor intensive and technology-based products. Knowledge-intensive imports from the European Union have also contributed to industrial realignment in the Central European countries. The trade liberalization between Eastern and Western European countries has lead to gradual normalization of trade relations,

---

[128] Rajan Ramkishen S (2005), Trade Liberalization and the new Regionalism in the Asia-Pacific: Taking Stock of Recent Events, *International Relations of the Asia-Pacific*, 5(2), 217-233.

[129] Söderbaum, Fredrik, StÅlgren, Patrik and Van Langenhove, Luk (2005), The EU as a Global Actor and the Dynamics of Inter-regionalism: a Comparative Analysis, *Journal of European Integration*, 27 (3), 365-380.

and liberalization within Central European Free Trade Agreement (CEFTA) has reversed the fall in trade intensity among Central European countries. The emerging markets in the developing countries have shown a strong potential for change in preferences during the late $20^{th}$ century. In most of the advanced countries, the birth rate is declining while it is increasing in the developing countries. The growing trade agreements in the countries indicate some likelihood of success because when the level of tariff and non-tariff barriers is already low, a preferential agreement is more likely to have an adverse impact than a beneficial one. However, the reduction in the tariff barriers, duties and liberalization process worldwide has further given a stimulus to the international marketing across the regional boundaries.

The economic reforms thus will not have a constant speed and will often be subject to modifications in the policies that bring changes in the performance and structure of economic activities. The economic reforms can be assessed by examining their corresponding policy measures and implications. However, entire economic progress may not be interpreted as an outcome of the reforms. The growth and development may result to be slower in a country or region in a normal process than stirred process of reforms. After years of poor economic management, many Latin American and Caribbean countries are experiencing a process of structural reforms that places them on a path to a superior economic performance[130]. Two basic principles identify this process of economic reforms - fiscal and monetary discipline, and reliance on market forces to determine the allocation and distribution of resources.

## Transition in Political Ideology

It is important to understand that the global political environment has greater role to play in all business and economic matters today, however, it remains in a constant flux. The political system of a country is shaped after passing through major processes of growth, decay, breakdown and a ceaseless ferment of adaptation and adjustment. The magnitude and variety of the changes that occurred in the world's political systems between the 20's and 80's of the $20^{th}$ century describe the complex dimensions of the problem. It may be observed that during the last century, great empires disintegrated; nation-states emerged, flourished briefly, and then vanished. The two consecutive world wars transformed the international system and seeded new ideologies that swept the world and shook established groups from power-grid nations. However, many developing countries experienced civil and political revolutions during the post-world-ward period in order to determine the most effective governing system and domestic politics in every system was contorted by social strife and economic crisis. In the middle of the $20^{th}$ century the nature of political life was changed everywhere by novel forms of political activity as the new means of mass communication, increase of popular participation in politics and the rise of new political issues offered better understanding towards international politics and popular governance in reference to global integration. Besides, the extension of the scope of governmental activity and other innumerable social, economic, and technical developments in the developing countries urged for stability in the

[130] Easterly William and Sergio Rebelo (1993), Fiscal Policy and Economic Growth-An Empirical Investigation, *Journal of Monetary Economics*, 32 (3), 417-458.

government for effective implementation of the international development programs and the trade policies have been one among the international priorities.

There are many factors that influence the ideological transition, development and change in the world's political systems. In the recent past, industrialization, population growth, the "revolution of rising expectations" in the less developed countries, and international tensions have affected the political thinking to a large extent. However, the political instability generally occurs when the distribution of wealth fails to correspond with the distribution of political power. This situation may be described in reference to the classical school of political thought as the political stability in a country is largely based on a large middle class in a country. On the contrary, Marxist theories of economic determinism view all political changes as the result of changes in the mode of production. However, the neo-classical political thinkers discuss that the prime cause of revolutions and other forms of violent political changes are due to power polarization and alienation with the capitalistic economic countries. The majority of the world's political systems have experienced one form or another of internal warfare leading to violent collapse of the governments in power and certain crisis situations seem to increase the likelihood of breakdown in the governing politics of a region or a country. In the politico-economic scenario the economic crisis are another common stimulus to the political setbacks as may be witnessed in the recent Argentinean crisis. Brazilian economy was also at the cliff in the late 90's due to internal economic instability. The political situation of a country may be explained in terms of economic growth as reflected in gross domestic product and also towards the social scarcity. However, the political environment of a country also contributes in building the social position of individuals. A sense of insecurity and uncertainty for the future, and an aggravation of the relationships among social classes also results in the politico-economic conflicts in a country. A severe national economic crisis develops distrust in the political system of the country and triggers outbreak of revolutions in the political systems. The political unrest in a country triggers the test conditions for the stability of political systems in extremely revealing ways, which often demand either for the change in the political leadership or the structure and process of governance in the system. Since the quality of the political leadership is often decisive, those systems that provide methods of selecting able leaders and replacing them possess important advantages towards internal and global political concerns. Unstable political systems are those that prove vulnerable to crisis pressures and that break down into various forms of internal warfare. The fundamental causes of such failures appear to be the lack of a widespread sense of the legitimacy of state authority and the absence of some general agreement on appropriate forms of political action.

The political sovereignty may be referred as country's desire to assert its authority over foreign business through various sanctions. Political sovereignty is the assertion of self, determination of its citizens, and the manifestation of their freedom. It is in and through the determination of its sovereignty that the order of the nation is constituted and maintained. Such sanctions are regular and evolutionary, and therefore predictable *e.g.* increase in taxes over foreign operations. Many of the developing countries impose restrictions on foreign business to protect their independence. These countries are jealous of their political freedom and want to protect it at all costs, even if it means a slow economic pace without the help of MNCs. Thus, the problem of political sovereignty exists mainly in developing countries.

The political philosophy and the legal environment of a nation largely influence the practice of international marketing. The political environment of a country comprises the international environment, host-country environment and the home-country environment. Many studies have shown that dealing with problems in the political arena is the principal challenge facing international managers in developing pro political strategies to run the business successfully in the host country. It is observed that each country has its own set of national goals; most countries also share many common objectives. Nationalism and patriotism refer to citizens' feelings about their country and its interests. Such feelings exist in every country and the multinational firms, individually or collectively, may be perceived as a threat to that sovereignty. The foreign firms perceive greater threats if they are larger in size and more in number in a country. At the time of any political turmoil, the foreign firms may be targets for attack. Many countries seek "national solutions" to help troubled companies to retain what are perceived to be national champions. International firms need to be sensitive to these issues and to be careful not to be too "foreign." This includes advertising and branding policies as well as ownership and staffing. Establishing local research and development activities would be perceived favorably in this context.

The international political environment involves political relations among the countries of common ideologies. The foreign firm need to make all adjustments with the host country's international relations, no matter how non-aligned it may try to be. Such strategic adjustments in tune to the international environment of the host country are required as its operations are frequently related also to the neighboring countries, either on the supply or demand side or both. Another critical factor affecting the political environment is the diplomatic relations of the host countries with others in the region or beyond. If a country is a member of a regional group, such as the EU, NAFTA, ASEAN, its political identity influences the firm's operational and expansion opportunities. If a nation has particular friends or enemies among other nations, the firm must modify its international logistics to comply with how that market is supplied and to whom it can sell. For example, the United States limits trade with various countries and Arabian countries do not entertain any business activities with Israel. The participation of the host country in the regional trade agreements or with the international trade organizations may affect patents, communication, transportation, and other items of interest to the international marketer. As a rule, the more international organizations a country belongs to, the more regulations it accepts, and the more dependable is its economic, political and legal environment. The political environment at home-country is also an important indicator for a firm to decide its entry to the host country. However, an adverse environment therein may constrain its international operations as well as its domestic operations. The best-known example of the home-country political environment affecting international operations used to be South Africa. Home-country political pressures induced more than 200 American firms to leave that country altogether. In the private sector, the bottom line is shareholder value. In government, the objectives can be harder to pinpoint due to being clouded by political agendas, turf battles, special interests and economics. Some of the key issues in reference to measuring the performance of the government in the given political environment of the home country may be considered by the firm as described below:

- *Measuring performance:* Governments need to continue to focus on gauging performance by what is achieved. Leaders should strive to understand the real results that are being delivered, and how much real progress is being made.
- *Improving through competition:* Government's position is often perceived in a fix by the social pressures. The issues of trade protection, allowing foreign companies to

participate in the host country, repatriation of profits and other economic issues are subject to the prevailing political ideology in the host country.

- *Streamlining operations:* It is necessary for a foreign firm to examine the conduct of government activities in the home country. Many government operations can be performed by third parties often at lower cost and with equal or higher quality.
- *Promoting efficiency:* Most government employees are smart, industrious people. But like any workforce, their behavior is largely driven by the organization's rewards and incentives.

Many multinational companies face uncertainty in political environment due to instability of political leadership, coalitions and external pressures. Even if the home country and the host country give them no problems, they can face threats in the neighboring markets. Firms that do not have problems with their home government or the host government may be bothered or boycotted in neighboring countries. Escalation of political conflict in many developing countries and their impact on economic development has been a topical issue in recent development literature. The overwhelming emphasis on 'ethnic conflicts' in this literature has, however, precluded looking at political conflict in the wider context of the development process, going beyond the ethnic dimension. In particular, because of the preoccupation with the ethnic roots as the prime source of these conflicts, reverse causation running from economic policy to political conflict has been virtually ignored in the debate[131]. The effectiveness of the political systems in a country may be analyzed by the foreign firms in reference to the following indicators:

- Democratic effectiveness: capable of deepening democracy and democratic citizenship;
- Policy effectiveness: capable of tackling fundamental developmental problems of poverty and social equality
- Conflict-management effectiveness: capable of channeling conflicts and rendering them less destructive.

Political conflict in general could be defined as dynamic and manifest conflict processes consisting of certain phases. In this case the term conflict is used in a more specific meaning: a political process (dynamic situation) in which engaged political parties have incompatible attitudes and behaviors. Internal as well as international conflicts have three interrelated components:

- Conflict situation, manifested in expressing various political aims or conflict of interest that cannot be simultaneously achieved and for that reason can be qualified as mutually exclusive;
- Conflict behavior (in the first place aimed at achieving the aforementioned political aims); and
- Conflicting attitudes and perceptions having an emotional dimension (feeling of anger, mistrust, fear, scorn, hatred, etc.) as well as a cognitive dimension.

[131] Sirimal Abeyratne (2002): Economic Roots of Political Conflicts- A Case of Sri Lanka, Australian National University, Australia South Asia Research Centre, Working Paper #03.

Many countries in different parts of the world undergo political conflict of various natures like turmoil, internal war, and conspiracy that can be irregular, revolutionary, and/or sporadic. Turmoil refers to instant upheaval on a massive scale against an established political regime. The internal unrest in a country refers to large-scale, organized violence against a government, such as guerrilla warfare. The example may be cited of Vietnam's actions in Cambodia and internal violence by the self proclaimed people's groups like in north-eastern states in India.

As a social system, *communism* would be a type of egalitarian society with no state, no private property and no social classes. In communism, all property is owned by the community as a whole, and all people enjoy equal social and economic status. Perhaps the best known principle of a communist society is *from each according to his ability, to each according to his need.* As an ideology, the word communism is a synonym for Marxism and its various derivatives. In terms of ideology and politics, communism is a sub-category of socialism. Communist ideology is a specific branch of socialist ideology and the communist movement is a specific branch of the larger socialist movement. A person who calls himself or herself a "communist" is a certain kind of socialist; in other words, all communists are socialists but not all socialists are communists. In terms of socio-economic systems, communism and socialism are two different things.

> After World War II, a centrally planned socialist system was transplanted to Poland from the Soviet Union without any consideration for the differences in the level of development of the country, its size, resource endowment, or cultural, social, and political traditions. In 1947 Poland became a Communist People's Republic and the elections were denounced by the US as undemocratic. The county went through internal unrests, economic disorders and political problems with its communist ideologies. In 1989 the round-table talks between Solidarity, the Communists and the church took place that allowed having the partially free elections that could achieve widespread success for solidarity, which helped form a coalition government. In the same year Poland became the first of the eastern European countries to overthrow Communist rule. In the following year market reforms, including large-scale privatization were implemented in the country as the new political policies. The Soviet troops made a gradual move to leave Poland and the reformed communists started entering the coalition government. They pledged to continue market reforms and implementation of institutional reforms towards achieving the new goals of the country. Poland ultimately joined NATO in 1999 and the European Union in May 2004[132]. The inception of the democratic transformation in Poland in 1989 evoked high hopes concerning the future of the Polish society. Majority of Poles seemed to expect that incoming changes will consist in expansion of personal freedom and realization of civil rights, introduction of the rules of law and social justice, empowerment of ordinary people, attaining national sovereignty, economic progress and significant increase in standards of life. In the post-communist political system people of Poland fostered a development of entrepreneurial spirit and economic (market) rationality that resulted in increase in productivity, decrease in the rate of employment, and dramatic increase in economic polarization. They led to establishment of the strong interdependency between the world of politics and the world of business. As a result, they have faced a fast growth of so called political capitalism[133].

[132] The Economist: Country Profile – Poland, The Economist, 19th October 2004.

[133] Janusz Reykowski (2003): Unexpected Traps of the Democratic Transformation, Conference on Social Change in Poland, University of Michigan, Ann Arbor, 24-26 September 2003, USA.

It is sometimes difficult to ascertain whether the people and the government of a country are in accord. However, media, religious leaders, and internal intelligence of a country can provide some insights into the feelings of the citizens. Among various political systems across the countries state-centric international politics, pluralistic national politics, bureaucratic organizational politics, or transnational politics are important. The *state-centric political model* of international politics assumes that national governments seek power and status in relation to one another, that they do so in the context of a competitive, decentralized international political system, and that they utilize whatever international political resources are available in pursuit of their international objectives. The *pluralistic model of national politics* assumes that national governments are responsive to the diverse and conflicting interests and pressures of multiple interest groups within a political system. The assumptions of the *bureaucratic organizational political behavior* hold the notion that the actions of the national government are the result of organizational processes within the bureaucratic setup of the government while the transnational *politics model* emphasizes the increasingly important role played in the world politics by organizations other than those of national governments.

## Political Interventions in Transitional Economies

Political intervention may be described as a decision taken on the part of the government of host country intended to force a change in the operations, policies, and strategies of a foreign firm in the interest of the country. Such interventions may range from enforcing control to complete takeover, or annexation of the foreign enterprise. The magnitude of intervention would vary according to the company's business existing in the host country and the nature of political decisions taken thereof. In countries where foreign investment plays a significant role in the economy, the possibilities of political interference in the operations of foreign firms would be higher and stringent. Besides, the political system of a country like democracy, communism or mixed economies, also indicates the nature of intervention. If a foreign company is prominent in the economy in developing countries as Zambia, Guinea, Iran, and Tanzania, the possibilities of government intervention are relatively greater in reference to the public policies of the country. The political intervention may affect the marketing-mix functions of a firm in the host country in several ways. The intervention may be observed in a host country to the extent of local content law, technology content, and restrictions on the sale of some products, products' functional range, and design of products, useful life, and adaptability to local conditions, patent life, local manufacturing and assembling leading to product strategies of a foreign firm. The political directions may also govern the functions related to transfer pricing, price ceiling and price floor, price contracts, price paid for local raw materials and price paid for imported raw materials to be used in production in the host country. Besides the activities of distribution and product, retailing may also be subject to political interventions in many developing countries. Advertising and communication is another important area for a foreign firm that is affected by political interference in a country. Of these, local production of commercials, local artists, type of message, type of copy, availability of media and time restrictions on the use of certain media are significant political interventions faced by a foreign firm.

## Expropriation, Domestication and Nationalization

The developing countries generally intervene directly in the operations of foreign firms engaged in business in order to pursue their own special interests of their country. Of many different forms of political intervention expropriation, domestication, exchange control, import restrictions, market control, tax control, price control, and labor restrictions are the common ones. *Expropriation* is one of the most stringent and pervasive political intervention that a foreign firm may face in a host country. It may be described as official seizure of foreign property by a host country whose intention is to use the seized property in the public interest. Such intervention is recognized by international law as the right of sovereign states, provided the expropriated firms are given prompt compensation, at fair market value, in convertible currencies[134]. The act of expropriation without offering any compensation to the foreign or local firms may be described as *confiscation*. In legal terms it may be explained that expropriation occurs when a government takes over property for a purpose deemed to be in the public interest, even though the owner of the property may not be willing to sell it. Any interest in land, plant and machinery and/or value additions thereof, such as permanent constructions, may be expropriated. The business capital may also be subject to expropriation in many countries. However, technology can serve as the defense against expropriation, if the technology of the enterprise cannot be transferred to or duplicated by the host country or despite transfer of technology it cannot be made operational by the expropriators. Further, if a firm is not holding an independent status in the host country and is vertically integrated with the parent firm wherein the supplies for production or the market for the product is controlled by the parent firm located elsewhere, such firms an unlikely to be targeted for expropriation. *Domestication* is another form of expropriation, which may be also be conceived as creeping expropriation. In this process of political intervention the controls and restrictions placed by the host country authorities on the foreign firm, gradually reduce the control of owners. The domestication is a slow process of expropriation and a foreign firm may lose its control in all financial, operational and management areas over a period of time. Domestication involves several measures, including gradual transfer of ownership to nationals, promotion of a large number of nationals to higher levels of management, greater decision-making powers accorded to nationals, more products produced locally rather than imported for assembly and specific export regulations designed to dictate participation in world markets.

Traditionally expropriation (in the foreign investment sense) referred to the seizure of property by the host government *e.g.* forced *nationalization* of assets. In recent years, extensive definitions of expropriation have appeared, such as "creeping expropriation", "regulatory taking over" and "measures tantamount to expropriation", which can sometimes be used as strategy against government measures that might simply dent a foreign investor's profitability. The clause on "measures tantamount to expropriation" has been particularly controversial in the investment related details of NAFTA. The clause argues that expropriation may not necessarily be a taking over of the companies in public interest as it may be unreasonable and do not justify the political interference. However, the regional trade agreements stress on the investor rights to protect the undue losses to the investing companies

---

[134] Eiteman David k and Stonehill Arthur I (1979): Multinational Business Finance, Addison-Wesley, Reading MA, 184-188.

in the host country. The governments of countries (Canada, USA and Mexico) under NAFTA are required to compensate the investor for the full market value of the property.

On the contrary, *nationalization* may be described as taking over of assets into state ownership. The process of nationalization refers to a transfer of entire industry within the country from private to public ownership with no discrimination to the foreign or local ownership of firms. This may be explained as policy of bringing a country's essential services and industries under public ownership. It was pursued, for example, by the Labour party ruled government in United Kingdom during 1945–51. Assets in the hands of foreign governments or companies may also be nationalized; for example, Iran's oil industry and US-owned fruit plantations in Guatemala, during 1950s. The Communist states of Eastern Europe nationalized all industry and agriculture in the period following World War II. Under the Labour government of the period 1945 to 1951, Great Britain nationalized a number of important industries, including coal, steel, and transportation. In non-Communist countries, it has been common practice to compensate the owners of nationalized properties, at least in part; however, in the Communist countries, where private ownership is opposed in principle, there usually has not been such compensation. Nationalization of foreign properties has occurred, especially in underdeveloped nations, where there is resentment of foreign control of major industries. Instances include Mexico's seizure of oil properties owned by U.S. corporations (1938), Iran's nationalization of the Anglo-Iranian Oil Company (1951), the nationalization of the Suez Canal Company (1956) by Egypt, and Chile's nationalization of its foreign-owned copper-mining industry (1971). The government of India nationalized fourteen major private commercial banks in 1969 and six more in 1980. Nationalization forced commercial banks increasingly to meet the credit requirements of the weaker sections of the nation and to eliminate monopolization by vested interests of large industry, trade, and agriculture. However, a key issue in nationalization is whether the private owner is properly compensated for the value of the institution.

## Exchange Control

In addition to expropriation and domestication, there are various other means of government intervention in foreign enterprise, usually in the form of legislative action or a decree enacted in the best national interest. It has been observed that many countries exercise restrictions on foreign exchange in order to discourage the free and flexible operations of foreign firms. Such strategy may be describes as a government policy designed to restrict the outflow of domestic currency and prevent a worsened balance of payments position by controlling the amount of foreign exchange that can be obtained or held by domestic citizens. Often results from overvalued exchange rates. The process of exchange control emerges as a system of controlling inflows and outflows of foreign exchange, devices include licensing multiple currencies, quotas, auctions, limits, levies and surcharges. Many countries face serious deficits in their balance of payments and are short of foreign exchange. Hence, they restrict the use of foreign convertible currency according to their priorities. Foreign firms may be low on that priority list and have difficulty getting foreign exchange for needed imports or profit repatriation. The exchange control regulations are generally introduced by the monetary authorities of governments to control the flow of money. Restriction on the free use of foreign exchange is generally imposed by the countries having imbalances in the import – export ratio leading to problems in the balance of trade. Such countries may enforce restrictions on the remittances from the country involving international convertible currency like US Dollars, Euros and Pounds. This type of exchange control may also be an effort to encourage domestic industry. The exchange-control measures have two major consequences on the foreign business in terms of repatriation of profits and capital to the parent company at will and free imports of raw materials, machinery, spare parts, and the like from other destinations for operating purposes. The foreign exchange restrictions are also imposed by some countries for the off-shore investment by firms of home countries. The State Administration of Foreign Exchange (SAFE) of China has implemented the ceiling on foreign exchange administration in pilot cities to examine foreign exchange sources. It has been found that upon imposing such restrictions in foreign exchange transactions the domestic investment[135] is increased from US$1 million to US$3 million in 2003.

## Import Restrictions

Import restriction, is the type of political intervention that primarily intends to support the native industries. Consider a foreign apparel manufacturing company traditionally importing certain synthetic yarn and dyes from the parent company. If the host country places restrictions on imports, the company may be forced to depend on local sources of supply for these new materials. The import restrictions would help the country to encourage domestic industry as a matter of industrial policy; however, such measures tend to jeopardize the functions of foreign business. The globalization and emergence of new international trade order with the emergence of World Trade Organization has reduced the occurrence of import restrictions in many countries. The Chinese government had authorized only a limited number of companies to act as agents for restricted import and export of steel, natural rubber, wool, acrylic fibers and plywood till 2004. After joining WTO in 2001, the Chinese government is gradually relaxing the import restrictions and the above products have been opened for the free trade as an obligation to the WTO agreements. Import restrictions in a country are also subject to the cultural and religious requirements. In Kuwait alcoholic beverages, pork and bacon products, and pigskin are banned for imports on cultural and religious grounds. The general agreements in reference to WTO have emphasized on elimination of the import restrictions on all competitive goods and services. Accordingly, in the member countries of WTO, the tariffs on all agricultural products are now bound. Almost all import restrictions that did not take the form of tariffs, such as quotas, have been converted to tariffs, a process known as *"tariffication"*. This has made markets substantially more predictable for agriculture. Previously more than 30% of agricultural produce had faced quotas or import restrictions[136]. However, intervention of WTO in pursuing the member countries towards eliminating the import restrictions had mixed impact in the trade environment of Romania. The development of textile and clothing exports has benefited from link-ups between Romanian production units and companies in France, Germany and Italy. The external environment also became more favorable due to the elimination of long-standing import restrictions by the European Union and Norway; Canada and the United States are two

[135] Official website of Government of China, SAFE www.chinaonline.com/minitry_profiles
[136] World Trade Organization (2004): Tariffs- More Binding and Closer to Zero, WTO, Geneva.

potentially large markets, but they still restrict imports from Romania[137]. The non-tariff barriers imposed by a country also discourages the firms to import the goods. The country's quotas and tariffs limit the firm's ability to import equipment, components, and products, forcing a higher level of local procurement than it may require.

## Market Control

The government of a country sometimes imposes market control to prevent foreign companies from competing in certain markets. The market control may be imposed by a country at various phases of the business operations of a foreign form. If allowed to enter the country, the firm may be restricted to the types of industries it may enter. It may be prohibited from acquiring a national firm. It may not be allowed to have total ownership but may be required to enter a joint venture with a national firm. The firm may also be restricted by the government to choose its areas of operation and sell its products. It has been observed that Japanese government indirectly discourages the foreign firms conducting their business in the country. Until the fall of 20$^{th}$ century, Japan prohibited foreign companies from selling sophisticated communications equipment to the Japanese government. Thus, AT&T, GTE-Sylvania, and ITT could perform in limited way in Japan. Besides the operational controls in the market, one of the most common controls that the foreign firms may face is price controls, which limits the profitability of foreign firms in inflationary situations in the host country. Gerber left Venezuela because a decade of price controls prevented a profitable operation. Other regulations may affect advertising or other marketing practices of the firm.

> The Export and Import Controls Bureau (EPD) is responsible for administering the *Export and Import Permits Act* (EIPA) which was first enacted in 1947. The EIPA delegates to the Minister of Foreign Affairs (referred to as "the Minister") wide discretionary powers to control the flow of goods contained in specified lists provided for under the Act. Under authority of the *Department of Foreign Affairs and International Trade Act*, the Minister for International Trade provides policy direction in most areas involving market access and trade policy. The Bureau regulates trade in military and strategic dual-use goods, prevents the proliferation of weapons of mass destruction, as we are obliged to do under multilateral agreement, and protect vulnerable Canadian industries such as clothing manufacturing and fulfils other international obligations. The control goods for imports in Canada are textile and clothing, agricultural products, steel products and defense goods while the export restrictions are imposed on agricultural products, textiles, forest timber and wood products, miscellaneous goods including goods of U.S.-origin, items with medical value and all goods destined for countries on the area control list of Angola and Myanmar. Most controlled goods require an Individual Permit for import or export, although some goods may enjoy facilitated treatment under a General Permit. General Permits are not specific to an individual importer or exporter in the manner of Individual Permits. General Permits allow for the pre-authorized export or import of certain eligible goods to/from certain eligible countries, by a simplified process. For instance, the import or exports of household goods are treated in this manner[138].

---

[137] World Trade Organization: Trade Policy Review- Romania, WTO, Geneva, 1999, Press Release, PRESS/TPRB/115.

[138] Government of Canada: Export and Import Controls, Export and Import Controls Bureau, Official Web Site, http://www.dfait-maeci.gc.ca/eicb/eicbintro-en.asp

Sometimes the conflicting political ideologies also let the countries exercise the market controls without strong economic arguments. One of the examples, to be cited in this context may be of the Arabian countries which boycott companies doing business with Israel. The Arab states had not accepted Israel's right to exist and hoped that the boycott eventually would bring about its collapse, which does not seem to be realistic. In April 1998 China ordered all direct-sales operations to cease immediately. The ban, instituted last April, outlawed the direct-sales operations of companies including Avon, Amway, Mary Kay Cosmetics, and Sara Lee. However, China announced provisional plans to phase out ban on direct selling imposed during 1998 by the year 2003. The elimination of such ban on direct sales is contingent upon the development of direct-selling regulations. The consideration of Chinese government on lifting the ban on direct selling has been thought of after the U.S. support in World Trade Organization negotiations[139].

### Tax and Human Resources Controls

The governments of some countries may also impose tax control by means of excessive and non-traditional taxes on foreign firms. For example, a new form of tax imposed on foreign firm towards excessive levy on volume of production, for which no precedent may be placed. Imposing such taxes on the foreign business houses may hold reasons like an out-of-the-way monetary burden on foreign companies, to explore additional sources of revenue to meet the fiscal deficit of the country without putting pressure on the citizens of the country and to construct a tax barrier as a retaliatory measure to voice against the international policies or general dissatisfaction in diplomatic relations with other countries. In many countries like China, labor unions play significant role in political decisions and have great political clout. In such countries, labor restrictions are an effective form of government intervention. Traditionally, labor unions in America have been able to prevent layoffs, plant shutdowns, and the like, even when business could not afford to meet their demands.

## Macroeconomic Factors

The monetary system of a country defines the standards for measuring the value of its currency whereas the internationalization of monetary system determines such standards across the countries for exchange of money concerning the trading and investment activities. The efforts towards international financial arrangements emerged as preventive measures of the hard-learned lessons from Great Depression in the 1930's. It was understood by many countries that the economic policies, which might seem logical from the viewpoint of an individual economy, such as protectionism, can have a devastating effect when pursued by large number of countries. The framework of international monetary system established at the end of World War II was designed to revive international trade in goods and services — and it succeeded brilliantly. There were many factors responsible for internationalization of finance during the post second world war period as many countries began attempting structural adjustments in order to reform their economies and expand the international trade.

[139] Institute of Global Ethics: http://www.globalethics.org

The growth of international trade has been one of the prime forces behind economic growth in the post-World War II period, as many countries have availed themselves of access to global markets to grow at historically unprecedented rates. In real terms world GDP rose by 4.3 per cent a year on average between 1950 and 1999, driven and outstripped by growth in world trade averaging 5.7 per cent a year.

In the recent past the international monetary system has been driven largely by the concept of privatization that has been oriented towards faster growth of private international capital flows. The international financial system had to adapt to the increasing role of private capital flows. Such process was evident in the shift towards flexible exchange rates among the major currencies three decades ago, and it continues today, as we absorb and react to the lessons of the emerging market crises of the last decade[140]. This process was evident in the shift towards flexible exchange rates among the major currencies three decades ago, and it continues even today. In the past, the monetary policy was focused on controlling either the price or quantity of credit or both though the direct policy instruments that included interest rate controls, credit ceilings and guided lending. Interest rate control and credit ceilings were governed by state regulation though both mandatory and discretionary powers. The guided lending practices involved the state interventions towards priority sectors, allocation of subsidies and discounts. Country risk has been an issue of prime concern all through the years after World War II for the international financial community. There have been various methods used by the risk rating agencies to determine the extent of country risk, integrating a range of qualitative and quantitative information on alternative measures of political, economic and financial risk to evolve composite risk indices. Country risk analysis is a complex task and it demands a holistic vision, expert skills and consistency in measurements. The analyst must follow standard procedures to assure coherency in its studies, using reliable and useful sources of data, including rating agencies, official institutions and other several sources. The country risk analysis show the strengths and weakness of a country, after dealing with the macroeconomic, socio-political and financial aspects in order to define a risk level and, consequently, a related price for the asset in risk. Managing the risk of a portfolio demands a systematic follow up concerning the external and internal environment, governmental policies' outlook provided by rating agencies, and so on.

The structural reforms have been initiated in the macro areas including economic activity, international trade, financial markets, generation and use of public resources, governance, and labor markets. It has been observed in the previous studies that the economies that have advocated for open international trade have gained higher rates of growth influenced by the higher rate of investment and factor productivity[141]. The tariff and quantitative restrictions often impede the process of trade liberalization. The higher is the average level of dispersion of tariffs and para-tariffs in terms of custom duties and taxes; more is the distortion of international trade. The measure applied to evaluate the level of tariffs and para-tariffs is the weighted average rate of tariff and para-tariff charges that is used to weigh their respective shares in regional or global imports[142].

---

[140] Fischer Stanley: Managing the International System, speech delivered at International Law Association Biennial Conference, London, July 26, 2000 (Text documented by International Monetary Fund, Speeches, 2000).

[141] Harrison A (1996), Openness and Growth – A Time-series, Cross-country Analysis for Developing Countries, *Journal of Development Economics*, 48 (2), 419-447.

[142] Pritchett L and Sethi G (1994), Tariff Rates, Tariff Revenue and Tariff Reforms- Some New Facts, *World Bank Economic Review*, 8 (1), 1-16.

The most common pattern of economic reforms in Latin America has been, first, radical liberalization, and second, implementation of prudential norms that moderated the initial liberalization. The policy changes related to the financial system (namely, the removal of interest-rate controls, elimination of mandated credit to "priority" sectors, privatization of state banks, liberalization of the foreign investment regime, and more recently, improvements in the regulatory framework) have improved both the banking system and the stock market. The traditional view about fiscal and monetary policies in developing countries (and particularly in LAC) is that they are pro-cyclical, contributing to deepen business cycles[143]. Trade policy reform in LAC in the 1990s has been both widespread and extensive, and the region now shows a fairly open trade regime. Such a sharp policy reversal clearly had an impact on trade flows, and those effectively underwent significant changes in the past decade[144]. The Latin American countries with higher GDP, faster growth, more cropland and a longer period of time since reform had more empathy to support free trade[145]. The effects of the economic crisis of 90's among the larger countries of Latin America, Brazil appears as the most vulnerable economy. It has been observed that move towards liberalization stimulated privatization in Latin American Countries. However, most cases of privatization failure can be linked to poor contract design, opaque processes with heavy state involvement, lack of re-regulation and a poor corporate governance framework[146].

## DEBT MANAGEMENT IN TRANSITIONAL ECONOMIES

The sharp increase in the oil prices, followed by worldwide inflation, a collapse in commodity prices, global recession and high interest rates wallop the economies of the developing countries world over during 1970s. When oil prices shot up, these countries borrowed heavily at high interest rates to prevent the economic downfall. The international financial institutions lent money to developing countries along with official subsidies and such aid grew very rapidly during this period. As a result of the irresponsibility of creditor and debtor governments (e.g., corruption, private projects benefiting only the rich, etc.), the countries did not use the money for productive investment; rather, they spent these new dollars on immediate consumption and the countries were unable to repay such amassed debt. Consequently, the total medium and long-term debt of developing countries quadrupled in nominal terms, from about $140 billion at the end of 1974 to about $560 billion in 1982. The debt trap got stiffer for these countries and the borrowings reached to the level of $ 2.4 trillion by the end of 1998.

The debt crisis has had a deep impact and consequences on the economic growth of the developing countries. This situation became alarming and of major concern to international community and international institutions, including IMF and World Bank took steps to find

143 Talvi Ernesto and Végh Carlos (2000), *Tax Base Variability and Procyclical Fiscal Policy*, NBER Working Paper, No. 7499, January.

144 Loser Claudio M and Guerguil Martin (1999), Trade and Trade Reform in Latin America and the Caribbean in the 1990's, *Journal of Applied Economics*, 2 (1), 61-96.

145 Beaulieu, Eugene, Yatawara, Ravindra and Wang, Wei Guo (2005), Who Supports Free Trade in Latin America?, *The World Economy*, 28 (7), 941-958.

146 Lopez de Silanes, Florencio and Chong, Alberto (2003): *The Truth about Privatization in Latin America*, Yale ICF Working Study No. 03-29, October.

ways of reducing the impact of continuing debt of the developing countries. A framework to reduce the burden of debt has been evolved at two levels wherein the debtors need to grow faster and export more and to pull down the cost of debt service. During the process of overcoming the debt crisis, most countries have sought IMF assistance for debt relief. As a crisis managing institute, the Fund assumed a new role as financial organizer for the troubled debtor nations. The IMF required "structural adjustment programs" in these countries. Debtor governments had to agree to impose very strict economic programs on their countries in order to reschedule their debts or borrow more money. Put simply, countries had to cut spending to decrease their debt and stabilize their currency. The governments limited their costs by slashing social spending (e.g., education, health, social services, etc.), devaluing the national currency (via lowering export earnings and increasing import costs), creating strict limits on food subsidies, cutting workers' jobs and wages (especially workers in government industries and services), taking over small subsistence farms for large-scale export crop farming and promoting the privatization of public industries. Most countries have experienced the economic trauma of a recession and often a depression; and the poorest of the poor have been most affected. In 1982, Mexico declared that it was unable to repay its debts. Mexico owed vast sums of money to commercial banks in the west and default posed a serious threat to the stability of the international financial system. The commercial banks, in conjunction with the International Monetary Fund (IMF), worked out a system whereby indebted countries could spread out or reschedule their debts rather than default. It was during this time that the IMF and World Bank began to take over much of the debt owed to commercial banks. These institutions offered developing countries new loans with strict conditions attached. Since the 1980s the IMF and the World Bank, have been in control of the debt crisis. Indebted countries were required to follow policies favored by the IMF and World Bank to get new loans or even aid money. These policies have directly affected the lives and livelihoods of people in indebted countries.

The Highly Indebted Poor Countries (HIPC) initiative was first launched in 1996 by the IMF and World Bank, with the aim of ensuring that no poor country faces a debt burden it cannot manage. The initiative to create a framework for all creditors, including multilateral creditors, to provide debt relief to the world's poorest and most heavily indebted countries, and thereby reduce the constraint on economic growth and poverty reduction imposed by the debt build-up in these countries, was laid by the international financial institutes in the above period. The HIPC initiative entails coordinated action by the international financial community, including multilateral organizations and governments, to reduce to sustainable levels the external debt burdens of the most heavily indebted poor countries. Following a comprehensive review in September 1999, a number of modifications were approved to provide faster, deeper and broader debt relief and to strengthen the links between debt relief, poverty reduction and social policies.

Ethiopia is a landlocked country located in the Horn of Africa. With a per capita GDP of about US$100 (one fifth of the sub-Saharan average), Ethiopia is among the poorest countries in the world. Recent national household surveys find 44 percent of the people below the basic needs poverty line. Following the overthrow of the socialist-oriented Derg regime in 1991, the Ethiopian government with the support of the Fund and the World Bank has been implementing the economic reforms policies. The measure of economic reforms aimed at raising real GDP growth and reducing poverty, while maintaining macroeconomic stability.

> Real GDP growth averaged about 5 percent per year during 1991-2002 while inflation has been relatively contained. These positive developments were achieved despite the border war of 1998-2000 with Eritrea, and the continued decline in coffee prices since 1997-98. Ethiopia's economic circumstances adversely affected its debt sustainability, raising the net present value (NPV) of debt-to-exports ratio at end of 2002-03 substantially above the 150 percent threshold established under the enhanced HIPC framework. Further, the track record of the Ethiopian authorities in policy and reform implementation has been strong, and the authorities have borrowed prudently despite being adversely affected by a severe drought and lower coffee prices. The Net Present Value (NPV) of debt is the discounted sum of all future debt-service obligations (interest and principal). It is a measure that takes into account the extent of subsidy of a country's debt stock. Whenever the interest rate on a loan is lower than the market rate, the resulting NPV of debt is smaller than its face value, with the difference reflecting the grant element. The International Monetary Fund (IMF) and the World Bank's International Development Association (IDA) have agreed that Ethiopia has made sufficient progress and taken the necessary steps to reach its completion point under the enhanced Heavily HIPC initiative[147]. The completion point under the HIPC initiative is reached by the country when creditors commit to deliver debt relief fully and irrevocably. The decision point, which precedes the completion point, is when debt relief is committed and begins on an interim and voluntary basis. Ethiopia is the thirteenth country to reach this point, joining Benin, Bolivia, Burkina Faso, Guyana, Mauritania, Mali, Mozambique, Nicaragua, Niger, Senegal, Tanzania, and Uganda.

The debt sustainability analysis of the country is carried out to determine the debt relief needs of the country as a process of measuring the extent of international indebtedness. If a country's external debt ratio after traditional debt relief mechanisms is above a threshold for the value of debt to exports (or, in special cases, the value of debt to fiscal revenues), it qualifies for assistance under the Initiative. Once a country has made sufficient progress in meeting the criteria for debt relief, the Executive Boards of the IMF and World Bank formally decide on a country's eligibility, and the international community commits to reducing debt to the sustainability threshold. This is called the *decision point* and upon reaching this point, it may immediately begin receiving *interim relief* on its debt service falling due. The countries under the category of HIPC initiative may receive the full and irrevocable reduction in debt available provided the country establishes a further track record of good performance under IMF- and World Bank-supported programs. Once a country has met these criteria, it can reach its *completion point*, at which time lenders are expected to provide the full relief committed at the decision point.

In total, more than forty countries in Asia, Africa, and Latin America sought relief from their external debts. Negotiations among the debtor countries, creditor countries, private banks, and international organizations continued throughout the rest of the 1980s. Earlier to the intervention of the global institutions including the IMF and World Bank, various approaches were used to resolve the crisis. The 1985 Baker Plan (named after then U.S. Treasury Secretary James Baker) stressed the importance of debt rescheduling, rigid controls imposed by the Fund over domestic monetary and fiscal policies, and continued lending to debtor countries in hopes that economic growth would allow them to repay their creditors. In

[147] The World Bank: IMF and World Bank Support Ethiopia's Completion Point and Approve Topping-Up of Debt Relief Under the Enhanced HIPC Initiative, Development News Media Center, News Release No:2004/331/PREM.

response to the debt crisis of Mexico, the IMF agreed to provide a loan package only if private foreign banks holding Mexican debt agreed to reschedule their loans and provide Mexico with additional financing. However, the debtor nations made little progress in repaying their loans. Debtors and creditors alike agreed that a new approach was needed. The 1989 Brady Plan[148] focused on the need to reduce the debts of the troubled countries by writing off parts of the debts or by providing the countries with funds to buy back their loan below face value. The international debt crisis tend to recede in 1990s as the debt servicing requirements of debtor countries have been made more manageable via a combination of IMF loans, debt rescheduling, and changes in governmental economic policies. However, the impact of debt crisis of 1980s has made long-run damages to the economies of affected countries and many experts consider this phase as "lost decade" for economic development in Latin America.

In 1997 the national currency of Thailand (Bhat) jeopardized following a series of economic repercussions, most evidently the loss of competitiveness in labor intensive products that became very apparent in 1996, when total export declined by 0.2%, compared to increases by over 20% per annum in prior years. Exports of some key items, such as medium to low end garments and shoes, declined by about 30-40% in 1996. Apart from over-investment in sectors that did not generate much foreign exchange such as infrastructures, real estates and heavy industries, other factors also contributed to Thailand's gradual loss of competitiveness. The Bank of Thailand spent huge amount of funds to try to shore up weak financial institutions during the late 1990s, which went in the opposite direction to the need to maintain strict monetary discipline to solve the problem of the current account deficit. In the past, the Thai public sector had very effective management system to control the size and maturity structure of public sector debt, ranging from foreign debt ceiling, currency mix, to management of the repayment schedules. However, when most of the debt was private, there was no effective overall debt management mechanism. All these factors led to lower confidence of the international financial market in the Thai economy. The foreign reserve situation became critical after the Bank of Thailand used vast amount of reserves to defend the Baht against speculative attacks. In total, 23.4 billion US$ in forward purchases of the Baht was made up to the middle of 1997. This meant that Thailand's net foreign reserve position became much lower than the 41 billion US$ reported in Table 1. When considered in comparison to the outstanding short-term debt position of the country, there was no choice but to let the Baht float on July 2, 1997, and eventually to ask for IMF assistance, with all the implied tough policy conditions. In simple terms, the IMF package had a number of rationales:

- Medium-term loans in the amount of 17.2 billion US$ (with contributions from mostly Asian countries led by Japan) to shore up the foreign reserve position.
- Expenditure reduction in the overall economic system, whether the public sector, private sector and the population at large, in order to reduce the current account deficit, which was of the order of 14 billion US$ per annum in 1995 and 1996.
- Expenditure switching through weaker exchange rates in order to also helps the current account deficit.

[148] The plan was named after the Bush administration's treasury secretary, Nicholas Brady.

- Rehabilitation of the financial system in light of large amount of non-performing loans in the system, and huge amount of private debt. The end result would be that new foreign money would come in to take shares in or take over assets in the country.

Thailand has managed to achieve all the key IMF targets as of the end of 1997 such as fiscal cash position, monetary and foreign exchange targets as well as current account deficit target and moved carefully ahead to resolve the debt crisis. These crises did not come as a surprise to those analysts who had been watching for danger signs. The balance of payment (BoP) accounting system provided clear warning of the deteriorating performance of the countries in crisis and the increasing risk of their overextended external debt positions. A careful reading of BoP statistics could have protected international bankers from bad investments and risky loans.

In 1999, the World Bank and International Monetary Fund called on the governments of the poorest countries to prepare Poverty Reduction Strategy Papers (PRSP). Based on the Comprehensive Development Framework approach, these are comprehensive and transparent plans aimed directly at fighting poverty and are used by all donors to determine assistance and, where applicable, debt relief. There is no blueprint for building a country's poverty reduction strategy. The process however should reflect a country's individual circumstances and characteristics. There are five core principles underlying the development and implementation of poverty reduction strategies[149]. The strategies should be:

- Country-driven : involving broad-based participation by civil society and the private sector in all operational steps;
- Results-oriented : focusing on outcomes that would benefit the poor;
- Comprehensive in recognizing the multidimensional nature of poverty;
- Partnership-oriented: involving coordinated participation of development partners (bilateral, multilateral, and non-governmental);
- Based on a long-term perspective for poverty reduction.

Mexico strengthened the process of macroeconomic stabilization and structural transformation from 1988 to 1993, with the active support of the IMF, which began in the wake of the 1982 debt crisis. The macroeconomic strategies of the country were aimed at attaining external viability and laying the foundations for private-sector-led growth conceived on tight financial policies; the use of the exchange rate as a nominal anchor; comprehensive structural reforms, including privatization and trade and exchange liberalization; and a major restructuring of external debt. The result was remarkable success on many fronts. A reduction in the fiscal deficit was achieved that should be an inspiration for many countries. Inflation was reduced from 160 percent in 1987 to 8 percent in 1993. The restructuring of externaldebt paved the way for a resumption of access to international financial markets, and private capital inflows surged, contributing to a large increase in international reserves. Mexico therefore entered 1994 with a strengthened economy, and an economy more deeply integrated into global markets, with its membership in NAFTA and impending accession to membership of the OECD as well as its commitments to an open exchange and trade regime promising to lock in many of the important reforms it had implemented. In particular, the external current account deficit, running at 6.5 percent of GDP in 1993, was very large by most standards, and was being financed largely by short-term capital inflows. A steep real appreciation of the peso and a major deterioration in the private sector's saving performance had contributed to the emergence of this deficit[150].

Among many other highly indebted poor countries of Africa, some of the countries of Latin America had also experienced the debt trap. In 1995, Mexico ran into deep economic problems, since the Mexican leaders pushed the orrowing of the country too far ahead of its economic growth resulting into a catastrophic economic slump in the country. The value of Mexican currency (Peso) went down 30 percent within a week, as foreign investors lost confidence in the economic stability of the country. Mexico has been growing consistently in the late 1980s and early 1990s and its fiscal and monetary conditions were sound during the triennium beginning of 1990s. The balanced federal budget over the years attracted considerable foreign and domestic investment. However, foreign lenders, mainly American banks, pension, and mutual funds, overdid it as they advanced capital to Mexican enterprises during 1991-93 and to the government $15 billion to $25 billion a year, which was more than what Mexican exports was contributing to the gross national income of the country. These creditors recognized the problems and stressed on part repayment of the money lent and Mexico had no way to pay. The reason was that Mexico had $28 billion in dollar-denominated Treasury notes becoming due in 1995, of which $16 billion was owned by Americans[151]. A large proportion of Mexican loans were owned by thousands of U.S. mutual and pension funds, retirement accounts, and the country had legal obligations to pay benefits to millions of Americans, mostly small savers. There was no practical way to demand new loans from them to liquidate the existing sum and further plunge into the debt trap. Therefore, the IMF and the U.S. government had to come to their rescue. The IMF committed $17.8 billion to help Mexico to resolve the currency crisis with strict measures to restore the economic growth of the country and US government offered $40 billion in loan guarantees.

> The recent economic history of Mexico is marked by the severe recession that started in the fall of 1994. Theoretically, the problem may be explained as a race between a foreign investment that led to the demand boom and the anticipated expansion in supply. The outcome of such a race is inherently uncertain. If, in an exchange rate based stabilization program, supply does not keep pace with demand, competitiveness problems will eventually result in lower output, and consequently the government might be tempted to devalue[152]. The recession deepened following the 15% devaluation of the national currency, the peso on December 20th. By the end of December, the peso had fallen by 30%, stock prices collapsed and interest rates increased sharply. As a consequence of this crisis, GDP fell by 6.2% in 1995, the rate of inflation on a 12-month basis climbed to 52% in December 1995 and short-term interest rates reached a level of 71.5% in April 1995. The Mexican Crisis had such a large impact globally because it was a period of global recession and many other countries were running large debts

[149] The World Bank: Overview of poverty reduction strategies, www.worldbank.org

[150] Camdessus Michel: Drawing Lessons from the Mexican Crisis: Preventing and Resolving Financial Crises--the Role of the IMF, Address delivered at 25th Washington Conference of the Council of the Americas on "Staying the Course: Forging a Free Trade Area in the Americas" Washington, D.C., May 22, 1995, Referred from the speech documents available with the International Monetary Fund, www.imf.org

[151] Rich Thomas (1995): How to save face and trade, Newsweek, February 06, 34.

[152] Irwin Gregor and Vines David (1995): The macroeconomics of the Mexican Crisis: A simple two period model, Center for Economic Policy Research, Working Paper 1241, London.

> and were financially vulnerable. The Mexican experience weakened bank and investor confidence overall and decreased the amount of funds available to many middle-income countries that were at the time in desperate need of capital. The crisis highlighted the weaknesses of the international financial system. Mexico's crisis hurt banks' confidence in lending to Latin America in general. This was extremely harmful for many countries in the region, especially Brazil that was in need of capital. Other countries besides Brazil, like Costa Rica, Ecuador, Bolivia, and Chile were all running major deficits and the cutting off of funds would only lead to insolvency and more economic downturn. A radical version of gainers and losers in the debt crisis of a country critically puts the fact as a financial crisis, when it springs from the foreign investors' fear that others are pulling their capital out of a developing country, as was the case in Mexico, the world's central banks can contain the crisis by providing liquidity and support. In such "liquidity crises", those providing support do not lose. They make money[153].

The crisis in Asia has occurred after several decades of outstanding economic performance. During the three decades preceding the crisis, per capita income levels had increased tenfold in Korea, fivefold in Thailand, and fourfold in Malaysia. Moreover, per capita income levels in Hong Kong and Singapore now exceed those in some industrial countries. Asia attracted almost half of total capital inflows to developing countries--nearly $100 billion in 1996. Asia's success has also been good for the rest of the world. The developing and emerging market economies of Asia have not just been major exporters; they have been an increasingly important market for other countries' exports. The crisis emerged with the failure to dampen pressures in large external deficits and property and stock market bubbles. Also, the exchange rates encouraged external borrowing and led to excessive exposure to foreign exchange risk in both the financial and corporate sectors and the financial oversight that led to a sharp deterioration in the quality of banks' loan portfolios. Largely, the problems in these countries were grown mostly on domestic platforms and the developments in the advanced economies and global financial markets contributed significantly to the buildup of the imbalances that eventually led to the crises. The economies of Indonesia and Korea were also affected alike Thailand and suffered from the amount of exchange rate adjustment that had taken place. The situation exceeded beyond any reasonable estimate of what might have been required to correct the initial overvaluation of the Thai *baht*, the Indonesian *rupiah*, and the Korean *won*, among other currencies. They all had suffered a loss of confidence, and their currencies were deeply depreciated.

## FREE TRADE AGREEMENTS

There have been varying arguments on the impact of trade agreements on the economy and welfare measures. It has been concluded in one of the studies that the preferential trade agreements are mostly welfare reducing since the partner countries might end up with severe welfare losses due to substantial amount of trade diversion[154]. Another study finds that Free

[153] Bradford De Long, Christopher De Long and Sherman Robinson: The Mexican Peso Crisis – In defense of US policy towards Mexico, Economic Affairs, May-June, 1996.

[154] Bhagwati, J. and A. Panagariya (1996): Preferential trading areas and multilateralism: strangers, friends or foes?, in J. Bhagwati and A. Panagariya (eds.), *Free Trade Areas or Free Trade? The Economics of Preferential Trading Agreements* AEI Press.

Trade Areas constitute a potential threat to the world trading system because these types of agreements are; in general, trade diverting and they lead to formation of new interest groups who oppose the multilateral tariff reductions. The examination of the compatibility of exchange rate systems across trading partners is also very revealing. Part of the success of NAFTA since the late 1990s and the "impasse" of Mercosur during 1999-2001 had to do with the choices of exchange rate regimes. In both trade areas, the share of trade among the partners is very high, and in NAFTA, this includes significant financial transactions while another study draws attention on the historical context of economic institutions in the region, and on how these institutions have influenced competition policy enforcement[155].

New estimates of export and import equations are studied using a broader set of variables than previous studies and distinguishing trade between the member countries of Mercosur and trade with non-Mersocur member countries. It has been observed that Latin American countries are moving in sensible directions by emphasizing well-publicized actions against price fixers, by undertaking competition advocacy programs, and by targeting public sector restraints on competition[156]. In a study it has been reveled that Mercosur is not likely to develop supranational governance institutions present in the European Union, as policy elites in Mercosur member states desire to maintain a great deal of domestic policy autonomy. However, Latin American countries have recently made impressive progress in trade reforms; there has been limited use of competition policies[157].

## Trade and Monetary Reforms

The impact of increased global economic integration on national and regional environmental standards has been studied in general by a large number of researchers. However not many studies are available on the institutional reforms in reference to the Latin America. A study reveals the role of market mechanisms in facilitating the dissemination of environmental standards from greener nations to less green ones and the impact of international agreements on trans-border environmental problems). The traditional view about fiscal and monetary policies in developing countries (and particularly in LAC) is that they are pro-cyclical, contributing to deepen business cycles. It has been argued that governments relax their policies during booms and restrict them during busts, due to weak institutions, unfavorable political-economic equilibrium, and volatile access to international capital markets. However, international exchange-rate regimes became less persistent than hard pegs and floats in LAC after the Asian crisis. The choice of exchange-rate regimes and their transitions do matter for inflation and growth[158]. Although some studies have found that openness has a positive impact on economic performance, others have seriously questioned

---

[155] Rojas-Suarez, Liliana (2002): Toward a Sustainable FTAA: Does Latin America Meet the Necessary Financial Preconditions? Institute for International Economics Working Study No. 02-4.

[156] Owen, Bruce M (2003): *Competition Policy in Latin America*, Stanford Institute for Economic Policy Research (SIEPR) Stanford Law and Economics Olin Working Study No. 268, October.

[157] Rajapatirana Sarath (1994): *The Interface of Trade, Investment and Competition Policies: Issues and Challenges for Latin America*, World Bank, Latin America and Caribbean Department, Report # 009.

[158] Rajagopal (2005): Institutional Reforms and Trade Competitiveness in Latin America, *Applied Econometrics and International Development*, 5 (1), 45-64.

the significance of this result. One of the studies on Latin American trade issues emphasizes that openness involves more than just trade liberalization[159].

## REGIONAL TRADE AND ECONOMY OF EEC

In the beginning of transition process it was presumed that the newly liberalized economies in Central and Eastern Europe would experience high rates of sustained economic growth, with rapid convergence towards trade and economy of the major industrialized economies in the West. However, Hungary, Poland, Lithuania and Latvia have experienced transition recessions and have grown at a relatively slower rate. There has been considerable heterogeneity in outcomes, with some transition economies recovering rapidly so that by the end of the 1990s their level of output was at or above pre-transition levels. A key factor of the transition process is the structural change consisting in the reallocation of resources on the basis of market incentives. Product variety is therefore a potentially useful concept in analyzing the structural changes that have actually occurred in Eastern European transition economies. Using contemporary econometric methods and data which provide a new dimension for testing the implications of alternative growth models, an empirical study reveals that there exists a strong evidence of export fostering in economic growth of the East European transition economies. The results show that export in capital-intensive industries and investment are spearheading the growth process in an export-led growth model[160].

**Table 4.1.Growth of GDP in Eastern European Countries (in percent)**

| Country | 1990 | 1995 | 1999 | 2002 |
|---|---|---|---|---|
| Czech Republic | -1.2 | 6.0 | -0.2 | 2.5 |
| Estonia | -8.1 | 4.2 | -1.4 | 5.7 |
| Hungary | -3.5 | 1.4 | 4.4 | 3.2 |
| Poland | -11.6 | 7.1 | 4.0 | 1.3 |
| Russia | -3.0 | -4.1 | 3.2 | 4.3 |
| Slovenia | -8.1 | 4.2 | 4.9 | 3.2 |

Source: UNEEC (2003) and IMF (2000).

It may be observed from the above Table 4.1 that the transitional economies of Central and Eastern Europe suffered severe transitional recessions with negative growth of GDP. Among the Central and Eastern European countries the Polish transition can be viewed as the most successful one in terms of growth levels. It was the first of the transition economies to record positive levels of growth following the recession, growing by 2.7 percent in 1992. Slovenia entered its recovery a year later, but Hungary and the Czech Republic did not show positive growth until 1994, and Estonia until 1995. Russia recorded weak positive growth for the first time in 1997, but the financial crisis of 1998 pushed it back into recession. The

[159] Cuardos Ana, Orts Vicente and Algnacil Maite (2004): Openness in Growth: Reexamining Foreign Direct Investment, Trade and Output Linkages in Latin America, *The Journal of Development Studies*, 40 (4), 167-192.

[160] Ventura J (1997): Growth and interdependence, *Quarterly Journal of Economics*, 112, 57–84.

growth of aggregate GDP in Eastern Europe was lower (3.0 per cent) than in the CIS but was basically unchanged from the previous year. The flexibility of domestic demand induced future prospects of these economies on the part of both consumers and investors. This also reflects the considerable progress that some of these countries have made in their market reforms, as evidenced by the invitation to eight east European countries to join the European Union in 2004.

The recent reduction of tariffs in Eastern Europe is consistent with welfare-maximizing trade policy in response to the substantial changes in the market structure of these countries[161]. It has been observed in a study that impact of disintegration on trade among the former constituent republics of three demised federations in central and Eastern Europe, the Soviet Union, Yugoslavia, and Czechoslovakia has been followed by a sharp fall in trade intensity, although the legacy of a common past remains strong. However, the process of integration into the world economy has not been uniform across transition countries. Integration has been rapid and deep in the countries of Central Europe and Baltic states. The countries of South-eastern Europe and Commonwealth of Independent States (CIS) are far less integrated into the world's product and capital markets for different reasons. CIS trade is limited by obstructive domestic and regional policies and distance from other markets. Restrictions to market access remain significant in several sectors compared with those faced by many other countries. Moreover, with the completion of accession, remaining EU trade barriers against the accession countries will be lowered. As a result, trade with the non-accession countries may be reduced unless their market access is improved[162].

The Central –European Free Trade Agreement (CEFTA) has been instrumental for sub-regional trade alliance and cooperation, however, the constraints to both further internal and external development of CEFTA are such that it is unlikely to move to a redefined role in the future (Dangerfield, 2001). After long inward-looking trade policies and import-substituting industrialization, several Latin American countries undertook comprehensive trade liberalization and macroeconomic adjustment in the 1980s and the experience of these countries has been relevant for the economies in Eastern Europe and the former Soviet Union in transition from socialism to market economies. The inward-looking trade policies have been the principal attribute of Latin American economy, which has gradually transformed towards trade openness. Similar situation prevailed in the countries Eastern Europe and the former Soviet Union as they belonged to the Council for Mutual Economic Assistance (CEMA), a regional trading arrangement with many limitations on outward movements[163]. Russia did trade significantly, but largely with other members of the CMEA. Such trade rarely reflected underlying comparative advantages and soon disappeared once the transition process began[164].

CEMA was officially dissolved in early 1991 and future trade among the former CEMA countries has taken place on a radically different basis, and the region will be in search of new partners. The reorientation of Central European trade is likely to be gradual rather than

---

[161] Egli Dominik and Westermann Frank (2004): Optimal Tariffs and Subsidies and Changes in Market Structure, *Review of Development Economics*, 8 (3), 406-412.

[162] European Bank for Reconstruction and Development (2003): *Trade and Integration in Transition Countries*, Transition Report, European Bank for Reconstruction and Development, 73-88.

[163] De Melo Jaime and Dhar Sumana (1992): *Lessons of Trade Liberalization in Latin America for Economies in Transition*, Policy Research Working Paper Series #1040, World Bank, November.

[164] Michalopoulos C(1999): *The integration of the transition economies into the world trading system*, World Bank Policy Research Working Paper # 2182, World Bank.

dramatic, as trade negotiation in the western countries may not be easy. It has been observed that the trade reforms policies in former CEMA countries would be able to drive changes in production as these countries begin to produce according to their comparative advantage alike countries in Latin America. In addition, the traditional state trading structures are being dismantled, with individual enterprises increasingly able to search out their own foreign partners. Since the start of economic transformation more than a decade ago, a number of east European economies have had massive inflows of FDI, a significant part of which have been undertaken by large, export-oriented multinational companies. These new and expanding capacities exploit the comparative advantages of these economies in low-cost labor (particularly, low-cost skilled labor) as well as their proximity to the major markets of Western Europe. This fundamental competitive edge appears to have been one of the factors that allowed east European exporters to continue to gain export market share in some particular products despite the weakness of western demand.

## Trade and Economic Growth in Latin American Countries

In the 1990s, macroeconomic policies improved in a majority of developing countries, but the growth dividend from such improvement fell short of expectations, and a policy agenda focused on stability turned out to be associated with a multiplicity of financial crises[165]. The economic advancement of a country may be reviewed in reference to its fiscal, monetary, and exchange rate policies over time, and the effectiveness of the changing policy framework in promoting stability and growth. There are large differences in gross domestic products by sectors among Latin American countries, and the majority of these differences are due to the value of industrial and service sectors. Although the sectoral economic activity has been increased, in per capita terms this value decreased due to the demographic growth that Latin American countries (mainly Mexico and Brazil) had experienced during the last decades. In terms of external trade, it has been found that the outward orientation as the ratio between total exports and gross domestic product (GDP) increased from 16.1% in 1990 to 32.7% in year 2000. Panama had the highest level in this area (66.5%). Modest growth returned to Latin America and the Caribbean in 2003 and regional GDP advanced by an average 1.3 percent, after a contraction of 0.6 percent in 2002. Argentina continued recovering rapidly after its acute crisis. Brazil and Uruguay shared in the broadening of economic recovery during the year while Chile, Colombia and Peru recording growth above 3 percent. However, ongoing political uncertainties caused Venezuela's economy to deteriorate further during the first half of the year. Central America grew by an average 3.1 percent and looks set to sustain growth, thanks to the recently signed Central America Free Trade Agreement (CAFTA). The rate of change in the merchandize export in the Latin American countries during 2002 shows that most of the countries in the region except Costa Rica and Peru, other have shown a downward trend[166]. The Latin American and Caribbean countries that have shown low growth in exports have suffered from macroeconomic imbalance and in

[165] Luis Servén, and Peter J. Montiel (2004): *Macroeconomic Stability in Developing Countries: How Much Is Enough?* Working Study # 3456, World Bank, November.

[166] World Bank: Report on Latin America and Caribbean, Regional Overview, 2003.

some cases a virtual economic chaos in the pre-reform period. In many countries inflation rates evolved into hyperinflations during the 1980s, while fiscal deficits continued to burst.

The Central American Free Trade Agreement (CAFTA) negotiated between the U.S. and Central America offers opportunities and challenges for the five countries including El Salvador, Guatemala, Honduras, and Nicaragua that joined in 2003 and Costa Rica that was included in January 2004. Mexico, Nicaragua, Jamaica and Honduras always were over the mean. During the years 1990, 1995 and 2000, Mexico, Cuba, Panama, Argentina, Brazil, Chile and Uruguay reached incomes above 2000 dollars per capita in the service sector[167]. On the other hand, there are some countries like Haiti, Honduras, Nicaragua and Bolivia with incomes below 500 dollars per capita. Latin America's merchandise exports increased slightly as the decline in intra-regional trade was balanced by increased shipments to other regions. The recovery of commodity prices in the course of the year and the upturn in the US economy contributed to this rise. While most Latin American countries saw a reduction or stagnation in their imports, those of Costa Rica increased by 9 per cent. Mexico benefited from the recovery of the US market while for Costa Rica, the recovery in semi-conductor shipments boosted both imports and exports. Despite the continuation of low prices for a number of primary commodities, exports of many Central American and Caribbean countries recovered strongly. Economic activity in Western Europe remained subdued as Germany, the largest economy, experienced declining domestic demand. Domestic demand growth remained positive in the rest of the region, but was sluggish in several other countries. In the euro zone, public consumption was the most dynamic expenditure category while private consumption slowed down and fixed investment in the enterprise sector fell nearly 3 per cent. In the midst of this poor economic situation, further progress was made in the process of European integration[168].

Starting in the mid-sixties of the 20$^{th}$ century, the European example inspired a number of trade-oriented integration arrangements in the Latin American region such as the Latin American Free Trade Association, which later became the Latin American Integration Association (ALADI), the Central American Common Market (MCCA), the Caribbean Community and Common Market (CARICOM), the Andean Group, later the Andean Community; and more recently, the Southern Common Market (Mercosur), the Group of Three (G3) and the Association of Caribbean States (ACS). The main objective of Mercosur is to improve the efficiency of the four member economies through the process of opening markets and accelerating economic development. The common history shared by the member countries facilitates the integration process and the group is recognized as the third largest regional trading bloc in the world.

There are many bilateral alliances as well. Latin American countries have been living a renaissance since 80's. Most economies are stabilized, living standards are higher, direct foreign investment has surged, democracy has been institutionalized and most countries have demonstrated a desire to integrate themselves into the new global economy by opening their economies to international trade and investment. In the 90's the Latin American countries have liberalized their economies, which has been followed by a significant increase in their

[167] Guisan, M C and Aguayo (2000): Education, Industary, Trade and Development of American Companies in 1980-99, *Applied Econometrics and International Development*.2(1), 83-106.

[168] World Trade Organization: World Trade Report 2003, 30-42.

imports. This improvement was due primarily to three factors including lower inflation, less government intervention, and fewer trade barriers.

International trade has been the key indicator of the overall economic growth of Latin American countries. Several regional free trade agreements signed over the past decade--such as Mercosur, the Central American Common Market, the Andean Community, and the Caribbean Common Market-demonstrate the region's understanding of the benefits of free trade. Countries like Chile have gone even further in their trade liberalization efforts, signing bilateral agreements with Mexico and Canada after being unable to sign an agreement with the entire NAFTA bloc. In terms of scope, sectors of interest and coverage, there are three levels of sub-regional arrangements: (i) customs unions currently being finalized, e.g., the Andean Community, Mercosur, MCCA and CARICOM, (ii) first-generation free trade accords with a commercial emphasis, and (iii) new-generation free trade pacts encompassing such sectors as services, investment, intellectual ownership, and state acquisitions. Chile successfully engaged in negotiations for broader scope aimed at furthering their association with Mercosur, establishing free trade areas and bringing other sectors and issues into the accords.

With investor confidence returning in Latin America and domestic conditions improving, gross private financial inflows in 2003 increased by 40 percent over 2002. Moreover, interest rate spreads on sovereign bonds over US treasuries reached record lows. Net foreign direct investment (FDI), however, continued its decline from a peak of $88 billion in 1999 to an estimated $36 billion in 2003. This is partly explained by the end of the privatization boom and the profit crisis in Brazil and Argentina. Export growth outpaced import growth for most countries in 2003, leading to surplus positions on trade and a big improvement in the region's current account deficit, down to 0.5 percent of GDP (compared to 4.5 percent in 1998). Tourism revenues and workers' remittances also improved, and commodity prices were generally strong. Consequent upon falling trade and investment barriers and high growth prospects, the countries of Latin America represent attractive alliance prospects for an increasing number of global firms. The typical objective for these strategic alliances is a basic trade-off wherein local firms seek access to technology and capabilities that are critical for their survival in an environment of increased competition and in return, they offer prospective multinational partners access to a large and growing market.

The macroeconomic policy refers to the top-down strategy developed and implemented in a country by the government and central banks, usually intended to maximize growth while keeping down inflation and unemployment. The growth factors determining the incentives towards investing in human capital for developing new products include government policies. Countries with broadly free-market policies, in particular free trade and the maintenance of secure property rights typically have higher growth rates. By 1990, most developed countries reckoned to have long-term trend growth rates of 2-2.5% a year. Elsewhere, among Latin American countries, the reforms did bring lasting benefits. In Chile, an early reformer, fast growth saw poverty halved, to 23%, between 1987 and 1996.

A positive trend in the behavior of trade flows has been observed during the reforms period, resulting from the increased openness of these economies to international markets. There is a striking difference between the behavior of export and import volumes around the devaluation episodes. Exports tend, on average, to increase in the year of the devaluation and the following two years. Only in Argentina, Peru and Venezuela do we observe negative export growth in the second year after the devaluation, and this probably has more to do with the circumstances in world markets at that time, especially in the United States. In all other cases, exports continue to increase. Import volume, in contrast, behaves quite differently. In most of the devaluation episodes import volume contracted e.g. devaluation of currency in Brazil in the mid 1990s has driven substantial growth in imports. In all other cases, the import contraction was short-lived. Exports increase faster than average to countries in the region, and especially towards countries that are partners in regional trading agreements. Brazil and Argentina increased their trading flows with each other significantly, and also with other countries in the region such as Chile and Paraguay.

## TRADE AND TARIFF STRUCTURES

The trade among the Latin American and East Asian countries certainly exhibit enormous potential and apart from the trading of physical goods the services trade in terms of consultancy, transfer of technology and managerial training may also be explored bi-regionally. However, there exist differences among both the regions in factor endowment between the generally natural-resource-abundant Latin America and the natural resource-scarce Asia-Pacific Geography (*i.e.* distance) and differences in the availability of capital, knowledge (*e.g.* Japan, South Korea and Taiwan) and labor (China) also have been major drivers of the bilateral trade. It has been observed by many researchers that Latin America is aggressively opened up to world trade and investment in the late 1980s and its mixed results have emerged over two decades in expansion, diversification and upgrading its exports. The Asia-Pacific countries have shown extraordinary success in diversifying their exports and in raising their stakes in the world economy, while at the same time their domestic market is largely protected against import competition. Such trade policies of this region have also alarmed the concerns for global partnering and business expansions. Instruments such as tariff, non-tariff barriers, trade related investment measures (TRIMS) and barriers to domestic distribution still play an import role in these countries, although there are important cross-country differences in their timing, scope and importance.

The last several years have witnessed deep changes in trade policy in the Latin American region; this process has generally been accompanied with other far-reaching macroeconomic reforms. The overhaul of the tariff structure included the reduction of the average rate as well as the reduction in its dispersion. Though the gains along this dimension are not very notable throughout the nineties, there is a significant reduction relative to the levels observed during the second half of the eighties. Relative to the Chile's structure –which is almost flat- there is still some room to reduce tariff dispersion by the Mercosur member countries. The Table 4.2 exhibits the tariff dispersion structure among the Mercosur countries.

It may be observed from the results exhibited in the above Table that tariff structure had high variations in all the countries under study except Chile during 1985 while in the post reforms period such variation in the tariff structure in Latin American countries was reduced. The dramatic change may be experienced when the deviation in the tariff was found to be 7.8 in 1999 as against 36.7 during 1985. It may be seen from the Table that Chile has been the pioneer of trade liberalization since the mid 1980s as it has liberated the tariff regime to lead globalization..

**Table 4.2. Tariff Dispersion among Latin American Countries (Standard deviations)**

| Trade Bloc | Country | 1985 | 1986 | 1987 | 1988 | 1989 | 1990 | 1991 | 1992 | 1993 | 1994 | 1995 | 1996 | 1997 | 1998 | 1999 |
|---|---|---|---|---|---|---|---|---|---|---|---|---|---|---|---|---|
| Mercosur | Argentina | 14.5 | 20.5 | 20.5 | 21.5 | 21.5 | 8.6 | 8.6 | 7.4 | 5.0 | 6.7 | 7.6 | 7.0 | 6.8 | 6.9 | 8.3 |
| | Brazil | 36.7 | 30.0 | 30.0 | 26.2 | 17.2 | 19.8 | 17.3 | 14.2 | 9.5 | 8.2 | 6.9 | 8.5 | 7.7 | 7.3 | 7.8 |
| | Paraguay | - | 15.2 | 15.2 | 15.2 | 15.2 | 13.0 | 1.4 | 7.8 | 6.8 | 7.7 | 6.9 | 7.1 | 6.7 | 6.5 | 7.4 |
| | Uruguay | 16.2 | 18.8 | 18.8 | 14.4 | 14.4 | 9.7 | 9.7 | 5.9 | 5.9 | 5.9 | 7.1 | 7.3 | 6.9 | 7.9 | 4.3 |
| Prospecting for Mercosur | Chile | 3.2 | 1.7 | 1.7 | 1.0 | 1.0 | 0.9 | 0.9 | 0.7 | 0.7 | 0.7 | 0.7 | 0.7 | 0.7 | 0.7 | 0.7 |
| | Colombia | 28.2 | 16.8 | 16.8 | 17.6 | 17.6 | 14.2 | 8.3 | 6.3 | 6.3 | 6.3 | 4.9 | 6.3 | 6.3 | 6.2 | 6.2 |
| | Peru | 26.8 | 25.9 | 25.9 | 27.4 | 27.4 | 22.6 | 22.6 | 4.4 | 4.4 | 4.4 | 4.4 | 4.4 | 4.4 | 2.9 | 2.5 |
| | Venezuela | 28.6 | 30.2 | 30.2 | 31.4 | 31.4 | 17.1 | 17.1 | 11.3 | 11.3 | 11.3 | 4.8 | 4.8 | 6.1 | 6.1 | 5.9 |

Source: Computed on the data available with ECLAC, UNCTAD, WTO and IDB for the referred periods.

**Table 4.3. Exports from Latin American Countries to Asia-Pacific (1990-2003) in US $ millions**

| Trade Bloc | Country | Japan | Korea Republic | China | Hong Kong | Taiwan | Singapore | ASEAN | Asia-Pacific (A) | World (B) | Percent Share (A/B) |
|---|---|---|---|---|---|---|---|---|---|---|---|
| Mercosur | Argentina | 344<br>(395) | 434<br>(51) | 2478<br>(241) | 98<br>(60) | 126<br>(48) | 10<br>(409 | 1098<br>(329) | 4588<br>(1164) | 29566<br>(12352) | 15.5<br>(9.4) |
| | Brazil | 2311<br>(2349) | 1223<br>(543) | 4533<br>(382) | 694<br>(271) | 689<br>(432) | 338<br>(250) | 1113<br>(790) | 10900<br>(5016) | 73084<br>(31412) | 14.9<br>(16.0) |
| | Paraguay | 5<br>(21) | 0<br>(6) | 17<br>(67) | 9<br>(17) | 12<br>(3) | 1<br>(5) | 9<br>(5) | 53<br>(123) | 1242<br>(1708) | 4.3<br>(7.2) |
| | Uruguay | 12<br>(21) | 6<br>(6) | 95<br>(67) | 14<br>(17) | 5<br>(3) | 2<br>(5) | 63<br>(5) | 197<br>(123) | 2198<br>(1708) | 9.0<br>(7.2) |
| Prospecting for Mercosur | Chile | 2243<br>(1384) | 1006<br>(258) | 1817<br>(34) | 0<br>(41) | 583<br>(279) | 39<br>(33) | 254<br>(132) | 5922<br>(2162) | 20077<br>(8522) | 29.5<br>(25.4) |
| | Colombia | 202<br>(259) | 76<br>(13) | 82<br>(2) | 16<br>(16) | 52<br>(1) | 11<br>(3) | 18<br>(9) | 456<br>(303) | 13092<br>(6765) | 3.5<br>(4.5) |
| | Peru | 390<br>(420) | 176<br>(65) | 675<br>(55) | 30<br>(19) | 147<br>(50) | 16<br>(0) | 76<br>(18) | 1511<br>(628) | 8749<br>(3313) | 17.3<br>(19.0) |
| | Venezuela | 135<br>(505) | 15<br>(6) | 165<br>(6) | 11<br>(34) | 37<br>(57) | 201<br>(125) | 9<br>(44) | 571<br>(777) | 24974<br>(18044) | 2.3<br>(4.3) |
| Overall | LAC | 6473<br>(6958) | 3367<br>(1091) | 10470<br>(866) | 1278<br>(507) | 1786<br>(967) | 832<br>(495) | 3029<br>(1376) | 27234<br>(12261) | 363707<br>(120916) | 7.5<br>(10.1) |

Figures in parentheses indicate values for 1990

Source: IDB-INT calculations based on UN/COMTRADE data published in the official document AB-2370, March 21, 2005: “Asia and Latin America and the Caribbean: Economic Links, Cooperation and Development Strategies”

Venezuela, and to a lesser extent, Brazil, made considerable progress in trade reform in the late 1980s; all of the remaining countries conducted major trade reforms in the early 1990s. Whereas Brazil and Venezuela liberalized their tariff regime over a few years, Argentina, Colombia, and Peru conducted faster trade liberalizations.

It may be stated that the higher the average level and dispersion of tariffs and para-tariffs such as duties and customs fees, the more distorted the trade development. In the specific case of agriculture, although the coverage of non-tariff barriers did fall considerably, in some countries it nevertheless remained for a time more significant than in other sectors. This can be attributed in part due to the desire of governments to protect their farm sectors from world price fluctuations and to counteract export subsidies. Latin America's total exports grew by an annual average 8.9 percent between 1990 and 2003 raising its share of world exports from 3 to 5.4 percent as exhibited in Table 4.3. It may be observed from the data that Chile has the largest share of its exports (29.5 percent) to the Asia- Pacific countries in terms of percent share to the world exports followed by Peru (17.3 percent) during 2003. Mexico has been the indisputable driver of Latin America's export growth, with its share of the regional total rising from a fifth in the early 1980s to 45 percent in 2003. It may be observed from the exhibited data that four big countries which include Brazil, Argentina, and Venezuela-today generate more than three-fourths of Latin America's exports. Even with Latin America struggling with anemic economic growth, the region's imports rose by more than exports (an annual average of 10.1 percent in 1990-2003), perhaps reflecting the region's rather aggressive opening and episodes of exchange rate appreciation.

The dynamism of trade notwithstanding, the volume of Latin American exports to Asia-Pacific starts from a relatively low base and is well below the region's exports to North America, the European Union, and intra-regional commerce. In fact, while increasing substantially up to 1991, the importance of Asia-Pacific as a market for Latin America has declined over the past decade. Latin American exports to Asia-Pacific stood at $24 billion in 2003, with the Asia-Pacific accounting for 6.6 percent of Latin America's total exports to the world-a marked drop from Asia-Pacific's share of 9 percent in 1990. Central America did, however, experience slight growth in the share of the Asia-Pacific in total exports in 1990-2003. Of the individual countries, Argentina, Chile, Colombia, Paraguay, Peru, Uruguay, and Venezuela have experienced a rise in the share of Asia-Pacific in their exports between 1990 and 2003.

The importance of the Asia-Pacific is most marked for Chile, which exported 29 percent of its exports to Asia-Pacific, as well as for the Mercosur countries, which sent 15 percent of their exports to the Asia-Pacific basin in 2003. Arguably, the most vulnerable region right now is Latin America, where most countries are trying to cope with an environment of high economic fragility, partly resulting from the current global slowdown but also reflecting internal political trouble and policy mismanagement. The region's problems are of a more long-term nature than merely cyclical and therefore need to be tackled accordingly, taking into account country-specific circumstances. Latin America's large distance from world markets, the region's complicated topography, and the tropical climate pose particularly important challenges. On the macroeconomic front, the fiscal policy stance has deteriorated significantly in several countries, sending them into a dangerous spiral of increasing debts and deficits despite important efforts to generate primary surpluses in the public budget. However, that encouraging reforms have been implemented in some areas, notably regarding foreign trade and financial liberalization. As a result, exports have deepened and become more diversified, which bodes well when the external environment becomes more favorable again.

## EXPANSION OF LATIN AMERICA-ASIA TRADE LINKS

The trade performance of Asian and Pacific countries had been outstanding up to 1997. In 1980, the region exported less than US$ 280 billion, by 1990 that total had increased to almost US$ 700 billion and in 1995 more than US$ 1,230 billion. Results on the export side were matched by an exceptional performance on the import side. Total imports jumped from US$ 292 billion in 1980 to more than US$ 700 billion 10 years later and over US$ 1,300 billion in 1995. These values indicate an average annual growth rate between 1990 and 1995 of about 12 per cent for exports and over 13 per cent for imports. However, the Asian crisis had a negative effect on the region's trade performance. Between 1996 and 1998, the average annual growth of total exports was -0.2 per cent, while on the import side the decrease was more pronounced, at -4.2 per cent. The result for the period 1990-1998 shows that annual growth for exports reached only 7.5 per cent as compared to 11.5 per cent for the period of 1980-1990. Growth of Asian and Pacific exports to the countries belonging to Latin American Integration Association (LAIA) increased 19 per cent a year between 1990 and 1995, growth that was even more pronounced than intra-Asian trade. This was a clear indication that trade liberalization in Latin America offered a special opportunity for Asian and Pacific countries to increase their share in this expanding market.

Inter-regional cooperation has intensified on the trans-Pacific agenda in recent years. Latin America and Asia-Pacific have created various fora to deal with bilateral economic and political issues. The most comprehensive in terms of bi-regional membership is the Forum for East Asia-Latin America Cooperation (FEALAC) launched at a Ministerial Meeting in March 2001 in Santiago, Chile. Comprising of 17 Latin American and 15 Asia-Pacific economics, FEALAC is an informal mechanism for dialogue and cooperation among the countries of the two regions to meet political, cultural, social, economic and international issues of common concern. Two further major venues of trans-Pacific cooperation are the Pacific Basin Economic Council (PBEC) and the Pacific Economic Cooperation Conference (PECC). The Latin American partners in each are Colombia, Chile, Ecuador, Mexico and Peru. PBEC is an association of senior business leaders from more than 1,100 major corporations in 20 economics around the Pacific Basin Region aimed at expanding trade and investment flows through open markets. In its next International General Meeting (IGM) in June 2005 in Hong Kong, PECC will focus on the Pacific Basin's role in the next stages of globalization, such as the Doha Development Round. Meanwhile, the 25-member PECC promotes trade, investment, financial stability, and development around the Pacific Rim. It comprises senior representatives from business, government, and the academia. PECC has recently focused on the proliferation of regional integration agreements as a potential way for achieving the Bogor Convention Goals of APEC[169].

Japan and Latin America have deep-seated cooperation. Japan has alone, contributed to Latin America's development through economic and technical cooperation aimed particularly

[169] Inter-American Development Bank (2005): IDB Official document # AB-2370, March 21, 2005: "Asia and Latin America and the Caribbean: Economic Links, Cooperation and Development Strategies".

at economic reform, poverty reduction, and environmental protection. It is one of Latin America's main sources of Official Development Assistance (ODA). Japan was one of the key actors in helping Latin America debt crisis of the early- 1980s, and also involved in the Central American peace processes. More recently, Japan has supported the electoral processes in Latin America, including joining the dispatch of election observers from the Organization of American States (OAS). Japan has also pursued active cooperation with the Caribbean through the Japan-CARICOM Consultation, which centers on fostering bilateral relations, and economic cooperation, cultural exchanges, and collaboration in international fora.

It is interesting to note that this was the highest rate of growth compared to other regions. On the other hand, Asian and Pacific imports from LAIA were the most affected among the regions. Even before the Asian crisis, Latin America was a minor partner in Asia's export and import flows. In 1998, only 2.2 per cent of total Asian and Pacific exports went to Latin America, and only 1.8 per cent of their imports originated in LAIA countries. It is even more significant that 18 years earlier, the share of LAIA countries in total Asian and Pacific exports and imports was higher. During the first five years of the 1990s, growth of exports from Asia and the Pacific to LAIA was high. Eight countries had annual average growth rates over 20 per cent during this period. Three countries that included China, Indonesia and Thailand had increases of over 40 per cent in their exports to the region.

The average annual growth rate for imports to East Asian countries from LAIA countries actually increased slightly over the rate for 1990-1995. However, New Zealand's imports from the world which had increased on average by 8 per cent between 1990 and 1995 decreased almost 6 per cent between 1996 and 1998. Before the crisis, the most dynamic Asian market for Latin American products was Malaysia, followed closely by Indonesia. The import demand of these two countries declined drastically after the crisis. During this period, Latin America represented more than 2 per cent of total imports for only five Asian and Pacific countries, Latin America absorbed more than 2 per cent of total exports for only three countries. Latin America had the highest average market share of total exports for Japan, while the region's imports were more relevant for the Republic of Korea. South Korea maintains important institutional ties with the countries of Latin America and the Caribbean. It was one of the first Asian countries to join the OAS as a permanent observer, and has made efforts to contribute to Latin America's economic and social development through ODA and technical cooperation. South Korea has recently sought to deepen its economic ties with Latin America. Besides the FTA with Chile, in 2003 South Korea staged with various Latin American countries the South Korea-Latin America and Caribbean Business Forum, which drew a host of government officials and analysts. South Korea and Mexico are joined by the 21st Century Commission, a private-level consultation forum created to explore possibilities for longer-term bilateral collaboration.

China and Latin America have strengthened cooperation ties markedly over the past decade. The Rio Group and China launched political dialogue in 1990, and in 1994 China became the first foreign country to be admitted as an observer to the Latin American Integration Agreement (LAIA or ALADI). In 1997, China was admitted to the Caribbean Development Bank. China has also held official talks with Mercosur following the establishment of a bilateral dialogue mechanism. Furthermore, much like Japan and South Korea, China collaborates with various Latin American countries in APEC and FEALAC. It also has expressed interest in a non-borrower membership in the Inter-American Development Bank.

India and Chile have signed a Preferential Trade Agreement (PTA) in early 2006 as part of initiatives to increase trade and investment between the two countries. The PTA strategically positions Chile to access and to capitalize on the Indian market and its technological assets. The agreement provides tariff preferences ranging from 10 to 50 per cent on 178 products to Chile and a similar range of preferences on 296 items to India. It would benefit 98 per cent of items being exported by Chile to India and 91 per cent of the goods being exported by India to Chile. The Indian products, which would benefit include textiles, chemicals, pharmaceuticals, engineering and agricultural machinery while Chilean products include copper, newsprint, iodine, fish meal and salmons. Both the countries have also discussed the draft reports of the Joint Study Group and agreed to submit their findings to consider further action on a Free Trade Agreement.

## BUSINESS DEVELOPMENT IN TRANSITIONAL ECONOMIES

The financial objectives of the multinational companies are aimed at measuring the performance on the capital employed. Capital employed is the sum of all assets along with the accumulated reserves for depreciation. The multinational companies, in their financial goals, may recognize that not all operations are directly comparable and state that targets for area profit centers and operations will take into account the nature of the operations and performance plans thereof. Emphasis on asset management by the multinational company at all levels is laid in reference to annual targets for cash generation, capital expenditures, and balance sheet items, including inventory and receivables management. The finance managers of the company draw special attention to the differences between actual cash generating capacity and book results. Each production group and profit center both of product categories and territorial develop net cash-generating capacity for its own requirements and also pools-up sufficient funds for the company to meet its high-priority investment commitments and opportunities. Financial objectives constitute the foundation for making financial decisions for a company. The companies should be able to integrate the financial objectives for both domestic and international business. Financial objectives also constitute the foundation for making financial decisions for a company. For example, in order to protect it against exchange rate fluctuations, it might require managers in overseas subsidiaries to forecast regularly the exchange rates month-by-month for the upcoming six months. On the basis of those forecasts, corporate funds in a currency likely to be substantially depreciated would be utilized before funds in stronger currencies.

> In most of the multinational companies, the cash management is centrally organized process. The major goal in this process is to concentrate overall group liquidity as much as possible and to a reasonable extent. Ideally, this pooling is done across banks and borders. In a broader sense, cash management comprises the organization of the process of all incoming and outgoing payments in the most efficient way. To achieve this, multinational companies depend on the, instruments like bank policy and cash pooling software intelligence. In reality the right mix of organizational and software intelligence probably leads to the best result. The quality of cash pooling can be measured by the gap between the forecasted and the realized cash position of a company. Smaller the difference between expectations and reality higher is the efficiency of cash management. Cash pooling is the standard instrument for efficient cash

management. There are two basic concepts available: the notional pooling is organized as interest compensation across the participating bank accounts; alternatively, the zero balancing approach requires physical concentration of all cash flows on one concentration account. The latter approach is the most used concept today. A logical further step in cash management is the organization of the payments in a centralized way. Such concepts are expressed as *payment factory* whereby all payments for all connected subsidiaries of a multinational corporate can be managed at a single place or a centralized station. This includes single payments as well as mass payments.

The goal of an international money manager may be to obtain finances for foreign project towards expansion, subsidiaries or strategic alliances with the companies of the host country in a way to maximize the resources availability and lower the after-tax interest costs and foreign exchange losses. The exchange rate parity theory suggests that international differentials in interest costs are offset by changes in foreign exchange rates; that is, the expected value for net financing costs will be equal for all currencies over any given time period, provided foreign exchange markets are efficient. However, the multinational companies are susceptible to the following risks related to money management[170]:

- The political risk of assets being taken over by the host country
- The exchange risk whereby the value of the US dollar changes with reference to the host country currency; and
- The translation risk whereby the corporate financial statements are required by the country specific regulations to be based on historical costs rather than current value.

In some countries, gains and losses from long-term exchange transactions are subject to preferential capital gains tax rates or reserves treatment. Conversely, many countries- Australia, Indonesia, South Africa, and Germany, have no taxes on gains or losses arising from most long-term exchange transactions. Traditionally, foreign investors foresee low opportunity for raising capital locally in the developing countries. However, there may be any inadequacy of the local capital in these countries. It has been experienced in India that often the initial public offers of multinational companies fetched encouraging response. The Honda Motor Company's issue was oversubscribed 165 times within a span of 72 hours. Similarly, Burroughs Corporation's stock and debenture issue was oversubscribed 30 times.

The financial management also involves significantly the matters of repatriation of funds and profits of a multinational organization. Repatriation may be explained as The return from abroad of the financial assets of an organization or individual. A multinational firm needs to formulate a strategy on remission of dividends from overseas affiliates to headquarters. The international dividend policy is determined by the following factors[171]:

- Tax implications.
- Political risk.

---

[170] Kwang Chul Lee and Cluik C Y Kwok (1988): Multinational corporation vs. domestic corporations: International environment factors and determinants of capital structure, Journal of International Business Studies, Summer, 195-218.

[171] Eitemann David, Stonehill Arthur J and Moffett Michael M (1995): Multinational Business Finance, 7th ed. Addison Wesley, New York, chapter 19.

- Foreign exchange risk.
- Age and size of affiliate.
- Availability of funds.
- Presence of joint venture partners.

The policy of Government of India is liberal with regard to the remittance of profits, dividends, royalties etc., but the Government is cautious of excessive remittance while approving foreign investment proposals and collaboration agreements. Thus foreign enterprises have complete freedom for the remittance of profit and repatriation of capital subject to exchange considerations. Remittance falling due under the collaboration agreements will however be subject to the approval of the Reserve Bank of India (RBI)[172]. On the contrary, Many multinationals operating in China have started to turn in profits, and, as they become more profitable, they are being frustrated by complex arrangements currently in place to deter repatriation. The strict regulations discourage transfer of funds out of China. Multinational companies operating in China are also restricted from lending intra-company[173].

The United States-Argentina Bilateral Investment Treaty (BIT) came into force in 1994. Under the treaty, U.S. investors enjoy national treatment in all sectors except shipbuilding, fishing, and nuclear power generation. An amendment to the treaty removed mining, except uranium production, from the list of exceptions. The treaty allows arbitration of disputes by the International Center for the Settlement of Investment Disputes (ICSID) or any other arbitration institution mutually agreed by the parties. Several U.S. firms have invoked the provisions of the treaty in on-going disputes with Argentine national or provincial authorities. Under the Convertibility Law of 1991, the exchange rate of the Argentine peso is fixed to the dollar at the rate of one to one, under a currency board type of arrangement called "convertibility." This rate is expected to remain unchanged in the medium term. Argentina has no exchange controls. Foreign investment receives national treatment under Argentine law. Firms need not obtain permission to invest in Argentina. Foreign investors may wholly own a local company, and investment in firms whose shares trade on the local stock exchange requires no government approval. There are no restrictions on repatriation of funds[174].

In the countries where political risk may not be an important factor, the repatriation policy will be based on availability and use of funds. For example, if funds are needed in the United Kingdom, headquarters might decide to transfer its retained earnings from a German subsidiary to the United Kingdom rather than transferring funds from the United States. An alternative to this action would be the investment of funds in Euro. In reference to the risk factors discussed above On the basis of the six factors just listed and discussed, a multinational firm may follow either a pooled strategy or a flexible strategy for distribution of earnings generated by foreign affiliates. The pooled strategy refers to a stated policy of remittance of profits to the parent on a regular basis. The flexible strategy leaves the decision on dividends to factors operating at the time. The flexible strategy permits the parent to make the most viable use of funds *vis-a-vis* its long-term global corporate objectives.

---

[172] Government of India: Ministry of Finance, Foreign investment policy, 2001.

[173] Asia Today Online: Corporate dilemma: Profits idle in China, 01 December 2003 www.asiatoday.com.au

[174] Bureau of Economic and Business Affairs: Country Reports on Economic Policies and Trade Practices of Argentina-2001, US Department of State, February 2002.

The business partnership strategies should be developed keeping in view the heterogeneity in economic development, culture and institutional modalities that exist in both regions, while seeking globally balanced relations. The relationship should be based on fundamental shared principles and values, which in turn can be translated into clear political messages and a general sustained process of dialogue and cooperation. Relationships can be deepened at the bi-regional, regional or bilateral levels, taking advantages of the special circumstances of country groupings. Building relationships should proceed at different levels and speeds among the countries of the region. Considering the multiplicity of forums it is necessary to focus the trade partnering negotiations at bilateral and multilateral levels and avoid overlap between distinct dialogues and similar initiatives taken at other forums.

Bilateral negotiations should be strategically pursued in removing/ reducing the non-tariff and investment barriers. The trade related negotiations among the Latin America-East Asian countries should also focus on the technical norms and standards; rules of origin, anti-dumping, subsidies, countervailing measures; other liberalization and deregulation measures (privatization); sub-regional, regional and hemispheric integration processes; and convergence and divergence between regional integration and multilateral trade regimes. The negotiations should also be dealt on simplifying the customs rules and procedures, including non-transparent and inefficient infrastructures; differing customs; improper application of rules of origin, customs valuation, pre-shipment inspection and import licensing. Customs problems can be especially difficult for small and medium enterprises that have less experience and fewer resources for handling these problems.

The trade integration between most of the largest Central and Eastern European countries and the euro area is already relatively advanced, while the Baltic countries as well as the South Eastern European countries still have significant scope for integration. The necessity of foreign investments in the transition countries is the result of industrial restructuring in post-socialist Eastern Europe and the Baltic countries. New markets, lower production costs and higher profit rates have been the main motivators in investing to the transition countries. Bi-regional multilateral trade need to be encouraged among the Latin America and East Asian countries which would enable them to promote liberalization which is conducive to increasing the traditional trade flows among the participating countries. The bi-regional diplomatic negotiations should be evolved towards developing an action plan aiming at reducing non-tariff barriers and transaction costs, as well as promoting trade and investment opportunities between the two regions. Such a plan could provide concrete goals to be achieved in identified priority areas such as customs procedures, standards, testing, certification and accreditation, public procurement, intellectual property rights and mobility of business people.

## REFERENCES

Allen, Franklin (2005), Corporate Governance in Emerging Economies, *Oxford Review of Economic Policy*, 21 (2), 164-177.

Das, Dilip K. (2006), The Chinese and Indian Economies: Comparing the Comparables, *Journal of Chinese Economics and Business Studies*, 4 (1), 77-89.

Dunis, Christian L; Shannon, Gary (2005), Emerging markets of South-East and Central Asia: Do they still offer a diversification benefit? *Journal of Asset Management*, 6 (3), 168-190.

Greenland, Steve; Coshall, John; Combe, Ian (2006), Evaluating service quality and consumer satisfaction in emerging markets, *International Journal of Consumer Studies*, 30 (6), 582-590.

Lall, Sanjaya; Weiss, John; Oikawa, Hiroshi (2005), China's Competitive Threat to Latin America: An Analysis for 1990-2002, *Oxford Development Studies*, 33 (2), 163-194.

Martin, Philippe; Rey, Hélène (2006), Globalization and Emerging Markets: With or Without Crash? *The American Economic Review*, 96 (5), 1631-1651.

Michael G. Papaioannou, George Tsetsekos (1996), *Emerging Market Portfolios: Diversification and Hedging Strategies*, New York, Irwin.

Sokil-Milnikiewicz, Catherine (2006), Investment Strategies in Emerging Markets, *Comparative Economic Studies*, 48 (2), 387-389.

Swanson, Burton E. (2006), Extension Strategies for Poverty Alleviation: Lessons from China and India, *Journal of Agricultural Education and Extension*, 12 (4), 285-299.

Tsukuda, Yoshihiko; Miyakoshi, Tatsuyoshi; Shimada, Junji (2005), Dynamic Efficiency in the East European Emerging Markets, *Financial Engineering and the Japanese Markets*, 12 (2), 159-179.

# PART II: THE STUDY

*Chapter 5*

# REVIEW OF RESEARCH CONTRIBUTIONS

Sustainable development is a prime global concern of all nations. It has been emphasized that the business sector will only be more effective if it incorporates social and environmental responsibilities into its policies. Poverty and environmental damages affect the business sector and thus, need to be resolved and prevented to create a good and prosperous business environment. It is also noticed that global competitiveness is the key element to survive in business and it is a task that the business sector along with governments have to confront. Since the latter half of eighties and all through the decade of 90's, issues of reforms have swept the economies of Latin America and Caribbean countries. The development strategy has been based extensively on the policies of import substitution and strong intervention of the state in production of goods, functioning of the marketing and redistribution of income. The economic reforms in a country are complex and multi-dimensional process that involves the development and implementation of many public policies at intermediate levels during the reforms. The economic reforms thus will not have a constant speed and will often be subject to modifications in the policies that bring changes in the performance and structure of economic activities. The economic reforms can be assessed by examining their corresponding policy measures and implications. However, entire economic progress may not be interpreted as an outcome of the reforms. The growth and development may result to be slower in a country or region in a normal process than stirred process of reforms. After years of poor economic management, many Latin American and Caribbean countries are experiencing a process of structural reforms that places them on a path to a superior economic performance[175]. Two basic principles identify this process of economic reforms - fiscal and monetary discipline, and reliance on market forces to determine the allocation and distribution of resources.

The social perspectives of economic growth have also been discussed in some studies. A study discussed the importance of education on a sustained economic development strategy, having into account inter-sector relations and the influence of education in the growth of production per head using three cross-country models[176]. The study recommends

---

175 Easterly William and Sergio Rebelo (1993): Fiscal Policy and Economic Growth-An Empirical Investigation, *Journal of Monetary Economics*, 32 (3), 417-458.

176 Guisan M Carmen, Aguayo Eva and Exposito Pilar (2001): Economic Growth and Cycles: Cross-Country Models of Education, Industry and Fertility and International Comparisons, *Applied Econometrics and International Development*, 1 (1), pp 1-18.

the need for evolving new international policies for improving the educative level of population in less developed countries. Some researchers specialized in economic growth analyze the export-led growth in many countries and insist upon the importance of openness to increase real gross domestic product. In this context, one of the studies discusses the important role of human capital, manufacturing and imports to increase real income per inhabitant and non-agrarian employment[177]. This study argues that beyond increasing the degree of openness in order to increase foreign demand, it is also necessary to relate foreign trade with supply side having into account the general positive effects of imports on the domestic growth of industry, building and services.

Although Latin America has been intensively debating appropriate institutional designs for more than two decades, little progress has been made. One of the key challenges, therefore, will be to provide explanations as to why institutional reforms have succeeded in some policy areas but not in others. Today, most of the Latin American countries are well-respected democracies, with a multi-party political system, the division of powers, a working parliament and regular elections. But at the same time, there is a strong crisis of confidence, not only towards governments, but in the whole political class and representation in general. The increasing lack of confidence in the political elite in Latin America has fostered new forms of opposition in several countries, leading to a significant number of Latin American presidents[178] not being capable of completing their terms of office during the 1990s. Although political shifts are a constant feature of democracy and generally indicate the strengths of democratic institutions, a more stable political system in the region would have helped to pursue reforms processes in a more effective way. Specifically, a strong macroeconomic stabilization will, after some short-run recessive effects, provide a framework that has less distortion for economic indicators than the pre-reforms period. The failure of market reforms in Latin America to produce sustained growth and equitable prosperity is demonstrated most clearly by Argentina's most recent economic and political meltdown. But economic difficulties, poverty and searing inequality has continued to plague the Mexican case as well. Latin American policy makers themselves have begun to contribute to the growing discussion of policies necessary to confront the lingering economic and social challenges. Included among the recommended policy prescriptions are: increased social spending supported by tax reforms, assistance to small and medium enterprises, and an end to corruption. Such policy reforms require governments that are autonomous from particular business interests with established institutional channels capable of securing generalized business cooperation and support[179].

---

[177] Guisan M Carmen, Malacon C and Exposito Pilar (2003): *Effects of Integration of Mexico into NAFTA on Trade Industry, Employment and Economic Growth*, University of Santiago de Compostela, Economic Development Series, Working Paper No. 68, 1-24.

[178] World Economic Forum (2002): Latin America Agenda, Latin America Business Summit, Rio de Janeiro, Brazil, 20-22 November 2002.

[179] Teichman J (2002): Private Sector Power and Market Reforms – Exploring the Domestic Origins of Argentina's Meltdown and Mexico's Policy Failures, *Third World Quarterly*, 23 (3), June, 491-512.

## Macroeconomic Factors

The structural reforms have been initiated in the macro areas including economic activity, international trade, financial markets, generation and use of public resources, governance, and labor markets. In the early reforms period shift in economic policy, most were suffering from both low growth and serious macroeconomic disequilibria - high inflation, fiscal deficits, current account deficits, and financial sectors in critical trouble associated in part with the foreign debt crisis of the early 1980s. Not only were economic reforms pushed by an ideological impulse toward smaller governments, but agricultural trade reforms were implemented in this context of fiscal deficits and large foreign debt. It has been observed in the previous studies that the economies that have advocated for open international trade have gained higher rates of growth influenced by the higher rate of investment and factor productivity[180]. Trade leads to specialization, contributes to the total factor productivity (TFP), and offers comparative advantages for the other countries. It also expands potential markets that allow the domestic companies to take advantage of economies of scale and to diffuse technology, innovation and managerial practices through close alliances with the foreign firms. The TFP growth rates in the long run are higher for the countries that exhibit more open and less distorted international trade sector. The TFP growth improves after the reforms on trade liberalization. Chile has been more benefited from trade liberalization as compared to other countries (Mexico) in the region because of faster economic and structural reforms. Chile pioneered the trade liberalization in the 70's and has also led the process all through the 80's and early 90's. Bolivia, Mexico, Venezuela, Brazil (to a lesser extent) experienced the trade reforms considerably during the late 80's and all other countries in the Latin America and the Caribbean (LAC) region began the trade reforms process in early 1990's. Brazil and Venezuela liberalized their tariff- administration and Argentina, Colombia and Peru have also been dynamic in conducting the trade liberalization process. The task of liberalization of international trade has been achieved through a balanced reduction of all trade restrictions, sharp decrease in tariff and para-tariff, and reduction of non-tariff barriers. The non-tariff barriers have been even withdrawn in the Chile and Peru in the process of liberalization.

Although the processes of structural reforms throughout the region have shared the same principles, they have differed in their time of initiation and in the breadth and depth of their specific reforms. Regarding the time of initiation, Chile was the pioneer of market-oriented reforms in the mid-1970s. In the mid-1980s and after a macroeconomic crisis topped by hyperinflation, Bolivia took important steps in ensuring fiscal and monetary stability, and it liberalized its financial system and trade regime. This pattern of crisis followed by economic reforms was repeated in Mexico in the late 1980s, in Argentina, Peru, and Nicaragua in the early 1990s, and, more recently, in Brazil, El Salvador, and Venezuela. Colombia and Costa Rica stand out as cases where structural reforms were not implemented in a crisis environment. The process of structural reforms has also been heterogeneous in other related aspects. While the region as a whole has advanced in certain reforms areas more than in others, the sequencing, depth and contents of the reforms have differed from country to

[180] Harrison A (1996): Openness and Growth – A Time-series, Cross-country Analysis for Developing Countries, *Journal of Development Economics*, 48 (2), March, 419-447.

country. Improving economic integration is only a part of the measures that a government should adopt to improve increases in real GDP per inhabitant and in socio-economic welfare.

The reduction in the average level and dispersion of tariff and para-tariff charges as well as the sharp reduction of non-tariff barriers is where reforms have been the deepest and most generalized in the region. These policy changes have brought about a marked increase in the trade intensity of the reforming economies. For the early reformers, among them Bolivia, Chile, Costa Rica, and Mexico, the expansion of international trade as a share of GDP, occurred mostly in the 1986-89 period. In the 1990s, the Argentina, Brazil, Paraguay, and Uruguay constituents of Mercosur experienced very high growth rates of the volume of trade. While the respective trade shares of Colombia, Mexico, and Peru increased rapidly (certainly as result of the liberalization process), the improvement was not as large in the oil-exporting economies of Ecuador and Venezuela despite a liberalization program similar to that of the former countries (especially Colombia). However, the tariff and quantitative restrictions often impede the process of trade liberalization. The higher is the average level of dispersion of tariffs and para-tariffs in terms of custom duties and taxes; more is the distortion of international trade. The measure applied to evaluate the level of tariffs and para-tariffs is the weighted average rate of tariff and para-tariff charges that is used to weigh their respective shares in regional or global imports[181]. The trade reforms in the LAC countries seeded the privatization concept. Consequently, Mexico during 1987 and Argentina during 1991-92 had showed *ad hoc* steep rises in the basic economic indicators as a result of the privatization programs. A study on diffusion of technology via international trade from industrial countries to Latin America evaluates the role played by international trade within the region in this process of technology diffusion. The estimates of the study suggest the existence of trade-related technology diffusion from the North. The results are robust for different specifications of the model. Evidence is also found suggesting that trade among the Latin American countries serves as an additional mechanism by which the technology from the industrial countries is indirectly diffused across the region[182]. Latin American countries which had previously planned tariffs were left without the benefits of special safeguards. Nevertheless, the impulse to trade liberalization in many countries was reinforced by that Agreement. The later emergence of numerous regional trade agreements (notably MERCOSUR, the Andean Group, the Central American common market, the Caribbean Group, Mexico entering NAFTA) and bilateral accords (Chile with Mexico, Canada and several countries) also contributed to a reduction in the levels of protection in many sectors, including agriculture.

The most common pattern of economic reforms in Latin America has been, first, radical liberalization, and second, implementation of prudential norms that moderated the initial liberalization. The policy changes related to the financial system (namely, the removal of interest-rate controls, elimination of mandated credit to "priority" sectors, privatization of state banks, liberalization of the foreign investment regime, and more recently, improvements in the regulatory framework) have improved both the banking system and the stock market. The traditional view about fiscal and monetary policies in developing countries (and

[181] Pritchett L and Sethi G (1994): Tariff Rates, Tariff Revenue and Tariff Reforms- Some New Facts, *World Bank Economic Review*, 8 (1), 1-16.

[182] Blyde Juan (2004): Trade and Technology Diffusion in Latin America, *The International Trade Journal*, 18 (3), Fall, 177-197.

particularly in LAC) is that they are pro-cyclical, contributing to deepen business cycles[183]. It has been argued that governments relax their policies during booms and restrict them during busts, due to weak institutions, unfavorable political-economic equilibrium, and volatile access to international capital markets. The most common pattern of financial reforms in the LAC countries has been towards radical liberalization and implementation of prudential norms that moderated the initial process of liberalization. However, growth has been inadequate in the post-reforms period not because of the failure of reforms to yield the expected growth payoff on the basis of international experience, but because of the combination of an unfavorable external environment with the insufficient depth and breadth of reforms. A common feature in Latin America during the early phases of the reforms was the appreciation of exchanges rates. Changes in exchange rates can have differing effects across farm sizes, and therefore longer-term changes in exchange rates can affect the size distribution of the agricultural sector.

The performance of the LAC countries since the reforms were initiated in the mid-eighties had shown mixed results. Their annual growth rate for the referred period was 3.9 percent though the performance widely differed. During 1950-1980, the region witnessed relatively higher growth rates of 5.0 percent per annum on an average. The decennial growth of GDP among the Latin American countries is exhibited in Table 5.1.

**Table 5.1. Growth of GDP in Latin American Countries (In percent)**

| Countries/Period | 1951-60 | 1961-70 | 1971-80 | 1981-1990 | 1991-2000 | 2003 |
|---|---|---|---|---|---|---|
| Argentina | 2.9 | 4.4 | 2.8 | -0.6 | 4.6 | 8.6 |
| Brazil | 6.8 | 6.1 | 8.7 | 1.7 | 2.6 | -0.4 |
| Chile | 4.0 | 4.3 | 2.7 | 3.2 | 6.0 | 3.3 |
| Colombia | 4.7 | 5.2 | 5.4 | 3.7 | 2.6 | 3.7 |
| Costa Rica | 7.3 | 6.8 | 5.5 | 2.3 | 4.4 | 6.4 |
| Ecuador | 5.0 | 4.8 | 9.0 | 1.8 | 1.8 | 2.5 |
| Mexico | 6.1 | 7.0 | 6.7 | 1.9 | 3.3 | 1.2 |
| Paraguay | 2.8 | 4.7 | 8.7 | 3.1 | 2.8 | 2.5 |
| Peru | 5.5 | 5.1 | 3.9 | -0.8 | 4.7 | 4.1 |
| Uruguay | 2.2 | 1.6 | 3.1 | 0.2 | 3.2 | 2.3 |
| Venezuela | 7.6 | 6.0 | 1.9 | -0,5 | 2.1 | -9.3 |

Source: Economic Commission for Latin America and Caribbean (ECLAC).

Evidence from Latin America and the Caribbean countries show that in the late 1980s and 1990s a transition occurred from industrial policies associated with the import substitution model to industrial policies suitable for outwards-oriented economies. Measures such as export processing zones, grants and fiscal incentives aimed at promoting technological modernization, and policies to promote small and medium enterprise development replaced traditional direct subsidies and fiscal incentives[184]. During the 1990s, the outward orientation strategy has become significant among the countries with emerging markets. Latin America and Africa, unsatisfactory performance in the transitional economies

[183] Hausmann R., Alberto R, Rudolf Hommes and Stein Ernesto H (1996): *Budget Institutions and Fiscal Performance in Latin America,* NBER Working Papers, WP-W5588, May.

[184] World Trade Organization (2006): World Trade Report-2006, World Trade Organization, Geneva.

and the financial crisis in Asia raised doubts regarding the capacity of outward orientation to promote development. Empirical work regarding the growth benefits of openness looked more promising initially, but this work has been challenged more recently on methodological grounds. Interest in the linkages between trade reforms, inequality and poverty has also revived, and results have confirmed there can be no simple general conclusion about the relationship between trade liberalization and poverty[185].

There has been a steep decline in the growth rates to the extent of 1.4 percent per annum in the LAC countries during the decade of 1980. The growth resumed in 1990's, that was lower than the growth rate of 3.4 percent per annum achieved during 1951-81 period. One of the factors that contributed significantly to the collapse of the economy of Latin American countries during 90's was the region's dependence on volatile capital flows. Growth before 1997 coincided with record capital inflows, some attracted by privatization. As a result, currencies became overvalued, hurting exports and local producers, and leading to big current account-deficits. The economy of the region was fist hit in 1994-95, with Mexico's devaluation followed by emerging-market investors suffered big losses in mid-1998when Russia defaulted. Among the reforms leaders, Argentina, Bolivia, Chile and Uruguay emerged as star performers with an average growth rate of 4.4 percent per annum during 1991-2000 as against the average annual growth rate of 3.2 percent achieved during 1951-1980 period. These countries also stood above the average growth of the LAC region that accounted for 3.4 percent during 1991-2000. The other countries of the region including Brazil, Columbia, Ecuador, Jamaica, Mexico, Paraguay and Venezuela have shown a declining trend in the referred period. The growth rate for this group of countries has fallen from 5.7 percent in 1951-1980 to 2.0 percent per annum during 1991-2000, which was even below the average growth rate of the LAC region. Costa Rica has been growing at the pace of 6.5 percent per annum during the base period but had shown only 4.4 percent growth rate during the latter period. The decline in the growth rate was caused largely due to the instable political conditions and lower contribution of factors of production to GDP.

The trade policy in Latin America and the Caribbean (LAC) had involved very high levels of protection and of government intervention in the pre-reforms period. The active pursuit of import substitution policies reduced the openness and efficiency of the regional economies. It also increased their external vulnerability, as they became dependent on a narrow range of export products, with little ability to absorb external shocks. This state of affairs changed markedly in the 1980s and 1990s, when most countries of the region moved to liberalize their trade regime. Trade policy reform in LAC in the 1990s has been both widespread and extensive, and the region now shows a fairly open trade regime. Such a sharp policy reversal clearly had an impact on trade flows, and those effectively underwent significant changes in the past decade[186]. The Latin American countries have not had much experience with competition policies in the past. Combined with restrictive trade policies, the absence of competition policies has often led to monopolized domestic markets.

The strong trade liberalizations in Latin America during the 1980s and the 1990s have introduced a good measure of import competition, but trade policies alone are not sufficient to create a competitive environment in an economy. The presence of non-traded goods, vertical

---

[185] Winters, L.A., McCulloch, N. and McKay, A. (2004): Trade liberalization and poverty: the evidence so far, *Journal of Economic Literature*, 42, 72-115.

[186] Loser Claudio M and Guerguil Martin (1999): Trade and Trade Reform in Latin America and the Caribbean in the 1990's, *Journal of Applied Economics*, 2 (1), 61-96.

integration, monopolized distribution systems, the limited use of trade policies to foster competition, and sometimes the use of anti-dumping measures, countervailing duties, and safeguards as protective devices have constrained the effectiveness of trade policy as an instrument of competition policy. Competition policies, such as anti-trust, merger controls, and other regulatory means, can prevent the abuse of market power, dominance, exclusionary practices, and complicity among competitors and domestic competition is found increased by foreign ownership and liberalized investment regimes. These latter provisions provide a market presence that enhances competition. A study discusses that trade, competition policies are essential complements, and when used together they can lead to higher levels of welfare. There are of course tensions between these two policies that arise from globalization, regional policies, technical barriers, certain forms of industrial policies, and macroeconomic exigencies[187].

A study examines individual trade policy preferences across 17 countries in Latin America with the focus on whether skilled or unskilled workers are more likely to support liberalized trade and the country characteristics, such as factor endowments, alter the preferences of skilled and unskilled workers. Based on the standard Heckscher-Ohlin model and the Stolper-Samuelson theorem, wage inequality in developing countries will decrease under free trade and unskilled workers will benefit. The findings of the study discusses that on average skilled workers are more likely than unskilled workers to support free trade in Latin American countries. Separate country regressions reveal that this pattern is only statistically significant in 8 out of 17 Latin American countries. However, there are no countries in our sample in which unskilled workers are statistically more likely to support free trade than skilled workers, not even in the lowest skill-endowed country in the sample. The analysis of the study also reveals that people from Latin American countries with higher GDP, faster growth, more cropland and a longer period of time since reform were more likely on average to support free trade[188].

## International Economic Environment

The effects of the economic crisis of 90's among the larger countries of Latin America, Brazil appears as the most vulnerable economy. Brazil needs to take further steps to reduce its twin deficits in the current account and the public budget, to make its exchange rate policy flexible and to implement additional structural reforms. Chile, though hit hard by a terms of trade shock, is structurally healthy. Weaker regional demand and the loss of competitiveness associated with the Asian crisis will deteriorate Argentina's external accounts and provoke a significant slowdown. Because of its heavy dependence on the Brazilian market, Argentina will face severe problems if Brazil falls into a crisis. Mexico benefits from its significant export diversification and its close integration to the U.S. economy but faces severe pressures from lower oil prices and, especially, from its weak banking sector. Capital controls, though popular, are no solution at times of crisis. A correction of the fundamental macroeconomic

[187] Rajapatirana Sarath (1994): The Interface of Trade, Investment and Competition Policies: Issues and Challenges for Latin America, World Bank, Latin America and Caribbean Department, Report # 009.

[188] Beaulieu, Eugene, Yatawara, Ravindra and Wang, Wei Guo (2005): Who Supports Free Trade in Latin America?, *The World Economy*, 28 (7), 941-958.

imbalances, on the other hand, is a necessary but not sufficient condition to prevent currency crises[189]. The privatization policies emerging as a driver of globalization in Latin American countries has received much criticism in terms of ineffective management of corporate ventures, lack of proper resources management and political interventions. The success of privatizations is enhanced by two complementary policies: re-regulation or deregulation of industries previously shielded from competitive forces; and an effective corporate governance framework that facilitates privatized firms' access to capital at lower costs. Overall, the empirical record shows that privatization leads to increased profitability and productivity, firm restructuring, fiscal benefits, output growth and even quality improvements. Most cases of privatization failure can be linked to poor contract design, opaque processes with heavy state involvement, lack of re-regulation and a poor corporate governance framework[190].

The process of structural reforms has also been heterogeneous in other related aspects. While the region as a whole has advanced in certain reforms areas more than in others, the sequencing, depth and contents of the reforms have differed from country to country. Improving economic integration is only a part of the measures that a government should adopt to improve increases in real GDP per inhabitant and in socio-economic welfare. The reduction in the average level and dispersion of tariff and para-tariff charges as well as the sharp reduction of non-tariff barriers is where reforms have been the deepest and most generalized in the region. These policy changes have brought about a marked increase in the trade intensity of the reforming economies. For the early reformers, among them Bolivia, Chile, Costa Rica, and Mexico, the expansion of international trade as a share of GDP, occurred mostly in the 1986-89 period. In the 1990s, the Argentina, Brazil, Paraguay, and Uruguay constituents of MERCOSUR experienced very high growth rates of the volume of trade. While the respective trade shares of Colombia, Mexico, and Peru increased rapidly (certainly as result of the liberalization process), the improvement was not as large in the oil-exporting economies of Ecuador and Venezuela despite a liberalization program similar to that of the former countries (especially Colombia). However, the tariff and quantitative restrictions often impede the process of trade liberalization. The higher is the average level of dispersion of tariffs and para-tariffs in terms of custom duties and taxes; more is the distortion of international trade. The measure applied to evaluate the level of tariffs and para-tariffs is the weighted average rate of tariff and para-tariff charges that is used to weigh their respective shares in regional or global imports[191]. The trade reforms in the LAC countries seeded the privatization concept. Consequently Mexico during 1987 and Argentina during 1991-92 had showed *ad hoc* steep rises in the basic economic indicators as a result of the privatization programs. A study on diffusion of technology via international trade from industrial countries to Latin America evaluates the role that international trade within the region plays in this process of technology diffusion. The estimates of the study suggest the existence of trade-related technology diffusion from the North.

---

[189] Esquivel, Gerardo and Larrain, Felipe (1998): *Latin America Confronting the Asian Crisis*, Pontificia Universidad Catolica de Chile, Working Paper, December.

[190] Lopez de Silanes, Florencio and Chong, Alberto (2003): *The Truth about Privatization in Latin America*, Yale ICF Working Paper No. 03-29, October.

[191] Pritchett L (1996): Measuring Outward Orientation in LDCs- Cant it be Done? *Journal of Development Economics*, 49 (2), 307-335.

# FREE TRADE AGREEMENTS

There have been varying arguments on the impact of trade agreements on the economy and welfare measures. It has been concluded in one of the studies that the preferential trade agreements are mostly welfare reducing since the partner countries might end up with severe welfare losses due to substantial amount of trade diversion[192]. Another study finds that Free Trade Areas constitute a potential threat to the world trading system because these types of agreements are, in general, trade diverting and they lead to formation of new interest groups who oppose the multilateral tariff reductions[193]. Interestingly, some researchers present a completely different picture about the implications of bilateral trade agreements. Regional trade agreements might provide trading blocs with stronger incentives to pursue multilateral trade liberalization since establishing these types of agreements allows small countries to deal more effectively with large trading blocs in the form of Free Trade Associations wherein member countries can choose their external tariff rates freely.

A study focuses on identifying preconditions that will ensure the sustainability of a Free Trade Area of the Americas (FTAA). It argues that the macro, micro, and political conditions advanced in the literature to measure a country's ability to compete internationally, while necessary, are not sufficient to ensure the success and permanence of a free trade agreement. Instead, two additional financial conditions are needed. The study discusses that each partner in the free trade area needs to have sustainable public debts as determined by the achievement of credible and sustainable structural fiscal balances and the exchange rate regimes across trading partners should be compatible in the sense that adverse shocks in one country do not generate a policy dilemma in other partners between abandoning their exchange rate system or the free trade area. A preliminary analysis of the evidence in the Latin American and Caribbean region as discussed in the referred study shows the importance of these two preconditions. An analysis of debt sustainability reveals that there are a number of countries in the region that need to deal with potential solvency problems before reaching the status of credible partners in a regional trade arrangement. Argentina is already deemed insolvent, and countries such as Ecuador and Venezuela rank high on the list of countries where the issue of debt sustainability can become a serious problem. Not resolving this before reaching a regional trade agreement can threaten its long-term stability. The examination of the compatibility of exchange rate systems across trading partners is also very revealing. Part of the success of NAFTA since the late 1990s and the "impasse" of Mercosur during 1999-2001 had to do with the choices of exchange rate regimes. In both trade areas the share of trade among the partners is very high, and in NAFTA, this includes significant financial transactions[194]. While Mexico was able to use the flexibility of the exchange rate to improve competitiveness following the sharp decline of portfolio flows from US investors into Mexico following the Asian and Russian crises, Argentina had no mechanisms to deal with an adverse shock from Brazil.

---

[192] Bhagwati, J. and A. Panagariya ( 1996), Preferential trading areas and multilateralism: strangers, friends or foes?, in J. Bhagwati and A. Panagariya (eds.), *Free Trade Areas or Free Trade? The Economics of Preferential Trading Agreements* AEI Press.

[193] Krueger, A O (1995), *Free Trade Agreements versus Customs Unions*, NBER WP# W5084

[194] Rojas-Suarez, Liliana (2002): Toward a Sustainable FTAA: Does Latin America Meet the Necessary Financial Preconditions? Institute for International Economics Working Paper No. 02-4.

The share in world GDP of countries that are members of the Latin American Integration Association (LAIA) has increased over the past decade, and so has their participation in international trade, although at a slower pace. In 1998, Mexico was among the world's 20 major importers and exporters of merchandise. Latin America is rich in natural resources, a feature that makes the region one of the most important suppliers to world markets. However, since mid 1980s, the Latin American countries have dramatically transformed their trade regimes as an integral part of economic reforms. This has contributed to the creation of a stronger, more market-friendly climate for both domestic and foreign economic business people. Over the years, the absolute tariff levels and dispersion around the mean have been greatly reduced, while a great number of administrative measures and non-tariff barriers have been eliminated. In these countries, anti-export biases have been removed and enterprises are stimulated towards the production of tradable goods or services. They have also made significant progress in making their export promotion systems compatible with norms established by the WTO. In another global development lower economic growth, recessions in most countries and declining commodity prices, coupled with fears about the effects of devaluations in Asian countries on the competitiveness of Latin American countries have led some countries in the region to protectionist measures. In response to external and internal imbalances, some countries have applied unilateral measures to increase import tariffs, while others have not modified their tariffs or reduced import tariffs even further.

Several emerging market economies have experienced large and persistent trade deficits, following the liberalization reforms of the late 80s and early 90s. The Argentine experience has endorsed the extent to which trade imbalances in the 1990s resulted from income and relative price movements were associated with structural changes from shifts in foreign trade elasticity during the reforms period. New estimates of export and import equations are studied using a broader set of variables than previous studies and distinguishing trade between the member countries of Mercosur and trade with non-Mersocur member countries[195]. The results reveal that considerable export sensitivity to world commodity prices, domestic absorption, and economic activity in Brazil, combined with a high income elasticity of imports, are key determinants of Argentina's trade balance. In particular, a study draws attention on the historical context of economic institutions in the region, and on how these institutions have influenced competition policy enforcement. The study delineates three conditions necessary for competition policy enforcement in Latin American countries- (a) to achieve efficiency and innovation development goals through the promotion of a pro-market policy agenda (b) institutional incentives placed on competition agencies, and (c) the challenge of adverse anti-market social values where the policy is to be implemented. On the contrary, another study reveals that the Coordination and regional integration of competition policy, both generally and within the context of the various customs unions (MEROSUR, Andes Pact, Caricom, FTAA, and WTO) remains an unachieved objective. This is a problem because relevant geographic markets in merger and monopoly cases are not, in general, contained in national boundaries and also because benign international mergers are penalized and delayed by the necessity to undergo review in multiple jurisdictions[196]. No Latin American country appears to focus explicitly on the potential for helpful positive and negative incentive effects on

[195] Catao Luis and Falcetti Elisabetta (2002): Determinants of Argentina's External Trade, *Journal of Applied Economics*, Vol. 5, No. 1, pp 19-57.

[196] Leon Igancio de (2001):, *A Market Process Analysis of Competition Policy in Latin America*, Catholic University of Adres Bellow (UCAB), Venezuela, Working Paper.

economic behavior, and none appears to be engaged in systematic evaluation and measurement of the effects of its policies. Throughout the region, antitrust and other government policies are undercut by the inability of governments and courts to make credible commitments to consistent, transparent decision-making. Still, many Latin American countries are moving in sensible directions by emphasizing well-publicized actions against price fixers, by undertaking competition advocacy programs, and by targeting public sector restraints on competition[197].

In international trade, coalitions have been traditionally formed within countries, and occasionally, among countries, in order to protect the domestic production of particular goods, services, or sectors of the economy. However, oil and interest rate shocks in the world economy during the 1980s, coupled with debt crises and the rise of a more market oriented economic philosophy, brought about a dismantling of organized protectionism in many countries, eroding the coalitions which had so tightly resisted trade liberalization. Alongside regionalism, the world trading order In the last decade has been marked by increased Institutionalization. This has opened up a new, wider set of issues and interests around which future coalitions of countries may well form. Prior to the UR, and during the pre-negotiations of that round, developing countries had formed a coalition of 'the South'. The Group of Ten (G-10), led by a 'Big Five' comprising Argentina, Brazil, Egypt, India and Yugoslavia, formed as soon as the US began its push to launch a new round of trade negotiations. The coalition of developing countries successfully blocked some aspects of the US initiatives. However, the G-10 soon found itself split in trying to formulate negotiating positions on the various aspects trade[198].

The change in economy has taken place through the free trade policies in Latin America since 1980's, and most of the region's economies have changed from restrictive to open policies. But unlike trade liberalization in Europe, most trade barriers in Latin America have been reduced unilaterally. Recently bilateral or multilateral agreements have been considered, especially preferential trade agreements within the region. A Study evaluates the relevance and desirability of multilateral free trade agreements (such as NAFTA) for the Latin American continent and the Caribbean, with an emphasis on how they affect trade flows[199]. Is a preferential trade agreement among some Latin American countries determined as an economic welfare driver? The evidence strongly suggests little likelihood that these agreements will succeed in Latin America. Paradoxically, the intense liberalization in recent years has made it less likely that such agreements would be beneficial except possibly for agreements between some countries and Brazil, Mexico, or (to a lesser extent) Argentina. The trade policy can be used for protection even without high tariffs or quantitative restrictions through anti-dumping measures, countervailing duties, and safeguard measures, which would limit, rather than promote, competition. Caution should be the guiding principle in the use of these measures and they should be GATT compatible in law, and competition promoting in spirit. However, Latin American countries have recently made impressive progress in trade

---

[197] Owen, Bruce M (2003): *Competition Policy in Latin America*, Stanford Institute for Economic Policy Research (SIEPR) Stanford Law and Economics Olin Working Paper No. 268, October.

[198] Narlikar A (2000): *Bargaining Together in Trade: Developing Countries in Coalition*, D Phil Thesis, Oxford University Press, Oxford.

[199] Michaely Michael (1999): *Trade Preferential Agreements in Latin America: An Ex-Ante Assessment*, The World Bank Policy Research Working Paper Series, No. 1583.

reforms; there has been limited use of competition policies[200]. The spatial attributes in a country make significant effects on trade and generally do not correlate with other determinants of income. However, merely examining the correlation between trade and income cannot identify the cause and effect relationship between these two variables. In this context a study constructed the measures of the geographic component of countries' trade and uses those measures to obtain instrumental variables estimates of the effect of trade on income. The results provide no evidence that ordinary least-squares estimates overstate the effects of trade, though they suggest that trade has a positive effect on income in developing countries[201].

A significant cross-section of commentators from countries in the weaker half of the Basin, particularly those that make up the Commonwealth Caribbean, has not persuaded that NAFTA and other macro-phenomena offer any hope for countries in the periphery. It is argued that the winners will be among those countries that restructure their political-economic base while rigorously negotiating their terms of entry into the free trade agreement area. Indeed, much of the outcome will be politically determined and cannot be entirely 'read off' from existing economic structures and relationships. The production sharing practice followed by the multinational companies in the LAC countries as a result of the globalization process also helped in gearing up the export competitiveness. A comparative case study approach has been conducted to explore the inter-organizational dynamics of the Mexican apparel industry's post-NAFTA export dynamism, and it assesses the upgrading prospects that this dynamism entails for exporters in Mexico. The results of fieldwork conducted in three apparel-producing clusters in north, central, and southern Mexico are discussed. The key finding from this commodity chain analysis of linkages between US clients and local producers is that NAFTA-inspired full-package networks provide opportunities for some apparel-manufacturing clusters to upgrade their operations beyond the assembly-export role traditionally associated with Mexico's *maquiladora* plants[202]. Evidence of industrial upgrading includes expanded employment opportunities in activities such as textile production, the generation of linkages to local suppliers, and improved working conditions in plants producing for brand-name clients.

Business plays a critical yet poorly understood role in trade policymaking. An analytical framework that focuses on the distribution of business trade preferences, discusses the forces that cause those preferences to change, and the ability of different groups to exert political influence over policy in reference to Mexico in the 1980s and 1990. Large exporting firms increased their weight due to shifts in the international context, the condition of the domestic economy, and previous government policies. Policymakers granted political access to players whose economic and political leverage had risen, typically those who controlled numerous investment resources and sought out a direct role in policymaking. Many of these players also favored free trade. Business participation in trade policy reflects these patterns. Large, outward-oriented firms played an increasingly important role in Mexico's adoption of free trade policies over the 1980s and early 1990s. Analytical explanations have been developed

---

[200] Rajapatirana Sarath (1994): The Interface of Trade, Investment and Competition Policies: Issues and Challenges for Latin America, World Bank, Latin America and Caribbean Department, Report # 009.

[201] Frankel Jaffery A and Romer David (1999): Does Trade Cause Growth? *American Economic Review*, Vol. 89, No. 3, 379-399.

[202] Bair Jennifer (2002): Beyond the Maquila Model – NAFTA and the Mexican Apparel Industry, *Industry and Innovation*, 9 (3), 203-205.

and tested in reference to the motivations that drove the process of economic integration known as Mercosur (Southern Cone Common Market). The hypotheses tested are those that focus on elite considerations of geo-political, political economic and domestic political factors when deciding to participate in international economic integration. The study found that policy elites in Mercosur member states have been primarily driven by domestic political considerations when they have furthered the integration process. This leads to the conclusion that Mercosur is not likely to develop supranational governance institutions present in the European Union, as policy elites in Mercosur member states desire to maintain a great deal of domestic policy autonomy[203].

Mercosur member states signed a Protocol for the Defense of Competition in 1996 but congressional approval is pending to make it enforceable. The Protocol provides mechanisms to curb business anti-competitive practices; calls for the convergence of domestic competition laws; and provides an agenda for surveying public policies that limit, restrict, falsify, or distort competition conditions and affect trade among member countries. The Protocol calls upon member countries to undertake preparations to set common standards and mechanisms. Argentina's enactment of a new Defense of Competition Law in 1999, which aligns the Argentine competition policy regime with that of Brazil, may help harmonization in this area. Both the Protocol for the Defense of Competition and the mentioned working group could form a basis from which to build regional disciplines on investment incentives. Thus, the task of introducing these disciplines should be closely related to the defense of competition, both at the national as well as the regional level, following the experience of the EU.

## Trade and Monetary Reforms

The impact of increased global economic integration on national and regional environmental standards has been studied in general by a large number of researchers. However not many studies are available on the institutional reforms in reference to the Latin America. A study reveals the role of market mechanisms in facilitating the dissemination of environmental standards from greener nations to less green ones and the impact of international agreements on trans-border environmental problems[204]. It argues that current regional and international governance mechanisms are adequate to enable nations which have the resources and the commitment to improve environmental quality to do so, either on their own or in cooperation with other nations with similar values and resources. The most common pattern of economic reforms in Latin America has been, first, radical liberalization, and second, implementation of prudential norms that moderated the initial liberalization. The policy changes related to the financial system (namely, the removal of interest-rate controls, elimination of mandated credit to "priority" sectors, privatization of state banks, liberalization of the foreign investment regime, and more recently, improvements in the regulatory framework) have improved both the banking system and the stock market. The traditional view about fiscal and monetary policies in developing countries (and particularly in LAC) is

---

[203] Kaltenthaler Karl and Mora Frank O (2002): Explaining Latin American Economic Integration – The Case of MERCOSUR, *Review of International Political Economy*, 9 (1), 72-97.

[204] Vogel David (1997): Trading Up and Governing Across – Transnational Governance and Environment Protection, *Journal of European Public Policy*, 4 (4), 556-571.

that they are pro-cyclical, contributing to deepen business cycles. It has been argued that governments relax their policies during booms and restrict them during busts, due to weak institutions, unfavorable political-economic equilibrium, and volatile access to international capital markets. The most common pattern of financial reforms in the LAC countries has been towards radical liberalization and implementation of prudential norms that moderated the initial process of liberalization. However, growth has been inadequate in the post-reforms period not because of the failure of reforms to yield the expected growth payoff on the basis of international experience, but because of the combination of an unfavorable external environment with the insufficient depth and breadth of reforms.

Despite an enormous literature, that has analyzed the comparative experiences of Latin America and Asia in post-World War II trade policy, almost no attention has been paid to the comparative experience prior to the wars. Even a cursory look at the best available empirical evidence reveals tremendous contrasts between the two regions. Latin America had the highest tariff barriers on earth before 1914; Asia had the lowest. Protected economy of Latin America showed an explosive growth performance during the post World-War II, while Asia registered some of the worst[205]. Generally, global economic downturns have led to regulation and contraction, generating a situation where the hegemonic leader has to recast the rules for the new 'post-crisis' order. Since 1914 but especially from the 1930s onwards, the US felt responsible for leading a crusade towards free trade. The trade liberalization has become mixed with other causes, including the conflation of markets and political freedoms under US leadership. Often a menace of an enemy was necessary to garner consensus on further liberalization. After the 1930 crisis, when countries adopted *beggarthy-neighbor* measures, US took the initiatives to halt the wave of protectionism and thereby reduce political tensions[206]. Such move had affected the Latin American countries to develop an economic nationhood concept and work on developing trade and economic policies for mutual benefit.

For over 40 years after the Second World War, Latin America together with developing countries did not perceive the GATT as a friendly, fruitful institution to promote their interests, for a mix of both ideological and pragmatic reasons. Inward-oriented Industrialization and nationalist Ideologies of development prevailed, turning trade relations into the crux of the North-South debate. Few Latin American countries were members of the GATT and the remaining were remained either detached altogether or were sleeping partners in the GATT, with a nominal exception to this general trend marked by contributions to the working of the trade and economic dispute settlement mechanism[207]. But by and large, the insignificance of developing countries' markets had so far been perceived as unworthy of the effort of pressing for their opening. The result was negligible obligations for developing countries together with disproportionately small trade liberalization in those sectors of immediate interest to them[208]. The trade negotiations had at best a marginal impact on the domestic policy process and by the mid-1980s this picture had changed significantly. To begin with, several Latin American countries became major exporters of manufactured goods,

---

[205] Clemens Michael A and Jeffery G Williamson (2002): Closed Jaguar, Open Dragon: Competing Tariffs in Latin America and Asia before World War II, NBER Working Paper #9401, December.

[206] Tussie, Diana (1987): *The Less Developed Countries and the World Trading System: A Challenge to the GATT*. New York: St. Martin's Press.

[207] Weston Ann and Valentina Delich (2003): Settling Disutes, in Tussie Diana (Ed.), *Trade Negotiations in Latin America- Problems and Prospects*, New York Palgrave-Macmillan, 2003.

[208] Tussie, Diana (1987): *op. cit.*

including in the sectors in which it was previously assumed they lacked comparative advantages. Further, as competition among the major trading players intensified, the continued opening and greater contestability of Latin American markets became a more valued asset. The Latin American countries overcame their former defensive policies and made a strategic shift in the 1990s when an institutional reforms approach to trade and financial liberalization was adopted. The countries of LAC region participated in the Uruguay round with a commitment towards unilateral reforms to signal the path to medium-term economic objectives and provide an anchor for reforms.

Most of the Latin American countries began to open their international business opportunities to the rest of the world in 80's. This process has made significant improvement in the structural adjustments program along with the debt management strategies. It has helped the Latin American countries to overcome the industrial and trade policy of import substitution of over four decades. During the late 80's and early 90's a large number of countries began to lower their levels of protection and bent their energies towards international trade reforms with the increasing assistance of the multilateral institutions. Trade reforms process proceeded at a faster pace and tariff barriers were reduced significantly. There has been a significant transition in the international relations and business partnering of Latin American countries with the rest of the world in the post 80's period that has reflected in the economic and technological growth of some countries like Mexico, Brazil, Chile and Peru. The recent trade liberalization policies of the Latin American countries have sought to reserve the protectionist policies and open the scope for foreign direct investment and joint ventures in the public and private sector industries. Regional integration such as NAFTA, Mercosur and FTAA has been flourishing in Latin American countries since the 1990s. In addition to these multi-countries FTAs, many bilateral FTAs have also emerged both among Latin American countries and extra-regional countries.

Liberalization originating in multilateral trade negotiations should in principle affect both Industrial and agricultural products in a balanced way. There is, for instance, no economic reason to limit offers of total tariff elimination to industrial products. In the same way that developing economies in the Uruguay round were expected to, and did, fall in line with more liberal trade regimes affecting industrial products, the new round should remove the obstacles that still affect agricultural trade at a much faster pace than further liberalization affecting industrial products. The information on gross national product at purchasing power parity rates (GNP-PPP) and total (imports plus exports) trade for most Latin American and Caribbean economies has been presented in Table 5.2 which reveals that the impact of further trade liberalization is likely to be greater in economies with greater trade flows.

It emerges from trade data exhibited in the above Table that Mexico is by far the most important trading economy in Latin America: its total trade in 1999 accounted for nearly 45 per cent of total Latin American trade, representing almost three times total trade from the second most important Latin American trading nation - Brazil - and 80 per cent more than total Mercosur trade. Mercosur's total trade was about 45 per cent of total trade in all other Latin American and Caribbean economies, Mexico excluded. The GNP- purchasing power parity (PPP) data (1999) of Mercosur represented 48.7 per cent of total GNP-PPP of the region of which Brazil accounts for 33.9 per cent, Mexico 24 per cent, the Andean Community (AC) as a whole about 16.7 per cent and Chile 4 per cent. All other economies together thus account for around 6 per cent of the aggregate. The data exhibited in the above Table reveals the countries' comparative leverage in negotiations, given the small size of all

Latin American and Caribbean economies compared to major developed economies. However, little indication of the importance of multilateral negotiations for each particular economy is made.

**Table 5.2. Latin American and Caribbean Gross National Product and Total Trade**

| Region/Trade Blocs | Country | GNP (in US$ billion) | Total Trade (in US$ billion) |
|---|---|---|---|
| Andean Community | *Andean Community* | *523.0* | *79.4* |
| | Bolivia | 17.8 | 3.3 |
| | Colombia | 237.2 | 22.2 |
| | Ecuador | 32.3 | 8.6 |
| | Peru | 110.7 | 12.7 |
| | Venezuela | 124.9 | 32.6 |
| Caribbean Community | *Caribbean Community* | *30.6* | *17.8* |
| | Bahamas | 3.0 | 3.8 |
| | Barbados | 3.3 | 1.4 |
| | Belize | 1.1 | 0.5 |
| | Dominica | 0.4 | 0.2 |
| | Grenada | 0.6 | 0.2 |
| | Guyana | 2.8 | 1.2 |
| | Jamaica | 8.5 | 4.4 |
| | St. Kitts | 0.3 | 0.1 |
| | St. Lucia | 0.7 | 0.1 |
| | St. Vincent and Grenadines | 0.5 | 0.6 |
| | Trinidad and Tobago | 9.4 | 5.3 |
| Central American Common Market | *Central American Common Market* | *109.7* | *39.6* |
| | Costa Rica | 20.7 | 13.6 |
| | El Salvador | 25.1 | 6.5 |
| | Guatemala | 39.0 | 9.3 |
| | Honduras | 14.3 | 8.1 |
| | Nicaragua | 10.6 | 2.2 |
| Mercosur | *Mercado Común del Sur (Mecosur)* | *1525.7* | *154.1* |
| | Argentina | 414.1 | 46.6 |
| | Brazil | 1061.7 | 98.1 |
| | Paraguay | 22.5 | 3.6 |
| | Uruguay | 27.4 | 5.8 |
| NAFTA | *NAFTA* | | |
| | Mexico | 752.0 | 278.4 |
| Other Latin American Countries | *Others* | | |
| | Chile | 125.7 | 29.9 |
| | Dominican Republic | 39.1 | 14.5 |
| | Haiti | 11.0 | 1.4 |
| | Panama | 14.1 | 5.0 |
| | Suriname | 1.7 | 1.0 |

GNP-PPP data for all 1999 except for Bahamas, Barbados, Belize and Surinam data represents for 1998.

Source: Word Bank 2000, Trade data from IMF, 1998, ECLAC statistics, 2001.

Economic recovery in Latin America remained subdued in 2003 as Brazil; the largest economy of the region stagnated and Venezuela's economy contracted by 9 per cent. Argentina's GDP recovered strongly which partially offset the decline of the previous years, while Mexico's economy continued to expand moderately. The volume of Latin America's merchandise exports rose by 5 per cent and the contraction of imports in 2001-02 was followed by only a moderate upswing. Nominal export growth of merchandise and commercial services, at 9 per cent and 7 per cent respectively, matched the average growth rates recorded in the 1990s. As the region's export expansion continued to exceed that of imports for both merchandise and commercial services, the regional trade surplus increased further.

The opening of business avenues to the other countries has posed many strategic control and legal issues in the South American region. A review of the antitrust activity in Latin America shows that all the larger countries have active competition agencies using modern economic theories and procedures that rely chiefly on administrative agencies rather than the courts. In many Latin American countries increased openness to international trade probably is more important to consumer welfare than increased local competition in tradable goods and services, but receives less attention[209]. However, no Latin American country appears to focus explicitly on the potential for helpful positive and negative incentive effects on economic behavior, and none appears to be engaged in systematic evaluation and measurement of the effects of its policies. Although Latin American and Caribbean countries have assigned a high priority to increasing exports in recent years substantially transforming their economies in the process - export performance in most cases remains deficient. The interplay between economic freedom, Foreign Direct Investment (FDI) and growth has been found positive during the post 80's period in the Latin American countries. A study reveals that economic freedom in the host country is found to be a positive determinant of FDI inflows into that nation and FDI is positively correlated with economic growth in the host countries of the sample considered[210]. Besides, the arguments in favor of linking labor and environmental standards to trade measures are much more controversial as there are significant doubts on what would be the end impact on exactly those targets which are thought to be worthwhile to pursue. Compulsory minimum standards enforced through trade retaliation measures may end up further hurting abused workers and the environment, a result which is directly in contradiction with the alleged aims of such trade measures[211].

The trade policy in Latin America and the Caribbean (LAC), for many years had involved very high levels of protection and of government intervention. The active pursuit of import substitution policies reduced the openness and efficiency of the regional economies. It also increased their external vulnerability, as they became dependent on a narrow range of export products, with little ability to absorb external shocks. This state of affairs changed markedly in the 1980s and 1990s, when most countries of the region moved to liberalize their trade regime. Trade policy reform in LAC in the 1990s has been both widespread and

[209] Bruce Owen M (2003): *Competition Policy in Latin America, Institute of Economic Policy Research*, Stanford University, Working Paper # 268

[210] Sanchez Blanca R and Clavo Marta Bengoa (2003): Foreign Direct Investment, Economic Freedom and Growth, *European Journal of Political Economy*, 19 (3), 529-545.

[211] Bhagwati J and Srinivasan T N (1996): Trade and Environment: Does Environmental Diversity Detract from the Case fro Free Trade? In Bhagawati J and Hudec (Eds.) *Fair Trade and Harmonization: Prerequisites for Free Trade, Vol 1, Economic Analysis*, The MIT Press, Cambridge, MA.

extensive, and the region now shows a fairly open trade regime. Such a sharp policy reversal clearly had an impact on trade flows, and those effectively underwent significant changes in the past decade. They also coincided with a number of other important changes in the LAC economies, including major structural reforms (with the privatization of many public enterprises and the deregulation of most domestic markets), a surge in investment (itself partly linked to the lower relative prices for capital goods resulting from higher openness), higher capital flows, and a more careful pursuit of macroeconomic policy aimed at preserving financial stability to foster sustainable growth[212].

Economic integration and growth in trade within the Latin American region have created a need for new and major business developments. In this context, the private sector has emerged as the driving force behind international trade and legal initiatives related to trade agreements such as the Andean Pact and Mercosur (Common Market of the South). A survey of the legal history of economic integration reveals that harmonization occurs in areas such as banking, environment protection, insurance, securities, liberal professions, international securities exchange regulations, and transportation[213]. The South American customs union known as Mercosur has contributed significantly to regional trade liberalization. However, by encouraging trade within the group at the expense of trade with nonmembers, Mercosur may limit member countries' access to high-technology imports, an important stimulus to growth. The foreign direct investment policies of the host countries significantly affect the trade movements and such dimensions may be observed in establishing the business relations with Japan- the giant of Asian business. The sets of relationships between the real exchange rate and foreign direct investment, and between foreign direct investment and trade, support two channels through which the real exchange rate affects trade: a direct effect on the relative price of goods and an indirect effect through foreign direct investment[214].

Serious challenges to the hegemony of neo-liberalism have been experienced as the dominant form of economic organization since the end of the Cold War. This resistance is not uniform, nor is it restricted to one site or group of actors. Besides, in many instances, resistance is more to practice than to principle. Events in Asia and Latin America represent low s triumph of liberalism in a post-Cold War era in the region[215]. These factors are more critical for bringing about productivity growth and structural change in the Latin American region. Even for Latin American countries with a more developed industrial base (Argentina, Brazil, Mexico), dynamic efficiency effects from trade liberalization do not come about automatically[216]. The scope for intra-Latin trade of dissimilar products based on comparative costs has expanded modestly in recent decades while exports of primary products have declined in importance for Latin America; they still play a significantly large role. The potential for trade of differentiated, but broadly similar, manufactures has increased among

212 Loser Claudio M and Guerguil Martin (1999): Trade and Trade Reform in Latin America and the Caribbean in the 1990's, *Journal of Applied Economics*, 2 (1), 61-96.

213 Buscaglia Edgardo and Long Clarisa (1996): *Analysis of he legal and Economic Determinants of Integration in Latin America – The Case of MERCOSUR*, School of Law, University of Virginia, Working Paper # 96-I.

214 Golderg Linda and Klevin Michael W (1997): *Foreign Direct Investment, Trade and Real Exchange Rate Linkages in Southeast Asia and Latin America*, NBER Working Paper # 6344.

215 Higgot Richard and Phillips Nicola (1999): *The Limits of Global Liberalization – Lessons from Asia and Latin America*, Center for the Study of Globalization and Regionalization, University of Warwick, Working Paper, 22-98.

216 Djistra A G (2000), Trade Liberalization and Industrial Development in Latin America, *World Development*, 28 (9), 1567-1582.

Argentina, Brazil, and Mexico, but not for intra-Latin bilateral trade involving smaller countries.

The financial investment and banking opportunities matter significantly, determining the international trade and economic growth. Foreign entry into domestic banking markets remains a contentious issue. Whether privatizing a state bank in Brazil or selling a failed bank in Japan, the proposed sale of a large domestic financial institution, possibly to a foreign acquirer, frequently results in a major controversy. Many Asian countries have yet to experience major foreign penetration of domestic banking markets, while Latin American countries have privatized many of their banks and have encouraged foreign banks to enter their domestic markets. Because many Latin American countries opened their markets during the 1990s, and because they have experienced exchange rate and banking crises as well as severe fluctuations in their macro-economies over this period, Latin American countries provide a good laboratory for understanding the effects of foreign bank penetration[217]. However, in building bilateral trade and common markets, it is necessary for the Latin American countries to resolve the regional economic disparities and look for partnering with potential countries in the rest of the world. Markets around the world are becoming more competitive because of changing operating and regulatory environments. One such change--the loosening of trade restrictions--is a macroeconomic policy shift that should have a microeconomic impact on industrial efficiency. Specifically, competitive pressure should discipline or eliminate inefficient producers[218].

The study done by Glick and Moreno (1999) analyzes the role of money, credit, trade and competitiveness variables in signaling currency crises in a sample of East Asian and Latin American countries over the period 1972-1997. The Bivariate tests administered in the study suggest that money and credit, as well as trade and competitiveness variables appear to behave differently around crisis episodes from the periods of tranquility, suggesting that they may help signal currency crises. In multivariate regressions, which allow for the identification of marginal contributions of individual variables, reductions in real domestic credit and in foreign reserves as well as appreciation in the real exchange rate imply increases in the probability of the monetary crisis and lead to the exports decline in the Latin American countries. The study revealed that real exchange rate appreciation appeared to play a greater role in predicting currency crises in East Asia, while foreign reserve losses play a greater role in Latin America due to shrinking exports and low trade competitiveness[219].

Multiple exchange rates, multiple interest rates, protection of domestic products with licenses, quotas, tariffs in the excess of what would have been necessary for infant industries, and a welter of regulations and bureaucratic obstacles to normal business in general have detrimental effects on economic growth. Mainstream economic theory suggests that economic welfare would be maximized when distortions are minimized. Accordingly, a removal of distortions of both macroeconomic and microeconomic nature would have beneficial effects

---

[217] Joe Peck and Rosengren Eric (2000): Implications of the Globalization of the Banking Sector – The Latin American Experience, *New England Economic Review*, Sep., 45-62.

[218] Alam Ila Semenik M and Morisson Andrew R ( 2000): Trade Reform Dynamics and Technical Efficiency – The Peruvian Experience, *World Bank Economic Review*, 14 (2), May, pp. 309-330.

[219] Glick Reuven and Moreno Ramon (1999): *Money and Credit, Competitiveness and Currency Crisis in Asia and Latin America*, Federal Reserve Bank of San Francisco, Pacific Basin Working Paper series No. 99-01, 7-38.

on economic activity and the rate of growth[220]. For the early reformers, among them Bolivia, Chile, Costa Rica, and Mexico, the expansion of international trade as a share of GDP, occurred mostly in the 1986-89 period. In the 1990s, the Argentina, Brazil, Paraguay, and Uruguay constituents of Mercosur experienced very high growth rates of the volume of trade. While the respective trade shares of Colombia, Mexico, and Peru increased rapidly (certainly as a result of the liberalization process), the improvement was not as large in the oil-exporting economies of Ecuador and Venezuela despite a liberalization program similar to that of the former countries (especially Colombia). However, the tariff and quantitative restrictions often impede the process of trade liberalization. The higher is the average level of dispersion of tariffs and para-tariffs in terms of custom duties and taxes; more is the distortion of international trade.

Kamin (1998) describes research comparing the response of inflation to changes in exchange rate competitiveness in various regions of the world with evidence that an empirical relationship between the rate of inflation and the level of the real exchange rate, which was documented for Mexico in previous research contributions, holds for a large set of other countries as well. He argues that such results may pose a dilemma for policy-makers, since it implies that it may not be possible to achieve low inflation and high export competitiveness simultaneously. However, the study demonstrates that the responsiveness of inflation to the real exchange rate has been much higher in Latin America and has distorted the growth of foreign trade despite institutional reforms that were introduced in early 90's by the LAC countries[221]. New empirical work by Hertel and Martin (1999) has shown that a standard tariff cut of 40 per cent in the next round of multilateral trade negotiations would relatively benefit developing more than developed economies. Possible welfare gains would amount to a maximum in the region of 1.5 to 2.0 per cent of total Income for some Asian economies contrasted to 0.1 to 0.2 per cent for most developed economics. Brazil's income would Increase by 0.5 per cent and the rest of Latin America's by 0.2 to 0.3 per cent. This difference between developing and developed countries reflects the fact that tariffs on industrial products in developed economies are much lower than those in developing economies[222].

## TRADE LIBERALIZATION AND PRODUCTIVITY

After decades of weak growth in Latin American countries, the manufacturing sector exports have shown optimistic results in recent years following the international trade agreements. The previous research studies find that the competitive base for export performance in the Latin America and Caribbean (LAC) countries is very narrow and is dominated largely by non-manufactured products like raw materials. However, the countries in the LAC region possess strength in low-end manufacturing and exporting, whereas it is

[220] Igor Paunovic (2000): *Growth and Reforms in Latin America and the Caribbean in the 1990s*, United Nations Economic Commission for Latin America and the Caribbean (ECLAC), Working Paper, Economic Division, May.

[221] Kamin Steven B(1998): *A Multi Country Comparison of the Linkages between Inflation and Exchange Rate Competitiveness*, Federal Reserve bank of US, International Finance Discussion Paper No. 603.

[222] Hertel T and Martin W (1999): *Would Developing Countries gain from Inclusion of Manufacturers in the WTO Negotiations?* Paper Presented at the WTO-WorldBank Conference on Developing Countries in a Millennium Round, Geneva, 20-21 September.

vulnerable to competitive entry and technological change. These processes have meant increasing competition for firms in national and international markets. The LAC countries are urged to increase competitiveness in order to increase employment, production and growth under a context of globalization. The region has been highlighted as an important player in both, as an important source of competitiveness for localized firms and in the reallocation of economic activity. Agglomeration economies and innovations are considered the most important forces in agglomeration leading to increasing competitiveness and to improving living conditions for people living in such regions. The relationship between trade liberalization and manufacturing labor productivity growth for 27 industries in seven Latin American countries from 1970 to 1998 has been studied with the variables export and import growth and a commercial reform index. The analysis of the study captures the various channels through which productivity and trade liberalization have been related. The study finds a significant positive correlation between all the three variables and productivity growth[223].

The factors, which determine the long-run real exchange rate in Argentina, Colombia and Mexico, may be distinguished as real and nominal determinants. Co-integration analysis is utilized to establish that the real exchange rate has an equilibrium relationship with real variables (the terms of trade, capital flows, productivity, and government share of GDP) which excludes nominal variables (nominal exchange rate, money) and central bank intervention. Variance decompositions reveal that among the real variables that determine the real exchange rate, the terms of trade and productivity explain much of the variation in the real exchange rates. The impulse response functions are broadly consistent with theoretical predictions and shocks to the nominal variables have only transitory effects on the real exchange rate[224]. The structural reforms have been initiated in the macro areas including economic activity, international trade, financial markets, generation and use of public resources, governance, and labor markets. Trade leads to specialization, contributes to the total factor productivity and offers comparative advantages for the other countries. It also expands potential markets that allow the domestic companies to take advantage of economies of scale and to diffuse technology, innovation and managerial practices through close alliances with the foreign firms.

The export competitiveness of a country is also significantly driven by the resources availability in the country and harnessing them. These resources may broadly be classified as natural, monetary, research and development, production and market infrastructure and human resources. The relationship between export competitiveness and investment in machinery, allowing for imperfect substitution between domestically produced and imported machinery has been analyzed in reference to the developing countries and a translog export-price function is estimated for developed, export-oriented developing, and import-substituting developing countries in a panel data setting. Between 1967 and 1990, imported machinery helped lower export prices for export-oriented developing countries. The study revealed that innovative effort based on imported technologies can be a precursor to the development of

---

223 Jorge Vera Garcia (2001): From Globalization to Upgrading Value in the Productive Chain in Specialized Agglomerations: Is Local Space Still Important? - Evidence from Mexico, ERSA Conference Paper, European Regional Science Association, Vienna, August.

224 Joyce Joseph P and Kamas Linda (2003): Real and Nominal Determinants of Real Exchange Rates in Latin America – Short-run Dynamics and Long-run Equilibrium, *The Journal of Development Studies*, 39 (6), 155-182.

domestic innovation capabilities, which may ultimately become the main nexus of a country's innovation efforts to boost the export competitiveness[225]. Changes in comparative advantage should reflect changes in factor endowment, but increasingly, changes in trade policies also affect a region's trade performance. Based on the arguments towards comparative advantage thesis, the performance of manufacture exports in a number of Asian and Latin American economies over the period 1981-1997, the revealed comparative advantage indices between economies in East Asia, Southeast Asia and Latin America has been constructed. Although the Revealed Comparative Advantages (RCA) measurement may not distinguish between the factor endowments effects from the trade policy effect, we argue that RCA measures provide indication on the movement in a region's comparative advantage. The evidence strongly suggests that despite the strong export performance experienced by East Asian economies, they are losing their comparative advantage to the lower-tier economies in Southeast Asia and Latin America. Changes in comparative advantage should reflect changes in factor endowment, but increasingly, changes in trade policies also affect a region's trade performance. Although the RCA measurement may not distinguish between the factor endowments effects from the trade policy effect, we argue that RCA measures provide indication on the movement in a region's comparative advantage. The evidence strongly suggests that despite the strong export performance experienced by East Asian economies, they are losing their comparative advantage to the lower-tier economies in Southeast Asia and Latin America[226].

## INVESTMENT ON TRADE

The inflow of market-seeking investments is largely determined by the size, growth rate and perspectives of the host market. Natural resources and labor force are relevant in resource-seeking, export-oriented investments. However, multinational corporations (MNCs) seem to be increasingly involved in so -called 'strategic-asset' seeking investments, in which the relevant location based advantages are related to the physical, communications and technological infrastructure, the skills of the labor force, and so on. Economic and political stability and a sound regulatory framework seem to be necessary but not sufficient preconditions to guarantee a steady flow of FDI when the above mentioned location based advantages are lacking.

In a 'Cournot duopoly' model of international competition between a domestic and foreign firm, it is shown that when the foreign firm has incomplete information about the marginal cost of the domestic firm then the domestic government can use an export subsidy to signal the competitiveness of its firm. This signaling effect strengthens the usual profit-shifting argument for an export subsidy. The optimal export subsidy in the signaling equilibrium may be twice as large as the optimal profit-sharing export subsidy under

---

[225] Mody Ashoka and Yilmaz Kamil(2002): Imported Machinery for Export Competitiveness, *World Bank Economic Review*, Vol. 16, June, 23-48.

[226] Bender, Siegfried and Li, Kui-Wai (2002) : *The Changing Trade and Revealed Comparative Advantages of Asian and Latin American Manufacture Exports*, March, Yale Economic Growth Center Discussion Paper No. 843.

complete information[227]. The subsidies on physical and financial resources including the fiscal incentives attract the foreign direct investments (FDI), which help in augmenting the export competitiveness of specialized goods and services in the region. The findings of one of the studies conducted on the impact of subsidies in FDI and export competitiveness reveal that linkages between the foreign and domestic sectors need to be improved if FDI is to be a vehicle for improving the competitiveness of domestic firms. The openness-growth connection is still an open question in the empirical literature. Although some studies have found that openness has a positive impact on economic performance, others have seriously questioned the significance of this result. One of the studies on Latin American trade issues emphasizes that openness involves more than just trade liberalization[228].

The increasing importance of international capital flows and especially FDI seems to be another relevant component of outward oriented policies. Based on the quarterly data from the late seventies to 2000, the study investigates the effects of liberalization in Mexico, Brazil and Argentina by taking into account trade and FDI growth links. The results suggest that it is important to consider both exports and FDI to ascertain the benefits associated to the outward oriented strategies followed by these countries. New growth-trade theories have emphasized the contribution of international trade to economic growth through its effect on capital accumulation. A study with this focus tests the hypothesis that export oriented sectors attain higher rates of investment using panel data techniques and sectoral data from the Mexican manufacturing industry between 1970 and 1990[229]. Despite the substantial variations in export shares across sectors and over time, the study can find no evidence supportive of the hypothesis that exports lead to capital accumulation. There is evidence that common determinants, such as the real exchange rate, may be behind the correlations between exports and investment rates found in cross-country studies. It has been observed in the previous studies that the economies that have advocated for open international trade gained higher rates of growth influenced by the higher rate of investment and factor productivity.

A study focused on the relationship between entrepreneurship and successful export marketing performance revealed after testing the hypothesis that entrepreneurship is positively related to such performance. The research reveals that entrepreneurial behavior is positively correlated with export marketing behavior, suggesting government actions to boost competitiveness[230]. Contemporary trends in the organization of multinational enterprises (MNEs), developments in regional economic integration, and evidence pertaining to the globalization of innovative activities are suggestive of the need to revisit the question of the contribution of overseas MNE affiliates to the technological capacity of developing countries. The study examining the contribution of European Union (EU) MNEs to the development of technological capacity in Mexico, drawing upon small-scale survey and case study evidence, reaffirms that the main contribution of EU MNEs is that of the long-standing one of MNEs in

---

[227] Collie David and Hviid Morten (1993): Export Subsidies as Signals of Competitiveness, *Scandinavian Journal of Economics*, 95 (3), 327-339.

[228] Cuardos Ana, Orts Vicente and Algnacil Maite (2004): Openness in Growth: Reexamining Foreign Direct Investment, Trade and Output Linkages in Latin America, *The Journal of Development Studies*, 40 (4), 167-192.

[229] Iscan Talan (1998): Exports and Capital Accumulation – Some Empirical Evidence from Mexican Manufacturing Industry, *Applied Economic Letters*, 5 (6), 355-360.

[230] Haar Jerry and Buonafina Moria Ortiz (2002): Entrepreneurial Exporters: The Canadian Experience, *The International Trade Journal*, 16 (1), 31-71.

enhancing aspects of technological know-how in developing countries[231]. Yet the export orientation and status of EU MNE affiliates in Mexico appears to have been enhanced with regional economic integration and the anecdotal evidence from company case studies hints at possibilities for the future generations of technological know-how.

This paper applies an economic approach to empirically investigate differences in inward foreign direct investment patterns between East Asia and Latin America and discusses the implication of regional trade arrangements. International production/distribution networks in East Asia effectively utilize the new economic logic of fragmentation, agglomeration, and optimal internalization and seem to greatly contribute to economic development. The paper examines statistical data for international trade as well as the activities of Japanese and U.S. multinational enterprises (MNEs) and argues that international production/distribution networks, particularly in machinery industries, are extensively developed in East Asia while remaining immature in Latin America. The impact of regional trade arrangements is substantially different depending on whether international production/distribution networks have already been developed or not. Our findings suggest that the impact of FTAA on FDI in Latin America by East Asian MNEs could be either positive or negative, depending on the content of FTAA and accompanying policies. If differentials between intra-regional tariffs and most favored nations based tariffs are kept large, import-substituting FDI from East Asia may stagnate or even decrease. With a proper policy package to nurture international production/distribution networks, on the other hand, FDI from East Asia could be accelerated and contributed to deeper integration of Latin America[232].

The private investment in developing countries is stimulated by real GDP growth, increases in government investment, improvements in financial intermediation, reductions in credit to the government, and declines in world interest rates. An interesting result of an empirical study relates to the important role played by educational development in stimulating private investment[233]. One of the studies suggests two possible outcomes regarding policy competition for FDI. The first is based on a 'positive-sum game', according to which competition produces net benefits for Investors and host economics alike. The reasoning is that governments know the high priority investors attach to the fundamentals' and thus seek to improve domestic supplies of human capital and Infrastructure as well as to ensure political and macro-economic stability. A corollary to this hypothesis is that intensified competition to attract FDI leads governments to 'do a better job on the fundamentals. Hence, in addition to inducing governments to take actions that enhance growth and Productivity levels (even in the absence of additional FDI), those actions are likely to increase the global supply of FDI[234]. The private investment in developing countries is stimulated by real GDP growth, increases in government investment, improvements in financial intermediation, reductions in credit to the government, and declines in world interest rates. An interesting result of an empirical study relates to the important role played by educational development in stimulating

[231] Laura E Martinez Solano and Phelps NA (2003): The Technological Activities of EU MNEs in Mexico, *International Planning Studies*, 8 (1), 53-75.

[232] Kimura Fukunari and Ando Mitsuyo (2005): The Economic Analysis of International Production /Distribution Ventures in East Asia and Latin America: The Trade Implication of Regional Trade Agreements, *Business and Politics*, 7(1).

[233] Ghura Dhaneshwar and Goodwin Barry (2000): Determinants of Private Investment – A Cross-regional Empirical Investigation, *Applied Economics*, 32 (14)1819-1829.

[234] Omen C (1999): *Policy Competition and Foreign Direct Investment*, OECD Development Centre, OECD, Paris.

private investment[235]. Nevertheless, statistically significant adverse effects of external debt on private investment found by other studies could not be confirmed by this study. In addition, the results for the full sample of countries are by no means common across the regions. While real GDP growth stimulated private investment in Asia and Latin America, its effect was not significant in Sub-Saharan Africa (SSA). Also, while government investment stimulated private investment in SSA, it had the opposite effect in Asia and Latin America. In addition, private investment was stimulated by increases in private sector credit in Asia and SSA, but not in Latin America. Also, increases in credit to the government had significant adverse effects on private investment in SSA and Latin America. The political economic consensus in Latin America has played significant role in crafting the trade and economy of the region. The splintering of the MERCOSUR following the Brazilian devaluation in early 1999 has given way to an important re-crafting of the regional vision and a significant expansion of the scope of the regional project. These trends can best be understood as coalescing into a new (and nascent) form of regionalist governance in the countries of the region, in which the MERCOSUR is reconfigured as a vehicle for a new set of developmentalist and strategic objectives). This emerging form of regionalist governance is both causative and indicative of a new political economy both of the sub-region and of the wider region of the Americas, and reflective of the crystallization of a new political economy of development[236].

Most competition to attract investments occurs within regions, not between them. Thus, any international cooperation among governments to help limit the potential damage caused by competition to attract FDI would probably be best envisaged at the regional level rather than the global level. Nonetheless, this being true for most projects, globalization allows increased mobility of investments; high-tech activities are mostly footloose, as illustrated by the case of the Intel investment in Costa Rica, for which the original 'short-list' included 13 Asian and Latin American countries (Spar, 1998). Mercosur has been remarkably successful at increasing intra-regional trade and attracting FDI. The participation of Mercosur member countries in world FDI inflows increased from 1.4 per cent in 1984-89 to 5.9 per cent in 1997-99. Interest in attracting investment flows has engendered competition mostly at regional or sectoral levels. Controversial cases like the automobile industry have led to arguments in favor of disciplines on incentives. Studies about the Impact of FDI on Argentina and Brazil have raised issues which call for more activists FDI related policies. Specifically, multi-national companies (MNC) tend to have huge deficits in their trade relations with developed countries. The contribution of FDI to the growing merchandise trade deficit in both Argentina and Brazil has thus become a critical Issue. While this situation may change In the future, so far only those MNCs engaged in resource-based investments are clearly net exporters. Second, technological spillovers seem to be minimal. MNCs do not devote significant resources to R&D activities, and have seldom created technological networks with suppliers, customers, competitors or research Institutions. In Argentina, a sort of 'rules-based' competition prevailed during 1991-2001, based on strict legal protection of property rights, predictability, and the adoption of market and investor friendly policies. Incentives based competition only surfaced in an automobile regime established in 1991, which included investment incentives and production resources for local producer and a mining regime

[235] Ghura Dhaneshwar and Goodwin Barry (2000): Determinants of Private Investment – A Cross-regional Empirical Investigation, *Applied Economics*, 32 (14), 1819-1829.

[236] Phillips Nicola (2001): Regionalist Governance in the New Political Economy of Development: Re-launching the "Mercosur", *Third World Quarterly*, 22 (4), 565-583.

adopted in 1993, including a 30-year guarantee of no tax increase for investors. Privatizations also had some specific features geared to attract foreign investors. Though the limited fiscal attributions of the Argentine provinces kept sub-national 'fiscal wars' under relatively low ceilings, there is significant anecdotal evidence showing an increase in the use of investment incentives in the late 1990s.

*Chapter 6*

# METHODOLOGICAL CONSTRUCT

The trade partnering between Latin America and Asia is yet to be explored while trade between the European Union and Latin America is growing in importance, currently amounting to $100 billion a year. However, there are potential problems for European businesses seeking to move into this market. North American Free Trade Agreement linking Canada and the USA with Mexico has had a serious impact on European trade with Mexico and the Free Trade Area of the Americas, which aims to further the economic integration of the western hemisphere, and an increasing tendency towards dollar orientation in Latin America will pose additional challenges to European trade and investment in the region.

The recovery in the region's merchandise trade was held back by the sluggish growth of shipments to North America, its principal market, and the failure of some countries in the region to grasp the opportunities provided by the rise in global demand for primary commodities, in particular fuels. The recovery in intra-regional trade, by 9 percent in 2003, did not fully offset its contraction in 2002. The share of intra-regional trade in exports stayed at 15.6 percent in 2003 or more than five percentage points below the 1977 peak level of 21 percent. Merchandise shipments to Western Europe and Asia advanced by 17 percent and 20 percent, to new record levels. Exports to China, the region's largest market in Asia, surged to $9.2 billion, only slightly less than the region's shipments to Africa and the Middle East combined. Exports to the transition economies and Africa rose by more than one third, but even combined account for less than 3 per cent of the region's merchandise exports. The relative growth status of exports and imports in the Latin American region and North America is exhibited in Figure 6.1 (A) and (B).

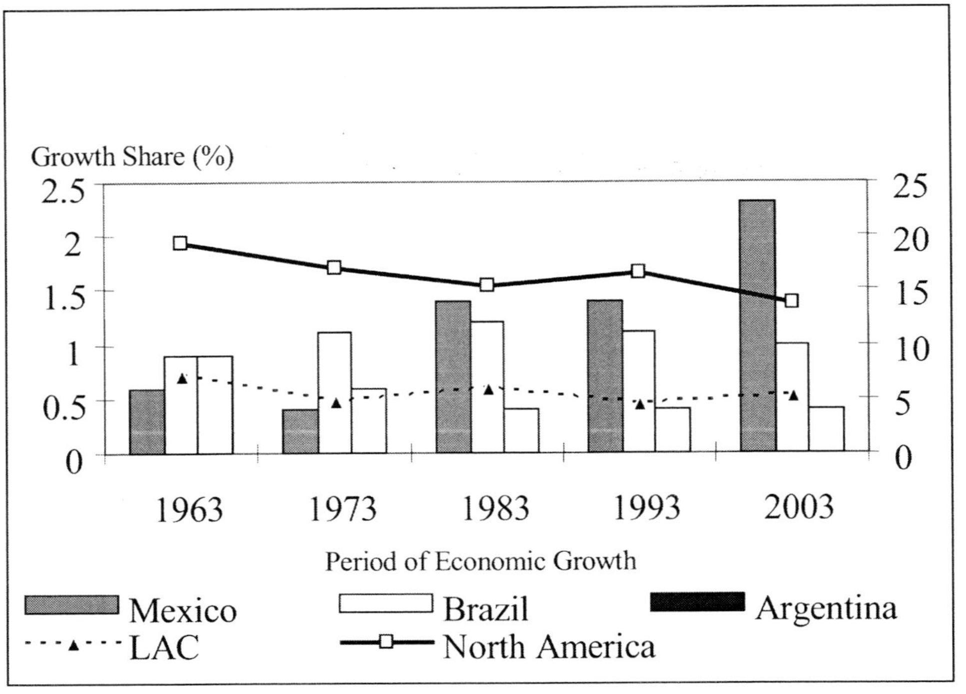


(A)

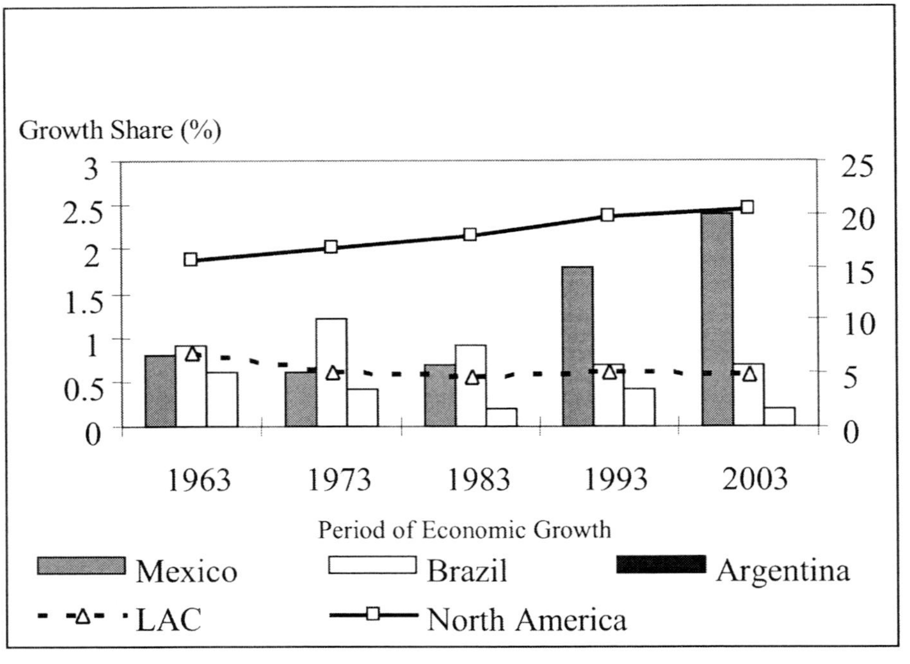


(B)

Figure 6.1. (A) Comparative Status of Exports in North America, LAC Region and Major Latin American Countries (1963-2003); (B) Comparative Status of Imports in North America, LAC Region and Major Latin American Countries (1963-2003).

## TRADE AGREEMENT PATTERN IN LAC COUNTRIES

There are large differences in gross domestic products by sectors among Latin American countries, and the majority of these differences are due to the value of industrial and service sectors. Although the sectoral economic activity has been increased, in per capita terms this value decreased due to the demographic growth that Latin American countries (mainly Mexico and Brazil) had experienced during the last decades. In terms of external trade, it has been found that the outward orientation as the ratio between total exports and GDP increased from 16.1% in 1990 to 32.7% in year 2000. Panama had the highest level in this area (66.5%). Modest growth returned to Latin America and the Caribbean in 2003 and regional GDP advanced by an average 1.3 percent, after a contraction of 0.6 percent in 2002. Argentina continued recovering rapidly after its acute crisis. Brazil, Mexico and Uruguay shared in the broadening of economic recovery during the year. The Andean countries performed well, with Chile, Colombia and Peru recording growth above 3 percent. However, ongoing political uncertainties caused Venezuela's economy to deteriorate further during the first half of the year. Central America grew by an average 3.1 percent and looks set to sustain growth, thanks to the recently signed Central America Free Trade Agreement[237] (CAFTA). The rate of change in the merchandize export in the Latin American countries during 2002 in most of the countries in the region except Costa Rica, Ecuador, Peru and St. Kitts Islands other have shown a downward trend.

The Central American Free Trade Agreement (CAFTA) negotiated between the U.S. and Central America offers opportunities and challenges for the five countries including El Salvador, Guatemala, Honduras, and Nicaragua that joined in 2003 and Costa Rica that was included in January 2004. Mexico, Nicaragua, Jamaica and Honduras always were over the mean. During the years 1990, 1995 and 2000, Mexico, Cuba, Panama, Argentina, Brazil, Chile and Uruguay reached incomes above 2000 dollars per capita in the service sector[238]. On the other hand, there are some countries like Haiti, Honduras, Nicaragua and Bolivia with incomes below 500 dollars per capita. Latin America's merchandise exports increased slightly as the decline in intra-regional trade was balanced by increased shipments to other regions. The recovery of commodity prices in the course of the year and the upturn in the US economy contributed to this rise. While most Latin American countries saw a reduction or stagnation in their imports, those of Costa Rica increased by 9 per cent. Mexico benefited from the recovery of the US market while for Costa Rica, the recovery in semi-conductor shipments boosted both imports and exports. The Table 6.1 exhibits the trade performed by the countries within the trade agreements as partnering countries.

Latin America's exports by product group varied in 2003 as exports of ores and minerals, iron and steel, fuels and food increased between 15 per cent and 21 per cent while exports of automotive products and clothing stagnated and those of office and telecom equipment contracted. The region's recovery in commercial services exports was driven by a sharp rise in transportation services, which increased by 13 per cent, to $12.1 billion. Other commercial services exports decreased to $15.5 billion in 2003, mainly due to a further sharp decline in Mexican exports. Looking at the merchandise trade performance of individual countries one

---

[237] World Bank: Report on Latin America and Caribbean, Regional Overview, 2003.

[238] Guisan, M.C. and Aguayo (2002): "Education, Industary, Trade and Development of American Companies in 1980-99". *Applied Econometrics and International Development*, 2 (1), 83-106.

notices that 30 out of 35 countries recorded positive value growth, the best result since 1997. The arithmetic average growth for exports and imports was also stronger than the weighted average of the region, indicating that many smaller traders performed better than the regional average in 2003. The variation in the trade performance of individual countries in the region continued to differ sharply in 2003. While Brazil, Chile, Uruguay and some oil exporters (such as Ecuador, Trinidad and Tobago and the Netherlands Antilles) reported merchandise export gains of between 16 per cent and 21 per cent, those of Venezuela and several Caribbean islands decreased. In respect of commercial services exports, the strength of the recovery in Argentina's exports and the double digit growth in Chile, Dominican Republic, Panama and Jamaica contrast with the stagnation of the services exports of Mexico and the decline of those of Columbia in 2003. Despite the continuation of low prices for a number of primary commodities, exports of many Central American and Caribbean countries recovered strongly. Economic activity in Western Europe remained subdued as Germany, the largest economy, experienced declining domestic demand. Domestic demand growth remained positive in the rest of the region, but was sluggish in several other countries. In the euro zone, public consumption was the most dynamic expenditure category while private consumption slowed down and fixed investment in the enterprise sector fell nearly 3 per cent. In the midst of this poor economic situation, further progress was made in the process of European integration[239].

**Table 6.1. Trade by Regional Trade Agreements (1990-2003)**

| Regional Trade Agreements | Share (in Percent) | | | Annual Percent Change (in percent) | | | |
|---|---|---|---|---|---|---|---|
| | 1990 | 1995 | 2000 | 1995-2000 | 2001 | 2002 | 2003 |
| NAFTA (3) | 19.6 | 19.8 | 25.8 | 11 | (-)6 | 1 | 8 |
| Mercosur | 0.8 | 1.6 | 1.4 | 2 | (-)6 | (-)26 | 10 |
| ASEAN | 4.6 | 6.9 | 5.7 | 1 | (-)8 | 4 | 10 |

Source : World Trade Statistics-2004, WTO.

In telecommunications, banking or other sectors that are strictly regulated and where politics plays a role, there's more of a need. Right now in Mexico, which has liberalized many of its rules and regulations and is part of NAFTA, the need for having a local partner has been greatly reduced over the years. Chile may also fall in this category. In other countries, such as Peru, Colombia, Venezuela, Argentina, and Brazil, it is probably more useful to have a strategic partner. The Latin America and Caribbean countries are at a critical juncture that carries risks and challenges but also hopes and motivation. Internationally, they supported the founding of the World Trade Organization (WTO) and hope that the new multilateral regulations will lay the essential ground rules for international trade. The merchandise trade of Latin America performed during 2003 is exhibited in Table 6.2.

An important feature of the region's trade developments was the sluggish growth of Mexican trade in 2003. Mexico is the region's largest trader and recorded a significantly more dynamic trade performance in the 1990s than other countries in the region. The weakness of US import demand for automotive products and the lack of competitiveness of Mexican goods in its major market contributed to this lackluster export performance. Brazil was

[239] World Trade Organization: World Trade Report 2003, pp 30-42.

particularly successful; expanding its merchandise exports by more than 20 per cent, partly due to commodity price increases and strong demand from China[240]. As imports recovered only marginally, Brazilian trade surplus rose to a record level of $25 billion in 2003. Central America and the Caribbean countries continued to record a large merchandise trade deficit, although exports expanded by about 10 per cent, much faster than imports.

**Table 6.2. Merchandise Trade of Latin America, 2003**
**(Value in billon US dollars and annual change in percentage)**

| Region/Country | Exports | | | | Imports | | | |
|---|---|---|---|---|---|---|---|---|
| | Value | Annual Change | | | Value | Annual Change | | |
| | 2003 | 2001 | 2002 | 2003 | 2003 | 2001 | 2002 | 2003 |
| Latin America | 377 | (-)4 | 0 | 9 | 366 | (-)2 | (-)7 | 3 |
| Mexico | 165 | (-)5 | 1 | 3 | 179 | (-)4 | 0 | 1 |
| Central America (6) | 14 | (-)8 | 0 | 10 | 28 | 3 | 5 | 6 |
| Caribbean countries (15) | 16 | (-)6 | (-)6 | 11 | 28 | 0 | (-)2 | 0 |
| South America | 181 | (-)2 | (-)1 | 14 | 131 | (-)1 | (-)18 | 7 |
| Argentina | 29 | 1 | (-)3 | 14 | 14 | (-)20 | (-)56 | 54 |
| Brazil | 73 | 6 | 4 | 21 | 51 | 0 | (-)15 | 2 |
| Chile | 21 | (-)4 | (-)1 | 14 | 19 | (-)4 | (-)4 | 13 |
| Venezuela | 24 | (-14) | (-)11 | (-)3 | 9 | 11 | (-)34 | (-)21 |

Source: World Trade Report- 2004, WTO.

## SCOPE OF THE STUDY

There is a fast change observed in the world markets resulting into the new emerging markets across the countries. In this century China, India and Latin America and the emerging market based economies in Eastern Europe promise new opportunities for global trade. The Pacific region had shown time-bending leap in the past four decades as significant Asian population participated in the rapid transition in response to the global movement of trade and services. Asia may be portrayed as the fastest growing market for the top brands of western companies and at the same time, the Asian companies began penetrating the western markets at low price-high quality strategy. While the luxury and fashion goods are dominating the Asian and Far-east markets, the specialized product like electronics and automobiles from Asian Markets are trying to capture considerable market share in Europe and North American countries. The emerging markets in the developing countries have shown a strong potential for change in preferences during the late 20th century. In most of the advanced countries, the birth rate is declining while it is increasing in the developing countries. It has been observed that the technology has homogenized the world markets for variety of customer and industrial needs. The reduction in the tariff barriers, duties and liberalization process worldwide has further given a stimulus to the international marketing across regional boundaries.

[240] The shipments of Brazil to China rose by 80 percent to US$ 4.5 billion in 2003.

This study is based on extensive survey of literature and statistical analysis of the data available from the secondary sources. The strategic partnership model will be developed on analyzing the functional gap map in reference to the political, economic, legal and trade related factors. The broad objectives of the study are as following:

1. The study proposes to analyze the leading factors that are behind the proliferation of intra-regional and inter-regional Free Trade Agreements (FTAs) of Latin American countries.
2. To discuss the prospects for bilateral FTAs between Latin America and Asia, particularly focusing on Japan-Mexico and Japan-Chile FTA, and develop a new approach to cooperation between East Asia and Latin America, the East Asia Latin America Forum (EALAF), will be examined.
3. This study is aimed at documenting and evaluating the process of trade reforms in Latin America from the mid-1980s until 1993 and providing an analytical and historical discussion of the consequences of industrial policies in the region, from the early 1950s when import-substitution ideas were supported by the Economic Commission for Latin America to the 1990s when liberal regimes were embraced.
4. To review the policies based on strict import substitution, which combines high import tariffs with export promotion. The study also focuses to analyze the extent of trade reform in Latin America and evaluate the role of supporting policies to assure the success of trade liberalization.
5. The study also focuses on the evolution of productivity and exports, and it deals with several countries' experiences. The role of real exchange rates in the trade liberalization process is studied, and the recent trend towards appreciation observed in many countries in the region is scrutinized.
6. Finally the study proposes to develop the business partnering model for the Latin American countries to optimize its business potentials, build effective international relations and improve its economic conditions

The analysis in the study concentrates on the evolution of productivity and exports, and discusses factors variability in the Latin American region. The role of strategic alliances in the trade liberalization and international partnering variables will be analyzed in reference to non-parametric measures and the recent trends towards economic appreciation observed in Latin American countries in the region will be put through the process of appropriate qualitative and quantitative test to support the development of the model.

## Sampling and Data Collection

This study aims at reviewing the approach to trade policy, economic reforms, role of RTAs and welfare gains in the region in reference to trading blocs in Latin America. The reference period for analysis of spatial and temporal data is 1950-2003. The aspects of trade and growth and problems of Balance of Payments and their relation with macroeconomic policy have also been discussed in the paper. Further, this study analyzes economic integration between two economies: one central, with a large local market, and the other peripheral, with a small local market and explore the possibility of building appropriate business partnering models among the Latin American and Asian countries. Each economy has an imperfectly competitive manufacturing sector. It has been observed in the discussion that the trade liberalization creates a strong incentive for the imperfectly competitive industry to concentrate in the central region, near the large market. The strategic partnership model has been developed on analyzing the functional gap map in reference to the political, economic, and legal and trade related factors. The analysis concentrates on the evolution of productivity and exports, and it deals with several countries' experiences in the Latin American region. The role of strategic alliances in the trade liberalization and international partnering variables has been analyzed in reference to non-parametric measures and the recent trends towards economic appreciation observed in Latin American countries in the region have been put through the process of appropriate qualitative and quantitative test to support the development of the model.

The study is limited to 11 countries of Latin American region selected on the basis of its GDP growth. The principal data sets have been used from the published resources of Economic Commission on Latin America and Caribbean (ECLAC), World Development Reports, World Trade Reports and World Economic Outlook for the reference period 1950-2003. This study will be based on extensive survey of literature and statistical analysis of the data available from the secondary sources. The data has also been collected for the above reference period on major variables like trade openness, FDI, production portfolios, debt, and terms of trade, GNP, foreign reserves, savings, exports share, imports and foreign exchange rates from the published public resources. Data has also been collected from INDSTAT3 released by UNIDO in 2005 which contains statistics about industrial performance of the countries region wise. In the report, the data has been arranged according to the international standards industrial classification (ISIC) of all economic activities during 1981-2003.

## HYPOTHESES

Economic reforms in a country are a complex and multi-dimensional process that involves the development and implementation of many public policies at intermediate levels during the reforms. Thus economic reforms will not have a constant speed and will often be subject to modifications in the policies that bring changes in the performance and structure of economic activities. The economic reforms can be assessed by examining their corresponding policy measures and implications. However, entire economic progress may not be interpreted as an outcome of the reforms. The growth and development may result to be slower in a country or region in a normal process than stirred process of reforms. After years of poor economic management, many Latin American and Caribbean countries are experiencing a process of structural reforms that places them on a path to a superior economic performance[241]. Hence, it may be hypothesized that:

*H1:* Trade reforms process has proceeded at a faster pace, tariff barriers have been reduced significantly and there has been a significant transition in the international

[241] Easterly William and Sergio Rebelo (1993): Fiscal Policy and Economic Growth-An Emperical Investigation, *Journal of Monetary Economics*, 32 (3), 417-458.

relations and business partnering of Latin American countries with rest of the world during 90's.

After the Uruguay Round, all signatories have agreed to incorporate antidumping laws into their trade policy. Both the Uruguay Round and the North American Free Trade Agreement (NAFTA) abolished or reduced tariffs and quotas, which have traditionally been the protectionist tools of choice. Now that these tools have been scaled back, antidumping laws have risen in importance, and are likely to become the most powerful and most often utilized tools of protectionism as domestic producers in more countries feel the pressure of international competition[242]. It is shown that in the last few years the Latin American countries have gone from having one of the most distorted external sectors, to having very low degrees of protectionism[243]. Hence, it has been hypothesized as:

*H2:* The trade liberalization policies of the Latin American countries have substantially put off the protectionist policies and opened avenues for foreign direct investment and joint ventures in the public and private sector industries.

The free trade areas for Americas (FTAA) on FDI in Latin America by East Asian multinational enterprises could be either positive or negative, depending on the content of FTAA and accompanying policies. If differentials between intra-regional tariffs and most favored nations based tariffs are kept large, import-substituting FDI from East Asia may stagnate or even decrease. With a proper policy package to nurture international production/distribution networks, on the other hand, FDI from East Asia could be accelerated and contributed to deeper integration of Latin America (Kimura and Ando, 2005). The new economic model in Latin America radically altered foreign direct investment inflows to the region. Previously restrictive national policies became ones that facilitated FDI in the context of new business opportunities. Transnational corporations (TNCs) took a new look at the region in the context of their evolving corporate strategies, examples being efficiency-seeking corporate strategies in the automotive (Mexico) and the apparel industry (Caribbean Basin) and the market access strategy for services in the telecommunications and electrical energy industries (Brazil). Two interrelated problems were observed in the process - (a) the objectives of TNCs were often attained but those linked to national development goals often were not, and (b) national policies did not channel FDI to priority development activities[244]. Hence, it has been hypothesized as:

*H3:* The interplay between economic freedom, Foreign Direct Investment (FDI) and growth has shown positive impact on the overall trade and economy status in the Latin American countries.

*H4:* The foreign direct investment policies and strategic alliances of the host countries significantly affect the trade movements in establishing the business relations with Asian counterparts.

---

[242] McGee Robert W (1998): *Application of the Antidumping Laws against Latin America*, Andreas School of Business Barry University, Working Paper.

[243] Edwards Sabastian (1993): *Trade Policy, Exchange rates and Growth*, NBER Working Papers, #4511.

[244] Mortimore M (2000): Corporate Strategies for FDI in Context of Latin America's New Economic Model, *World Development*, 28 (9), 1611-1626.

Enormous change has taken place in trade policies in Latin America: within a few years, most of the region's economies have changed from restrictive to open policies during 1990-2000. But unlike trade liberalization in Europe, most trade barriers in Latin America have been reduced unilaterally. Recently bilateral or multilateral agreements have been considered, especially preferential trade agreements within the region. Michaely evaluates the relevance and desirability of multilateral free trade agreements (such as NAFTA) for the Latin American continent and the Caribbean, with an emphasis on how they affect trade flows. Is a preferential trade agreement among some Latin American countries more or less likely to be meaningful than others in reference to their intensity of impact, or benefits, or both[245]? The evidence strongly suggests little likelihood that these agreements will succeed in Latin America. Paradoxically, the intense liberalization in recent years has made it less likely that such agreements would be beneficial except possibly for agreements between some countries and Brazil, Mexico, or Argentina. When the level of tariffs and non-tariff barriers is already low, a preferential agreement is more likely to have an adverse impact than a beneficial one (although in any case only a slight impact). The hypotheses hence may be framed as:

> *H5:* The regional trade agreements have not been effective due to economic policies of the member countries of Latin American region and the results were not found encouraging towards international trade and partnering.

Some studies discuss that the Latin American economies are predominantly private with functioning financial systems, substantial purchasing power and widespread understanding of how markets work[246]. Nevertheless, transitional and Latin American privatization share has similar problems: poor performing state firms, varied commitment to privatization, technical difficulties and adverse macroeconomic conditions. Five lessons from Latin America are particularly relevant for transitional economies: (a) privatization can help foster competition; (b) governments can build competent institutions for privatization despite weak capacity; (c) labor can benefit without majority control; (d) transparency and share distributions help win public support; and (e) selling profitable, efficient firms can benefit the economy.

On the contrary, research studies have also attempted to establish that the privatization policy faces increasing popular opposition in Latin America. A study uses the results of *Latinobarometro*-2002, a survey of a representative sample of 18522 individuals in 17 countries as our dependent variable of perception, and a privatization dataset on the same countries, including sectoral disaggregation of divestitures, time profiles, proceeds, and other variables for each country[247]. The main findings of the study reveal that disagreement with privatization is more likely when the respondent is poor, privatization was large and quick, involved a high proportion of public services as water and electricity, the country suffered adverse macroeconomic shocks, and there is high inequality of incomes. It has been observed that more the respondent is educated, the more adverse to privatization he or she is. This research suggests that these results depict a broadly consistent picture of privatization

---

[245] Michaely Michael (1999): *Trade Preferential Agreements in Latin America: An Ex-Ante Assessment*, The World Bank Policy Research Working Paper Series, No. 1583.

[246] Shirley Mary M (1994): Privatization in Latin America: Lessons for Transitional Europe, *World Development*, 22 (9), 1313-1323.

[247] Carrera Jorge, Chechhi Daniele and Florio Massimo (2005): *Privatization Discontent and its Determinants: Evidence from Latin America*, Discussion Paper# 1587, Institute for the Study of Labor (IZA), Germany.

discontent that points to distributional issues, probably because of tariff rebalancing not adequately addressed by policy makers and regulators, as suggested by earlier empirical papers.

However, there are studies that indicate liberalization policies in the post-reforms period of economic growth in the Latin America have induced privatization. The dynamic efficiency effects from trade liberalization do not come automatically. Hence, the hypothesis has been framed as:

*H6:* Privatization policy of the Latin American countries would offer favorable internationalization platform for developing effective business partnerships with the rest of the world.

The openness-growth connection is still an open question in the empirical literature. Although some studies have found that openness has a positive impact on economic performance, others have seriously questioned the significance of this result. The main point that we try to emphasize in this paper is that openness involves more than just trade liberalization. The increasing importance of international capital flows and especially foreign direct investment seems to be another relevant component of outward oriented policies. Therefore, by using quarterly data from the late seventies to 2000, we investigate the effects of liberalization in Mexico, Brazil and Argentina by taking into account trade and FDI growth links[248]. The results of the study suggest that it is important to consider both exports and FDI to ascertain the benefits associated to the outward oriented strategies followed by these countries.

## CONSTRUCT OF MODEL

The data has been subject to the TFP model discussed in the following sections. The GDP measures constructed by the Nehru and Dareshwar (1993) have been referred in the study to derive calculations for the TFP variables. The data has been analyzed using the dummy variables referring to the period of structural reforms in the region[249]. A similar procedure has been applied by Lefort and Solimano to measure the economic growth during the recessional period[250]. Similarly, Griliches and Lichetenberg made an assumption in a study measuring the long-run effects of technology transfer indicators on TFP growth[251].

The researchers' advocate of endogenous growth theory that claims that physical capital growth alone cannot explain per capita output growth and that the neoclassical model fails to capture a number of crucial variables that explain economic growth. Their main contributions

---

[248] Cuardos Ana, Orts Vicente and Algnacil Maite (2004): Openness in Growth: Reexamining Foreign Direct Investment, Trade and Output Linkages in Latin America, *The Journal of Development Studies*, 140 (4), 167-192.

[249] Nehru V and Dhareshwar A (1993): A New Database on Physical Capital Stocks – Sources Methodology and Results, *Revista de Analysis Economico*, 8, June, 37-59.

[250] Lefort F and Solimano A (1994): *Economic Growth after Market Based Reforms in Latin America: The Case of Chile and Mexico*, Working Paper, Macro Economic and Growth Division, World Bank, Washington DC.

[251] Griliches, Z. and F. Lichtenberg (1984): *R &D and Productivity Growth at Industry Level: Is There Still a Relationship?*, in Griliches Z. (ed.), R&D, Patents and Productivity, Chicago: University of Chicago Press, 465-501.

consist of including not only human capital, but also international trade in goods[252]. By incorporating technological change, these models consider the diffusion of technology between countries, and the ability of developing countries to adopt and implement foreign technology.

The decomposition of output growth demonstrates that factor growth generally proves much more important than either the improved quality of factors or total factor productivity growth in explaining output growth. The quality of capital positively and significantly affects output growth in all groups. The quality of labor has a negative and notable effect on the overall economic growth in Latin America. The economic growth thus, associates with the declining quality deployment factors and vice versa. A growth accounting method for productivity and competitiveness has been determined using an integrated production function. The justification to choose this approach is that during low growth period, which might have been contributed by economic recession and the firms, might have been forced to operate on the suboptimal manner with low levels of capacity utilization can be analyzed accurately. The construct of the model is explained below:

The Cobb-Douglas function determines the relative influences of the factors of production. This model has been further interpreted in reference to the impact of factor dynamics resulted out of the structural reforms measures in LAC region, in terms of change in technology, investment, productivity and international trade. These factors, when considered with specific industrial sectors say, manufacturing industry determining the productivity in terms of income will generate competition index that would reveal the industry competitiveness, upon pooling. The model may be described as:

$$\mathrm{Y}_t = \widehat{\mathrm{Z}}_t\left[\mathrm{K}_t^{\alpha} L_t^{(1-\alpha)}\right]\widehat{Q}_t^{\infty}\left[I_t^{\beta} R_t^{1+\beta}\right] \tag{1}$$

where, Y is the generated income out of factor productivity (pooled), $\hat{Z}$ is an index of TFP, $K$ and $L$ are the indicators of capital and labor availability and $Q^{\infty}$ is the projected output as a function of innovation ($I$) and change in technology ($R$). Dividing both sides by the intensity of change in factor "Yield" (y), taking Logs and first differentiating the rates of change per LAC countries, resulting into TFP ($\tilde{Q}$) the equation may be constructed as:

$$\ln\left[\frac{y_t}{y_{t-1}}\right] = \ln\left[\frac{\widehat{\mathrm{Z}}_t}{\widehat{\mathrm{Z}}_{t-1}}\right] + \alpha \ln\left[\frac{K_t}{K_{t-1}}\right] \tag{2}$$

It is assumed that the rate of growth of TFP can be expressed as a constant (λ) with a random error (ε). In the process of estimating the change in TFP that is reflected in the competitiveness in the manufacturing industry in LAC region, it is also assumed that (λ) suffers a break during the structural reforms and the process of economic integration. This leads to the following equation for estimation:

[252] Romer Paul M (1994), The Origins of Endogenous Growth, *Journal of Economic Perspectives*, Vol. 8, Winter, 2-22.

$$\ln\left[\frac{y_t}{y_{t-1}}\right] = \lambda + \alpha \ln\left[\frac{K_t}{K_{t-1}}\right] + D_{x(r1+r2)} + \varepsilon_t \tag{3}$$

Where $D_{xr}$ is the dummy variable activated in the years of structural reforms and economic integration. This variable has been calculated for recession period of reforms $D_{xr1}$ and during reforms when the productivity contribution went negative $D_{xr2}$. In all the equations, the demand function is assumed to have constant elasticity. The equation may be constructed as:

$$\ln x_t = \widehat{p}\ln(rp)_t + \widehat{y}\ln(m)_t + \varepsilon_t \tag{4}$$

Where $x$ denotes the exports from LAC region during the reforms period, $rp$ is relative prices, $m$ is foreign real expenditure on manufactured good, $\widehat{p}$ is price elasticity, $\widehat{y}$ is income elasticity and ε is the error term in the referred period.

## Trade Competitiveness

It is assumed that the rate of growth of TFP can be expressed as a constant (λ) with a random error (ε). In the process of estimating the change in TFP that is reflected in the competitiveness in the international trade in LAC region, it is also assumed that (λ) suffers a break during the structural reforms and the process of economic integration. The trade competitiveness in the study has been analyzed with reference to the variables openness, FDI, Portfolio, debt, Terms of Trade and export. The variability of ($\lambda$) may be explained in reference to the equation (ii).

This leads to the following equation for estimation:

$$\ln\left[\frac{y_t}{y_{t-1}}\right] = \lambda + \alpha \ln\left[\frac{K_t}{K_{t-1}}\right] + D_{x(r1+r2)} + \varepsilon_t \tag{5}$$

In the above equation, $D_{x(r_1+r_2)}$ is the dummy variable activated in the years of structural reforms and economic integration. This variable has been calculated for recession period of reforms $D_{xr_1}$ and during reforms when the productivity contribution went negative $D_{xr_2}$. In all the equations, the demand function is assumed to have constant elasticity. The equation may be constructed as:

$$\ln x_t = \hat{p}\ln(rp)_t + \hat{y}\ln(m)_t + \varepsilon_t \tag{6}$$

Where $x$ denotes the exports from LAC region during the reforms period, $rp$ is relative prices, $m$ is foreign real expenditure on manufactured good, $\hat{p}$ is price elasticity, $\hat{y}$ is income elasticity and ε is the error term in the referred period.

## Interplay of Trade Blocs

It has been established through previous research studies that trade agreements play significant role in developing a favorable environment for trade and economy among the participating countries[253]. In the model it is assumed that there are 'N' trading blocs, where in the countries freely trade with each other (*e.g.* NAFTA, CAFTA, MERCASUR). They could be a part of Free Trade Agreement (FTA), Customs Union (CU) or a simple N trading bloc condition. Assuming that there exist N Trading blocs in the LAC region and each bloc is endowed with a fixed amount of each commodity.

Let $B_j^i$ be the trading bloc *i* in the region with an endowment of the commodity *j*, chosen for transaction under the bi-lateral trade agreement.[254] The Cobb-Douglas performances exist in each trading blocs and the utility function, which can be derived out of the preferential trade agreements between the countries of trading bloc, may be described as

$$U^i = \sum_{j=1}^{M} \alpha_j^i \ln \hat{A}_j^i \tag{7}$$

Where $U^i$ is the utility of the trading bloc *i*, $\alpha_j^i$ is the weight that trading bloc *i* put on the commodity *j*, $\hat{A}_j^i$ is the aggregate consumption of j commodity in trading bloc *i* and M denotes different commodities that have the trade potential in the trading bloc. The volume of trade $V_j^i$ is described as $V_j^i = \hat{A}_j^i - B_j^i$, of which the positive values indicate imports from the point of view of trade competitiveness whereas the negative values represent exports in the trading bloc. The trading blocs impose a fixed value tariff *t* which may be defined as *advalorem duty* charged in each trading bloc *i* on import of *j* commodity $(t_j^i)$. Under such circumstances, the prevailing international price for *j* commodity may be described as $P_{rj}$. Accordingly the domestic price for the *j* commodity in trading bloc *i* would be $P_{rj} = (1 + t_j^i)P_{rj}$. Hence the equation may be derived as below:

$$\sum_{j=1}^{M} P_{rj}(1 + t_j^i)\hat{A}_j^i = Y_{j...n}^i = \sum_{j=1}^{M}(1 + t_j^i)B_j^i + [(P_{rj})(t_j^i)(V_j^i)] \tag{8}$$

Where in $Y_j^i$ is the revenue granted in the trading bloc *i* for the commodity *j* up to '*n*' potential commodities to be brought under trading. The equilibrium of the trade blocs within the given trade conditions, may be derived through the equations (7) and (8), we get:

---

[253] Phillips Nicola (2001): Regionalist Governance in the New Political Economy of Development: Re-launching the "Mercosur", *Third World Quarterly*, 22 (4), 565-583.

[254] If $B_j^i = 0.4$ it means trading bloc *i* is endowed with 40% of the regions endowment of commodity *j*.

$$\sum_{j=1}^{M} P_{rj}\hat{A}_j^i = \sum_{j=1}^{M} P_{rj}\hat{B}_j^i = 1 \tag{9}$$

And, towards the demand and supply, the equilibrium among the trading blocs may be achieved as described in the following equation.

$$\sum_{i=1}^{N} \hat{A}_j^i = \sum_{i=1}^{N} \hat{B}_j^i = 1 \tag{10}$$

At the equilibrium, the trade blocs would have aggregate expenditure equal to aggregate revenue, which may also be desired as endowment vector. Endowment may be explained as the sum of values of unilateral trade and consumption.

The measure of the economic welfare in reference to trade agreement has been computed using calibrated fraction δ which expresses the relationship between the fiscal allocation including taxes and gross revenue and trade equilibrium among the countries under study. Such equilibrium relationship is largely affected by the tariff regions of the participating countries. The welfare cost is derived using the following equation:-

$$B^{t}(x_1, x_2, x_3) = B^{ft}\left[(1-\delta)x_1, (1-\delta)x_2, (1-\delta)x_3\right] \tag{11}$$

Where $B^t$ denotes the benefits derived under an equilibrium with positive tariffs and $B^{ft}$ represents benefits derived in the given trade equilibrium emerged out of free trade agreements, common market structure or bilateral trade agreements.

## Trade Competitiveness

The principal variables used in the analysis are defined as below:

Gross national product *(V)*
Imports of goods and services *(M)*
Consumption of goods and services *(C)*
Savings *(S)*
Exports of goods and services *(E)*
Capital inflow $[F \equiv (M - E)]$
Gross domestic investment *(I)*
Reserves of foreign assets *(R)*
Growth rate of GNP *(r)*

In the analysis, imports and exports are measured as net flows of returns on investments. The study postulates that a constant capital-output ratio $(k')$ for directly productive net investment and a constant share $(z)$ of current gross income, oriented to replacement and social overhead investment. Hence, gross investment in a given period may be represented by the equation:

$$I_t = k'\Delta V + zV_t \tag{12}$$

Where, $\Delta V = V_{t+1} - V_t$. Since the traditional incremental capital-output ratio $(k_t)$ is defined as $I_t/_{\Delta V}$ and since the growth rate of the following year $(r_{t+1})$ is represented as $\Delta V/_{V_t}$, dividing equation (x) by $(\Delta V)$ yields an equation for $(k_t)$ as a decreasing function of $(r_{t+1})$ :

$$k_t = k' + \left(\frac{z}{r_{t+1}}\right) \tag{13}$$

In the above equation $(k')$ is the marginal capital-output ratio that is relevant to increase in the level of investment in a given period. The required imports of a country in a given time may be expressed as:

$$M_t = (M)_{t-1} + \mu\Delta V + \chi\Delta C + \phi\Delta\left(E/_V\right) + \pi\Delta\left(R/_V\right) \tag{14}$$

Where, $\Delta$ refers to changes between the previous and the current period. In the above equation $\mu, \chi, \phi, \omega$ and $\pi$ are the constants indicating propensity to import, additional consumption, additional basic investment, export shares and ratio of reserves respectively in reference to imports during the pre- and post-reforms periods in the selected countries. Either the pair of parameter $\chi$ and $\phi$ or the parameter $\mu$ is zero in any given application of the above equation.

The model used for the projections of export growth (2015) has been conceived as largely exogenous. An export sector responsive to the trade situation of the country is assumed for "high performance". The exogenous growth rate of exports has been derived through the following equation:

$$E_t = E_0(1 + \varepsilon'')^t \tag{15}$$

Where in, $(\varepsilon'')$ represents exogenous growth rate of exports *(E)*, $E_t$ denotes the exports of goods and services in the reforms period and $E_0$ exhibits the historical performance of the exports of the countries in the region. The equation for potential savings (S) is hence derived as:

$$(S)_t = (S)_{t-1} + \alpha\Delta V + \gamma\Delta\left(E/_V\right) \tag{16}$$

Where, $\Delta$ refers to the change between the pre-reforms period $(t-1)$ and the reforms period $(t)$. In the equation $\alpha$ represents propensity to save from additional GNP and $\gamma$ denotes the effect of changes in export share on savings.

***Revealed Comparative Advantages***

The analysis of the data has been carried out on the aggregate by computing four trade performance indices for the East Asia and Latin America regions instead of looking at individual trade policies adopted by individual countries. The two indices used to measure the structural change in the study are the Lawrence Index and the Beneficial Index. The Lawrence Index gives an index value that ranges from 0 to 1, and the index indicates a complete upheaval if it is close to unity, otherwise indicates little change if it is close to 0. This index has been computed using the following equation:

$$L=\left(\frac{1}{2}\right)\sum_{i=1}^{n}\left|S_{ij}-S_{i,t-1}\right| \tag{17}$$

$$\text{Wherein, } S_{i,t}=\left[\frac{X_{i,t}}{\sum_{i}X_{i,t}}\right] \tag{18}$$

In the above equation $S_{i,t}$ denotes the share of industrial sector *i's* export in the total exports of the country in a year $t$[255].

The Beneficial Index is used to measure whether a given structural change in export pattern is oriented to the most dynamic products demanded by the world. The beneficial structure change index (BSCI) has been computed using the formula as stated below:

$$\text{BSCI}=\sum_{i=1}^{n}\left\{\left[\frac{X_{i,t}\big/\sum_{i}X_{i,t}}{X_{i,t-1}\big/\sum_{i}X_{i,t-1}}\right]\bullet\left[\frac{\left(M_{I,t}\big/Mi_{i,t-1}\right)}{M_{I,T}\big/M_{i,t-1}}-1\right]\bullet\left(\frac{X_{i,t}}{\sum_{i}X_{i,t}}\right)\right\} \tag{19}$$

A positive value indicates a beneficial orientation, and that the structural change in exports favored the dynamic sectors. The higher the value of this index, the stronger is the beneficial change in export pattern. The other two indices relate to trade specialization[256]. The Michaely Index is the more traditional index, whose value ranges from 0 to unity with a value closer to 1 indicating a greater degree of trade specialization.

---

[255] Spar D (1998): Attracting High Technology Investment – Intel's Costa Rican Plant, *World Bank Foreign Advisor Service (FIAS), Occasional Paper #11*, FIAS, Washington DC.

[256] Amable Bruno (2000), International Specialization and Growth, *Structural Change and Economic Dynamics*, 11 (4), 413-131.

This index is defines as: $I = \left(\frac{1}{2}\right)\sum_{i=1}^{n}\left|\frac{X_i}{\sum_i X_i} - \frac{M_i}{\sum_i M_i}\right|$, (20)

Where $X_i$ and $M_i$ are respectively, exports and imports of sector "i" in a given year.

The Trade Specialization Index gives an improved version of the Michaely Index. In this case, the degree of specialization in each sector is weighted by its relative importance in the country's total trade. This index also ranges between zero and one, and the value of one implies a complete specialization in trade.

For the given sector I, its degree of specialization is unambiguously given by the following ratio:

$$\frac{|X_i - M_i|}{X_i + M_i}.$$

The value of 1 for this ratio indicates a complete specialization (to export or to import). Therefore, the aggregate measure of trade specialization can be obtained first by weighting all the individual sectors' measures and then summing over all sectors. Therefore, the trade specialization index[257] (TSI) is defined as:

$$TSI = \sum_{i=1}^{n}\left\{\left(\frac{(X_i + M_i)}{\sum_i (X_i + M_i)}\right)\frac{|X_i - M_i|}{(X_i + M_i)}\right\} = \sum_{i=1}^{n}\left\{\frac{|X_i - M_i|}{\sum_i (X_i + M_i)}\right\}, \quad (21)$$

Where the weights are = $\frac{(X_i + M_i)}{\sum_i (X_i + M_i)}$

Both the Michaely Index and Trade Specialization Index are inversely related to conventional Grubel-Lloyd (GL) intra-industry trade index. The industry variable "i" is defined in the GL index as below:

Defined for industry "i" as $GL_i = \left\{1 - \left[{|X_i - M_i|}/{(X_i - M_i)}\right]\right\}$ (22)

The GL indices for different periods convey some information on the structure of trade in each of these time periods, but it does not allow conclusions on the structure of the *change* in trade flows[258]. A generalized rise or fall of average GL indices in one or several countries may be due to *multilateral dimensions*, because it suggests trends towards more intra- or more

[257] For details, see Bender, Siegfried and Li, Kui-Wai: (2002) *The Changing Trade and Revealed Comparative Advantages of Asian and Latin American Manufacture Exports*, March, Yale Economic Growth Center Discussion Paper No. 843.

[258] Brulhart, M. and R. C. Hine (1999): *Intra-Industry Trade and Adjustment: The European Experience*, Centre of Research in European Development and International Trade (CREDIT), University of Nottingham, 1999.

inter-industry trade and specialization and it may thus indicate the importance of *aggregate* adjustment costs.

Trade competitiveness and its impact on the economic welfare measures in the Latin American countries have been analyzed using the above model. The analysis concentrates on measuring the economic growth of the Latin American countries through the major variables gross national product, imports of goods and services, consumption of goods and services, exports of goods and services, capital inflow, gross domestic investment, reserves of foreign assets, savings and growth rate of GNP in reference to the economic growth pattern emerged during 1950-2003. The single model equations and regression function have been used to measure the variability and economic growth and Nash equilibrium has been calculated to measure the economic welfare gains among the trading blocs in the Latin American region.

*Chapter 7*

# CRITICAL ANALYSIS AND DISCUSSION

In the beginning of the 1980s, the private sector in Latin America faced a very uncomfortable economic environment. including high inflation, sharp currency fluctuations, which in turn led to acute price volatility, low investment, low production prompted by import substitution , state intervention, large foreign debt and severe balance of payment deficits. The whole region suffered a strong macroeconomic state of imbalance, which required strong remedies. The subsequent stabilization and structural adjustment programs aimed to reduce fiscal deficits, open up economies, privatize state enterprises, reduce foreign debt, introduce flexible exchange rates and modernize the financial system.

**Table 7.1. Growth Decomposition in Periods of Reforms and No-Reforms of the Economy in Latin American Countries, 1950-2003 (In percent)**

| Country/ Status | GPD growth | | Productivity | | Contribution of Productivity in GDP | |
|---|---|---|---|---|---|---|
| | Pre-Reforms | Reforms | Pre-Reforms | Reforms | Pre-Reforms | Reforms |
| Argentina | 1.6 | 4.7 | -0.5 | 4.1 | -31.25 | 87.23 |
| Brazil | 5.2 | 2.5 | 0.9 | 0.2 | 17.31 | 8.00 |
| Chile | 2.3 | 5.2 | -0.3 | 2.3 | -13.04 | 44.23 |
| Colombia | 4.7 | 4.7 | 0.9 | 1.8 | 19.15 | 38.30 |
| Costa Rica | 4.3 | 5.9 | -0.1 | 0.8 | -2.33 | 13.56 |
| Ecuador | 1.8 | 5.5 | -0.9 | 1.6 | -50.00 | 29.09 |
| Mexico | 5.7 | 1.4 | 1.1 | -1.9 | 19.30 | -135.71 |
| Paraguay | 4.9 | 3.5 | -0.4 | -0.2 | -8.16 | -5.71 |
| Peru | 1.6 | 5.3 | -1.2 | 2.9 | -75.00 | 54.72 |
| Uruguay | 1.6 | 3.1 | 0.7 | 2.1 | 43.75 | 67.74 |
| Venezuela | 2.3 | 5.2 | -1.2 | 1.9 | -52.17 | 36.54 |

Source: Based on the data computation done by the author.

**Table 7.2. Total Factor Productivity Growth: Average in 1950-2003 and Change during Periods of Reforms, OLS Regressions (Percent)**

| Recession Dummy | None | | $D_{xr1}$ | | $D_{xr2}$ | |
|---|---|---|---|---|---|---|
| Country/ Period | 1950-2003 | $\delta_x$ | 1950-2003 | $\delta_x$ | 1950-2003 | $\delta_x$ |
| Argentina | -1.9 (0.161) | 6.7 (0.008) | 2.5 (0.001) | 3.9 (.005) | 2.8 (0.001) | 4.0 (0.005) |
| Brazil | -1.3 (0.245) | 1.9 (0.392) | 0.4 (0.651) | 1.4 (0.350) | 2.0 (0.010) | 0.7 (0.614) |
| Chile | -1.3 (0.229) | 2.9 (0.047) | 2.9 (0.059) | 1.8 (0.079) | 3.4 (0.483) | 0.6 (0.927) |
| Colombia | 0.7 (0.465) | 0.4 (0.503) | 0.8 (0.485) | 0.4 (0.593) | 2.3 (0.000) | -0.5 (0.271) |
| Costa Rica | -1.7 (0.201) | 1.3 (0.469) | 0.3 (0.786) | 1.6 (0.174) | 0.8 (0.316) | 0.9 (0.217) |
| Ecuador | -1.2 (.570) | 3.1 (0.159) | 1.3 (0.469) | 0.7 (0.740) | 1.5 (0.449) | 2.9 (0.227) |
| México | -3.7 (0.004) | 1.1 (0.372) | -0.7 (0.415) | 1.4 (0.556) | 1.2 (0.569) | 4.2 (0.899) |
| Paraguay | -1.3 (0.099) | 0.4 (0.784) | 0.2 (0.990) | -0.7 (0.536) | 1.5 (0.020) | 1.1 (0.248) |
| Peru | -1.9 (0.132) | 2.9 (0.16) | 0.8 (0.327) | 2.6 (0.152) | 2.5 (0.224) | 0.8 (0.947) |
| Uruguay | 1.4 (0.223) | 1.4 (0.537) | 2.8 (0.000) | 0.4 (0.785) | 3.3 (0.000) | -0.2 (0.822) |
| Venezuela | -1.2 (0.18) | 3.3 (0.072) | 0.4 (0.458) | 2.8 (0.395) | 3.6 (0.022) | 1.0 (0.440) |

$\delta_x$ = change during the reforms period.

Source: Based on the data computation done by the author.

*p* values are presented in parentheses, $D_{xr1}$ is activated when the GDP growth is negative while $D_{xr2}$ is activated when the growth rate of TFP is negative.

The decomposition results for the pre- and post-reforms period in the selected countries of the LAC region show that Brazil, Mexico and Uruguay had shown slower growth rate of GDP during the period of reforms.

The data presented in the Table 7.1 shows that these countries experienced average rate of output growth to the extent of 4 percent as compared to the 2.8 percent of the pre-reforms period. The contribution of productivity as a fraction of GDP growth has a steep decline in Mexico and a slow rate of decline in Paraguay during the post-reforms period. Out of the countries selected for the study, the contributions of productivity in Brazil and Mexico went down when corresponding economies were reformed. During the pre-reforms period 7 out of 11 countries had showed negative contributions of TFP to output growth, while such trend was found only in the Paraguay and Mexico during the stage of economic reforms.

**Table 7.3. Industry Competitiveness in the Latin American Countries (1970-2000)**

| Country | Regression Analysis[a] | | | | | |
|---|---|---|---|---|---|---|
| | Openness | FDI | Portfolio | Debt | Terms of Trade | Exports |
| Argentina | 0.72988** | 0.61124** | 0.54371** | 0.84319** | 0.30104** | 0.44134 |
| Brazil | 0.30145 | 0.79216** | 0.61112 | 0.82243 | 0.12769 | 0.37621** |
| Chile | 0.53661 | 0.20073 | 0.59721 | 0.88301 | 0.44166** | 0.39823 |
| Colombia | 0.19972** | 0.14217 | 0.39012 | 0.69931** | 0.37164 | 0.47159 |
| Costa Rica | 0.55374 | 0.49214 | 0.39822** | 0.47644 | 0.79331** | 0.61842** |
| Ecuador | 0.11498 | -0.11767 | 0.17632 | 0.53319 | 0.03467 | 0.15620 |
| México | 0.19833 | 0.57622** | 0.89831 | 0.73012** | 0.59217** | 0.48542 |
| Paraguay | 0.77971 | 0.39872 | 0.52761 | 0.61320 | 0.27643 | 0.29811 |
| Peru | 0.49321** | -0.0352 | 0.21984** | 0.71097 | 0.48711** | 0.30102 |
| Uruguay | 0.59136 | -0.0349 | -0.0127 | 0.29371 | 0.30891** | 0.20956 |
| Venezuela | 0.0234 | 0.35612 | 0.52019 | 0.76653** | 0.46522 | 0.71131** |

a : Dependent variable GDP ** Statistical significance at 5 percent level.
Source: Based on the data computation done by the author.

**Table 7.4. Pre-and Post Reforms Economic Growth in the Latin American Countries (5 years average basis)**

| Countries | Pre-reform period | | | Post-reform period | | |
|---|---|---|---|---|---|---|
| | Inflation | Fiscal Surplus | Overall Growth | Inflation | Fiscal Surplus | Overall Growth |
| Argentina | 1376.8 | -1.1 | 0.9 | 4.7 | -0.6 | 3.9 |
| Brazil | 1329.7 | -2.1 | 1.7 | 9.3 | -6.1 | 2.5 |
| Chile | 21.5 | 0.3 | 0.0 | 12.9 | 1.5 | 6.4 |
| Colombia | 25.6 | 0.5 | 3.8 | 20.8 | -1.3 | 2.7 |
| Costa Rica | 17.9 | -1.9 | 2.3 | 16.2 | -2.7 | 4.4 |
| Ecuador | 59.7 | 1.3 | 4.4 | 29.4 | -1.5 | 1.3 |
| Mexico | 87.9 | -9.6 | 2.6 | 20.9 | -0.4 | 3.7 |
| Paraguay | 24.9 | 0.5 | 2.7 | 16.9 | 0.3 | 2.1 |
| Peru | 2454.8 | -5.3 | 2.7 | 35.7 | -0.8 | 4.9 |
| Uruguay | 85.2 | -0.9 | 2.6 | 34.9 | -1.2 | 3.8 |
| Venezuela | 35.7 | -1.3 | 2.7 | 49.3 | -1.1 | 2.5 |

Source: For basic data- Economic Commission for Latin America and Caribbean (ECLAC), IMF, 2001. Growth rates are based on the data computation done by the author.

The long-run effect of reforms would prevail, if sustained during the process which might be influenced by the sum of the contemporaneous and the delayed impacts. If the latter is negative, some of the achievements of growth would be lost in the future. If positive, additional growth would occur effortlessly. The results including lagged reforms variables in the basic equation are reported in the coefficients that hold negative signs as compared to those of the corresponding contemporaneous variables. However, the lagged coefficients are quite small in absolute value, leaving substantial positive long-run effects for each of the reforms variables. None of the delayed effects has a clear statistical significance individually, but they have strong significance jointly. This dynamic specification marginally improves upon the static one according to standard statistical measures, as well as with regards to the qualitative features of the results. As measured by the adjusted R-square, the fit of this dynamic specification is slightly better than that of its static counterpart. Moreover, in the dynamic specification, education is statistically significant. The evidence thus suggests the presence of a minor partial offset to the beneficial growth effect of stabilization during the post -reforms years.

The coefficients of the constants and the dummy variables $D_{xr1}$ and $D_{xr2}$ derived from the ordinary least squares for each country and the average of rate of growth for total factor productivity during the periods of reforms have been exhibited in Table 7.2. The regression results show that there is upward growth in the total factor productivity for the six countries with and without the introduction of dummy variables. However, the economic reforms had a positive effect on the rate of growth of TFP that also reflected through the policy of trade liberalization in the Latin American countries.

Assuming low variation in the regional economic growth and taking the estimates at their face values, the income effect is immediate, the short term effect from relative prices is lagged, and the estimated short run price elasticity (-)0.3 is lower in absolute value than the long run elasticity (-)1.3. These results are common in the analysis of time-series data of foreign trade. The estimated long run coefficient of foreign imports is found to be 0.8 that implies a trend of increasing market share for Latin American countries on the basis of the pooled data at constant relative prices. Intra-regional trade is relatively small in general terms and it is negligible for Costa Rica. Mexico has traditionally absorbed only a tiny fraction of Central America's exports. In sum, regional trade flows are not very big - on an average, no more than 18% of the region's exports have gone to the region itself and Mexico. On an average 40% of all imports, come from the USA.

The Table 7.3 shows that the trend of exports in the selected countries is positive but with a slower rate of growth, as compared to the country debt and foreign direct investment (FDI). It may be observed that except 3 countries, others have shown a positive trend in the FDI. Manufacturing in LAC region faces severe competitive stresses as it integrates into the global economy. However, it was the first region in the developing world - in the post-war era to liberalize on international trade and investment flows and had the most advanced industrial base, it failed to fully realize the opportunities offered. The growth of economy in the countries of Latin America during 1950-2003 is exhibited in Table 7.4 in reference to long-run stability and its impact on structural reforms.

It may be observed from the above Table that In Argentina, Chile, Costa Rica and Peru, the post-reform growth is substantially higher than the one in the five years prior to reform. In addition, in Chile in the five pre-reform years there was no growth at all; while in Argentina it was very slow. In Brazil, Mexico and Uruguay, the post-reform growth is somewhat higher than in the five pre-reform years, while in the cases of Colombia, Ecuador, Paraguay and Venezuela, the post-reform growth is slower than in the five years prior to reforms. Perhaps even more important than the slowdown in growth was the magnitude of a macroeconomic imbalance and in some cases a virtual economic chaos in the pre-reform period. In many countries inflation rates evolved into hyperinflations during the 1980s, while fiscal deficits continued to burst[259]. The trend line for the growth of pre- and post-reforms for the Latin American countries has been exhibited in Figure 7.1. It may be seen from the data presented in the Table 7.4 that in many countries fiscal deficits were uncontrollable during the pre-reform period, which has been severe in Argentina, Brazil and Peru. However, among all, Brazil managed to lower inflation and improve the fiscal situation in the post-reform period and less severe, but still serious was cases of Mexico (both fiscal situation and inflation) and Uruguay (Inflation). The success of the East Asian countries with the export-oriented model of development, as well as the dynamic growth of Chile in the second part of the 1980s, contrasted sharply with the apparent inability of many countries in the region to put their house in order.

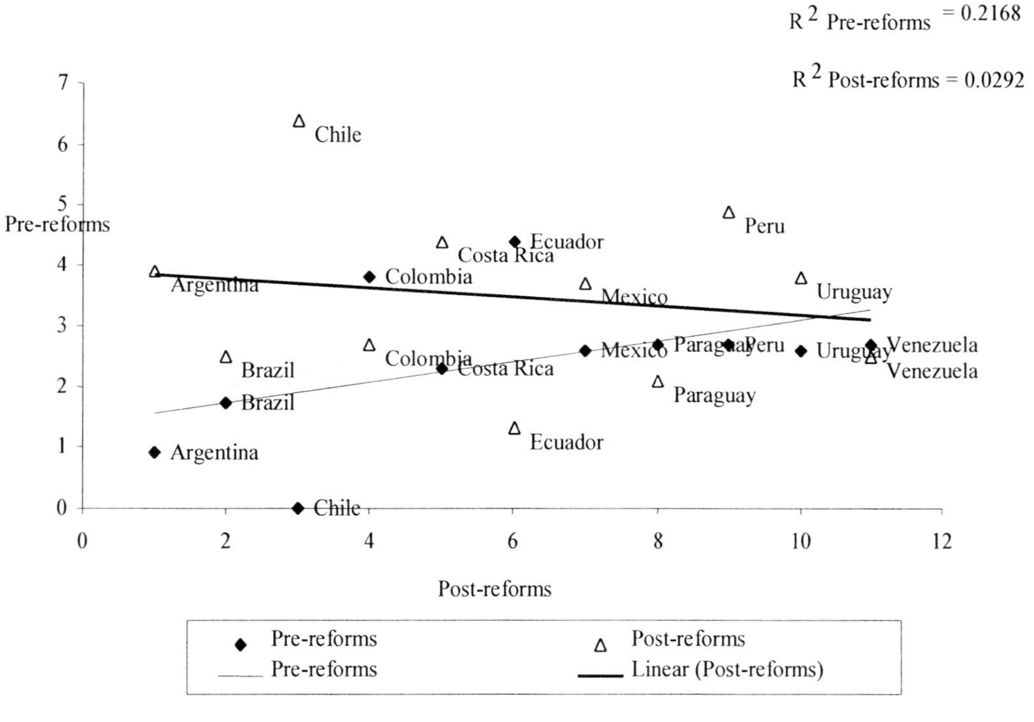


Figure 7.1. Pre- and Post Reforms Growth Rates in Latin American Countries.

Reviewing the impact of the structural reforms in the LAC region it may be stated that manufacturing is no longer the driver of growth in Latin America; a significant concentration has taken place in the industrial sector with a small number of large conglomerates controlling industrial production; small and medium enterprises are experiencing particular difficulty in adjustment; capital-intensive resource-based sectors are growing; and extensive reorganization of work on the shop-floor is taking place. It is also noted that the decline of vertically integrated firms in the region opens up new possibilities for smaller firms as sub-contractors, provided that appropriate infrastructure and markets are operating. The over-emphasis on political instability and ineffective governance issues has led policy makers to overlook key market failures that stand on the way to sustained productivity growth,

[259] Results of data analysis exhibited in the Tables 7.1 to 7.4 supports the hypotheses H1, H2, H3 and H4.

increasing technological capability and greater competitiveness. The historical parameters for the pre- and post-reforms period in the selected countries of the LAC region show that the change in growth rate of GNP $(r)$ had been higher during the period of reforms for Mexico, Brazil and Venezuela. The data presented in the Table 7.5 show that the growth rates vary from 2.8 for Argentina to 6.9 for Venezuela.

**Table 7.5. Historical Parameters and Growth Rates during of Reforms and Non-Reforms periods of the Economy in Latin American Countries, 1950-2003**

| Country | Imports | | | | | Exports | Capital Requirement | | GNP Growth |
|---|---|---|---|---|---|---|---|---|---|
| Status | $\Delta V$ $(\mu)$ | $\Delta C$ $(\chi)$ | $\Delta I$ $(\phi)$ | $\frac{\Delta E}{V}$ $(\omega)$ | $\frac{\Delta R}{V}$ $(\pi)$ | $(\varepsilon'')$ | Intercept $(k')$ | $(r_{t+1})$ | $(r)$ |
| Argentina | 0.016 | 0.025 | 0.264 | 228 | 119 | 0.036 | 2.13 | 0.149 | 0.028 |
| Brazil | 0.054 | 0.003 | 0.392 | 751 | 26040 | 0.047 | 2.19 | 0.055 | 0.059 |
| Chile | 0.051 | 0.141 | 0.412 | 2299 | 4423 | 0.041 | 2.04 | 0.041 | 0.033 |
| Colombia | 0.028 | 0.109 | 0.556 | 2196 | 1753 | 0.106 | 2.32 | 0.105 | 0.049 |
| Costa Rica | 0.035 | 0.265 | 0.468 | 433 | 77 | 0.067 | 2.41 | 0.066 | 0.054 |
| Ecuador | 0.036 | 0.054 | 0.763 | 489 | 337 | 0.074 | 2.00 | 0.072 | 0.039 |
| Mexico | 0.310 | 0.097 | 0.145 | 3642 | 8144 | 0.049 | 2.05 | 0.055 | 0.061 |
| Paraguay | 0.032 | 0.174 | 0.339 | 193 | 124 | 0.014 | 2.96 | 0.046 | 0.031 |
| Peru | 0.045 | 0.162 | 0.597 | 260 | 265 | 0.051 | 2.29 | 0.067 | 0.042 |
| Uruguay | 0.040 | 0.028 | 0.377 | 1103 | 542 | 0.016 | 2.58 | 0.047 | 0.054 |
| Venezuela | 0.250 | 0.194 | 0.482 | 1875 | 986 | 0.025 | 3.24 | 0.005 | 0.069 |

Source: Based on the data computation done by the author.

**Table 7.6. Economic Competitiveness in the Latin American Countries (1980-2003)**

| Country | Savings | | Export Growth | GNP Growth |
|---|---|---|---|---|
| | $\alpha$ $(\delta s / \delta V)$ | $\gamma$ $(\delta s / \delta E / V)$ | $(\varepsilon'')$ | $r$ |
| Argentina | 0.354 | 6624 | 0.036 | 0.054 |
| Brazil | 0.295 | 6541 | 0.047 | 0.067 |
| Chile | 0.247 | 1120 | 0.039 | 0.058 |
| Colombia | 0.286 | 2610 | 0.106 | 0.064 |
| Costa Rica | 0.255 | 966 | 0.057 | 0.066 |
| Ecuador | 0.266 | 139 | 0.074 | 0.057 |
| México | 0.284 | 9442 | 0.049 | 0.061 |
| Paraguay | 0.245 | 254 | 0.009 | 0.054 |
| Peru | 0.237 | 1233 | 0.041 | 0.066 |
| Uruguay | 0.311 | 536 | 0.019 | 0.061 |
| Venezuela | 0.310 | 995 | 0.025 | 0.077 |

Source: Based on the data computation done by the author.

**Table 7.7. Regression results for factors of economic growth in Latin American countries (1950-2003)**

| Country | Intercept | $V^a$ | $R^2$ | Intercept | $V^a$ | $\left(\frac{E}{V}\right)^a$ | $F^a$ | $R^2$ | Correlation with Time (1980-2003)[b] | |
|---|---|---|---|---|---|---|---|---|---|---|
| | | | | | | | | | $\left(\frac{E}{V}\right)$ | $F$ |
| Argentina | -998.3 | -0.30 (4.01) | 0.52 | -674.1 | 0.37 (6.99) | 5655.2 (2.02) | -0.54 (3.87) | 0.72 | -0.04 (-0.12) | -0.09 (0.37) |
| Brazil | 274.3 | -0.153 (6.43) | 0.29 | -203.0 | 0.241 (4.52) | 4721.6 (1.63) | 0.644 (1.99) | 0.66 | 0.58 (-0.36) | 0.61 (0.14) |
| Chile | 35.4 | 0.241 (3.72) | 0.46 | -383.3 | 0.143 (3.58) | 2715.3 (2.15) | 0.067 (1.33) | 0.48 | -0.37 (-0.64) | 0.43 (-0.27) |
| Colombia | 443.2 | 0.094 (3.15) | 0.36 | -471.2 | 0.127 (3.96) | 2652.5 (3.96) | -0.36 (1.84) | 0.73 | -0.83 (-0.97) | 0.11 (-0.19) |
| Costa Rica | 72.3 | -0.024 (1.16) | 0.12 | 16.5 | 0.052 (1.23) | 902.4 (1.44) | -0.27 (1.27) | 0.25 | -0.14 (-0-36) | 0.33 (-0.45) |
| Ecuador | 11.9 | -0.163 (9.63) | 0.92 | -34.6 | 0.172 (8.77) | -439.7 (1.77) | -0.145 (2.65) | 0.73 | -0.24 (-0.56) | -0.10 (-0.38) |
| México | 164.6 | 0.146 (5.63) | 0.66 | -936.3 | 0.223 (6.33) | 7633.7 (2.07) | -0.76 (3.49) | 0.92 | 0.56 (-0.34) | 0.55 (-0.21) |
| Paraguay | 12.4 | -0.134 (3.95) | 0.48 | 18.6 | 0.147 (3.64) | -554.7 (2.57) | 0.042 (2.66) | 0.39 | -0.14 (-0.58) | 0.42 (0.14) |
| Peru | 5.9 | 0.231 (6.94) | 0.76 | -46.3 | 0.262 (7.54) | 1422.9 (1.90) | -0.051 (3.67) | 0.63 | -0.39 (-0.44) | -0.49 (-0.59) |
| Uruguay | 34.8 | -0.124 (2.34) | 0.45 | -11.7 | 0.155 (3.22) | -342.7 (3.92) | -0.345 (2.41) | 0.42 | -0.63 (-0.74) | 0.19 (-0.27) |
| Venezuela | 692.4 | 0.091 (3.26) | 0.37 | 342.4 | 0.082 (3.74) | 126.0 (1.22) | 0.162 (1.14) | 0.54 | 0.22 (-0.32) | 0.29 (0.13) |

[a] Figures in parentheses are standard deviations.
[b] Figures in parentheses refer to the period 1950-1979.
Source: Based on the data computation done by the author.

However, the study revealed that capital requirements were also highest for Argentina (14.3) followed by Columbia (10.5), Ecuador (7.4) and Mexico (5.7). The capital requirement for Venezuela has been found to be the slowest (0.5). The export growth rate for Peru has emerged as the highest (5.5) while it has been held back for Argentina (3.6). The export growth rate for Mexico during the period of study was found to be above average (4.9). Other studies have also arrived at similar results. Mexico, a prominent liberalizer, failed to attain stellar gross domestic product (GDP) growth in the 1990s, and since 2001 its GDP and exports have stagnated (Tornell, *et.al*, 2004). Brazil, Mexico and Uruguay experienced average rate of output growth to the extent of 4 percent as compared to the 2.8 percent of the pre-reforms period. The contribution of productivity as a fraction of GDP growth has a steep decline in Mexico and a slow rate of decline in Paraguay during the post-reforms period.

The relationship between domestic savings *(S)* assumed to be the function of GNP *(V)*, the inflow of foreign capital *(F)* and the share of exports in GNP $\left(\frac{E}{V}\right)$ have been tested by fitting the regression equation. The Table 7.6 reveals that the impact of additional foreign capital on savings was found to be negative for all the countries in the study except Venezuela but the impact of export share was positive. In reference to the period of study, the inflow of foreign capital has increased for almost all countries covered in the study. The trend in export share rose during the post-reforms period (1980-2000) in all the selected countries. However, these results are not conclusive that the trade competition has been the dominant factor for most of the Latin American countries towards augmenting their export share.

The Central American countries have shown good growth results during the reforms period, though Chile has shown extraordinary growth during the referred period. Mexico, Argentina and Brazil also show an increasing trend in the economic growth which is largely influenced by the increasing exports share during the reforms period. The countries which experienced decline in the export share include Venezuela, Columbia and Paraguay. The model used for the projections of export growth (2015) has been conceived as largely exogenous. The regression results for the factors of economic growth have been exhibited in Table 7.7.

An export sector responsive to the trade situation of the country is assumed as "high performance". The exogenous growth rate of exports has been derived through the following equation:

$$E_t = E_0(1+\varepsilon'')^t \tag{1}$$

Where, $(\varepsilon'')$ represents exogenous growth rate of exports *(E)*, $E_t$ denotes the exports of goods and services in the reforms period and $E_0$ exhibits the historical performance of the exports of the countries in the region. The results exhibited in Table 7.7 reveal that all the countries selected in the study show faster growth in exports though the actual growth may be reflected by the trade policies of theses countries implemented through various types of agreements *e.g.* free trade agreement, common market or bilateral trade. As measured by the adjusted $R^2$, the fit of this dynamic specification is slightly better than that of its static counterpart. Moreover, in the dynamic specification, education is statistically significant. The evidence thus suggests the presence of a minor partial offset to the beneficial growth effect of stabilization during the post-reforms years[260]. Assuming low variation in the regional economic growth and taking the estimates at their face values, the income effect is immediate, the short term effect from relative prices is lagged, and the estimated short run price elasticity (-)0.3 is lower in absolute value than the long run elasticity (-)1.3. These results are common in the analysis of time-series data of foreign trade[261]. While using regression results to project savings behavior, it has been assumed that the observed coefficients on GNP and export share describe the coefficient on foreign capital. The equation for potential savings (S) is hence derived as:

$$(S)_t = (S)_{t-1} + \alpha\Delta V + \gamma\Delta\left(E/V\right) \tag{2}$$

[260] The results of the data analysis exhibited in Tables 7.6 and 7.7 and inferences drawn on the results support the hypotheses H2, H3, H4 and H5.

[261] Rajagopal (2005), Institutional Reforms and Trade Competitiveness in Latin America, *Applied Econometrics and International Development*, 5 (1), 45-64.

**Table 7.8. Welfare Equilibrium in Trading Blocs in Latin America**

| Trade Blocs | NE | FTA | CM | BT |
|---|---|---|---|---|
| 1 | 2.079 | 1.235 | 0.493 | 0.079 |
| 2 | 1.532 | 0.928 | 1.163 | 1.212 |
| 3 | 1.670 | 0.946 | 1.325 | 1.495 |
| LAC Region | 1.752 | 0.986 | 1.012 | 0.929 |

Trade Blocs 1 = NAFTA (FTA- Free Trade Agreement);
2 = Common Market (CM) – Mercosur;
3 = Bilateral Trade (BT) between two countries on mutually convenient agreement;
NE = Nash Equilibrium.

Where, $\Delta$ refers to the change between the pre-reforms period $(t-1)$ and the reforms period $(t)$. In the equation $\alpha$ represents propensity to save from additional GNP and $\gamma$ denotes the effect of changes in export share on savings.

Since the welfare measure leading to the economic benefit emerging out of foreign trade agreements has been computed in terms of tariff region (taxes) and revenue, it provides an estimate of percentage change in the revenue as an indicator of economic welfare through trade agreements. The economic welfare indicators associated with Nash equilibrium is discussed in the Table 7.8. The results reveal that NAFTA (Trading Bloc 1) has gained over the other two trading blocs in terms of revenue though the trading costs were higher. Each trading bloc approximately gains 1.5% higher in the LAC region, by changing optimal tariff. The trading bloc 2 has gained marginally lesser than the trading bloc 3 which is formed out of bilateral trade agreements. This leads to smaller tariffs and lower economic welfare gains. The analysis of economic welfare gains through Nash equilibrium allows critical examination of the optimal policy in an economy that evolves around take-off state, which is not necessarily efficient[262].

## REVEALED COMPARATIVE ADVANTAGE IN EAST ASIA AND LATIN AMERICA

In order to compute the RCA among the East Asian and Latin American countries, the ISCI data of UNIDO (2005) has been used for 11 Latin American countries and 8 East Asian countries. The Asian countries have been categorized into newly industrializing economies, trade partnering economies (ASEAN) and developed economy of the region. The East Asian Newly Industrializing Economics (EANIEs) consisted of Hong Kong, South Korea and Singapore, while the ASEAN4 is composed of the four economies (Indonesia, Malaysia, Philippines and Thailand) of the Association of Southeast Asian Nations (ASEAN). Together with Japan, East Asia contains a total of eight economies. Although we look specifically at three regions of EANIEs, ASEAN4 and LA, we first take an aggregated view on the export performance of the whole East Asia region. In order to achieve higher significance in the

[262] The data analysis presented in the Table 7.8 and inferences drawn on the results thereof supports the hypotheses H1 and H5.

analysis of the ISCI data of UNIDO-2005, the information has been aggregated into the clusters representing the three, five and ten main export clusters (EC) on a 3-digit industry classification, and the sector's corresponding global imports are used as an indicator of global demand. The Tables 7.9 and 7.10 exhibits the export performance of the East Asia and Latin America countries selected for the study, respectively. For the entire period 1981-2003, trade performances are reported on the basis of a triennium ending.

East Asia's share of the 10 main manufacturing export sectors is high, with an average exceeding 82 percent; similarly, their share in global total manufacturing imports is significant, with an average of more than 20 percent. Nonetheless, East Asia's manufacturing exports have concentrated in the high-value manufacturing sector groups. While their share of the 3 and 5 main export sectors increased, the 10 main export sectors showed a decrease beginning from the early 1990s. The performance of the exports of manufacturing sector in East Asia is exhibited in Table 7.9.

The share of East Asian exports in global manufacturing imports - for the 5 and 10 main and the total manufacture exports showed an increase of up to 4 percent in the 1990s. Therefore, an increase in East Asia's share in global manufacturing imports between 2 and 3 percent can be detected for the entire 1981-1997 periods. These increases are evidences of the successful trade policies that East Asian economics had pursued in the 1980s and 1990s. In term of the growth rates, two distinct periods can be identified. In the 1980s, with the exception of the 1981-1983 sub-periods, the global demand (the equivalent global imports) of the 3, 5 and 10 main export sectors showed a higher growth performance than their correspondent main export sectors. In the 1990s, on the contrary, East Asia's manufacturing exports had a much better growth performance than the correspondent global imports. For the whole period 1981-1997, East Asia's manufacturing sector exports growth outperformed the global demand growth for the corresponding manufacturing sectors. The success of East Asia trade exports reflected the suitable trade policies these economies had pursued, and their comparative advantage shows an improvement.

For the Latin American region, although their 10 main export sectors accounted for an average share of about 69 percent for the period 1981-1997, their share showed significant decrease over time. For example, their share of the 10 main exports decreased from 83.49 percent to 58.78 percent during 1981-1983 and 1996-1997 sub-periods, showing a decrease of 24.71 percent.

Compared to East Asia, however, Latin America's manufacturing exports are much less concentrated, their values are also much lower, and their share in global total manufacturing imports is only about 2.3 percent on average. The performance of the exports of manufacturing sector in East Asia is exhibited in Table 7.10. Beginning from the second half of the 1980s, however, their share showed a steady increase in global manufacturing imports. Similarly, an increase of the share in global manufacturing imports can also be detected for the 3, 5 and 10 main manufacturing export sectors. Evidences show that the shift of trade policies by Latin American economics in the 1990s had revived their export performance and a gain in export advantage is expected.

**Table 7.9. Analysis of Exports of Manufacturing Sector in East Asian Countries (1981-2003) (in US million dollars)**

| Performance | 1981-83 | | | | 1990-92 | | | | 2001-2003[a] | | | |
|---|---|---|---|---|---|---|---|---|---|---|---|---|
| Indicators | EC-1 | EC-2 | EC-3 | EC-4 | EC-1 | EC-2 | EC-3 | EC-4 | EC-1 | EC-2 | EC-3 | EC-4 |
| Average annual exports | 91.32 | 108.25 | 150.95 | 182.36 | 238.97 | 275.75 | 347.41 | 426.99 | 674.33 | 722.09 | 582.39 | 964.82 |
| Ave. annual global imports | 300.15 | 413.02 | 633.59 | 973.13 | 843.37 | 1089.6 | 15787.7 | 237.87 | 1964.76 | 2386.99 | 6329.33 | 4988.55 |
| Share in total exports | 50.7 | 59.36 | 82.78 | - | 55.97 | 64.58 | 81.36 | - | 64.12 | 73.34 | 87.92 | - |
| Share in global imports | 30.42 | 26.21 | 23.83 | 18.74 | 28.34 | 25.31 | 22.01 | 17.95 | 31.04 | 29.91 | 24.66 | 18.20 |
| Growth in main exports (in percent) | 1.5 | 0.74 | -3.09 | -2.83 | 27.59 | 22.39 | 22.71 | 26.53 | 25.31 | 28.54 | 27.77 | 29.52 |
| Growth in global imports (in percent | 0.48 | -1.57 | -5.10 | -4.00 | 16.09 | 13.65 | 12.05 | 11.99 | 18.02 | 15.45 | 14.86 | 15.03 |

EC-1: Export cluster-1 consisting of 3 main export sectors.

EC-2: Export cluster-2 consisting of 5 main export sectors next to EC-1.

EC-3: Export cluster-3 consisting of 10 main export sectors next to EC-2.

EC-4: Total manufacturing exports of the selected countries.

[a] Projected data by the author.

Principal source of information UNIDO statistics 2005.

**Table 7.10. Analysis of Exports of Manufacturing Sector in Latin American Countries (1981-2003) (in US million dollars)**

| Performance | 1981-83 | | | | 1990-92 | | | | 2001-2003[a] | | | |
|---|---|---|---|---|---|---|---|---|---|---|---|---|
| Indicators | EC-1 | EC-2 | EC-3 | EC-4 | EC-1 | EC-2 | EC-3 | EC-4 | EC-1 | EC-2 | EC-3 | EC-4 |
| Average annual exports | 8.35 | 10.13 | 17.51 | 20.97 | 18.86 | 231.14 | 30.08 | 38.24 | 32.19 | 422.84 | 54.96 | 66.21 |
| Ave. annual global imports | 251.79 | 423.26 | 606.82 | 973.13 | 578.49 | 1041.92 | 1370.34 | 2378.71 | 865.33 | 2311.56 | 2373.52 | 3984.66 |
| Share in total exports | 39.83 | 48.32 | 83.49 | - | 49.33 | 60.44 | 78.65 | - | 64.42 | 72.14 | 84.32 | - |
| Share in global imports | 3.32 | 2.39 | 2.88 | 2.15 | 3.26 | 2.22 | 2.19 | 1.16 | 2.04 | 3.69 | 2.55 | 1.84 |
| Growth in main exports (in percent) | -7.68 | -4.24 | 17,51 | 23.04 | 15.00 | 12.58 | 9.28 | 12.78 | 18.42 | 16.81 | 19.92 | 15.43 |
| Growth in global imports (in percent | .3.67 | -3.04 | -4.34 | -4.00 | 10.72 | 11.22 | 8.51 | 11.99 | 14.55 | 16.73 | 12.60 | 14.81 |

EC-1: Export cluster-1 consisting of 3 main export sectors.

EC-2: Export cluster-2 consisting of 5 main export sectors next to EC-1.

EC-3: Export cluster-3 consisting of 10 main export sectors next to EC-2.

EC-4: Total manufacturing exports of the selected countries.

[a] Projected data by the author.

Principal source of information UNIDO statistics 2005.

The pattern of Latin America's export growth rates, however, is different from East Asia. The percentage growth rates within each of the sub-periods are in general and in particular the 1987-89 and 1996-1997 sub-periods, higher than the global import growth rate for the same sectors. The two exceptions are the 3 and 5 main export sectors for the 1981-1983 and the 1993-1995 sub-periods when global imports performed much better than Latin America's export growth. Table 7.11 shows that the values of the Lawrence Index are very low, though they are constant over the sub-periods, suggesting that there was not an important structural change in the export pattern of East Asia in the whole period. The Beneficial Index did not suggest significant structural change in exports pattern. Both indices indicate that over the period 1981-1997, East Asia's export pattern remained constant. In other words, the same export structure was kept, even though East Asia had been oriented to the most dynamic product sectors in the global markets during this period. The two trade specialization indices show the same pattern. From the beginning of the 1980s to the second half of the 1990s, there was a steady decrease in trade specialization, and there were little movements to "diversify" exports (and imports).

Although there was an increase in intra-industry trade over the period covered by the data, the absolute value of these indices remained low, indicating that the degree of trade specialization was low since the beginning of the 1980s. This also meant that the extent of intra-industry trade had already reached the "maximum" level. The trade performance indices computed for the Lawrence index, beneficial index, Michaely index and Trade specialization index for the East Asian and Latin American countries are exhibited in Table 7.11.

An inference may be drawn from the above Table that for the East Asia region there was no significant change in revealed comparative advantage (RCA) of manufacturing sectors, but is affected by inter-country economic differences, as well as inter-industry disparities. The RCA is primarily based on relative export shares that could be biased due to distortions from various trade and non-trade barriers[263].

**Table 7.11. Trade Performance Index**

| Region | Performance Index | 1981-83 | 1990-92 | 2001-03 |
|---|---|---|---|---|
| East Asia | Lawrence Index | 0.03 | 0.04 | 0.03 |
| | Beneficial Index | 0.01 | 0.01 | 0.03 |
| | Michaely Index | 0.31 | 0.20 | 0.14 |
| | Trade Specialization Index | 0.29 | 0.24 | 0.22 |
| Latin America | Lawrence Index | 0.11 | 0.08 | 0.27 |
| | Beneficial Index | 0.03 | 0.01 | 0.09 |
| | Michaely Index | 0.61 | 0.43 | 0.39 |
| | Trade Specialization Index | 0.59 | 0.03 | 0.34 |

Data computed by the author based on the statistics of UNIDO, Indstat-2005.

[263] The results discussed in Tables 7.9 to 7.11 and inferences drawn accordingly supports the hypotheses H5 and H6 framed for the study.

Based on the statistical data from the UNIDO (1999) source, the empirical study supports the hypothesis of a comparative advantage shift between East Asia and Southeast Asia, and that Latin America also captured the loss in comparative advantage in East Asia. Despite East Asia's strong growth in exports in the 1980s and 1990s, its export pattern is losing its comparative advantage to the lower-tier major ASEAN-4 countries (EC-2) and Latin American countries. Between the 1980s and 1990s, the falling strength in East Asia's trade is captured by the growing strength in the exports of ASEAN-4 and Latin American countries.

## APPLIED INFERENCES OF DATA ANALYSIS

There are large differences in gross domestic products by sectors among Latin American countries, and majority of these differences are due to the change in the value of industrial and service sectors. The structural reforms Latin American countries have broadly focused in five major areas comprising international trade, financial markets, labor markets, and the generation and use of public resources. Consequently the financial development has improved, especially the depth of financial intermediation, private sector participation in banking, and the size and activity of stock markets. The economic integration and structural reforms in Latin America considered that import substitution in manufacturing sector would be synonymous with industrialization, which in turn was seen as the key to development. As far as the efficient generation and use of public resources are concerned, much has been done to make the value-added tax system efficient and to privatize public enterprises. In response to the liberalization of economies, there has been significant increase in the imports, primarily due to lower inflation, lesser government intervention, and fewer trade barriers. International trade has been the key indicator of the overall economic growth of Latin American countries. The study reviews the approach to trade policy in early reforms period and evolution of thoughts, integrating the economic and structural reforms in Latin America.

The institutional reforms towards trade liberalizations in Latin America during the 1980s and the 1990s have introduced a good measure of import competition, but trade policies alone are not sufficient to create a competitive environment in an economy. The change in economy has taken place through the free trade policies in Latin America since 1980's, and most of the region's economies have changed from restrictive to open policies. However, unlike trade liberalization in Europe, most trade barriers in Latin America have been reduced unilaterally. Many Latin American countries favored free trade to improve their economies in terms of savings, export share, foreign reserves and growth of GNP during the reforms period. Business participation in trade policy reflects these patterns in large, outward-oriented firms which played an increasingly important role in Mexico's adoption of free trade policies over the 1980s and early 1990s. After decades of weak growth in Latin American countries, the manufacturing sector exports have shown optimistic results in recent years following the international trade agreements. The proposed study examines the trends of export dynamism in the Latin American countries and attempts to analyze whether the current pace of growth is sustainable.

During the reforms, progress has been especially remarkable on trade and financial liberalization. However, these reforms proved largely successful in jump-starting economies they have not delivered long-term economic growth on a sustainable basis. Macro-economic reforms must be accompanied by institutional reforms, if they are to have a sustained impact on the economy. There is strong empirical evidence that better governance and higher quality institutions promote higher rates of economic growth. In this context, it is argued that structural and institutional differences between Latin America and South East Asia imply a difference of 2 per cent per annum in growth. It has been observed by the researchers in reference to LAC countries that the monetary and fiscal policies could be counter-cyclical in emerging countries[264]. Their cyclical stance depends on country fundamentals and policy credibility. Fiscal and monetary policies are counter-cyclical in emerging economies with low to moderate country-risk spreads. International exchange-rate regimes became less persistent than hard pegs and floats in LAC after the Asian crisis. The choice of exchange-rate regimes and their transitions do matter for inflation and growth. Inflation in LAC is lower if the regime is less flexible, whereas growth in LAC is higher if the regime is more flexible. The contribution of very successful structural reforms reflected in a massive growth jump in these countries.

Greater trade openness in Latin America would help to improve institutions. The opening up of markets can play an important role in weakening vested interests and reducing economic rents associated with long standing economic and institutional arrangements. Trade can thus spur improvement in domestic institutions that otherwise would not have been possible. In addition, international agreements can be an important external anchor and catalyst for institutional change by breaking through domestic impediments to reforms. Chile and Mexico provide important role models for the region. Institutional strengthening in both the countries has allowed them to establish a successful inflation targeting framework, to lower public debt, to open the trading regime, and to build a strong regulatory and oversight framework for the banking system. Both the countries also provide important lessons of targeted social spending. Chile's example, in particular, of institutional changes that limit the room for inconsistent fiscal behavior by the regional governance, provides an especially valuable lesson to other countries that have frequently witnessed high fiscal volatility.

Although Latin America has been intensively debating appropriate institutional designs for more than two decades, little progress has been made. One of the key challenges, therefore, will be to provide explanations as to why institutional reforms have succeeded in some policy areas but not in others. Today, most of the Latin American countries are well-respected democracies, with a multi-party political system, the division of powers, a working parliament and regular elections. However, at the same time, there is a strong crisis of confidence, not only towards governments, but in the whole political class and representation in general. The increasing lack of confidence in the political elite in Latin America has fostered new forms of opposition in several countries, leading to a significant number of Latin American presidents not being capable of completing their terms of office during the 1990s. Although political shifts are a constant feature of democracy and they generally indicate the strengths of democratic institutions, a more stable political system in the region would have helped to pursue reforms processes in a more effective way. Specifically, a strong macroeconomic stabilization will, after some short-run recessive effects, provide a framework that has less distortion for economic indicators than the pre-reforms period.

---

264 Cesar Calderon and Hebbel Klasu Schemidt (2003): *Macroeconomic Policies and Performance in Latin America*, Working Paper 217, Central Bank of Chile, June.

The failure of market reforms in Latin America to produce sustained growth and equitable prosperity is demonstrated most clearly by Argentina's most recent economic and political meltdown. Nevertheless, economic difficulties, poverty and searing inequality has continued to plague the Mexican case as well. Latin American policy makers themselves have begun to contribute to the growing discussion of policies necessary to confront the lingering economic and social challenges. Included among the recommended policy prescriptions are: increased social spending supported by tax reforms, assistance to small and medium enterprises, and an end to corruption. Such policy reforms require governments that are autonomous from particular business interests with established institutional channels capable of securing generalized business cooperation and support[265].

Latin American economy has gained substantial competitive advantage in the 1990s. Their improvement in RCA and trade diversification reflected more their government's trade and liberalization strategy than changes in factor endowment. One reason for the strong RCA improvement certainly is Latin America's initial low share in global export. That is, a relatively small increase in export value accounts for a relatively high increase in the RCA indices of Latin America. Several other factors are also responsible for improvements in Latin America. The North America Free Trade Agreement (NAFTA) concluded in the late 1980s welded together the economies of the United States, Canada and Mexico, thereby forming a solid regional trading block that benefited directly Mexico and indirectly other Latin American economies. Secondly, by the early 1990s, Argentina gained economic stability and an improved export performance emerged. During the 1970s and 1980s, Chile pursued a process of trade liberalization that reorganized and modernized the economy's production structure. All this reflected in a significant improvement in trade performance by the Chilean economy. Peru was also another Latin American country that succeeded in stabilizing the economy in the early 1990s, and improvement in economic conditions was reflected in an improvement in export performance. Argentina, Chile Peru and Mexico are the key Latin American economies in our RCA calculation. For the improvement of RCA to be sustainable, however, Latin American economies should maintain a period of stability and avoid economic or political shocks that devastated her hard-earned comparative advantage.

It is well established that inflation, for example, is costly and that its elimination is beneficial for the long-run growth. The same is true of structural reforms. Multiple exchange rates, multiple interest rates, protection of domestic products with licenses, quotas, tariffs in the excess of what would have been necessary for infant industries, and a welter of regulations and bureaucratic obstacles to normal business in general have detrimental effects on economic growth. Mainstream economic theory suggests that economic welfare would be maximized when distortions are minimized. Accordingly, a removal of distortions of both macroeconomic and microeconomic nature would have beneficial effects on economic activity and the rate of growth[266]. Therefore, there exists a mutual reinforcement of those benefits as the reforms process goes on. In other words, there might be a synergistic relationship between the effects of structural reforms and macroeconomic stabilization.

[265] Teichman J (2002): Private Sector Power and Market Reforms – Exploring the Domestic Origins of Argentina's Meltdown and Mexico's Policy Failures, *Third World Quarterly*, 23 (3), June, 491-512.

[266] Igor Paunovic (2000), *Growth and Reforms in Latin America and the Caribbean in the 1990s*, United Nations Economic Commission for Latin America and the Caribbean (ECLAC), Working Paper, Economic Division, May.

There is a wide disparity in the growth performance in the 1990s of the seventeen countries studied. There are "leaders" and "laggards" and to understand the effect of structural reforms on growth, it is necessary to explain the growth performance of both groups. The leading economies had a lower average rate of growth in the base period than in the 1990s, low or negative growth rates immediately before the reforms took place, and huge macroeconomic imbalances. That sparked the reform process and made it much more comprehensive than in other countries. "Laggards", in contrast, fared much better during the three post-war decades than during the 1990s. Also, their growth rates immediately before the adoption of reforms were not as low as the ones of the "leading" economies, and in most cases they did not experience hyperinflation. As a consequence, the pressure to change was not as strong as in the countries hit harder by the crisis. The economies with stronger growth record during the post-reforms had a much better macroeconomic stabilization record and have adopted deeper and more comprehensive structural reforms[267].

The countries that adopted far-reaching structural reforms and macroeconomic stabilization did well in the sense that they overcame the credibility problem. They managed to signal that the reform process is irreversible and that the rules of the game have changed for good, both at macroeconomic and microeconomic level. Others that lacked a combination of strong stabilization and strong reforms made things worse with partial reforms since the absence of positive results further undermined the support for reforms. The investment climate did not improve as expected, which further weakened the chances of future reformers. There were also some reinforcing elements that point towards the possibility of synergy between macroeconomic stabilization and structural reforms. Although reforms have had specific and unique characteristics in different countries, there are also some fundamental common threads. Specifically, Argentina, Chile and Peru are the examples of strong macroeconomic stabilization and intense reforms, and the payoff was formidable. On the other side of the spectrum are Ecuador and Venezuela, countries that have changed the course several times during the last fifteen years, increasing the uncertainty for economic agents and reducing the credibility of the policy makers. In addition, for still other economies (Mexico, Paraguay) the reforms did not work as expected, and the payoff has yet to materialize.

The high performance in savings, exports share and reserves of foreign assets would permit accelerated growth to occur with increase in the cumulative capital inflow. Hence, the Latin American countries may develop policies to identify resources, which would promote the domestic savings and growth of GNP. The increase in inflow of capital would help stimulating improved domestic development performance. The long-run accelerated growth at the cost of external resources may be less than the pre-reforms experience of the countries in resources management. The discussion in the study reveals that growth rates tend to fall only temporarily following a balance-of-payments crisis and then rebound to the pre-crisis levels in some of the Latin American countries. However, a balance-of-payments issue is often associated with a decline of growth rates and may run into the export crisis in the future.

The results of the study determine that international liquidity, financial soundness, real exchange rate depreciation and monetary policy play a critical role in reducing output losses and increasing the economic welfare gains. It has been discussed in the study that while

---

[267] Igor Paunovic (2000), *Growth and Reforms in Latin America and the Caribbean in the 1990s*, United Nations Economic Commission for Latin America and the Caribbean (ECLAC), Working Paper, Economic Division, May.

applying the Nash equilibrium, gains from trade liberalization rise through the various types of trade agreements, however, that stem from the impact of foreign economic activity on the domestic marginal cost of production. The trade competitiveness reflects significantly in reference to the welfare losses and gains. The variables that determine the efficacy of the trading blocs include exchange rates, foreign direct investments, total factor productivity and growth in exports. The interest rates in response to domestic inflation need to be adjusted to foreign inflation within the trading blocs in order to optimize the economic welfare gains. The growth impetus associated with the reforms in Latin America has been substantial and the estimated long-run growth effect of the 1990s reform is large for most countries in the region and amounts to almost 2 percentage points of additional annual sustainable growth in the aggregate, enough to double the real income expected in future.

## General Discussion

Economic integration and growth in trade in the Latin American region have created a need for new and major business developments. In this context, the international partnering has emerged as the driving force towards global trade and legal initiatives related to trade agreements. Globalization can be described as the combined influences of trade liberalization, market integration, international finance and investment, technological change, the increasing distribution of production across national boundaries and the emergence of new structures of global governance. Globalization is not new, but it is more pervasive than before and international partnering is a pivot of globalization process that drives the concepts of production sharing, strategic alliances and competitive advantages among the countries[268]. The fundamentals of effective partnering in an international context are the same as those applied to a local domestic relationship but are more complex. The whole process of building an effective international partnering relationship is likely to take longer to implement, consume more time and effort and involve more cost than a similar local arrangement. However, the potential opportunities from an international partnering relationship are likely to be significant provided there is a clearly articulated agreed plan of action. The advantages of the international partnering may be described in many ways, of these some significant determinants include:

- Diverting business from market saturation in home country
- Improving the production standards, manufacturing process and services
- Developing trade related international political relations
- Compensating trade deficit and long disequilibrium in the balance of trade
- Helping increase foreign competition for healthy market environment
- Explore the business opportunities by the emergence of new markets
- Functionally supporting globalization and free trade agreements, and
- Developing opportunities via foreign aid programs

[268] Rajagopal (2007): *International Marketing: Global Environment, Corporate Strategies and Case Studies*, Vikas Publishing House, New Delhi, 2005.

Most of the Latin American countries began to open their international business opportunities to the rest of the world in 80's. This process has made significant improvement in the structural adjustments program along with the debt management strategies. It has helped the Latin American countries to overcome the industrial and trade policy of import substitution of over four decades. During the late 80's and early 90's a large number of countries began to relax existing protection and bent their energies towards international trade reforms with the increasing assistance of the multilateral institutions. Trade reforms process has proceeded at a faster pace and tariff barriers have been reduced significantly. There has been a significant transition in the international relations and business partnering of Latin American countries with the rest of the world in the post 80's period that has reflected in the economic and technological growth of some countries like Mexico, Brazil, Chile and Peru. The recent trade liberalization policies of the Latin American countries have sought to reserve the protectionist policies and open the scope for foreign direct investment and joint ventures in the public and private sector industries. Regional integration such as NAFTA, CAFTA and MERCOSUR has been flourishing in Latin American countries since the 1990s. In addition to these multi-countries free trade agreements (FTA), many bilateral FTAs have also emerged both among Latin American countries and extra-regional countries. International partnering is necessary for global accessibility to the markets and may give a boost in determining the market opportunities as narrowing the trade barriers helped in deregulating certain sectors of trade such as financial services. Many Latin American countries have shown increased openness to international trade in the recent past but have received less attention towards international partnering in the form of joint ventures, strategic alliances and co-branding[269]. International partnering would bring many advantages to the countries that are described by the international development organizations like world Trade Organization, World Bank, International Monetary Fund and the United Nation's regional bodies like Economic Commission for Latin America and Caribbean (ECLAC). Of these, some of the principal benefits that attract the developing countries to look for strategic international alliance may include:

- Bringing together international partners from different socio-cultural backgrounds and technological advancement levels.
- Determining the optimal size and ambience of international trade between the two countries
- Exploring the global scope of business
- Establishing high profile of trade partnership for mutual benefit in production, branding, promotion, distribution and services
- To develop diplomatic relations and political alignment with the countries involved in globalization
- Developing overseas business bases for spatial expansion
- Introduce the global financial customs and practices
- Developing resources and infrastructure that are compatible for international operations

[269] Bruce Owen M (2003): Competition Policy in Latin America, Institute of Economic Policy Research, Stanford University, Working Paper # 268.

However, yet Latin American countries appear to focus explicitly towards the positive effects on economic behavior, and engage in systematic evaluation and measurement of the effects of its international trade policies encouraging the international partnering in the research and development, manufacturing, marketing and services areas. The institutional reforms process in Latin American countries showed that the rate of growth in Chile, Brazil, Costa Rica and Mexico were higher than other countries in the region. The success of institutional reforms resulted in lowering the tariff barriers, better international relations and business partnering of Latin American countries with rest of the world during 90's and further. The reciprocity of other countries towards business partnering with Latin American countries also needs to be studied at the same time[270].

The dramatic changes in trade policy in emerging economies have made a significant impact on the degree with which the emerging economies are being integrated into the world economy. The market openings around the world have created considerable opportunities for these countries to expand trade and to stimulate the growth of their economies. Trade liberalization has also done much to improve the competitiveness and as a result, the growth of trade has often been much faster than the growth of domestic output. In other words, trade has performed another important function - that of an engine of domestic growth. Given the extent of change that has taken place, we expect the period ahead to focus on consolidation of the reforms we have described (including implementation of the Uruguay Round commitments), rather than further rapid change. Some policies will have to be further refined at the national level to increase the speed of the supply-side response so that the welfare gains from the new liberalism can be felt by a wider section of the communities in emerging economies. Otherwise there is a danger of loosing fragile public support for the changes[271]. Thus, we perceive a need in many emerging markets to build on the reforms already undertaken and to strengthen the institutional and legal framework for trade and the national and international levels. The consequent increase in security of access and operating conditions in these markets should assist in attracting investment to provide the motor for future development. However, these countries also need improved access to developed domestic markets.

[270] Rajagopal (2005): Institutional Reforms and Trade Competitiveness in Latin America, Paper presented in the International Conference on Strategic Management in Latin America, Jointly organized by INACE and Journal of Business Research, Campus Walter Kissing Gam, INACE, Alajuela, Costa Rica, January 6-7, 2005.

[271] Zdenek Drabek and Sam Laird (1997), The New Liberalism: Trade Policy Developments in Emerging markets, Staff Working Paper # ERAD 9707-WFP, World Trade Organization, 2-30.

# Part III: Looking Ahead

*Chapter 8*

# STRATEGIC BUSINESS PARTNERING

There are large differences in gross domestic products by sectors among Latin American countries, and the majority of these differences are due to the value of industrial and service sectors. Although the sectoral economic activity has been increased, in per capita terms this value decreased due to the demographic growth that Latin American countries (mainly Mexico and Brazil) had experienced during the last decades. In terms of external trade, it has been found that the outward orientation as the ratio between total exports and GDP increased from 16.1% in 1990 to 32.7% in year 2000. Panama had the highest level in this area (66.5%). Modest growth returned to Latin America and the Caribbean in 2003 and regional GDP advanced by an average 1.3 percent, after a contraction of 0.6 percent in 2002. Argentina continued recovering rapidly after its acute crisis. Brazil, Mexico and Uruguay shared in the broadening of economic recovery during the year. Andean countries performed well, with Chile, Colombia and Peru recording growth above 3 percent. However, ongoing political uncertainties caused Venezuela's economy to deteriorate further during the first half of the year. Central America grew by an average 3.1 percent and looks set to sustain growth, thanks to the recently signed Central America Free Trade Agreement[272] (CAFTA). The rate of change in the merchandize export in the Latin American countries during 2002 shows that most of the countries in the region except Costa Rica, Ecuador, Peru and St. Kit Islands other have shown a downward trend.

The Central American Free Trade Agreement (CAFTA) negotiated between the U.S. and Central America offers opportunities and challenges for the five countries including El Salvador, Guatemala, Honduras, and Nicaragua that joined in 2003 and Costa Rica that was included in January 2004. Mexico, Nicaragua, Jamaica and Honduras always were over the mean. During the years 1990, 1995 and 2000, Mexico, Cuba, Panama, Argentina, Brazil, Chile and Uruguay reached incomes above 2000 dollars per capita in the service sector[273]. On the other hand, there are some countries like Haiti, Honduras, Nicaragua and Bolivia with incomes below 500 dollars per capita. Latin America's merchandise exports increased slightly as the decline in intra-regional trade was balanced by increased shipments to other regions. The recovery of commodity prices in the course of the year and the upturn in the US economy contributed to this rise. While most Latin American countries saw a reduction or stagnation in

---

[272] World Bank: Report on Latin America and Caribbean, Regional Overview, 2003.

[273] Guisan, M.C. and Aguayo (2000): Education, Industary, Trade and Development of American Companies in 1980-99, *Applied Econometrics and International Development* 2(1), 83-106.

their imports, those of Costa Rica increased by 9 per cent. Mexico benefited from the recovery of the US market while for Costa Rica, the recovery in semi-conductor shipments boosted both imports and exports. Despite the continuation of low prices for a number of primary commodities, exports of many Central American and Caribbean countries recovered strongly. Economic activity in Western Europe remained subdued as Germany, the largest economy, experienced declining domestic demand. Domestic demand growth remained positive in the rest of the region, but was sluggish in several other countries. In the euro zone, public consumption was the most dynamic expenditure category while private consumption slowed down and fixed investment in the enterprise sector fell nearly 3 per cent. In the midst of this poor economic situation, further progress was made in the process of European integration[274].

Starting in the mid-sixties of the 20$^{th}$ century, the European example inspired a number of trade-oriented integration arrangements in the Latin American region such as the Latin American Free Trade Association, which later became the Latin American Integration Association (ALADI), the Central American Common Market (MCCA), the Caribbean Community and Common Market (CARICOM), the Andean Group, later the Andean Community; and more recently, the Southern Common Market (Mercosur), the Group of Three (G3) and the Association of Caribbean States (ACS). There are many bilateral alliances as well. Latin American countries have been living a renaissance since 80's. Most economies are stabilized, living standards are higher, direct foreign investment has surged, democracy has been institutionalized and most countries have demonstrated a desire to integrate themselves into the new global economy by opening their economies to international trade and investment. During 1980, the Latin American countries have liberalized their economies, which have been followed by a significant increase in their imports. This improvement was due primarily to three factors: lower inflation, less government intervention, and fewer trade barriers. International trade has been the key indicator of the overall economic growth of Latin American countries. Several regional free trade agreements signed over the past decade--such as Mercosur, the Central American Common Market, the Andean Community, and the Caribbean Common Market-demonstrate the region's understanding of the benefits of free trade. Countries like Chile have gone even further in their trade liberalization efforts, signing bilateral agreements with Mexico and Canada after being unable to sign an agreement with the entire NAFTA bloc. In terms of scope, sectors of interest and coverage, there are three levels of sub-regional arrangements: (i) customs unions currently being finalized, e.g., the Andean Community, Mercosur, MCCA and CARICOM, (ii) first-generation free trade accords with a commercial emphasis, and (iii) new-generation free trade pacts encompassing such sectors as services, investment, intellectual ownership, and state acquisitions. Chile and Bolivia are successfully engaged in negotiations for broader scope aimed at furthering their association with Mercosur, establishing free trade areas and bringing other sectors and issues into the accords.

With investor confidence returning in Latin America and domestic conditions improving, gross private financial inflows in 2003 increased by 40 percent over 2002. Moreover, interest rate spreads on sovereign bonds over US treasuries reached record lows. Net foreign direct investment (FDI), however, continued its decline from a peak of \$88 billion in 1999 to an estimated \$36 billion in 2003. This is partly explained by the end of the privatization boom

[274] World Trade Organization: World Trade Report 2003, pp 30-42.

and the profit crisis in Brazil and Argentina. Export growth outpaced import growth for most countries in 2003, leading to surplus positions on trade and a big improvement in the region's current account deficit, down to 0.5 percent of GDP (compared to 4.5 percent in 1998). Tourism revenues and workers' remittances also improved, and commodity prices were generally strong. Consequent upon falling trade and investment barriers and high growth prospects, the countries of Latin America represent attractive alliance prospects for an increasing number of global firms. The typical objective for these strategic alliances is a basic trade-off wherein local firms seek access to technology and capabilities that are critical for their survival in an environment of increased competition and in return, they offer prospective multinational partners access to a large and growing market.

The region is becoming more attractive to multinationals, as product patent protection is implemented and, more importantly, enforced, in Latin American countries. Mexico, in particular, as a member of NAFTA, is attracting substantial inward investment. This is likely to grow even more rapidly in future, given the recent signing of a trade deal with the European Union. The recent recovery of oil prices has shown a positive sign of growth for a number of countries in the region, particularly Venezuela, Mexico and Colombia.

## INTERNATIONAL FINANCE AND ECONOMICS MANAGEMENT

Fiscal and monetary austerity attributes to lower GDP growth, perhaps slower rate of inflation and reduction in imports. Inflation may also be a significant issue of the fund but it is often less amenable to policy control. The financial programming in accordance with the status of balance of payments, fiscal and monetary accounts of the country is used as performance criteria by the Fund.

> In early 2000, the new Argentine government negotiated a three-year SBA to replace the extended arrangement that had fallen off track. The new arrangement, approved in March, provided SDR 5.4 billion ($7.2 billion) and was aimed at buttressing investor confidence and facilitating a sustainable recovery of the economy. Amid the unfavorable economic and political developments, Argentina effectively lost access to international capital markets. Although the arrangement had been treated as precautionary up to this time, the authorities recognized the gravity of the situation and requested exceptional support from the IMF[275]. By overlooking Argentina's growing indebtedness in the 1990s and continuing to lend the country money when its debt burden had become unsustainable, the fund significantly contributed to one of the most devastating financial crises in history. The crisis peaked when the Argentine government defaulted on nearly $100 billion in debt to private creditors and had to abandon the "convertibility" system that pegged the peso to the dollar at a one-to-one rate. The ensuing crash led to an 11 percent decline in Argentine output in 2002, sent the jobless rate soaring and toppled a series of presidents in a country that the IMF had once hailed as a model of free-market reform and development[276]. The crisis resulted from the failure of Argentine policy makers to take necessary corrective measures sufficiently early, particularly in the consistency of fiscal policy with their choice of exchange rate regime. The catastrophic collapse of the Argentine economy in 2001–02 represents the failure of Argentine policy makers to take

[275] International Monetary Fund: Report on the Role of IMF in Argentina- 1991-2001, Independent Evaluation Office, June 30, 2004, 63-80.

[276] Paul Blusterin (2004): IMF says its policies crippled Argentina, The Washington Post, Friday, July 30, E04.

> necessary corrective measures at a sufficiently early stage. The IMF on its part, supported by its major shareholders, also erred in failing to call an earlier halt to support for a strategy that, as implemented, was not sustainable. As the crisis deepened, the IMF was not able to engage the authorities in evolving an alternative strategy that might have helped mitigate the ultimate costs of the crisis, even though these would have been inevitably high. The IMF correctly identified the potential vulnerabilities inherent in the convertibility regime for a country like Argentina and the need for fiscal discipline and labor market flexibility as essential to the maintenance of the convertibility regime. The IMF pushed for corrective actions in both its surveillance activity and program design, but these efforts had mixed success and their impact declined over time as political commitment to the necessary adjustment waned[277].

There are some inflationary and contracting side effects that perpetuate in the institutional reforms strategy in the fiscal and monetary sector of the countries. The international institutions like IMF and World Bank should evaluate the reactions of implementing monetary solutions to rescue the falling economies. A core responsibility of the IMF is to provide loans to countries experiencing balance-of-payments problems. This financial assistance enables countries to rebuild their international reserves, stabilize their currencies, continue paying for imports, and restore conditions for strong economic growth. Unlike development banks, the IMF does not lend for specific projects. The volume of loans provided by the IMF has fluctuated significantly over time. The oil shock of the 1970s and the debt crisis of the 1980s were both followed by sharp increases in IMF lending. In the 1990s, the transition process in Central and Eastern Europe and the crises in emerging market economies led to further surges in the demand for IMF resources. Non-subsidized loans are provided through four main facilities: Stand-By Arrangements (SBA), the Extended Fund Facility (EFF), the Supplemental Reserve Facility (SRF), and the Compensatory Financing Facility (CFF). The IMF also provides emergency assistance to support recovery from natural disasters and armed conflicts, in some cases at subsidized interest rates. The Fund has created Special Drawing Rights (SDR) in 1969 as the resources providing short term benefits to the countries were not adequate. Sometimes called the SDRs have been analogized as paper gold as the SDR special account entry into the IMF books designed to provide additional liquidity to support the growing global trade requirements. The SDR is an international reserve asset, to supplement the existing official reserves of member countries. These drawing rights are allocated to member countries in proportion to their IMF quotas. The SDR also serves as the unit of account of the IMF and some other international organizations and its value is based on a basket of key international currencies.

The notion of SDR was considered in the Bretton Woods as the member countries in this system needed official reserves provided either by the government or central bank holdings of gold and widely accepted foreign currencies, which could be used to purchase the domestic currency in world foreign exchange markets, as required to maintain its exchange rate. However, the international supply of two key reserve assets - gold and the U.S. dollar proved inadequate for supporting the expansion of world trade and financial development that was taking place. The Fund thus created a new international reserve asset that has been termed as SDR. This right has only limited use as a reserve asset at present, and its main function is to serve as the unit of account of the Fund and some other international organizations. The SDR

---

[277] International Monetary Fund: Report on the Role of IMF in Argentina- 1991-2001, Independent Evaluation Office, June 30, 2004, 105-107.

is neither a currency, nor a claim on the IMF. Holders of SDRs can obtain these currencies in exchange for their SDRs in two ways: first, through the arrangement of voluntary exchanges between members; and second, by the IMF designating members with strong external positions to purchase SDRs from members with weak external positions. The value of the SDR was initially defined as equivalent to 0.888671 grams of fine gold-which, at the time, was also equivalent to one U.S. dollar. After the collapse of the Bretton Woods system in 1973, however, the SDR was redefined as a basket of currencies, today consisting of the euro, Japanese yen, pound sterling, and U.S. dollar. The Fund allocates the SDRs by way of General Allocations based on a long-term global need to supplement existing reserve assets and also by an application made by the countries for special one-time allocations subject to the approval of the IMF Board.

## Debt Crisis Management

Country risk has been an issue of prime concern all through the years after World War II for the international financial community. There have been various methods used by the risk rating agencies to determine the extent of country risk, integrating a range of qualitative and quantitative information on alternative measures of political, economic and financial risk to evolve composite risk indices. Country risk analysis is a complex task and it demands a holistic vision, expert skills and consistency in measurements. The analyst must follow standard procedures to assure coherency in its studies, using reliable and useful sources of data, including rating agencies, official institutions and other several sources. The country risk analysis reports show the strengths and weakness of a country, after dealing with the macroeconomic, socio-political and financial aspects in order to define a risk level and, consequently, a related price for the asset in risk. Managing the risk of a portfolio demands a systematic follow up concerning the external and internal environment, governmental policies' outlook provided by rating agencies, and so on.

The sharp increase in the oil prices, followed by worldwide inflation, a collapse in commodity prices, global recession and high interest rates wallop the economies of the developing countries world over during 1970s. When oil prices shot up, these countries borrowed heavily at high interest rates to prevent the economic downfall. The international financial institutions lent money to developing countries along with official subsidies and such aid grew very rapidly during this period. As a result of the irresponsibility of creditor and debtor governments (e.g., corruption, private projects benefiting only the rich, etc.), the countries did not use the money for productive investment; rather, they spent these new dollars on immediate consumption and the countries were unable to repay such amassed debt. Consequently, the total medium and long-term debt of developing countries quadrupled in nominal terms, from about $140 billion at the end of 1974 to about $560 billion in 1982. The debt trap got stiffer for these countries and the borrowings reached to the level of $ 2.4 trillion by the end of 1998.

The debt crisis has had a deep impact and consequences on the economic growth of the developing countries. This situation became alarming and of major concern to international community and international institutions, including IMF and World Bank took steps to find ways of reducing the impact of continuing debt of the developing countries. A framework to reduce the burden of debt has been evolved at two levels wherein the debtors need to grow faster and export more and to pull down the cost of debt service. During the process of overcoming the debt crisis, most countries have sought IMF assistance for debt relief. As a crisis managing institute, the Fund assumed a new role as financial organizer for the troubled debtor nations. The IMF required "structural adjustment programs" in these countries. Debtor governments had to agree to impose very strict economic programs on their countries in order to reschedule their debts or borrow more money. Put simply, countries had to cut spending to decrease their debt and stabilize their currency. The governments limited their costs by slashing social spending (e.g., education, health, social services, etc.), devaluing the national currency (via lowering export earnings and increasing import costs), creating strict limits on food subsidies, cutting workers' jobs and wages (especially workers in government industries and services), taking over small subsistence farms for large-scale export crop farming and promoting the privatization of public industries. Most countries have experienced the economic trauma of a recession and often a depression; and the poorest of the poor have been most affected. In 1982, Mexico declared that it was unable to repay its debts. Mexico owed vast sums of money to commercial banks in the west and default posed a serious threat to the stability of the international financial system. The commercial banks, in conjunction with the International Monetary Fund (IMF), worked out a system whereby indebted countries could spread out or reschedule their debts rather than default. It was during this time that the IMF and World Bank began to take over much of the debt owed to commercial banks. These institutions offered developing countries new loans with strict conditions attached. Since the 1980s the IMF and the World Bank, have been in control of the debt crisis. Indebted countries were required to follow policies favored by the IMF and World Bank to get new loans or even aid money. These policies have directly affected the lives and livelihoods of people in indebted countries.

The Highly Indebted Poor Countries (HIPC) initiative was first launched in 1996 by the IMF and World Bank, with the aim of ensuring that no poor country faces a debt burden it cannot manage. The initiative to create a framework for all creditors, including multilateral creditors, to provide debt relief to the world's poorest and most heavily indebted countries, and thereby reduce the constraint on economic growth and poverty reduction imposed by the debt build-up in these countries, was laid by the international financial institutes in the above period. The HIPC initiative entails coordinated action by the international financial community, including multilateral organizations and governments, to reduce to sustainable levels the external debt burdens of the most heavily indebted poor countries. Following a comprehensive review in September 1999, a number of modifications were approved to provide faster, deeper and broader debt relief and to strengthen the links between debt relief, poverty reduction and social policies.

Ethiopia is a landlocked country located in the Horn of Africa. With a per capita GDP of about US$100 (one fifth of the sub-Saharan average), Ethiopia is among the poorest countries in the world. Recent national household surveys find 44 percent of the people below the basic needs poverty line. Following the overthrow of the socialist-oriented Derg regime in 1991, the Ethiopian government with the support of the Fund and the World Bank has been implementing the economic reforms policies. The measure of economic reforms aimed at raising real GDP growth and reducing poverty, while maintaining macroeconomic stability. Real GDP growth averaged about 5 percent per year during 1991-2002 while inflation has been relatively contained. These positive developments were achieved despite the border war of 1998-2000 with Eritrea, and the continued decline in coffee prices since 1997-98. Ethiopia's economic circumstances adversely affected its debt sustainability, raising the net present value (NPV) of debt-to-exports ratio at end of 2002-03 substantially above the 150 percent threshold established under the enhanced HIPC framework. Further, the track record of the Ethiopian authorities in policy and reform implementation has been strong, and the authorities have borrowed prudently despite being adversely affected by a severe drought and lower coffee prices. The Net Present Value (NPV) of debt is the discounted sum of all future debt-service obligations (interest and principal). It is a measure that takes into account the extent of subsidy of a country's debt stock. Whenever the interest rate on a loan is lower than the market rate, the resulting NPV of debt is smaller than its face value, with the difference reflecting the grant element. The International Monetary Fund (IMF) and the World Bank's International Development Association (IDA) have agreed that Ethiopia has made sufficient progress and taken the necessary steps to reach its completion point under the enhanced Heavily HIPC initiative[278]. The completion point under the HIPC initiative is reached by the country when creditors commit to deliver debt relief fully and irrevocably. The decision point, which precedes the completion point, is when debt relief is committed and begins on an interim and voluntary basis. Ethiopia is the thirteenth country to reach this point, joining Benin, Bolivia, Burkina Faso, Guyana, Mauritania, Mali, Mozambique, Nicaragua, Niger, Senegal, Tanzania, and Uganda.

The debt sustainability analysis of the country is carried out to determine the debt relief needs of the country as a process of measuring the extent of international indebtedness. If a country's external debt ratio after traditional debt relief mechanisms is above a threshold for the value of debt to exports (or, in special cases, the value of debt to fiscal revenues), it qualifies for assistance under the Initiative. Once a country has made sufficient progress in meeting the criteria for debt relief, the Executive Boards of the IMF and World Bank formally decide on a country's eligibility, and the international community commits to reducing debt to the sustainability threshold. This is called the *decision point* and upon reaching this point, it may immediately begin receiving *interim relief* on its debt service falling due. The countries under the category of HIPC initiative may receive the full and irrevocable reduction in debt available provided the country establishes a further track record of good performance under IMF- and World Bank-supported programs. Once a country has met these criteria, it can reach its *completion point*, at which time lenders are expected to provide the full relief committed at the decision point.

In total, more than forty countries in Asia, Africa, and Latin America sought relief from their external debts. Negotiations among the debtor countries, creditor countries, private banks, and international organizations continued throughout the rest of the 1980s. Earlier to the intervention of the global institutions including the IMF and World Bank, various approaches were used to resolve the crisis. The 1985 Baker Plan (named after then U.S. Treasury Secretary James Baker) stressed the importance of debt rescheduling, rigid controls imposed by the Fund over domestic monetary and fiscal policies, and continued lending to debtor countries in hopes that economic growth would allow them to repay their creditors. In response to the debt crisis of Mexico, the IMF agreed to provide a loan package only if

[278] The World Bank: IMF and World Bank Support Ethiopia's Completion Point and Approve Topping-Up of Debt Relief Under the Enhanced HIPC Initiative, Development News Media Center, News Release No:2004/331/PREM.

private foreign banks holding Mexican debt agreed to reschedule their loans and provide Mexico with additional financing. However, the debtor nations made little progress in repaying their loans. Debtors and creditors alike agreed that a new approach was needed. The 1989 Brady Plan[279] focused on the need to reduce the debts of the troubled countries by writing off parts of the debts or by providing the countries with funds to buy back their loan below face value. The international debt crisis tend to recede in 1990s as the debt servicing requirements of debtor countries have been made more manageable via a combination of IMF loans, debt rescheduling, and changes in governmental economic policies. However, the impact of debt crisis of 1980s has made long-run damages to the economies of affected countries and many experts consider this phase as "lost decade" for economic development in Latin America.

Mexico strengthened the process of macroeconomic stabilization and structural transformation from 1988 to 1993, with the active support of the IMF, which began in the wake of the 1982 debt crisis. The macroeconomic strategies of the country were aimed at attaining external viability and laying the foundations for private-sector-led growth conceived on tight financial policies; the use of the exchange rate as a nominal anchor; comprehensive structural reforms, including privatization and trade and exchange liberalization; and a major restructuring of external debt. The result was remarkable success on many fronts. A reduction in the fiscal deficit was achieved that should be an inspiration for many countries. Inflation was reduced from 160 percent in 1987 to 8 percent in 1993. The restructuring of external debt paved the way for a resumption of access to international financial markets, and private capital inflows surged, contributing to a large increase in international reserves. Mexico therefore entered 1994 with a strengthened economy, and an economy more deeply integrated into global markets, with its membership in NAFTA and impending accession to membership of the OECD as well as its commitments to an open exchange and trade regime promising to lock in many of the important reforms it had implemented. In particular, the external current account deficit, running at 6.5 percent of GDP in 1993, was very large by most standards, and was being financed largely by short-term capital inflows. A steep real appreciation of the peso and a major deterioration in the private sector's saving performance had contributed to the emergence of this deficit[280].

Among many other highly indebted poor countries of Africa, some of the countries of Latin America had also experienced the debt trap. In 1995, Mexico ran into deep economic problems, since the Mexican leaders pushed the borrowing of the country too far ahead of its economic growth resulting into a catastrophic economic slump in the country. The value of the peso went down 30 percent within a week, as foreign investors lost confidence in the economic stability of the country. Mexico has been growing consistently in the late 1980s and early 1990s and its fiscal and monetary conditions were sound during the triennium beginning of 1990s. The balanced federal budget over the years attracted considerable foreign and domestic investment. However, foreign lenders, mainly American banks, pension, and mutual funds, overdid it as they advanced capital to Mexican enterprises during 1991-93 and to the government $15 billion to $25 billion a year, which was more than what Mexican exports was

[279] The plan was named after the Bush administration's treasury secretary, Nicholas Brady.

[280] Camdessus Michel (1995): Drawing Lessons from the Mexican Crisis: Preventing and Resolving Financial Crises--the Role of the IMF, Address delivered at 25th Washington Conference of the Council of the Americas on "Staying the Course: Forging a Free Trade Area in the Americas" Washington, D.C., May 22, 1995, Referred from the speech documents available with the International Monetary Fund, www.imf.org

contributing to the gross national income of the country. These creditors recognized the problems and stressed on part repayment of the money lent and Mexico had no way to pay. The reason was that Mexico had $28 billion in dollar-denominated Treasury notes becoming due in 1995, of which $16 billion was owned by Americans[281]. A large proportion of Mexican loans were owned by thousands of U.S. mutual and pension funds, retirement accounts, and the country had legal obligations to pay benefits to millions of Americans, mostly small savers. There was no practical way to demand new loans from them to liquidate the existing sum and further plunge into the debt trap. Therefore, the IMF and the U.S. government had to come to their rescue. The IMF committed $17.8 billion to help Mexico to resolve the currency crisis with strict measures to restore the economic growth of the country and US government offered $40 billion in loan guarantees.

> The recent economic history of Mexico is marked by the severe recession that started in the fall of 1994. Theoretically, the problem may be explained as a race between a foreign investment that led to the demand boom and the anticipated expansion in supply. The outcome of such a race is inherently uncertain. If, in an exchange rate based stabilization program, supply does not keep pace with demand, competitiveness problems will eventually result in lower output, and consequently the government might be tempted to devalue[282]. The recession deepened following the 15% devaluation of the national currency, the peso on December 20th. By the end of December the peso had fallen by 30%, stock prices collapsed and interest rates increased sharply. As a consequence of this crisis, GDP fell by 6.2% in 1995, the rate of inflation on a 12-month basis climbed to 52% in December 1995 and short-term interest rates reached a level of 71.5% in April 1995. The Mexican Crisis had such a large impact globally because it was a period of global recession and many other countries were running large debts and were financially vulnerable. The Mexican experience weakened bank and investor confidence overall and decreased the amount of funds available to many middle-income countries that were at the time in desperate need of capital. The crisis highlighted the weaknesses of the international financial system. Mexico's crisis hurt banks' confidence in lending to Latin America in general. This was extremely harmful for many countries in the region, especially Brazil that was in need of capital. Other countries besides Brazil, like Costa Rica, Ecuador, Bolivia, and Chile were all running major deficits and the cutting off of funds would only lead to insolvency and more economic downturn. A radical version of gainers and losers in the debt crisis of a country critically puts the fact as a financial crisis, when it springs from the foreign investors' fear that others are pulling their capital out of a developing country, as was the case in Mexico, the world's central banks can contain the crisis by providing liquidity and support. In such "liquidity crises", those providing support do not lose. They make money[283].

The crisis in Asia has occurred after several decades of outstanding economic performance. During the three decades preceding the crisis, per capita income levels had increased tenfold in Korea, fivefold in Thailand, and fourfold in Malaysia. Moreover, per capita income levels in Hong Kong and Singapore now exceed those in some industrial countries. Asia attracted almost half of total capital inflows to developing countries--nearly

---

[281] Rich Thomas (1995): How to save face and trade, Newsweek, February 06, 34.

[282] Irwin Gregor and Vines David (1995): The macroeconomics of the Mexican Crisis: A simple two period model, Center for Economic Policy Research, Working Paper 1241, London.

[283] Bradford De Long, Christopher De Long and Sherman Robinson (1996): The Mexican Peso Crisis – In defense of US policy towards Mexico, Economic Affairs, May-June.

$100 billion in 1996. Asia's success has also been good for the rest of the world. The developing and emerging market economies of Asia have not just been major exporters; they have been an increasingly important market for other countries' exports. The crisis emerged with the failure to dampen pressures in large external deficits and property and stock market bubbles. In addition, the exchange rates encouraged external borrowing and led to excessive exposure to foreign exchange risk in both the financial and corporate sectors and the financial oversight that led to a sharp deterioration in the quality of banks' loan portfolios. Largely, the problems in these countries were grown mostly on domestic platforms and the developments in the advanced economies and global financial markets contributed significantly to the buildup of the imbalances that eventually led to the crises. The economies of Indonesia and Korea were also affected alike Thailand and suffered from the amount of exchange rate adjustment that had taken place. The situation exceeded beyond any reasonable estimate of what might have been required to correct the initial overvaluation of the Thai *baht*, the Indonesian *rupiah*, and the Korean *won*, among other currencies. They all had suffered a loss of confidence, and their currencies were deeply depreciated.

## Exchange Rate Management

The forward market currency options and currency futures facilitate international trade and investment by allowing firms to hedge, or reduce the foreign exchange risks inherent in international transactions. The forward price of a foreign currency often differs from its spot price. If the forward price (using a direct quote) is less than the spot price, the currency is selling at a *forward discount* and in case the forward price is higher than the spot price, the currency is selling at a *forward premium*. The forward price represents the aggregate prediction of the spot price of the exchange rate in the future in the marketplace[284]. Thus, the forward price helps international businesspeople forecast future changes in exchange rates. These variations can affect the price of imported components as well as the competitiveness and profitability of the exports of a company. If a currency is selling at a forward discount, the foreign exchange market believes the currency will depreciate over time. Firms may want to reduce their holdings of assets or increase their liabilities denominated in such a currency. The currencies of countries suffering balance of payment (BoP) deficits or high inflation rates often sell at a forward discount. On the contrary, if a currency is selling at a forward premium, the foreign-exchange market assumes that the currency will appreciate over time. Firms may want to increase their holdings of assets and reduce their liabilities denominated in such a currency. The currencies of countries enjoying BoP surpluses generated of trade or low inflation rates often sell at a forward premium. Thus, the difference between the spot and forward prices of a country's currency often signals the expectations of a market regarding macroeconomic policies and prospects of the country.

In financial markets, uncertainty goes under the name of volatility that may express as how much asset prices are moving around. The issues that are of concern to traders and investors include their dealings ahead and movement of assets in the past. According to the latest survey

[284] Boris Antle and Richard Ensor (1982): Management of foreign exchange risk, Euromoney Publications, London, 43-45.

by the Bank for International Settlements, at the end of 2003 there was roughly $50 trillion-worth of options outstanding in the world. Many financial catastrophes have been caused by selling options. The most famous came in 1995, when a rising star at a British bank sold 34,000 options on Japan's Nikkei 225, driving implied volatility on the world's second-biggest stock market from 22% to 11%. However, share prices plummeted after the Kobe earthquake, volatility soared, and the bank went bust. There are, after all, many things that could go wrong for financial markets: tensions are still bad in the Middle East; the oil price is again over $40; and the Federal Reserve is raising interest rates when American households are more indebted than they have ever been[285].

Any individual or company engaged in overseas business should be aware of the risks of currency fluctuations. Customers without commercial contracts expressed in domestic currency (or fixed by an agreed rate of exchange) are fully exposed to what is known as an exchange risk. Exchange risk may arise because of exchange rate movements in the period from the original commercial contract, to the time of settlement of the domestic equivalent of the foreign currency amount. Although participants in the foreign exchange market are increasingly scattered around the globe, most transactions still take place in London, New York, and Tokyo. London dominates the foreign exchange markets, with 30 percent of all transactions; New York's share is 16 percent. Tokyo's share, now 10 percent, has been whittled away by the markets of Singapore and Hong Kong, which are fast gaining prominence. Singapore has become the world's fourth largest foreign exchange market, and Hong Kong has overtaken Switzerland to become the fifth largest. Despite the growing diversity of customers, market concentration has increased since 1992, as the proportion of trading carried out by the top banks continues to rise. This trend is most evident in the smaller markets, which are being abandoned by foreign banks seeking to consolidate their business in the major centers, but it is also being seen in the major centers [286]. Between 1992 and 1995, the market share of the top ten dealers in Tokyo rose from 44 percent to 51 percent, in New York from 41 percent to 47 percent, and in London from 43 percent to 44 percent. The foreign exchange market is highly liquid as transactions are large and executed frequently. The foreign exchange market has registered healthy increases in turnover and continues to be the most liquid of markets. However, the size and number of transactions, and the increased concentration of transactions in a handful of international banks place the foreign exchange market at the nexus of the global network of inter-bank payments.

A *fixed, or pegged,* rate is a rate the government (central or federal bank) sets and maintains the official exchange rate. A set price will be determined against a major world currency (usually the U.S. dollar, but also other major currencies such as the Euro, the Yen, or a basket of currencies). In order to maintain the local exchange rate, the central bank buys and sells its own currency on the foreign exchange market in return for the currency to which it is pegged. Unlike the fixed rate, a *floating exchange rate* is determined by the private market through supply and demand. A floating rate is often termed "self-correcting," as any differences in supply and demand will automatically be corrected in the market. Take a look at this simplified model: if demand for a currency is low, its value will decrease, thus making

[285] The Economist: An eerie calm, July 22, 2004.

[286] Laura E. Kodres (1996): Foreign exchange markets: Structure and systemic risks, International Capital Markets: Developments, Prospects, and Key Policy Issues, *World Economic and Financial Surveys,* (annex III) International Monetary Fund.

imported goods more expensive and thus stimulating demand for local goods and services. This in turn will generate more jobs, and hence an auto-correction would occur in the market. A floating exchange rate is constantly changing.

In reality, no currency is wholly fixed or floating. In a fixed regime, market pressures can also influence changes in the exchange rate. The Fixed regimes often lead to severe financial crisis since a peg is difficult to maintain in the long run. This was seen in the Mexican (1995), Asian and Russian (1997) financial crises: an attempt to maintain a high value of the local currency to the peg resulted in the currencies eventually becoming overvalued. This meant that the governments could no longer meet the demands to convert the local currency into the foreign currency at the pegged rate. Sometimes, when a local currency does reflect its true value against its pegged currency, a "black market" may develop which is more reflective of actual supply and demand,. A central bank will often be forced to revalue or devalue the official rate so that the rate is in line with the unofficial one, thereby halting the activity of the black market. In a floating regime, the central bank may also intervene when it is necessary to ensure stability and to avoid inflation; however, it is less often that the central bank of a floating regime will interfere. There was a global fixed exchange rate between 1870 and 1914, which suffocated the global economy during the great depression of 1930s. Currencies were linked to gold, meaning that the value of a local currency was fixed at a set exchange rate to gold ounces. This was known as the *Gold Standard* that was abandoned after the World War II. The optimal exchange rate regime may depend on whether prices are set in the currency of producers or the currency of consumers. When prices are set in consumers' currency, the variance of home consumption is not influenced by foreign monetary variance under floating exchange rates, while there is transmission of foreign disturbances under floating rates if prices are set in producers' currencies, or under fixed exchange rates[287].

## BUSINESS PARTNERING AMONG ASIAN-LATIN AMERICAN COUNTRIES

The Latin American and Caribbean countries have a long history of bilateral and sub-regional preferential agreements on trade and economic integration. Dating from the 1960s and early 1970s, the Latin American Free Trade Area (LAFTA), the Andean Community (AC), the Caribbean Common Market (Caricom) and the Central American Common Market (CACM) rarely met their goals, because of the inherent clash between integration and import substitution industrialization. However, a new wave of preferential agreements rocked the region in the 1990s, now linked to a re-hauling of trade and development strategies. Traditional arrangements, such as the Latin American Integration Association (LAIA) - LAFTA's successor - and the AC, gained strength and Mercosur broke off as an important sub-regional initiative in South America. Various bilateral agreements (many of them under the Montevideo Treaty that created LAIA in 1981) were struck, generally with the goal of establishing free trade areas. Moreover, Mexico negotiated NAFTA with the US and Canada during the 1990s.

[287] Devereux Michael B and Engle Charles (1998): Fixed vs. floating exchange rates – How price setting affects the optimal choice of exchange rate regime. NBER Working Papers # W6867, December.

**Table 8.1. Concluded Trade and Economic Partnership among the Latin American and Asian Countries (1980-2004)**

| Trade and Economic Agreements | Year of Entry |
|---|---|
| Asia-Pacific Economic Cooperation (APEC) | 1989 |
| South Korea-Chile | 2003 |
| Taiwan-Panama | 2004 |
| Japan –Mexico | 2004 |

In the process of bi-regional business negotiations among the Latin American and Asian countries, the Free Trade Agreements (FTAs) were up until recently and signed mainly in reference to the geographically proximate countries. Today, however, FTAs are becoming trans-continental, Reflecting this trend are, for example, the US-Australia, US-Singapore, and Mexico-Israel FTAs, as well as the EU's FTAs with Chile, Mexico, and South Africa. Also Latin America and Asia have established trans-continental FTAs. In 2003, Chile and South Korea signed the first comprehensive FTA between an Asian and Latin American country; the agreement went into effect in April 2004. Japan and Mexico have also recently concluded FTA talks. Latin American and East Asian partners have launched negotiations for three further bi-regional FTAs, including Chile-Singapore-New Zealand, Mexico-South Korea, and Mexico- Singapore FTAs. Chile and Japan have formed a joint study group to explore the feasibility of launching formal FTA negotiations. Latin America-Asia trans-continentalismn has spanned the Asia Pacific basin, with Brazil and India negotiating an FTA. Moreover, plans have been expressed for Chile-Japan, Mexico-New Zealand, Mercosur-India, Mercosur-China, and Chile-China FTAs. The Table 8.1 exhibits the successful trade and economic negotiations since 1980 among the Latin American and Asian countries.

These agreements often managed to form sub-regional free trade areas; many even explicitly seek to become common markets. For example, Mercosur was created with the intention of gradually evolving towards a common market and the AC has reaffirmed its goal of forming a common market in 2005. Neither has the Caricom abandoned its strategic goal of building a common market, evidenced by member statements in the Protocol of Guatemala in 1993. With ambitious integration goals and modest results, taken together the initiatives present similar trends and prospects, most remain in a free trade, a stage incapable of turning into full-fledged customs unions. Divergent foreign policies, domestic political and economic restraints, and border conflicts plague nearly all. Conflicts flare up from disparities in size, economic structure and patterns of trade, in addition to often contradictory cost-benefit evaluations of undertaking a common external tariff. Moreover, regional agreements risk being drowned out by the deepening of unilateral preferential trade schemes in the US and the EU that benefit the small economies of Central America and the Caribbean.

The economic integration arrangements in the Latin American and Asian regions have been established mainly at the sub-regional level. There are initiatives in the Latin American region to link together some of the Sub-regional arrangements. This leads to the question of what are the possibilities for economic integration arrangements linking the two regions. In the Asian and Latin American regions, some cross-regional free trade areas are almost at the point of being established. The one between Chile and the Republic of Korea is more advanced, but other bilateral initiatives are under way between Japan and Chile, Colombia and Mexico. Preferential arrangements have also been envisaged between Taiwan Province of

China and some countries in Central America. Besides the countries of Asia, membership in APEC includes Mexico, Peru and Chile. However, their membership has so far been only a consultation forum and not an integration arrangement. The trade and economic negotiations which are lying under process and newly planned have been exhibited in Table 8.2.

The best opportunity for countries of Asia and Latin America may be to intensify their commercial exchanges by continuing to rely on non-discriminatory trade relations. To expand interregional trade, the countries of the two regions should look at barriers to trade for products of interest to them from countries of the other region and negotiate for reduction or elimination on the basis of MFN at a future round of multilateral trade negotiations. Apart from this, other cooperative action could be taken to overcome impediments due to such factors as distance, lack of traditional trade relations and even linguistic differences that have inhibited interregional trade exchanges. Consultative forums among governments and among businesses should be set up where they do not exist. Such forums have to be strengthened where they already exist. Periodic consultations have to be coordinated with full use of the internet to disseminate information about production capabilities and the supply needs in the two regions.

**Table 8.2. Trade and Economic Negotiations among the Latin American and Asian Countries: In Process and Newly Proposed**

| Latin American Country | Asian Countries | |
|---|---|---|
| | Negotiations in Process | Newly Planned Proposals |
| Chile | Singapore-New Zealand | Japan |
| | China | - |
| Guatemala | Taiwan | - |
| Panama | Singapore | - |
| Peru | Singapore | - |
| | Thailand | |
| Mexico | Singapore | New Zealand |
| | - | South Korea |
| Mercosur | - | China |
| | - | India |

Source: IDB, Integration and Regional Programs Department.

## EXPANSION OF LATIN AMERICA-ASIA TRADE LINKS

The trade performance of Asian and Pacific countries had been outstanding up to 1997. In 1980, the region exported less than US$ 280 billion, by 1990 that total had increased to almost US$ 700 billion and in 1995 more than US$ 1,230 billion. Results on the export side were matched by an exceptional performance on the import side. Total imports jumped from US$ 292 billion in 1980 to more than US$ 700 billion 10 years later and over US$ 1,300 billion in 1995. These values indicate an average annual growth rate between 1990 and 1995 of about 12 per cent for exports and over 13 per cent for imports. However, the Asian crisis had a negative effect on the region's trade performance. Between 1996 and 1998, the average annual growth of total exports was -0.2 per cent, while on the import side the decrease was more pronounced, at -4.2 per cent. The result for the period 1990-1998 shows that annual growth for exports reached only 7.5 per cent as compared to 11.5 per cent for the period of 1980-1990. Growth of Asian and Pacific exports to the countries belonging to Latin American Integration Association (LAIA) increased 19 per cent a year between 1990 and 1995, growth that was even more pronounced than intra-Asian trade. This was a clear indication that trade liberalization in Latin America offered a special opportunity for Asian and Pacific countries to increase their share in this expanding market. In the following three years, Asian and Pacific exports to Latin America increased over 7 per cent per year[288].

Inter-regional cooperation has intensified on the trans-Pacific agenda in recent years. Latin America and Asia-Pacific have created various fora to deal with bilateral economic and political issues. The most comprehensive in terms of bi-regional membership is the Forum for East Asia-Latin America Cooperation (FEALAC) launched at a Ministerial Meeting in March 2001 in Santiago, Chile. Comprising of 17 Latin American and 15 Asia-Pacific economics, FEALAC is an informal mechanism for dialogue and cooperation among the countries of the two regions to meet political, cultural, social, economic and international issues of common concern. Two further major venues of trans-Pacific cooperation are the Pacific Basin Economic Council (PBEC) and the Pacific Economic Cooperation Conference (PECC). The Latin American partners in each are Colombia, Chile, Ecuador, Mexico and Peru. PBEC is an association of senior business leaders from more than 1,100 major corporations in 20 economics around the Pacific Basin Region aimed at expanding trade and investment flows through open markets. In its next International General Meeting (IGM) in June 2005 in Hong Kong, PECC will focus on the Pacific Basin's role in the next stages of globalization, such as the Doha Development Round. Meanwhile, the 25-member PECC promotes trade, investment, financial stability, and development around the Pacific Rim. It comprises senior representatives from business, government, and the academia. PECC has recently focused on the proliferation of regional integration agreements as a potential way for achieving the Bogor Convention Goals of APEC[289].

Japan and Latin America have deep-seated cooperation. Japan has alone, contributed to Latin America's development through economic and technical cooperation aimed particularly at economic reform, poverty reduction, and environmental protection. It is one of Latin America's main sources of Official Development Assistance (ODA). Japan was one of the key actors in helping Latin America debt crisis of the early- 1980s, and also involved in the Central American peace processes. More recently, Japan has supported the electoral processes in Latin America, including joining the dispatch of election observers from the Organization of American States (OAS). Japan has also pursued active cooperation with the Caribbean through the Japan-CARICOM Consultation, which centers on fostering bilateral relations, and economic cooperation, cultural exchanges, and collaboration in international fora.

It is interesting to note that this was the highest rate of growth compared to other regions. On the other hand, Asian and Pacific imports from LAIA were the most affected among the regions. Even before the Asian crisis, Latin America was a minor partner in Asia's export and import flows. In 1998, only 2.2 per cent of total Asian and Pacific exports went to Latin America, and only 1.8 per cent of their imports originated in LAIA countries. It is even more

[288] World Trade Reports, 1999, 2001, 2003 and 2004, World Trade Organization.

[289] Official document Inter-American Development Bank (IDB) # AB-2370, March 21, 2005: "Asia and Latin America and the Caribbean: Economic Links, Cooperation and Development Strategies".

significant that 18 years earlier, the share of LAIA countries in total Asian and Pacific exports and imports was higher. During the first five years of the 1990s, growth of exports from Asia and the Pacific to LAIA was high. Eight countries had annual average growth rates over 20 per cent during this period. Three countries that included China, Indonesia and Thailand had increases of over 40 per cent in their exports to the region.

The average annual growth rate for imports to East Asian countries from LAIA countries actually increased slightly over the rate for 1990-1995. However, New Zealand's imports from the world which had increased on average by 8 per cent between 1990 and 1995 decreased almost 6 per cent between 1996 and 1998. Before the crisis, the most dynamic Asian market for Latin American products was Malaysia, followed closely by Indonesia. The import demand of these two countries declined drastically after the crisis. During this period, Latin America represented more than 2 per cent of total imports for only five Asian and Pacific countries, Latin America absorbed more than 2 per cent of total exports for only three countries. Latin America had the highest average market share of total exports for Japan, while the region's imports were more relevant for the Republic of Korea. South Korea maintains important institutional ties with the countries of Latin America and the Caribbean. It was one of the first Asian countries to join the OAS as a permanent observer, and has made efforts to contribute to Latin America's economic and social development through ODA and technical cooperation. South Korea has recently sought to deepen its economic ties with Latin America. Besides the FTA with Chile, in 2003 South Korea staged with various Latin American countries the South Korea-Latin America and Caribbean Business Forum, which drew a host of government officials and analysts. South Korea and Mexico are joined by the 21st Century Commission, a private-level consultation forum created to explore possibilities for longer-term bilateral collaboration.

China and Latin America have strengthened cooperation ties markedly over the past decade. The Rio Group and China launched political dialogue in 1990, and in 1994 China became the first foreign country to be admitted as an observer to the Latin American Integration Agreement (LAIA or ALADI). In 1997, China was admitted to the Caribbean Development Bank. China has also held official talks with Mercosur following the establishment of a bilateral dialogue mechanism. Furthermore, much like Japan and South Korea, China collaborates with various Latin American countries in APEC and FEALAC. It also has expressed interest in a non-borrower membership in the Inter-American Development Bank.

Business between East Asia and Latin America is small. East Asia is largely represented by the countries Brunei, Cambodia, Indonesia, Laos, Malaysia, Myanmar, the Philippines, Singapore, Thailand and Vietnam, along with Australia, China, Japan, South Korea and New Zealand. Latin-American countries export only $23 billion worth of products to East Asia from total annual exports of $350 billion with an even smaller amount of Asian exports going the other way. Total trade, on the other hand, between the Philippines and Latin America was around $800 million in 2002. Trade between the Philippines and Mexico paced these economic ties. Our other major export markets are Panama, Brazil, Chile and Costa Rica. The relations between the Philippines and Mexico started with the Galleon Trade. Through the centuries, bilateral trade ties have developed between Manila and Latin-American capitals. There was a time when the Philippines was considered part of the Hispanic community. The potential for bigger trade and investments is great. Latin America with 500 million consumers is a major market for Philippine goods and services. Manila promises to be a big investment partner and regional headquarters for Latin America in Asia. Philippine visibility is strong in most of Latin America, although there is a need to establish full-fledged embassies in many countries to speed up economic and cultural ties.

In fact, Latin America was the only region that presented positive growth rates for exports from Asia and the Pacific. The solid nature of Latin American import demand has at its roots the process of deep transformation in the region. The depth in the recent crisis in Latin America has not entirely stopped this process. However, Latin American exports to Asia and the Pacific were the most strongly affected by the crisis. This creates a challenge for countries of both regions to find ways to establish solid trade and economic relation that are less vulnerable to fluctuations in the international economic environment. During the 1990s, Latin America improved its trade ties with most regions of the world. From 1990 to 1998, total exports increased from US$ 113 billion to US$ 248 billion. Total imports, which stood at US$ 83 billion in 1990, reached US$ 282 billion in 1998. These values indicate an average annual increase of almost 17 per cent for imports and 11 per cent for exports. These statistics represent a drastic change from the 1980s when the debt crisis caused a slowdown for Latin America's external trade, particularly in imports. As shown in the tables, LAIA imports stagnated in the period 1980-1990, growing at an average of 4 per cent annually. In the same period, the yearly average increase of world exports was 6 per cent.

## Global Financial Trends and Banking System

One of the apparent movements noted in the late 1990s that is still in vogue in the global finance is the unstable performance financial institutions of the countries as well as the open markets. There were longer-run trends that have set the backdrop for much of the work of central banks in international forums dealing with financial efficiency and stability. Financial instability connotes the presence of market imperfections or externalities in the financial systems that are substantial enough to create significant risks for real aggregate economic performance. Over the past few decades, economic research has identified a variety of imperfections inherent in markets, such as moral hazard, asymmetric information, and externalities. On occasion, these imperfections can become so widespread and significant as to result in outcomes that threaten the functioning of the financial system and adversely affect real economic variables. History suggests that these imperfections reach this advanced and disruptive stage when they are exacerbated by large external shocks. Such outcomes include panics, bank runs, severe market illiquidity, and excessive risk aversion. These outcomes are highly undesirable for society because they can be accompanied by a variety of economic distortions: Financial prices can diverge sharply and for prolonged periods from fundamentals, and their correction is likely to impose great cost on society; the availability and pricing of credit may be too lax at times and at other times too restrictive relative to underlying macroeconomic conditions. It has been observed that many nations are trying to overcome the structural defects in financial markets that left their economies prone to boom-and-bust cycles. In some cases, central banks were seen as part of the solution in addressing the results of such market imperfections[290]. The Federal Reserve, for example, owes its existence in large measure to the financial panics in the late nineteenth and early twentieth centuries in the United States that increased public recognition of the need for a lender of last resort, for more-effective bank supervision, and for greater efficiency in the payment system.

> Asset-based financing has become a more commonly accepted tool in the capitalization structure than it was in the past. There has been a transition in the marketplace with respect to traditional money center banks and some companies keep hedging their financing bets by securing both asset-based and cash-flow-based financing. In many organizations, finding sources of capital that are flexible has become a top priority, and asset-based arrangements can help achieve this goal. In general, asset-based financing offers more flexible liquidity than bank financing because it is driven more by collateral and less by covenants. In most cases, asset-based financing involves fewer and more flexible covenants than cash flow loans. In many cases, the only covenant focuses on the borrower's liquidity level. A company's access to asset-based financing often increases, as its working capital needs increase because that's when assets are growing. There are some disadvantages of asset based financing strategy as in general, borrowers must provide monthly or quarterly reports to show that they are meeting loan covenants. Strong performance and high liquidity enable companies to negotiate more flexible rules of reporting. The asset-based arrangements cost more than cash flow loans, but pricing depends on the borrower's creditworthiness. In recent years, interest rate spreads between asset-based and cash flow-based loans have remained steady, but fees on collateralized loans have increased in some cases.

The finance function has two principal aspects to provide the monetary resources to do business and to ensure an adequate financial return on the assets of the firm commensurate with its objectives. Even in a strictly domestic business, the able management of funds and investment aims at solving all sorts of problems related to issues including the adequacy of the financial returns, sources and availability of funds, raising supplementary resources and strategies for effective utilization thereof. In the international arena, the problems multiply and so the finance management must not only deal with different currencies and their fluctuating rates, but should also allow for the vagaries of the economic and political environments of nations with varying perspectives. The market concentration in the banking sector and in other sectors of the financial services industry has been increased in the recent past. The trend also marks towards steady increasing share of total credit provided directly through markets rather than through intermediaries like banks. Another important trend has been the expanding scope and availability of financial instruments. The global financial system is still well short of the theoretical ideal of complete financial markets, but clearly, it is moving in that direction. The financial system dominated by market-based finance has likely reinforced the status of the market for financial assets as the most important channel of monetary policy transmission. The market dynamic suggests that gauging the overall effect of monetary policy requires an assessment of broad financial conditions, including policy rates, long-term interest rates and foreign exchange rates.

The international investments demand total transparency at both the ends- investor and the host country governance. The Organization for Economic Cooperation and Development

---

[290] Roger W Ferguson Jr (2004): The Role of Central Banks in Fostering Efficiency and Stability in the Global Financial System, National Bank of Belgium Conference on Efficiency and Stability in an Evolving Financial System, Brussels, Belgium, May 17, 2004.

(OECD) report "Foreign Direct Investment for Development: Maximizing Benefits, Minimizing Costs" envisages that the host country transparency and the legal protection are among the top concerns of investors[291]. As an example, the case of Tanzania can be cited where in red tape in the investment establishment in the country is a prevalent hurdle for investors. Most decisions related to investment are made at the central level; investors interact with local government only during the consultation process and following establishment of the businesses in their area of jurisdiction[292].

**Table 8.3. Trend of FDI inflows into major Asian emerging market countries (In US$ million)**

| | 1990-94 | 1995 | 1996 | 1997 | 1998 | 1999 | 2000 | 2001 | 2004[a] |
|---|---|---|---|---|---|---|---|---|---|
| China | 16,062 | 35,849 | 40,180 | 44,237 | 43,751 | 38,753 | 38,399 | 44,241 | 49,308 |
| India | 375 | 2,144 | 2,246 | 3,57 | 2,635 | 2,169 | 2,315 | 3,403 | 3,449 |
| Indionesia | 1,693 | 4,34 | 6,194 | 4,677 | -356 | -2,745 | -4,550 | -3,278 | -1,513 |
| Malaysia | 4,172 | 4,178 | 5,078 | 5,137 | 2,163 | 3,895 | 3,788 | 554 | 3,203 |
| Pakistan | 322 | 723 | 922 | 716 | 506 | 532 | 308 | 383 | 823 |
| Philipines | 826 | 1,478 | 1,517 | 1,222 | 2,287 | 1,725 | 1,356 | 982 | 1,111 |
| Thailand | 1,9448 | 2,068 | 2,336 | 3,895 | 7,315 | 6,103 | 3,366 | 3,820 | 969 |
| Vietnam | 714 | 2,336 | 2,395 | 2,220 | 1,671 | 1,412 | 1,298 | 1,300 | 1,200 |
| Total | 26,112 | 53,122 | 61,048 | 65,681 | 59,972 | 51,844 | 46,629 | 51,405 | 58,550 |

a = up to June 30, 2004.
Sources: IMF, UNCETAD and World Bank.

In recent years, economic growth has been driven mainly by consumption, contributing more than 75% of the growth of the country's gross domestic product. Increased investment is one of major factors to allow the country to restore its economic growth rate from 3%-4% levels used over the past couple of years to the pre-crisis levels of 6%-7% and to help create more jobs for millions of the unemployed including new entrants entering the market each year. Investment approvals, however, have been declining since the country was hit by the 1997-98 financial crises. The Table 8.3 exhibits the inflow trend of foreign direct investment in Asian countries. Good public governance has two key ingredients: transparency and accountability. Recognizing the importance of improving transparency in the public sector, the economic reform package emphasized the Government's commitment to institutional reforms to generate transparency in a wide front. A main goal of public policy should be to rebuild key public institutions that would strengthen the nation's capacity to implement economic and social policies with popular support, transparency and good governance.

In 2002, FDI approvals plummeted by 35% and domestic investment approvals dropped by 57%. However, the declining trend continues and approved FDI of about $6.0 billion up to September this year was less than one third of pre-crisis level about $34 billion in 1997.

291 Organization for Economic Development and Cooperation: Foreign Direct Investment-Maximizing Benefits, Minimizing Costs, OECD, Paris, 2002.

292 Mathur Rajive D and Chaterjee Sanchita (2003): "Encouraging governance and transparency for investment", Paper presented in the Global Forum on Investment on Encouraging modern governance and transparency for investment, Hosted by Government of South Africa, November 17-18, 2003, Johannesburg.

Despite current stability in the country's macroeconomic indicators, legal uncertainty, security concerns, labor relations, the difficult process of decentralization and the weak global environment in the past two years are cited among the problems that have delayed the recovery of investment[293]. The international investors' community and international financial institutions have determined a number of general factors that consistently determine the attractiveness of the countries on foreign direct investment. These factors include, market size, growth prospects of the country, wage adjusted productivity of labor, availability of infrastructure and tax incentives.

## BALANCE OF PAYMENTS

The balance of payments is a record of one country's trade dealings with the rest of the world. This is an indicator of the international economic health of a country. Its data help government policy makers plan monetary, fiscal, foreign exchange, and commercial policies. The balance of payments of a country summarizes all the transactions that have taken place between its residents and foreigners in a given period, usually a year. The term *transaction* refers to exports and imports of goods and services, lending and borrowing of funds, remittances, and government aid and military expenditures. Such data can also provide information for decisions in international marketing. Two important decisions for a firm are the choice of location of supply for foreign markets and the selection of markets to sell to. Balance-of-payments analysis explains that which nations are strong importers and exporters of the products in the international arena. A multinational company can identify accordingly its own best import and export targets, that is, countries to sell to and countries to supply from. The balance of payments reflects the totality of a country's economic relations with the rest of the world: its trade in goods, its exchange of services, its purchase and sale of financial assets, and such important governmental transactions as foreign aid, military expenditures abroad, and the payment of reparation.

Certain forces determine the volume of these transactions, how they are brought into balance, what problems arise when they fail to balance, and what policies are available to deal with those problems. Longitudinal analysis of the balance of payments can help to track the international product life cycle. When the firm is considering foreign market opportunities, it finds a country's import statistics for its products to be a preliminary indicator of market potential. The balance-of-payments record is made on the basis of rules of debit and credit, similar to those in business accounting. For example, receipts are entered as credits and payments as debits. Thus, exports, like sales, are entered as credits; imports, like purchases, as debits. Dealings which result in money entering the country are *credit* (plus) items while transactions which lead to money leaving the country are *debit* (minus) items. The balance of payments can be split up into two sections:

---

[293] Hutagalung Jannes (2003): "Indonesia's efforts to enhance transparency for improving the investment climate: Achievements and challenges", Paper presented in the Global Forum on Investment on Encouraging modern governance and transparency for investment, Hosted by Government of South Africa, November 17-18, 2003, Johannesburg.

- The *current account,* which deals with international trade in goods and services;
- *Transactions in assets and liabilities,* which deals with overseas flows of money from international investments and loans

All transactions affecting increases in assets, like direct investment abroad, or decreases in indebtedness, like the repayment of external debts, are recorded as credits. However, decreases in assets, like liquidation of foreign securities, and increases in liabilities, like borrowing abroad, are treated as debits. Adding the balance of trade and balance on invisibles together gives the *balance on the current account.* A *deficit* on the current account means that more goods and services have been imported into the domestic country than have been sold abroad. A *surplus* on the current account means more goods and services have been exported than imported. The transactions in assets and liabilities section of the balance of payments show all movements of money in and out of the country for investment. This may be *direct investment* - investment in productive capacity, or *portfolio investment* - investment in shares or other assets. These flows will be debits to the Balance of Payments of the country.

Conceptually the balance of payments should always balances because of *official financing.* However, a balance of payments deficit means a persistent and large negative balance for official financing. This can be the result of excessive purchases of foreign goods and services or excessive investment overseas of a country. In the short term, a balance of payments deficit can be corrected by:

- Continued borrowing of foreign currency;
- Increasing interest rates to attract overseas investors;
- Imposing exchange controls;
- Imposing tariffs and import quotas.

However, in the long run, the government can correct a balance of payments deficit by reducing demand in the economy for all goods including imports. Conversely, a reduction in interest rates or restrictive exchange controls will correct the surplus.

## SUCCESSFUL BUSINESS PARTNERING

The trade policy in Latin America and the Caribbean (LAC), for many years had involved very high levels of protection and of government intervention. The active pursuit of import substitution policies reduced the openness and efficiency of the regional economies. It also increased their external vulnerability, as they became dependent on a narrow range of export products, with little ability to absorb external shocks. This state of affairs changed markedly in the 1980s and 1990s, when most countries of the region moved to liberalize their trade regime. Trade policy reform in LAC in the 1990s has been both widespread and extensive, and the region now shows a fairly open trade regime. Such a sharp policy reversal clearly had an impact on trade flows, and those effectively underwent significant changes in the past decade. They also coincided with a number of other important changes in the LAC economies, including major structural reforms including the privatization of many public enterprises and the deregulation of most domestic markets, a surge in investment partly linked to the lower relative prices for capital goods resulting from higher openness, higher capital flows, and a more careful pursuit of macroeconomic policy aimed at preserving financial stability to foster sustainable growth[294].

Let us look into the process of international partnering arrangements after analyzing the attributes of economic and trade transition issues in LAC region. The concept of international collaboration, by its very nature, operates in the realm of the global economy. The scale of the enterprises concerned and the nature of the competition encountered are fundamentally greater and more diverse than that encountered in a domestic situation. International partnerships need to be developed with sensitivity to the culture and mutual regard to the nationalistic feeling of both partners. However, the following stages of building bilateral trade relations may offer maximum benefit to the countries involved in the business game:

- Strengthen the macroeconomic policies of the country; develop industry attractiveness and comparative advantage in reference to production resources, infrastructure, technology and managerial know-how.
- Relax the tariff and non-tariff barriers to a considerable level to initiate the international trade proposals.
- Ease the immigration regulation for enabling the corporate partners to get the expatriates to work in respective countries. This would not only provide a culture-blend but also offer the potential for transfer of technology at either end.
- Identify the purpose of business partnership and develop the partnership strategy. Select and prioritize the products, markets and services to initiate the partnering relationship. Also the market research advice at this point from the professional consultant would be beneficial at this level.
- Develop an action plan and sell the idea within the firm and to the authorities in the home country as well as in the host country to facilitate the chosen corporate partner to develop strategic congruency.
- Screen the details of the international partner in reference to the state of economy in the host country, industry attractiveness and professional skills in the identified business activity. Define the strategies of identifying the corporate partner.
- Choose an appropriate corporate partner and develop a good blend of nationality, a different culture and often a different language.
- Negotiate on the major functional issues of business including financial management, investment and revenue sharing. The decisions on the foreign direct investment; resource sharing and stockholder management should also be negotiated with the international corporate partner.
- Develop a memorandum of understanding on the pattern of relationship, tangible and intangible functional dimensions in the selected business.
- Keep it simple – simplicity is a key to success, never more so than in an international relationship. This applies particularly to agreeing the measures of success – keep them to a minimum, focused on the major issues and review performance against them jointly on a regular basis.

---

[294] Loser Claudio and Guerguil Martine (1999): Trade and Trade Reforms in Latin America and the Caribbean in the 1990s, *Journal of Applied Economics*, Vol.2, May, pp. 61-96.

- Commit to the partnering and initiate process on all functional activities including, production, operations, marketing, monitoring and evaluation. Trigger off the business alliance work in accordance with the terms of reference.
- Conduct periodical review and audit, extend the partnering program and develop new avenues for future collaborations. Evaluate the rate of success in international partnering and emphasize on the business principle that *success breeds success*.
- Evolve an exit strategy – knowing how to get out of a relationship is as important as knowing how to get in. Sometimes things do not work out as planned and you may wish to exit the relationship or possibly the market. There is also a natural life cycle to any relationship and for this reason too it is advised to plan how it might end or change.

The rationale of international marketing is governed by factors of comparative advantages, sustained product life cycle, production sharing and extent of internalization. The concept of comparative advantages states that even if a country is able to produce all its goods at lower costs than that of another country, the trade still benefits mutually based on the comparative costs. It may be stated that the comparative costs may help in determining the companies to produce goods in the foreign countries that have comparative advantages over the others and decide either to export goods and services or produce therein. The global market place is becoming economically, culturally and technologically inter-dependent as the convergence of marketing activities have become more effective due to telecommunication and popularity of the electronic commerce. Leading corporations around the world have turned their attention towards expansion of their business activities in order to maintain their competitive edge and retain the customer loyalty. The conduct of global business activities trough international partnering has been described as the *third discipline*, the first and second being the regional trade cooperation and telecommunication boom respectively.

## REFERENCES

Anderson, Allice H, *Jack Kochanowicz and Lance Taylor : The Market Meets its match,* Harvard University Press, Cambridge, Massachusetts, 1994.

Caves Richard E : *Multinational Enterprise and Economic Analysis,* 2nd edition, Cambridge University Press, Cambridge, 1996.

Devlin Robert : *Debt and Crisis in Latin America : The Supply Side of the Story,* Princeton University Press, Princeton, New Jersey, 1989.

Eatwell John : International Finance Liberalization : The Impact of World Development, United Nations Development Program, *Discussion Paper Series,* Office of the Development Studies, UNDP, New York, 1996.

International Monetary Fund : *World Economic Report,* 2004.

Organization for Economic Cooperation and Development : *Country Economic Surveys*, 2001, OECD, Paris.

Panic Mica : The Bretton Woods System : *Concept and Practice, in Michie J and Smith Grieve (ed), Managing the Global Economy,* Oxford University Press, Oxford, 1995.

Patnaik Prabhat : *Macroeconomics,* Oxford University Press, Delhi, 1995.

Shapiro Alan C: *Multinational Financial Management,* 4th edition, Allyn & Bacon, Boston, 1995.

The Economist: *Sisters in the Woods: A Survey of IMF and the World Bank,* October 12, 1991, pp 5-48.

*Chapter 9*

# LESSONS AND VISIONS

It may be seen from the international trade arrangements that the trade structure of the Western Hemisphere's intraregional trade is significant but excessively concentrated in bilateral trade between a few countries; the United States with Mexico and Canada, and Argentina with Brazil. In 1999, almost all countries in this region either reported a sharp decline in economic growth or were in full recession, displaying a regional growth rate close to nil for that year. The value of exports from the region fell in 1998 for the first time in over 10 years. While total exports of the region recovered slightly in 1999, intraregional trade in the case of Mercosur and the Andean Community fell markedly in 1999. However, there have been some favorable external factors, such as strong economic growth in the United States; continued economic expansion in Europe; possible recovery of Japan from recession; more favorable prospects for international financial flows to the region; and the recovery of commodity prices. ECLAC forecasts for the region that there will be a significant recovery with an average growth rate of 3.6 per cent for 2000. Latin American exports to Asia and the Pacific, however, accounted for only 2 per cent of Asian and Pacific imports, showing a steady decline from a share of more than 3 per cent of Asian and Pacific imports in 1970. This meant that Asia and the Pacific had become one of the most important trade partners for Latin America as a whole, while the relative importance of LAIA countries for Asia and the Pacific was small, in terms of both their imports and exports.

The import and export markets for both regions have become more diversified a process that is expected to continue in the future. Among the LAIA countries, Argentina, Brazil, Chile and Mexico accounted for more than 80 per cent of the total interregional trade flows. Generally, the economic contraction in 1998 for major trade partners, Japan and the Republic of Korea, had a strong negative effect on the LAIA import demand. The share of LAIA in total imports was highest for Japan, but at only 3.2 per cent; while the Republic of Korea showed the highest LAIA participation in total exports at 3.5 per cent during 1990-2000. In the same period Peru, Mexico and the four Mercosur countries absorbed imports from Asia and the Pacific at a rapid rate, in some cases close to 40 per cent a year.

The exports from Asia and the Pacific to Latin America have achieved a higher degree of diversification. Asia and the Pacific entered the Latin American market with a variety of goods produced by industries operating at great advantages of scale and with advanced technology (automobiles and their components, home appliances and electronic products). Meanwhile, Latin America provides Asia and the Pacific with primary products such as copper, iron, steel, zinc, wood, soybeans, coffee, fish and meat, plus a few semi-manufactured products such as soybean oil, refined copper and fish meal. Sometimes, Latin American producers are able to compete with Asian and Pacific producers in their own markets. In this context, it is clear that manufactured products from LAIA countries have had better access to sub-regional and hemispheric markets than Asian and Pacific products.

The product composition of LAIA exports differs substantially according to its trading partners. Manufactures prevail in LAIA exports to the United States as well as in intraregional trade. In fact, close to 65 per cent of LAIA intraregional trade consists of manufactures. Food products predominate in LAIA exports to the European Union. In contrast, LAIA exports to Asia and the Pacific show a very different product composition. Minerals, metals and food have a large share in LAIA exports to this region. There has been a marked increase in the trade share of food. It is also interesting that manufactured exports to Japan are very limited, while exports to other Asian and Pacific countries and areas have a relatively high share of manufactures and semi-manufactures. Due to the increasing relative importance of food products and metals and minerals, the share of manufactures and fuels in LAIA exports to Asia and the Pacific has declined throughout the 1990s. The principal LAIA export items to Asia and the Pacific are by and large primary commodities, whose depressed prices recently has resulted in much lower values of exports. The major export items include copper; iron ore; iron and steel; aluminum; crude oil; wood, paper and pulp; soybeans and soybean products; coffee; fish and its products and meat; and leather. LAIA countries could be expected to play an increasingly important role as bases providing several primary commodities to Asia and the Pacific. The product composition of Asian and Pacific exports is dominated by manufactured goods, regardless of the importing region.

External trade with Asia and the Pacific appears to exhibit the most traditional features of the Latin American export model. The competitiveness of this model continues to depend on natural resources, while it gradually starts to incorporate products with a higher value-added. For instance, in the case of Chile, a decline in exports of the mining sector has been replaced with an increasing share the forest industry and its by-products (pulp and paper), fish industry and agro-industry. Brazil has developed a processed food industry and some progress can also be observed in the metal industry, especially steel and tin. Argentina has achieved a better trade position by exporting steel pipes to Asian markets, especially to ASEAN-member countries. Mexico has developed industries in the cement and glass sectors. All these products, which have been called "industrial commodities", indicate that a slow diversification process of trade between Latin America and Asian economies (Akio, 1999) began to appear in the 1990s and projected to be in the early decade of 2000.

Both regions have made commendable progress in reducing barriers to trade through multilateral trade negotiations, regional efforts, bilateral efforts and unilateral measures. In Asia and the Pacific, average tariffs have declined substantially in recent years. The simple average applied tariff in 1996 was below 15 per cent for 10 of the 12 countries considered, of which eight were below 10 per cent and three below 5 per cent. Liberalization efforts in more recent years have brought the rates even lower. The LAIA countries have also registered remarkable reductions in tariffs and tariff dispersion in recent years, and their average of MFN rates now fall in the range of about 10 to 14 per cent. The majority of the countries in both regions are taking a "Uruguay Round Plus" approach. High tariffs affecting some industries and numerous non-tariff barriers (NTBs) still exist in both regions, despite the benefits of liberalized trade, and this substantially reduces mutual comparative advantages. In fact, although tariffs have gradually been reduced, NTBs are still prevalent, including quotas, import licensing, discriminatory customs procedures, burdensome testing and certification requirements.

The recent proliferation of trade agreements in Latin America and Asia and the Pacific has not only brought realignments in tariff and non-tariff measures, but also dynamic effects on trade and investment flows, the cost structure of production, competition patterns and the creation and diffusion of technology. These agreements have contributed to better articulation of transport, telecommunications, energy, water and other infrastructure capacities at the regional level. It is expected that they will also lead to a more homogenous system of trade-related services, investment, intellectual property rights, factor mobility, rules of origin, anti-monopoly laws, anti-dumping and safeguards, sanitary and phytosanitary regulations. These efforts to enhance the systemic competitiveness of each region will, in turn, enable each country to more efficiently participate in the world market.

## New Dimensions of Competitive Growth

In view of the economic development of the countries involved and in their political, social, legal and administrative systems, and with equal respect for the views of all participating countries, future business partnering and economic cooperation between Latin America and East Asian countries may be guided by the following strategies:

### General Trade Negotiations

- The countries of each region should exhibit multidimensionality by giving priority to strengthening their relations with one another, through efforts that carry forward on the political, economic and social dimensions, particularly in areas of trade, investment, social development, science and technology, education, culture and institutional development.
- The business partnership strategies should be developed keeping in view the heterogeneity in economic development, culture and institutional modalities that exist in both regions, while seeking globally balanced relations. The relationship should be based on fundamental shared principles and values, which in turn can be translated into clear political messages and a general sustained process of dialogue and cooperation. Relationships can be deepened at the bi-regional level, regional or bilateral levels, taking advantages of the special circumstances of country groupings. Building relationships should proceed at different levels and speeds among the countries of the region.
- Considering the multiplicity of forums, it is necessary to focus the trade partnering negotiations at bilateral and multilateral levels and avoid overlap between distinct dialogues and similar initiatives taken at other forums.
- In order to promote the private and public sectors in both regions to take advantage of trade and investment opportunities, Asia and Pacific and Latin American countries

should have a framework for discussing and harmonizing common trade and investment interests.

- Economic issues should be a key part of the cooperation process between the two regions in view of the current low levels of economic exchange and the great potential for expansion. Close and growing economic ties are an important element for recovery and sustained growth in both regions. Both regions should work together to develop priorities, policies and measures in economic cooperation and thus maximize interregional synergy, based on the following principles: (i) closer cooperation and dialogue between government and the private sector, with the latter as the engine of growth; (ii) non-discriminatory liberalization, transparency and open regionalism; and (iii) consistency and compliance with applicable international rules, particularly those of the WTO.
- Increased trade and investment based on open markets and firm adherence to applicable international rules would contribute to early restoration of broad-based economic growth in both regions. The policies should be framed to remove the existing bottlenecks such as information exchange and knowledge sharing to intensify the bi-regional/ bilateral trade and investment flows

## Operational Issues in Business Partnering Model

Bilateral negotiations should be strategically pursued in removing/ reducing the non-tariff and investment barriers. The trade related negotiations among the Latin America-East Asian countries should also focus on the technical norms and standards; rules of origin, anti-dumping, subsidies, countervailing measures; other liberalization and deregulation measures (privatization); sub-regional, regional and hemispheric integration processes; and convergence and divergence between regional integration and multilateral trade regimes. The negotiations should also be dealt on simplifying the customs rules and procedures, including non-transparent and inefficient infrastructures; differing customs; improper application of rules of origin, customs valuation, pre-shipment inspection and import licensing. Customs problems can be especially difficult for small and medium enterprises that have less experience and fewer resources for handling these problems.

Bi-regional multilateral trade need to be encouraged among the Latin America and East Asian countries which would enable them to promote liberalization which is conducive to increasing the traditional trade flows among the participating countries. The bi-regional diplomatic negotiations should be evolved towards developing an action plan aiming at reducing NTBs and transaction costs, as well as promoting trade and investment opportunities between the two regions. Such a plan could provide concrete goals to be achieved in identified priority areas such as: (a) customs procedures, standards, testing, certification and accreditation; (b) public procurement; (c) quarantine and SPS procedures; (d) intellectual property rights; and (e) mobility of business people. The detailed descriptions on the above issues are discussed below:

## Customs Procedures

- Accelerated alignment and harmonization of tariff nomenclatures with the World Customs Organization(WCO) standards;
- Accelerated implementation of obligations under the WTO Customs Valuation Agreement;
- Endeavor to start negotiations on customs co-operation and mutual administrative assistance agreements between the Latin American and Asian business partners;
- Promotion of transparency through mutual access to existing databases such as customs duties and nomenclature, tariff quotas, import and export procedures and formalities, rules of origin, customs legislation, etc.;
- Improvement of predictability for the business community through publication, and clarification upon request, of customs regulations and procedures in force taking into account, where appropriate, the relevant international customs Conventions, such as the Kyoto Convention;
- Promotion of standardized and simplified documentation taking into account the existing international standards and the ongoing discussions in various international fora.

## Standards, Testing, Certification, Accreditation and Technical Regulations

In supporting and enhancing the bi-regional trade related cooperation in the areas of standards, testing, certification, and accreditation bodies, the deliverables which may need to be considered during evolving the trade policies or tenure agreements are discussed as below:

- Close consultation, where appropriate, in relation to the work of international bodies dealing with standards such as the International Organization for Standards (ISO) and the International Electrotechnical Commission (IEC) and to the WTO –Technical Barriers to Trade(TBT) discussions;
- Work towards the improvement of mutual understanding of each other's systems of testing, accreditation and certification of conformity, and the development and dissemination of information materials on national standards, certification and accreditation procedures in SME friendly format;
- Accelerated alignment of national standards to international standards, ensuring that national standards thus aligned are embodied in national laws and regulations, and periodic reporting thereon;
- Identification of sectors of priority interest with a view to the consideration of entering into Mutual Recognition Arrangements (MARS); and
- Establishing cooperation in the promotion of technical and institutional capacity-building in relation to standards, testing, certification, accreditation and technical regulations, including the exchange of information on existing programs, the identification of possible gaps, and the enhancement of cooperation programs as appropriate.

## Public Procurement

The governments of Latin America-East Asian countries may develop a Trade Facilitation Action Plan (TFAP) with a focus providing transparency in public procurement, in particular through exchanging information on public procurement procedures, statistics, and opportunities. The plan may include exchange of information on central government procurement procedures and making them available in a format suitable to the business community; sharing inventory of existing database and promoting mutual cooperation on exploring the technical support on public procurement projects.

## Quarantine and Sanitary and Phytosanitary (SPS) Measures

The bi-regional trade agreements should also discuss the issues related to promotion of simplification and rationalization in procedures and documentation considering international best practice, and enhancement of transparency on electronic media. This would help enhancing the trade among the partnering countries in plant genetic engineering and value added trade of flora based products. Such negations would facilitate enhancement of transparency in key quarantine and SPS areas including inspection and approval procedures, quarantine requirements and normal inspection processing time.

## Intellectual Property Rights (IPR)

The TFAP should also focus on cooperation in technical, institutional and human capacity-building in relation to IPR awareness and enforcement including exchange of information on existing programs, the identification of possible gaps in these programs, and their enhancement as appropriate.

## Mobility of Business People

With a view to facilitating direct business-to-business contacts between the two regions, the negotiating countries should draw administrative measures to examine and report on concerns identified by the business community with respect to formalities for business travel and temporary stay.

## Trade in Private Sector

The role of private sector organizations and chambers of commerce can be assumed in the creation of a private sector network linking Asian and Latin American companies. The integration process also involves mutual perceptions that are cultural, with an aim to replace the conventional agreements with contacts among actual business people and the possibility of creating common policies and benefits.

# Political and Residual Risks in International Business

Political, economic, religious and other tensions can shift at a moment's notice and disrupt business operations for exporters, traders, investors, banks and other organizations involved in international commerce. Companies can be subject to the discriminatory actions - or inaction - of foreign governments and third parties, potentially leading to forced shutdowns, relocations and other unexpected expenses. The political risks in international business are developed with illegitimate use of political power. The way political power is exercised determines government action and the degree of risk that threatens a firm's value. For example, a dramatic political event may pose little risk to a multinational enterprise, while subtle policy changes can greatly impact a firm's performance. Firm-specific political risks are the risks directed at a particular company in reference to its country of origin, nature of activities in the host country, social and economic goals etc. and such risks are by nature discriminatory. The risks specific to the firms may be concerned with the governmental policies as well as due to the instability in the political system governing the country. The following risks may emerge from such situations:

## Government Policy Based Risk

- Discriminatory regulations
- "Creeping" expropriation
- Breach of contract
- National security
- Structural adjustment
- Internal economic policies

## Risk off Shooting due to Political Instability

- Sabotage
- Civil unrest
- Anti-globalization movements
- International relations of the host country
- Firm-specific boycotts

On the contrary, the country-specific political risks are not directed at a firm, but are countrywide, and may affect firm's performance. An example in this context may be given as the decision of the government to forbid currency transfers or the outbreak of a civil war within the host country. The political risks also include government risks and stability risks. The government risks are those that arise from the policies of a governing authority, in reference to the use of authority. A legitimately enacted tax hike or an extortion ring that is allowed to operate and is led by a local police chief may both be considered as government risks. Indeed, many government risks, particularly those that are firm-specific, contain an ambiguous mixture of legal and illegal elements. Instability risks, on the other hand, arise from political power struggles. These conflicts could be between members of a government fighting over succession, or mass riots in response to deteriorating social conditions. The country level risk in reference to the government policies and political instability may vary in its intensity. However, following factors may affect the risks due to government policies and political instability in a country:

## Government Policy Based Risk

- Mass nationalizations
- Regulatory changes
- Currency inconvertibility

## Risk off Shooting due to Political Instability

- Labor unrest
- Urban rioting
- Protest on international relations
- People's movement on diplomatic moves
- Civil wars

Besides the apparent political risk, a foreign firm may also get exposed to a bundle of different risks. Many of these risks are not unique to the asset owned by a firm but reflect broader possibilities, such as that the stock market average will rise or fall, that interest rates will be cut or increased, or that the growth rate will change in an entire economy or industry. Residual risk, also known as alpha, is what is left after the firm takes out all the other shared risk exposures. An exposure to such risk can be reduced by the firm through strategic diversification decisions. The comprehensive political risks in a country may have many dimensions as exhibited in Table 9.1.

Hence, political risk assessment (PRA) is necessary for the foreign firms in order to identify countries that may turn out to be unsafe tomorrow and to identify the actual situation in the countries avoiding any biasness. For example, doing business in Vietnam and Haiti now may not be that unsafe as was felt earlier. Assessing the political risk of a country may also provide a framework to identify the degree of political risk in the selected countries for firm's entry. The political risk may be assessed through some effective methods. In one of the PRA methods, an executive or a team of executives is advised to visit the country in which investment is being considered. A preliminary market research is done to support the visit of the executives in the country. Upon arrival, there are usually meetings with government officials and local businesspersons. This approach is known as *grand tour*. The results emerging out of this approach may be very shallow, representing only selected pieces of information and therefore possibly camouflaging undesirable aspects of the market. The other method relies on the advice of an outside consultant or a person deemed to be an expert. Usually such persons are seasoned educators, diplomats, local politicians, or businesspersons. The capability and experience of the advisor is the factor determining the quality of this report. This approach of political risk assessment, by its very nature is termed as *the old hand*.

In another similar approach known as the *Delphi technique*, a few selected experts are asked to share their opinions independently on a given problem, in a form that can be scored in order to produce a statistical distribution of opinion. The experts are shown the resulting distribution and given the chance to alter their original views. In the process of the study, the experts are given the task of rating different political factors such as the stability of government, internal and external security issues of the country, and the existing political conflicts. The process is repeated several times and then the results are synthesized. Based on the final expert opinion, the firm takes an entry decision. In addition to the above discussed methods many firms conducts the inquiry into the risk factors in a country using *quantitative methods*. In such studies, the statistical analysis is done on the basis of the time series data collected on identified variables. The multivariate analysis, correlations and trend analysis are conducted to measure the magnitude and direction of political risk in a country. The foreign firms decide on the basis of the trend of political risk in a country and its magnitude, which emerges out of the quantitative studies. However, while assessing political stability, the focus should be on the legitimacy of state authority, the ability of that authority to impose and enforce decrees, the level of corruption that spread through the system of authority and the degree of political fractionalization that is present. Where economic policy is concerned, the focus would be more along the lines of the degree of government participation in an economy, the government's external debt burden, and the degree to which interest groups can successfully obstruct the decision-making process.

**Table 9.1. Political Risk Platforms in a Country**

| Area | Risk Factors |
|---|---|
| Demography | Size and occupational distribution, Economic growth and per capita income, Population growth and control, Income distribution. |
| Human Resources | Size and composition, Sectoral and geographic distribution, Productivity, Migration and urban unemployment. |
| Politico-economic | Natural resources, Economic diversification, Topography and infrastructure, Sources and structure of government revenues, Size and growth of the budget deficit, Social expenditure, Price indices, Wage rates, Interest rates, money supply, etc. |
| International economics and Trade Related Risk | Current account balance and composition, income and price elasticity of exports and imports, Price stability of major imports and exports, Terms of trade, Geographic composition of trade, Outstanding foreign debt, absolute and relative levels, Terms and maturity profile, Debt servicing to income and exports, Size and relative importance, Capital account, Reserve position, Exchange rates (official and unofficial). |
| Culture and Religion Based Risk | Underlying cultural values and beliefs, Religious and moral values, Sense of alienation with foreign or modem influences, Constitutional principles and conflicts, Resilience of national institutions. |
| Leadership, International alignment and diplomatic relations | Key leaders' background and attitudes, Main beneficiaries of the status quo, Role and power of the internal security apparatus, Strength, sources of support, effectiveness of opposition political parties, Level and frequency of internal disturbances, Riots and terrorist acts, Bureaucracy and extent of official corruption, International treaties and alignments, Position on international issues, Preferential economic and trade linkages, Border disputes, Diplomatic or commercial conflict with home country. |

## MICROECONOMIC ENVIRONMENT

An environment surrounding a specific product or market concerning the competition rather than a country's overall economic environment refers to the microeconomic environment. A careful analysis of a microenvironment indicates whether a company can successfully enter a specific market. It may be hypothesized that rising prosperity of a nation depends on the productivity with which it uses its human, capital and natural resources. This is manifested in the way in which a nation's firms compete. Productivity, in turn, is a function of the interplay of three factors: the Political, Legal and Macroeconomic Context; the Quality of the Microeconomic Business Environment; and the Sophistication of Company Operations and Strategy. Together they determine the capacity of a nation to produce internationally competitive firms and support rising prosperity. A context that creates pressure for firms continuously to upgrade the source and sophistication of their advantage and at the same time supports the upgrading process is a favorable microeconomic context. Pressure for upgrading is supplied by *demand conditions* featuring sophisticated and demanding customers, whose demands spur the local firms to innovate in order to upgrade their product/service offerings. Particularly valuable is pressure from local customers that anticipate the nature of demand elsewhere in the world. Different competitors, however, might aim to satisfy different types of demand: existing, latent, or incipient. *Existing demand* refers to a product bought to satisfy a recognized need. *Latent demand* applies in a situation where a particular need has been recognized, but no products have been offered. *Incipient demand* describes a projected need that will emerge when customers become aware of it sometime in the future.

Competition may be analyzed in reference to the characteristics of products as breakthrough, competitive, and improved. A *breakthrough product* is a unique innovation that is mainly technical in nature, such as the digital watch, VCR, and personal computer. A *competitive product* is one of many brands currently available in the market and has no special advantage over the competing products. An *improved product* is not unique but is generally superior to many existing brands. For example, let us assume Aubrey Organics is interested in manufacturing shampoo for tender hair in Turkey and seeks entry into the emerging market in the middle-eastern countries. The company finds that in addition to a number of local brands, Johnson & Johnson's baby shampoo and Helene Curtis Industries' Suave Shampoo are the competitive products in the market. Proctor and Gamble has recently entered the market with its Pantene Pro-V brand, which is considered as an improved product. Most of the competition appears to be addressing the existing demand. However, no attempts have been made to satisfy latent demand or incipient demand. After reviewing various considerations, Aubrey Organics may decide to fulfill latent demand with an improved offering through its Camomile Luxurious brand. Based on market information, the company reasons that a hair problem most consumers face in that part of the world is dandruff. No brand has addressed itself to that problem. Even Proctor & Gamble's new entry mainly emphasizes health of hair. Thus, analysis of the competition with reference to product offerings and demand enables Aubrey Organics to determine its entry point into the market of middle-eastern countries. The companies need to analyze some important issues as below while examining the micro-economic environment:

- Who is the competition now, and who will it be in the future?
- What are the key competitors' strategies, objectives and goals?
- How important is a specific market to the competitors, and are they enough to continue to invest?
- What unique strengths do the competitors have?
- Do they have any weaknesses that make them vulnerable?
- What changes are likely in the competitors' future strategies?
- What are the implications of competitors' strategies on the market, the inc. and one's own company?

One of the appropriate ways to examine the competition is to draw up a demographic profile of the industry. Markets dominated by small, single-industry businesses or small regional competitors differ significantly from those dominated by national or multi-industry companies. The competitor strengths may be measured by analyzing various functional indicators in marketing as described below:

- Market share
- Differential advantages
- Cost advantages
- Reputation
- Distribution capabilities
- Core competencies
- Perceptions of target buyers
- Competitors' financial strength, which determines their ability to spend money on advertising and promotions, among other things
- Competitor's ability and speed of innovation for new products and services

It is necessary to list the strengths and weaknesses of the competitors from the customer's viewpoint and analyze how a company can capitalize on their weaknesses and meet the challenges represented by their strengths. The information on the competitor information might be easily obtained by getting a copy of their annual report. It might take analysis of many information sources to understand competitors' strategies and objectives. In an international market, the business takes place in a highly competitive, volatile environment, so it is important to understand the competition. Some questions as illustrated below can help the marketer to map the micro-economic variables in reference to a competitor:

- Who are your five nearest direct competitors?
- Who are your indirect competitors?
- Is their business growing, steady, or declining?
- What can you learn from their operations or from their advertising?
- What are their strengths and weaknesses?
- How does their product or service differ from yours?

The competition in the photo film products has been increasing with competitive price and promotion strategies among the major international brands like Kodak and Fuji. The consumers have found a bona fide competitor to Kodak in the name of Fujifilm. Clearly, Fujifilm has emerged from a minor player in the early 1980's in American market to take a solid number two position within the US market and has caught the attention, as well as the fury, of Kodak. The success of low priced super stores such as Wal-Mart has taught retailers that diversification, scrambled marketing and "one-stop" shopping are important to consumers. As consolidation in retail industry sweeps in mass marketing, food and drug accounts, retailers realize they must maintain their competitive advantage or close shop. To survive, they are squeezing manufacturers for quality products at competitive prices to capture profit margins for expansion within the industry. This environment has provided an opportunity for Fujifilm to prosper in an otherwise stable and mature photographic industry. Though Kodak and Fuji fight for market share, the real winner and benefactor is the consumer, both the companies officially deny that they are engaging in a price war, but for each move Fuji makes, Kodak counters with a strategic move. Kodak and Fuji traditionally enjoyed healthy margins and treated the market as a mutually profitable duopoly[295]. Then in the spring of 1996, Fuji cut prices on film by 10 to 15 percent after Costco Wholesalers decided to go exclusively with Kodak. Fuji had excess inventory of 2.5 millions rolls of film. They distributed the heavily discounted film to other retailers to avoid "expiring" film and thus began a correlation between price cutting and market share. Once consumers tried Fuji, they found they liked the product as long as it was priced lower than Kodak. By 1998 the severe pace of competition between Kodak and Fuji seemed to slow down, with the exception of value packs. However, still the companies are on neck-to-neck competition in the market, though other brands like *Agfa, Konica* have made a dent in the global retailing including American markets.

Competitor analysis is an ongoing process that allows the new entrants to identify their respective strengths and weaknesses. Analyzing the movements of competitors, a firm may develop better understanding of what products or services to be offered in the segmented market; how to market them effectively; and positioning them appropriately in the given market. One way to gauge the strength of a given competitor in your market is to measure its online presence. How often does the competitor's brand appear in all forms on the Internet? In particular, how often does it appear in reference to your market, relative to yours and other companies? There are other, almost limitless, ways to learn about competitors. Competitive intelligence involves legal methods of data collection and analysis, from scouring securities filings and news reports to database research to schmoozing with representatives of rival companies at trade shows.

The soundness of the economy of a country largely governs the consumer confidence, which further determines the buying plans of the consumers. A favorable economic environment helps consumers to optimize their buying decisions and augment propensity to spend money. The reverse occurs when economic conditions are unfavorable. The economic environment in Brazil was not encouraging for the various segments of consumers during period 1998-1999 though the inflation was under control. The credit restrictions have had a negative impact on consumption during the above referred period. However, after the country

---

[295] Finnerty C Thomas: Kodak vs. Fuji: The Battle for Global Market Share, Institute of Global Business Strategy, Lubin School of Business, Pace University, 2000, pp 4-23.

exercised appropriate economic measures to stabilize the economy of the country in the recent past, it has been observed that foreign business corporations consider Brazil to be Latin America's most attractive investment target. International marketers should examine the extent to which their business is vulnerable to economic conditions. For example, in a booming economy, consumers tend to buy durable goods, on the contrary in recession they would avoid spending money. The prevailing economic environment is just an indicator to review the business fit in the given region or country. Even if the short-run economic environment is not conducive to profits, a company may decide to enter an overseas market in anticipation of favorable long-term economic prospects in country such as growing political stability, declining inflation or the low wage rates. However, the long-run perspective is the most critical decision factor, which provides the firm sufficient resources to endure waiting for the future favorable environment. The market attractiveness of Brazil may be described from this point of view.

The microeconomic environment of a product or market also plays a significant role in its market performance in overseas market. A very successful Asian electronics company, for many years a leader in electronic home appliances market, launched a cheaper version of its traditional product almost simultaneously in south-east Asia and in Europe. The marketing approach comprising product design, pricing, and advertising was quite similar in both areas. However, the product has been very successful at home market, but in Europe, sales fell far below expectations. Product in the home market was successful as the company's product strategy was in the mature phase of its life cycle, while in Europe it was at its beginning. The brand had stronger penetration in the home market than in European market that led to the weak consumer perception on the innovativeness of the product in Europe. Besides, the low price without explaining the product concept in south-east Asian countries market was sensible but this strategy had a negative impact on the European consumers. It may be observed from the above example that the Asian company got into problems in Europe because it could not be competitive in Europe and had a low market share. Besides, the product was new to the European market and at the beginning of the product life cycle; it presented an unfamiliar concept in the market. In other words, the Asian company did not orient its marketing program with the product/market environment existing in Europe.

## NEW VISIONS OF EMERGING MARKETS

There are many new hybrid business cultures emerging across the countries. Of these, the regional ones are re-emerging through international partnering under the aegis of globalization. The evolution of trade partnerships with the companies of the other countries is a phenomenon that often reflects deep structural changes in the whole economic system of a country. It usually takes long time to unfold since comparative advantages in international business partnering have long-term gains. Globalization has increased the access to the markets as the remote markets have been reduced following the political and economic changes world-wide. The structural reforms in Latin American countries have broadly focused in five major areas comprising international trade, financial markets, labor markets, and the generation and use of public resources. Consequently the financial development has improved, especially the depth of financial intermediation, private sector participation in banking, and the size and activity of stock markets. The economic integration and structural reforms in Latin America considered that import substitution in manufacturing sector would be synonymous with industrialization, which in turn was seen as the key to development.

The market access has also been improved by growing trade blocks at the regional level. Such accessibility to the markets is further reinforced by reducing the trade barriers through far-reaching business communication strategies, product and market development programs, and customer relations. This situation has given a boost in determining the market opportunities as narrowing the trade barriers helped in deregulating certain sectors of trade such as financial services. However, there may be some exceptions to this common pattern. The global market place equipped with the application of global communications has become the focus of the global business arena that makes the world markets remain open and involve in the fair competitive practices. At the same time the anti-globalization moves also exist in the process of development that protest against the hazards of suppressive strategies of the global companies affecting the regional trade entities. The globalization moves have opened up high comparative advantages in many manufactured goods through partnership deals to explore the business in the emerging economies. They generally display an increasing specialization trend and high consumer values. The leading alliances between the major multinational enterprises may be seen in reference to production, finance, and technology and supply chain along with other complementary activities.

Production sharing is the contemporary global economic trend based on the concepts of comparative advantages that offers economic advantages by stages of the production process. The strategy of production sharing has emerged as a solution to an economic problem in developing countries where the absorption of the surplus manpower in industry is a national economic issue. Consequently, the developing countries turn to the developed countries as major cost effective labor market in order to share production of labor oriented products. Investment in production sharing operations has become an integral part of global efforts to reduce manufacturing costs and has contributed to the accelerated pace of cross-border integration of manufacturing in North America and the Caribbean Basin. Currently, production sharing seems to be a growing practice that helps in building and strengthening the international partnerships with global firms like Volvo, a Swedish automobile company having its manufacturing partners for heavy duty engines in India and Mexico. This practice offers both the developed and developing countries a scope to share their resources and strengths for the mutual benefits of international partnering.

Markets today not only provide the multiple goods and services to the customers but also expose their behavior to the cross-cultural differences and innovations. The specialization of production process has also brought such cultural changes by business penetrations in the low production skills regions across the countries. Apparel from Asian countries like Indonesia, Korea and all types of consumer goods from China, electronics from Japan and perfumery from France may be some good examples to explain the specialization and cross-cultural sharing of consumer behavior. Conducting business is a creative enterprise and doing it out of one's own country is more demanding. The industry structure varies dramatically across the countries in the world and a global enterprise to strive against odds requires strong adaptation behavior. In the international business, a company needs to best prepare itself to achieve competitive advantage in the marketplace. International partnering in reference to production technology, co-branding, distribution and retailing may bring a high success to the companies of home country in increasing the market share in the region as well as augmenting the customer value for mutual benefit.

Emergence of virtual shopping and liberalization of economic policies in the developing countries all over the world competition has become like a traditional derby in which many companies participate for neck to neck race. In this business game the rules are subject to change without notice, the prize money may change in short notice, the route and finish line is also likely to change after the race begins, new entrants may join at any time during the race, the racers may form strong alliances, all creative strategies are allowed in the game and the state legislation may change without notice and sometimes with retrospective effect. Hence, to win the race any company should acquire the strategies of outwitting, outmaneuvering and outperforming the competitors. In this process, a company must understand thoroughly all the moves of the rival firms from various sources. The locales of business rivalry have to be spotted to assess their strengths. Under the given situation it may be necessary for a firm to hold the shoulder of a strong brand to swim across the competitive safely enhancing the reach to the markets. To do so, international partnering may prove to be one of the most popular and low risk strategies. Companies of Latin American region may look into this concept not only for growing their market share in the region, also to acquire long-term sustainability in the international business.

Economic globalization is a new worldwide economic order, in which a majority of nations prescribe to the free enterprise system. The triad market refers to the United States and Canada, Japan and Western European countries. This group of countries accounts for approximately 14 percent of the global population and represents about 70 percent of world gross product and absorbs the major proportion of capital and consumer products. However this may not be uniform for all the companies of the triad region and there may be some exceptions. For many European companies like Volkswagen, Latin America may be more attractive market than Africa and for a British Chocolate company like Cadbury's; India, Australia, Africa and part of Canada may be more attractive market than others. Some American companies heavily depend on the Middle-east markets. The relative strengths of Triad partner countries also reflect on their resources allocation and corporate spending on the research and development and strategic alliances in terms of capital tie-ups, joint ventures and technical tie-ups with the multinational companies of the partnering countries. The General Motors (GM) has increased its equity stake in Japanese automaker Suzuki to 20 percent in 2000 but has sized down in 2003 as GM reduces its total equity in Isuzu to 12 percent but acquires majority ownership of Isuzu's diesel engine businesses and technologies thereof. The Chevrolet Cruze is launched in Japan in 2001 that has been designed and developed by GM and its alliance partner Suzuki. The Cruze is the first GM vehicle to be built in Japan since the 1930s.

Some of the examples of successful partnering globally and in the Latin American countries may be discussed to emphasize the mutual advantage. In 1997 Telmex, a premier telecommunication company of Mexico and Sprint of USA entered into the joint venture to market long distance service to the growing U.S. Hispanic market. This alliance has aimed at catering to the special needs of this large and influential population by offering conveniently packaged calling plans and products. CIFRA Mexico is a holding company operating in the retail sector through 229 outlets that includes good number of units under a joint venture agreement with Wal-Mart, a USA retail mammoth, in the fields of goods and services. The association with Wal-Mart helps CIFRA to project global image of its services to the Mexican consumers and sustain the local competition. In another venture one of the largest branded food companies, ConAgra of Canada, entered into business partnering with Sigma Alimentos (Sigma), a leading Mexican refrigerated and frozen food marketer in creation of a frozen foods joint venture. ConAgra Foods has acquired 50 percent of Sigma's frozen processed foods subsidiary, Sigma Alimentos Congelados, S.A. de C.V., as part of the joint venture. Sigma Alimentos retains ownership of the other 50 percent. The frozen processed foods joint venture manufactures markets and distributes Sigma's Mexican frozen brands such as El Cazo Mexicano, Menu del Sol and Sugerencias del Chef products. El Cazo Mexicano is a market leading variety of authentic Mexican frozen prepared food in distribution throughout Mexico. Menu del Sol is a line of authentic Mexican food intended primarily for the American retail market. Sugerencias del Chef consists of pizzas and chicken nuggets, among other products, sold in Mexico's retail and foodservice channels. In addition to Sigma's existing Mexican brands, the new joint venture company will market and distribute ConAgra Foods' Banquet, Healthy Choice and Kid Cuisine products, as well as other ConAgra Foods' frozen products, throughout Mexico and Central America[296].

The international partnering also plays a significant role in research and development in manufacturing sector in Latin America. CamBioTec (the Canada–Latin America Initiative on Biotechnology, Environment and Sustainable Development) was launched in January 1995 by the International Development Research Centre (IDRC) of Canada. The objective of the Initiative is to promote the introduction of biotechnology-based products and applications to respond to critical needs in the agrifood and environmental management sectors of selected Latin American countries. The initiative has targeted four Latin American countries for the initial phase of its work: Argentina, Colombia, Cuba, and Mexico. Together, these countries possess a vibrant biotechnology sector and offer a range of opportunities for the application of biotechnology and for the development of partnerships with Canadian firms and institutions. Besides, Latin American countries have been strengthening development partnerships in Asia since the free trade agreements between Chile and Korea and between Mexico and Japan established in 2003. There also have been enhanced cross-investment and increased trade relations between China and several countries in the region. Latin America offers Japanese investors access to resources and markets that can support the growing needs of the Japanese economy.

The opening up of markets can play an important role in weakening vested interests and reducing economic rents associated with long standing economic and institutional arrangements. Trade can thus spur improvement in domestic institutions that otherwise would not have been possible. In addition, international agreements can be an important external anchor and catalyst for institutional change by breaking through domestic impediments to reforms. Chile and Mexico provide important role models for the region. Institutional strengthening in both countries has allowed them to establish a successful inflation targeting framework, lower public debt, open the trading regime, and build a strong regulatory and oversight framework for the banking system. The native companies of Latin America to explore the partnerships with the global companies towards developing research and development, co-branding, technology, distribution, production sharing activities, retailing and business consultancy services. Such partnership would prove beneficial not only in augmenting the corporate image of the Latin American countries but also capturing higher

[296] ConAgra Foods Inc. Home page http://www.conagrafoods.com/

market share for the products and services in the Latin American markets. The retail partnering with foreign retailing companies would also be a profit worthy propositions for the fast moving consumer goods like dairy products, processed meet, Latin carbonated beverages and the like. The retail size is represented by the pull effect on consumer shopping based on the unique sales proposition of the company, like Wal-Mart's retail philosophy of *every day low prices*. There may also be possibility of engaging the strategic international relationship with two or more companies to cooperate out of mutual need and to share the risk in achieving common objectives. The star alliance in aviation industry and multiple alliances in e-commerce *e.g.* Microsoft, Telmex-Podigy in Mexico as internet service provider company, may be described as the success agents of multiple international partnering strategy. Such alliances would offer opportunities for rapid expansion into new markets, access to new technology and the scope of profit optimization. However, it is advisable that the Latin American companies may do a strategic introspection of their organization before developing the partnership proposals in reference to clarity of partnering value proposition to the customer, its relevance to the end customer and the way the value proposition differentiates the company from its main competitors. However, the challenge for retail management is to generate value for the customer that is distinctive and, at the same time, profitable.

There are several other ways of international partnering that may allow the Latin American companies to expand into other countries. However, the most common and perhaps the least complex but risky approach is to transfer a powerful, *'tried-and tested'* format with the international companies that are less known to the region. It is necessary for the home companies to keep its core business elements intact but certain adjustments need to be tailored to the needs of the new context of partnership. *Carrefour* has successfully adapted its hypermarket format in its 21 foreign markets. Many international partnership format elements such as range structure, location characteristics, production, plant layout/size and innovative merchandising may be identical in face lifting the image of the brand, consumer perception and referrals. However, some elements such as product range, price and communications are to be customized to each country.

## ECONOMIC AND CULTURAL INTEGRATION IN EMERGING MARKETS

International marketing encompasses people from different cultures and thus every business activity in another country is subject to cultural challenges. The extent of cultural influence varies in accordance with the nature of industrial and consumer products and services. Consumer Products, by virtue of their marketing process such as mass advertising, sales promotion and personal selling tend to require a strong degree of cultural awareness since this knowledge relates to the human communication in the selling process. On the contrary, industrial products may have lesser requirements for cultural awareness, as sometimes negotiation in business to business or industrial marketing segment is based on a situation beyond cultural adaptation process. For example, the technical specifications for an industrial ceramic automotive component might be the same in New York as they are in Tokyo or Moscow. Under such circumstances what is important, to make this sale, is the price of the component and its fit within required specifications of the component.

> The traditional high esteem for the word in Europe is reflected for instance in the elaborate business correspondence. Europeans not only love to talk extensively in negotiations, they also draw up long minutes of meetings and letters of confirmation. They strive to put the progress of their business in exact words in order to keep going. Japanese enterprises, on the other hand, are not especially fond of correspondence. Compared to European business letters, Japanese letters tend to be brief and, in the European view, sometimes not sufficiently precise. Even differences in detail of communication may cause problems in business relationships. In Europe, contracts as a principle are put in writing, and written contracts are minutely drafted. In this way one tries to provide for all conceivable problems of the contractual relationship in advance. In Japan, a 1987 survey revealed that in practice 71% of business contracts are concluded only orally. But even if Japanese contracts are put in writing, they are often only of a summary nature. In Europe such summary contracts will be of little use. For example, a German labor contract frequently comprises 10 pages. A Japanese company followed Japanese practice in Germany and concluded a 1-page employment contract with a German employee. For this reason alone, the Japanese company stood no chance of winning when it was sued by the employee before a German labor court. Sometimes there is the impression that Japanese enterprises do not readily enter into written contracts because they want to retain their freedom of action and flexibility in the future. According to traditional Japanese thinking, a good personal relationship between the parties reinforced by *giri* obligations is more important than a written contract. *Giri* is a moral obligation to loyalty incurred by a special favor which is borne by the beneficiary until he has satisfied it by a definite but unspecified act of gratitude[297].

Corporations of any kind cannot escape the social environment that surrounds all their activities in the host countries. With the ever-increasing internationalization of companies the role of national culture in business is argued. It has been observed that some multinational companies experience serious culture shocks because of their cultural blindness. However, the most efficient ones are all well prepared to make good use of the cultural differences within the organization.

Market integration allows consumers to buy goods from all over the world in their local shops and supermarkets. While local businesses must compete with these foreign goods on their home turf, they also have new opportunities to develop their export markets by selling in a multitude of other countries. Cultural goods and services are no exception to these new patterns of production, consumption and trade. Cultural markets are increasingly going global as may be observed by the trends in cultural goods trade in the post 1980 period across the countries in different regions. As consumption of cultural goods and services spreads all over the world, production itself tends to concentrate. This results in an oligopolistic market with a highly asymmetric structure. The effects of this market profile are as yet unknown: while we are aware that a large share of the cultural products circulating in most countries are produced elsewhere, we know very little about the impact of this global cultural market on citizens, audiences, businesses and governments. The past few years have seen the emergence of a powerful interest in culture resulting from a combination of diverse phenomena such as globalization, regional integration processes and cultures claiming their right to express themselves - all this in a context where cultural industries are progressively taking over traditional forms of creation and dissemination and bringing about changes in cultural

[297] Guntram Rahn (1990): Cultural Differences and Doing Business in Europe and Japan, Discussion, University of Munich, C.H.Beck, Munich 1990.

practices. The issue of "culture and trade" has now acquired prime strategic significance. Cultural goods and services convey and construct cultural values, produce and reproduce cultural identity and contribute to social cohesion; at the same time they constitute a key free factor of production in the new knowledge economy. Culture is an essential dimension of business development. The business solutions should be tailored to locally relevant traditions and institutions and these activities should make use of local expertise and knowledge. The international company entering the host country should ensure that people, their cultures and society, and their organizations and institutions are taken into account in formulating the business goals and operational strategies. Such development coordination with local culture improves the lives of people, especially the poor, and builds the social capital for a company to sustain long in the host country.

An international firm makes its market oriented decisions in reference to the various customer perspectives that are determined by customer lifestyles and behavior patterns. The cultural aspects largely affect the products that people buy, the attributes that value, and the referrals that govern the buying decisions of the consumers. It is observed that a person's perspectives or resources, problems, and opportunities are generated and conditioned by cultural values to a considerable extent. Culture creates the system of communication among consumer about acceptance and rejection of the products and services, say in regard to food. Italian cultural influence in global markets plays an important role for the creation or expansion of markets for Italian products. One example is a collaboration project between the Italian government and the Japanese government called the "Italian Year in Japan, 2001". Utilizing this kind of event, Italy succeeded in generating a sophisticated brand image in the Japanese market. An important part of this event is the generation of a network system through the internet. Through this network, information about Italian technological products like automobiles and cultural products like paintings are distributed to members of the network[298].

## GLOBAL WRAP-UP

There is a fast change observed in the world markets resulting into the new emerging markets across the countries. In this century China, India and Latin America and the emerging market based economies in Eastern Europe promise new opportunities for global trade. The Pacific region had shown time-bending leap in the past four decades as significant Asian population participated in the rapid transition in response to the global movement of trade and services. Asia may be portrayed as the fastest growing market for the top brands of western companies and at the same time, the Asian companies began penetrating in the western markets at low price-high quality strategy. While the luxury and fashion goods are dominating the Asian and Far-east markets, the specialized product like electronics and automobiles from Asian Markets are trying to capture considerable market share in Europe and North American countries. The emerging markets in the developing countries have shown a strong potential for change in preferences during the late 20$^{th}$ century. In most of the advanced countries, the birth rate is declining while it is increasing in the developing

[298] Tadashi Yagi (2003): Effect of Cultural Influence on Market Expansion, Working Paper, Doshisha University, Kyoto, Japan, December.

countries. It has been observed that the technology has homogenized the world markets for variety of customer and industrial needs. The reduction in the tariff barriers, duties and liberalization process worldwide has further given a stimulus to the international marketing across the regional boundaries.

International companies, in order to be better among the competition involve significantly in assessing, monitoring and responding to the global competition by offering competitive values, developing superior brand image and positioning the product appropriately, keeping broader product line, adjustable price and keeping the quality of the products relatively high. Thus, it may be stated in brief that for competing globally the international companies should configure their marketing operation as discussed above, coordinate effectively with the domestic and neighboring markets and establish linkage of various marketing activities in different regions in order to sustain growing competition. Networks have made integration systems an essential aspect of doing business. Businesses rely on significant integration of servers to address the business needs of division, partners, distributors, and other affiliated groups to achieve efficient information access, enterprise-wide communication, and business process systems automation. Changing composition of world trade has been accompanied by a shift in production structures and the composition of domestic output. In industrial countries, growth in the information technology sector is rapidly changing with technology and services while developing countries are specializing in areas like apparel, metal products and electronics.

The Pacific Rim offers a variety of opportunities for American and European companies for the products and services that range from telecommunication instruments to the aircraft seats and banking services and a host of other products. Although it is a competitive market, the region is growing economically cohesive that attracts production sharing possibilities with the industrial countries. The Asian producers outside Japan have gained more than one fourth of the global market share for personal computers. Japan and the Pacific emerging triad comprising Singapore, Taiwan and South Korea provide most of the capital and expertise for the rest of the countries of the region that have enormous labor and natural resources. Hong Kong also contributes significantly for the development of international trade in the pacific region. Japan is Canada's second largest national trading partner (after the United States), taking 2.1% of total exports, and is the fifth largest source of foreign direct investment (FDI) in Canada. Canada is a leading supplier to Japan of a number of products of key export interest, such as lumber, pulp and paper, coal, meat, fish, oilseeds and prefabricated housing. While resource-based exports continue to represent much of our trading relationship, Canada is an increasingly important source of sophisticated, value-added, technology-driven products and services imported by Japan. In 2003, Canada's total merchandise trade with Japan was $22 billion. Canadian exports to Japan have declined steadily since the mid 1990s, Canadian exports to Japan declined again to $8.1 billion in 2003 from $8.4 billion in 2002 while imports from Japan decreased by 10% in 2003 to $14 billion. In 2003, Canada exported $1.4 billion in services and imported $1.9 billion[299]. The long-term trend in Japan is toward a growing demand for cost-competitive and innovative imports, which represents a significant market opportunity for Canadian exporters. The Asia Pacific region has been the fastest growing trade block over past three decades though it had experience downturn in 1998 and

[299] Government of Canada: Report on Canada's International Market Access Priorities- 2004, Department of Foreign Affairs and International Trade, Opening doors to the world, Chapter 6, 2004.

extended after shocks. East Asia is the principal export market for American goods. The transpacific trade has grown over 50 percent of its transatlantic trade by the end of $20^{th}$ century.

# SELECT REFERENCES


Barro Robert J (1991), Economic Growth in a Cross Section of Countries, *Quarterly Journal of Economics*, 106, pp 407-443.

Beaulieu, Eugene, Yatawara, Ravindra and Wang, Wei Guo: Who Supports Free Trade in Latin America?, *The World Economy*, Vol. 28, No. 7, 2005, 941-958.

Brown D, Deardorff A and Stern R (1996): International Labor Standards and Trade: A Theoretical Analysis, In Bhagawati J and Hudec (Eds.) *Fair Trade and Harmonization: Prerequisites for Free Trade, Vol 1, Economic Analysis*, The MIT Press, Cambridge, MA.

Collie David and Hviid Morten(1993), Export Subsidies as Signals of Competitiveness, *Scandinavian Journal of Economics*, Vol.95, No.3, pp 327-339.

Eaton Jonathan and Samuel Kortum (1995), Engines *of Growth – Domestic and Foreign Sources of Innovation*, National Bureau of Economic Research Inc., NBER Working Paper 5207.

Eaton Jonathan and Samuel Kortum (1996), Measuring Technology Diffusion and the International Sources of Growth, *Eastern Economic Journal*, 22 (4), pp 401-410.

Edwards Sabastian (1993): *Trade Policy, Exchange rates and Growth*, NBER Working Papers, #4511.

Esquivel, Gerardo and Larrain, Felipe (1998): *Latin America Confronting the Asian Crisis*, Pontificia Universidad Catolica de Chile, Working Paper, December.

Feenstra Robert C (1996): Trade and Uneven Growth, *Journal of Development Economics*, 49 (1), April, pp 229-256.

Fernandez-Arias Eduardo and Montiel Peter (2001): Reforms and Growth in Latin America: All Pains, No Gains? *IMF Staff Working Paper*, 48 (4), pp 1-25.

Finnerty C Thomas : Kodak vs. Fuji: *The Battle for Global Market Share, Institute of Global Business Strategy*, Lubin School of Business, Pace University, 2000, pp 4-23.

Gavin Michael and Hausmann Ricardo (1996): *The Roots of Banking Crisis: The Macroeconomic Context*, in Hausmann R and L Rojas- Suárez (Eds.), Banking Crisis in Latin America, Washington, Inter-American Development Bank.

Grossman Gene M and Elhanan Helpman (1991): *Innovation and Growth in the Global Economy*, MIT Press, Cambridge.

Guisan, M.C. and Aguayo (2000): Education, Industary, Trade and Development of American Companies in 1980-99, *Applied Econometrics and International Development.* Vol. 2-1, pp. 83-106.

Harrison A (1996): Openness and Growth – A Time-series, Cross-country Analysis for Developing Countries, *Journal of Development Economics*, 48 (2), March, pp 419-447.

Hausmann R., Alberto R, Rudolf Hommes and Stein Ernesto H (1996): *Budget Institutions and Fiscal Performance in Latin America,* NBER Working Papers, WP-W5588, May.

Joyce Joseph P and Kamas Linda (2003), Real and Nominal Determinants of Real Exchange Rates in Latin America – Short-run Dynamics and Long-run Equilibrium, *The Journal of Development Studies*, Vol.39, No. 6, pp 155-182.

Jun K W and Singh H (1996): The Determinants of Foreign Direct Investment in Developing Countries: New Empirical Evidence, *Transitional Corporations*, 5 (2), Geneva.

Kimura Fukunari and Ando Mitsuyo (2005): The Economic Analysis of International Production /Distribution Ventures in East Asia and Latin America: The Trade Implication of Regional Trade Agreements, *Business and Politics*, 7(1).

Krugman Paul (1994), Competitiveness – A Dangerous Obsession, *Foreign Affairs*, Vol. 73. No.2, 28-44.

Laplane, M. and F. Sarti (1997): *Investimento Direto Estrangeiro e a Retomada do Crescimento Sustentado nos anos 90*, Economia e Sociedade, No. 8, Sao Paulo.

Sarti F., Hiratuka C. and Sabbatini R. (2001): EI caso brasileño in D. Chudnovsky (ed.), *EI boom de la inversión extranjera directa en el Mercosur* (Buenos Aires: Siglo Veintiuno).

Leaderman Daniel, Perry Guillermo and Suescun Rodrigo (2002): *Trade Structure, Trade Policy and Economic Policy Options in Central America*, The World Bank, Office of the Latin American and Caribbean Region, Working Paper, November.

Marshall Don D (1998), NATFA/FTAA and the New Articulations in Americas – Seizing Structural Opportunities, *Third World Quarterly*, Vol. 19, No. 4, pp 673-700.

Mody Ashoka and Yilmaz Kamil(2002), Imported Machinery for Export Competitiveness, *World Bank Economic Review*, Vol. 16, June, pp 23-48.

Narlikar A (2000): *Bargaining Together in Trade: Developing Countries in Coalition*, D Phil Thesis, Oxford University Press, Oxford.

Nordstrom, H., (1995), Customs Unions, Regional Trading Blocs and Welfare, in R. Baldwin, P. Haaparanta, and J. Kiander (eds.), *Expanding Membership of the European Union*, Cambridge University Press, pp 54-78.

Omen C (1999): *Policy Competition and Foreign Direct Investment*, OECD Development Centre, OECD, Paris.

Paus Eva, Reinhardt Nola and Robinson Michael (2003), Trade Liberalization and Productivity Growth in Latin American Manufacturing, *The Journal of Policy Reforms*, Vol. 6, No.1, pp 1-15.

Perroni Carlo and Whalley John (1996), How Severe is the Global Retaliation Risk under Increasing Regionalism, *American Economic Review*, Vol. 86, No. 2, pp 57-61.

Rogowski R (1989): *Commerce and Coalitions*, Princeton University Press, Princeton, NJ.

Sanchez Blanca R and Clavo Marta Bengoa (2003): Foreign Direct Investment, Economic Freedom and Growth, *European Journal of Political Economy*, Vol. 19, No. 3, September, pp. 529-545.

Solow Robert (1956): A Contribution to the Theory of Economic Growth, *Quarterly Journal of Economics*, 70, February, pp 65-94.

Thacker Storm C (2000): Private Sector Trade Politics in Mexico, *Business and Politics*, Vol. 2, No.2, pp 161-187.

Tornell, Aaron, Westermann, Frank and Martinez Trigueros, Lorenza (2004): *NAFTA and Mexico's Economic Performance*, Center for Economic Studies and Institute for Economic Research, Working Paper Series No. 1155, March..

Tussie, Diana (1987): *The Less Developed Countries and the World Trading System: A Challenge to the GATT*. New York: St. Martin's Press.

(2003): *Trade Negotiations in Latin America- Problems and Prospects*, New York Palgrave-Macmillan.

Vogel David (1997): Trading Up and Governing Across – Transnational Governance and Environment Protection, *Journal of European Public Policy*, Vol.4, No.4, pp 556-571.

Weston Ann and Valentina Delich (2003): Settling Disutes, in Tussie Diana (Ed.), *Trade Negotiations in Latin America- Problems and Prospects*, New York Palgrave-Macmillan, 2003.

Zheng Ping, Siler Pamela and Giorgioni G (2004): FDI and the Export Performance of Chinese Indigenous Firms: A Regonal Approach, *Journal of Chinese Economic and Business Studies*, Vol. 2, No.1, pp 55-71.

# INDEX

## A

## B

## C

## D

## E

## F

## G

## H

## I

## M

## N



## O

## P

## Q



## R

## S

## T